THE SCOTT AND LAURIE OKI SERIES
IN ASIAN AMERICAN STUDIES

ENDURING CONVICTION

FRED KOREMATSU
AND HIS QUEST
FOR JUSTICE

LORRAINE K. BANNAI

University of Washington Press · *Seattle and London*

This book is published with the assistance of a grant from the Scott and Laurie Oki Endowed Fund for publications in Asian American Studies.

A full listing of the books in the Oki Series can be found at the back of the book.

© 2015 by Lorraine K. Bannai
Printed and bound in the United States
Composed in Utopia, a typeface designed by Robert Slimbach
Design: Dustin Kilgore
19 18 17 16 15   5 4 3 2 1

University of Washington Press
www.washington.edu/uwpress

Library of Congress Cataloging-in-Publication Data

Bannai, Lorraine K., author.
Enduring conviction : Fred Korematsu and his quest for justice / Lorraine K. Bannai.
    pages   cm. —   (Scott and Laurie Oki series in Asian American studies)
Includes bibliographical references and index.
ISBN 978-0-295-99515-1 (hardback : alk. paper)   1. Korematsu, Fred, 1919–2005—Trials, litigation, etc. 2. Japanese Americans—Evacuation and relocation, 1942–1945. 3. Japanese Americans—Civil rights—History—20th century.   I. Title.
KF228.K59B36 2015
341.6'7—dc23
                                                                2015020142

The paper used in this publication is acid-free and meets the minimum requirements of American National Standard for Information Sciences—Permanence of Paper for Printed Library Materials, ANSI Z39.48–1984.∞

For my parents, Paul and Hideko Bannai
For my children, Dana and Eliot Mar
And, of course, for Fred

—LKB

CONTENTS

PREFACE

THIS BOOK TELLS THE STORY OF FRED KOREMATSU, WHO, AS A young man during World War II, refused to comply with military orders that led to the incarceration of over 110,000 individuals of Japanese ancestry living on the West Coast. There had been no charges against them; they had no hearings; they were rounded up and sent to desolate camps in the interior United States simply because the country was at war with Japan, and they looked like the enemy. This story about Fred's wartime challenge to the mass removal, his quest for justice forty years later, and his tireless work speaking out against the targeting of minority communities after 9/11 continues to have haunting relevance today as the country still grapples with the extent to which it must sacrifice civil liberties to ensure national security.

In 1942, Fred was one of a handful of individuals who chose not to obey the wartime orders;[1] he chose instead to remain with the woman he loved in the community that had always been his home, exercising the freedoms and rights he possessed as an American citizen. In 1944, in what has become one of the most infamous cases in American legal history, the Supreme Court upheld his conviction and the constitutionality of the government's actions. Decades later, however, in 1983, with the assistance of a dedicated team of volunteer lawyers, Fred went back to court and cleared his name based on proof that the government had suppressed, altered, and destroyed material evidence when it was arguing Fred's case before the wartime Supreme Court. In reopening his case and in his years thereafter traveling the country to speak about the wartime incarceration, Fred helped to lift the implication of guilt that had hung over the Japanese American community and to remind the country of the enormous price to be paid if it is not vigilant in protecting civil rights.

In 1982, as a young lawyer fairly fresh out of law school, I had the privilege of serving on the legal team that represented Fred in reopening his case. During that time, I was able to get to know both him and his family, and in the years since, I have had the opportunity to write and speak about the wartime Japanese American incarceration, Fred's case, and their present-day relevance. When I've given talks, I've often been asked if I was going to write a book about his life and cases. Time and time again, I'd say that was a great idea, and it has taken until now to finally write it.

Other books written about Fred have been primarily for younger audiences. This book seeks to both provide a deeper and more nuanced understanding of his life and cases, as well as set his story in a broader context. First, this book draws on a wide range of sources, giving, I think, greater insight into Fred and the meaning and impact of his decisions. I have, for example, been able to draw on rich archival sources, including documents in the National Archives, such as immigration files, camp records, and court documents; records from local libraries, museums, and government offices, including jail registries and property records; the files of the Northern California ACLU, including wartime letters between Fred and his ACLU advocate, Ernest Besig; and the *Fred T. Korematsu v. United States* Coram Nobis Litigation Collection at UCLA, which holds the files of Fred's legal team related to the reopening of his case.

In addition, this book draws, as much as possible, on Fred's own words and on first-person interviews of those who knew him. I have had the benefit of not only Fred's published interviews and speeches but also previously unpublished interviews he (and others) gave in connection with the making of the documentaries *Unfinished Business* by Steven Okazaki and *Of Civil Wrongs and Rights* by Eric Paul Fournier. I've further been able to interview members of Fred's family, family friends, members of his legal team, and other people who came to know him. These individuals, many of whom have never been interviewed before, and some of whom, sadly, have passed, told of Fred's life and experiences and the way he touched others, often through inspiring, tender, and sometimes funny stories. There were many interviews during which tears from laughing mixed with tears from missing Fred. These recollections from those who knew Fred provide a tangible, human view of the events that made up his remarkable life, as well as the person he was.

Second, this book seeks to provide a deeper understanding of Fred and the significance of his actions and case by setting his story in a broader historical, social, cultural, political, and legal context. For example, setting Fred's life in the context of the history of the larger Japanese American community aids in understanding his experiences growing up, fighting his case, and joining the community's quest for redress for the wartime wrongs. It also, I hope, provides a more textured view of the community's history by underscoring that, while members of the Japanese American community, like members of other communities of color, share a common history and culture, they are far from homogenous; their lived experiences and perspectives are varied and complex.

Further, it is critical to understand the Japanese American incarceration not simply as an isolated historical event of the past, involving one ethnic minority in a unique and unusual set of circumstances. This book seeks to set Fred's case within the context of a broader legal history in which the American legal system has too often responded to public pressure in ways that harm minority communities. In this respect, the forced expulsion and imprisonment of Japanese Americans was, in many senses, an ultimate exclusion after a history of laws aimed at preventing their full and equal membership in American society. It is further important to understand the wartime incarceration and Fred's case in light of their present-day relevance to a range of issues that continue to confront this country. Fred never saw his case as simply about him or Japanese Americans; he understood that what happened to Japanese Americans during World War II was important because it spoke about larger themes. Throughout this discussion of Fred's life, the life of his community, and their struggles as an ethnic minority in this country are themes concerning the dangers of intolerance and stereotyping, the importance of checks on exercises of government discretion, and the need to be vigilant in protecting civil rights—all very much current issues as the country continues to struggle with questions of race and how to preserve civil liberties in a post-9/11 world.

In its broadest sense, Fred's story is really about the American promise—what America aspires to and where it has failed in that promise. Fred was an American citizen who so believed in what this country stood for that he challenged it to keep its promises of freedom and equality. In so doing, he showed that being an American carries with it an obligation to make the country what it professes to be and to always seek justice, no matter that others may disagree or that it may take years, even decades, to achieve.

The events in this book have deep personal meaning to me. I am a third-generation Japanese American—a Sansei. My parents, grandparents, aunts, and uncles were incarcerated at Manzanar in the California Mojave Desert during the war. The pages of this book, in many respects, tell their story, and, in turn, mine. Further, I knew and came to have great admiration and affection for Fred. This narrative very much reflects my own sense of who he was as I came to know him—the clarity of his resolve, his voice, his favorite anecdotes, and his generous spirit, dry wit, quick smile, and warm and gentle manner. I cannot purport to be a truly neutral reporter. At the same time, however, I give, I hope, a valuable first-person perspective. And I have sought to ensure accuracy in this work through my research, through interviews with those who knew Fred, and by including a range of voices and perspectives to tell as full a story as possible.

While my purposes in writing this book are many, my main intent is that others know and remember Fred, not only know who he was but also what he stood for—that, in the end, we are each responsible for advancing justice and need to do our part to ensure it, just as he did.

ACKNOWLEDGMENTS

THANK YOU FIRST TO THE KOREMATSU FAMILY—ESPECIALLY Fred's wife, Kathryn, daughter Karen, and son Ken—not only for the time they spent speaking with me, but, more importantly, for allowing me to tell Fred's story. I hope I've done right by it. Karen has become a cherished friend and has been a crucial resource. Kathryn, sadly, passed away in October 2013. I treasure the days I spent interviewing her, and I wish she could have seen the results of that time together. I also count as part of the "Korematsu family" and thank my fellow members of Fred's legal team, including Dale Minami, Peter Irons, Don Tamaki, Dennis Hayashi, Karen Kai, Bob Rusky, Leigh-Ann Miyasato, Marjie Barrows, Ed Chen, and Eric Yamamoto, for their extraordinary work on Fred's behalf and their friendship all these years. Special thanks to Peter and Eric— as accomplished scholars and writers, their suggestions and support have been particularly meaningful to me.

This book would also not be possible without the support of the Seattle University School of Law and my colleagues there. Thank you to Dean Annette Clark, my former Deans Mark Niles and Kellye Testy, and Associate Deans Steven Bender and Natasha Martin for providing institutional, as well as personal, support to this project, and to colleagues Margaret Chon, Bob Chang, Anne Enquist, Laurel Oates, and David Skover for their counsel and friendship at every stage. I also greatly appreciate Jonathan LeBlanc's and Laurie Wells's great work transcribing interviews.

I cannot sufficiently thank reference librarians Bob Menanteaux and Stephanie Wilson for the skill, commitment, tenacity, and understanding they brought to the research on this book. And I had the help of an outstanding team of research assistants; thank you in particular to Hozaifa Cassubhai, Tina Meade, Rachel Schaefer, Blake Kumabe, and Ashwin Kumar.

Archivists, librarians, and others at numerous institutions helped me greatly in my research, as well. Special thanks to the National Archives at San Francisco; the California Historical Society; the Department of Special Collections, Charles E. Young Research Library at UCLA; Densho: The Japanese American Legacy Project; the Japanese American National Library; the Japanese American National Museum; the San Leandro Public Library; and the San Leandro History Museum.

I owe a special debt of gratitude to the individuals I interviewed for this book, including Kathryn, Karen, and Ken Korematsu; Fred's sister-in-law, Kay Korematsu; his nieces Joanne Kataoka and Connie Wirtz; his son-in-law, Donald Haigh; and Yuri Yokota, Walt Hermann, Frank and Amy Eto, Rev. Lloyd Wake, Chizu Iiyama, Paul Takagi, Tom Kometani, Bruce Kaji, Elma and Mas Takahashi, Aiko Herzig-Yoshinaga, John Tateishi, Peter Irons, Norman Mineta, Rev. Saburo Masada, John Ota, Eric Fournier, and Leigh-Ann Miyasato. I thank them for sharing their recollections and thoughts and for their candor.

Many thanks to the University of Washington Press and its talented and dedicated team. Special thanks to Ranjit Arab for his commitment to this book and for the care and support he has given this project at every stage; to Mary Ribesky and Kerrie Maynes for their editorial assistance; and to Dustin Kilgore for his striking jacket design. Two anonymous reviewers read the manuscript, and I have greatly appreciated their suggestions.

Countless others have been part of the making of this book in a myriad of other ways. My sister Kathryn Bannai and brother Don Bannai have been constant, encouraging supports. Terry Tan provided me my home away from home in the Bay Area. Kathryn, Terry, and Sam Eng so generously read drafts and provided valuable feedback. I am also grateful to Steven Okazaki, Eric Fournier, Lane Hirabayashi, Elaine Elinson, Stan Yogi, Greg Robinson, Roger Daniels, Philip Gotanda, Don Horowitz, Diane Wong, and Gaye Chinn for their friendship and contributions to this effort.

Finally, thank you, Fred, for the privilege of knowing you, the honor of working on your case, and for teaching me, and all of us, about living one's truth.

ABBREVIATIONS

ACLU   American Civil Liberties Union

BAAR   Bay Area Attorneys for Redress

CWRIC   Commission on Wartime Relocation and Internment of Civilians

FBI   Federal Bureau of Investigation

FCC   Federal Communications Commission

JACL   Japanese American Citizens League

NCRR   National Coalition for Redress and Reparations

NCJAR   National Council for Japanese American Redress

ONI   Office of Naval Intelligence

WRA   War Relocation Authority

ENDURING CONVICTION

PROLOGUE

A SAN FRANCISCO

COURTROOM

THE COURTROOM WAS SO BIG—BIGGER THAN ANY HE HAD SEEN before. Its rich oak walls stretched up to a ceiling that was two floors high. The judge's bench seemed so far away, past galleries flanking each side of the wide expanse of carpet and guarded by the clerks and bailiff. Above and behind the bench, almost floating above it, it seemed, was the Great Seal of the United States: "E pluribus unum," it read, "Out of many, one." This courtroom was so much larger than the dreary courtroom he had been in before, forty years earlier and only a few blocks away. As he had back then, in 1942, he stood in the front at a table reserved for counsel and their clients. As he had back then, he waited for the judge to emerge from chambers, and he hoped for justice. And, to him, the issue this day in November 1983 was the same as it had been before. He had been in court back then because, months after the bombing of Pearl Harbor, Japanese Americans like him had been ordered to leave their West Coast homes, rounded up, and corralled into camps. He, like them, had committed no crimes—no acts or threatened acts of espionage or sabotage; they just looked like the "enemy." He was a loyal American who loved this country. But he had chosen freedom, and, in doing so, had violated the law. How could he have been charged with a crime based simply on the color of his skin?

Back then, he had stood virtually alone. Only his lawyers, the judge, the prosecutor, and the court staff had witnessed his trial. His family had gone; they were among the 110,000 persons of Japanese ancestry, lawful immigrants and American citizens alike, who had been herded into race-tracks and fairgrounds, and then desolate camps, and held under armed guard. Even if his family and other members of the Japanese American, or Nikkei, community could have been present, however, he wondered how many would have stood behind him in that courtroom. His family had been shamed by his arrest. And he felt that others within the community had rejected him for his refusal to comply with the government's orders. Most of the public had seen him as they saw all Japanese Americans, as potential saboteurs; many others had at least passively allowed the incarceration to occur.

But this time he was not alone. Slowly, the courtroom filled. One by one or in small groups, other Japanese Americans quietly entered: men and women now in their 60s and 70s, with graying hair and neatly dressed. They, like Fred, had suffered the camps, and today they took their places behind him. They came this day because they sought what he sought: recognition that they had been wronged. They were accompanied by younger Japanese Americans, sons and daughters who wanted to know why their parents had been incarcerated and now joined them in seeking justice. Slowly, the room filled to capacity. Those present murmured softly among themselves, respectful both of the formal courtroom environment and of the importance of the case they were about to hear.

In 1942, Fred Korematsu was among a few who had resisted orders that culminated in sending Japanese Americans into concentration camps in the Western interior, and his case was one of four that had been fought to the United States Supreme Court. He had been convicted of a federal crime and jailed. He had been moved to live in a horse stall in a hastily converted racetrack and then in a guarded, dusty, and desolate camp at Topaz, Utah. And, with the firm belief that the orders removing Japanese Americans from the West Coast violated their constitutional rights, he had challenged the government's orders all the way to the United States Supreme Court. In his case, *Korematsu v. United States*, the court had held in 1944 that the orders did not run afoul of the U.S. Constitution. The orders were lawful, the court reasoned, because the government had reason to believe that Japanese Americans, as a people, had close ties with an enemy nation and posed an imminent threat to the country's security. Fred had lived for decades with having lost that case. Today, he came to a new court to clear his name.

Some might have been nervous to stand before the courtroom, under the weight of expectation of the crowd. But Fred was not. While he was a soft-spoken man who had never sought the public eye, he had a calm strength that came from his firm belief that the government had wronged him. He didn't know everything about the U.S. Constitution, but he did know that the wartime incarceration had violated the essential principles of freedom and equality for which, he believed, America stood. Those principles were worth fighting for, even if it meant resisting the very government entrusted with protecting them. Fred had never wavered in his belief in those principles, and today sought again to hold his country to them.

Fred's story is about his own quest for justice, but it is also about more than that. It is also about the determination and perseverance of the Japanese American community, as well as the many and conflicting ways in which that community responded to, and survived, adversity. And even more than that, it is a story about America and the frailty of its promises of freedom and equality in times of crisis—then, as well as now.

CHAPTER 1

THE SON OF IMMIGRANTS,

BUT ALL-AMERICAN

LIKE THOSE OF MANY AMERICANS, FRED'S SPIRIT, HOPES, AND dreams grew from the spirit, hopes, and dreams of immigrant parents. His father, Kakusaburo Korematsu, was born in Maibara-machi, Fukuoka, Japan, on June 11, 1876. The late 1800s were hard for farming families like his, and, just after the turn of the new century, Kakusaburo joined the wave of young men leaving Japan in search of greater opportunity. Lured by the prospect of work on the sugar plantations of Hawai'i, at the age of twenty-eight, he boarded the *SS Doric* in Yokohama on October 8, 1904. The ship's manifest listed Kakusaburo's occupation as "farm laborer," the same as every other young man on that ship.[1]

Kakusaburo made his way to the island of Kaua'i and became part of the Issei, or first, generation of Japanese in this country; he did not, however, last long there. Housing was poor, compensation was meager, and working conditions were often abusive. News of higher wages beckoned workers to the mainland United States, and on April 26, 1905, less than a year after his arrival, Kakusaburo headed to San Francisco on the *SS Alameda*.[2]

Life on the mainland, however, would not be easy, either. Even as the country sought Asian immigrants as cheap labor, it did not welcome them. Arriving Issei recalled being called "Japs" or "Chinks" and being pelted with rocks and spat upon.[3] The refrain that Japanese Americans were different and foreign, and thus a race not capable of being American, began with their arrival in this country, grew in intensity, and ultimately became integral to

7

the call for their mass incarceration decades later. That refrain had early expression in comments like those by San Francisco Mayor James Duval Phelan, who, in May 1900, addressed the first large-scale protest against Japanese in California: "The Chinese and Japanese are not bona fide citizens. They are not the stuff of which American citizens can be made. . . . Personally we have nothing against Japanese, but as they will not assimilate with us and their social life is so different from ours, let them keep at a respectful distance."[4] Phelan's comments ignored, however, that any failure of Japanese Americans to assimilate was not truly of their own choosing. Their social isolation was largely externally imposed. Racism, discriminatory practices, and laws that denied them the incidents of full citizenship excluded them from mainstream society.[5]

The popular press warned of the "yellow peril" that Asian immigrants posed to the country and fanned the flames of racism.[6] In May 1905, delegates from sixty-seven organizations met in San Francisco to form the Asiatic Exclusion League, arguing for the exclusion of Japanese as threats to white society and its economic well-being: "We cannot assimilate with them without injury to ourselves. . . . We cannot compete with a people having a low standard of civilization, living and wages. . . . It should be against public policy to permit our women to intermarry with Asiatics."[7] The exclusionists won an early victory when, in 1907, President Theodore Roosevelt barred further Japanese immigration from intermediate points in Hawai'i, Mexico, and Canada. That victory became more complete when Roosevelt's "Gentlemen's Agreement" with Japan banned all further immigration of Japanese laborers.[8]

Despite the animosity toward them, the Issei endeavored. Economic opportunities, however, were limited. While there was a demand for low-wage laborers, racism and exclusion in the labor market denied the Issei access to other, better jobs. Many took their entrepreneurial spirits and became shopkeepers, merchants, and small businessmen. Kakusaburo was one of those entrepreneurs. In later years, Kakusaburo's daughter-in-law, Kay Korematsu, described him as having both an easygoing manner and an air of confidence—even conceitedness and recklessness—and these traits likely served him well as he struck out on his own.[9]

Kakusaburo started a flower nursery in an industrial area of East Oakland, across the bay from San Francisco, joining a vibrant community of

Japanese immigrant families who had found a niche in the West Coast flower industry. While most of these Issei had no experience growing flowers, their ingenuity, innovation, and hard work combined to make them important players in the business.[10] Property records suggest that Kakusaburo purchased the land for his nursery in 1913, before the effective date of the state's Alien Land Law. That law, which went into effect August 10, 1913, prohibited "aliens ineligible for citizenship" from purchasing property or entering into long-term leases on agricultural land. Because the Issei were barred from citizenship, the law prevented them from owning the land they worked. Kakusaburo likely obtained title to his nursery just under the wire.[11]

Kakusaburo's nursery soon became a going concern. His thoughts turned to marriage and family, and he sent for a bride. While the Gentlemen's Agreement had stopped the flow of male laborers from Japan, women could still enter to join them. Some men returned to Japan to find a bride or to bring a wife they had left behind, but most, lacking the financial means to travel, sent word to their families that they would like to marry, and their families found them brides to join them in the United States. Thus began the emigration of large numbers of "picture brides" to America—a system of "photo marriages," or *shashin kekkon*, which developed naturally in a country where marriages were routinely arranged by family. While, in a traditional marriage, or *omiai kekkon*, a go-between would facilitate the match, a meeting would be arranged, and a ceremony held, those formalities were not essential to a legal union. Instead, a marriage was legal when the bride's name was entered into the husband's family register, making her a member of his household. The extension of the practice of *omiai kekkon* thus allowed young men like Kakusaburo to marry brides who then joined them in their new land.[12]

Kotsui Aoki was from a farming family in Kakusaburo's home town of Maibara-machi and married him in Japan on August 11, 1913, although he was not present. Never having met her new husband, and bound for a country she did not know, she made the long trip to the United States on the SS *Siberia*, arriving in San Francisco on January 12, 1914. It's not possible to know what was in Kotsui's heart and mind as she prepared to travel across the Pacific; her daughter-in-law, Kay Korematsu, recalled Kotsui saying that she arrived excited to live in America. On her arrival, Kotsui met someone very different from herself. Kakusaburo was thirty-seven years old;

FIGURE 1.1. Fred's mother, Kotsui Korematsu, on her arrival in the United States, circa 1914. Courtesy of National Archives and Records Administration at San Francisco.

FIGURE 1.2. Fred's father, Kakusaburo Korematsu, circa 1914, included as part of Kotsui Korematsu's immigration file. Courtesy of National Archives and Records Administration at San Francisco.

she was twenty-two. In portraits submitted with Kotsui's immigration application, Kotsui is serene—dressed in a beautiful kimono with her hands neatly folded in her lap. Kakusaburo cut a dapper, contrastingly modern figure in his black suit, white shirt, and polished shoes. She, having been a teacher in Japan, was more educated than her husband-to-be.[13]

At Kotsui's entry interview at the immigration station on Angel Island, California, in January 1914, Kakusaburo stated that he had little money, but the Japanese Consul certified that "he [was] a man of good character, and [had] means to support his family." Because the "photo marriage" was not recognized in California, Kotsui was admitted to the country on the condition that she and Kakusaburo marry lawfully. The day she was released from Angel Island, January 15, 1914, they were married again by a Buddhist minister.[14]

Seeing Japanese continue to immigrate, anti-Japanese activists intensified the call for their exclusion, including the exclusion of picture brides and denial of citizenship, even for second-generation Japanese Americans born on U.S. soil.[15] In March 1924, the influential former publisher of the *Sacramento Bee*, V. S. McClatchy, and others carried the exclusionist banner to Washington. In testimony before the Senate Committee on Immigration, McClatchy argued the now-familiar "yellow peril" refrain, warning of the economic threat the Japanese posed to the nation:

> Of all the races ineligible for citizenship under our law, the Japanese are the least assimilable and the most dangerous to this country. . . . They come here specifically and professedly for the purpose of colonizing and establishing here the proud Yamato race. . . . In pursuit of their intent to colonize this country with that race they seek to secure land and found large families. . . . They have greater energy, greater determination, and greater ambition than the other yellow and brown races ineligible to citizenship, and with the same low standard of living, hours of labor, use of women and child labor, they naturally make more dangerous competitors in an economic way.[16]

The Nikkei were hardly the threat that McClatchy portrayed them to be. By 1930, there were 97,456 Nikkei in California, representing only 2.1 percent of the total population of the state, and only .10 percent of the population of the continental United States.[17] Nevertheless, the fight to end Japanese immigration—another significant step in the exclusionist's cause—was finally won: on June 30, 1924, Congress completely banned the immigration of any "alien ineligible to citizenship." Despite the seemingly neutral phrasing of the prohibition, it was clear that the ban was enacted to bar further immigration from Japan.[18]

The Nikkei, however, could not be deterred by the anti-Japanese vitriol that sounded in the chambers of government. They had, after all, no voice in those halls and had to attend to their livelihoods. Through hard work over long hours, Kakusaburo and Kotsui established a successful business; their greenhouses bloomed with Bouvardia, roses, and, later, carnations. And their family grew with the birth of four boys. As part of the Nisei, or second, generation, all of the boys were born American citizens. The Japanese names that Kotsui and Kakusaburo gave them were shed as cumbersome as the boys ventured out from the family home. Hiroshi, the first born, came to be called Hi. Takashi, the next, later went by Harry. The youngest, Junichi, was later called Joe. Fred was born on January 30, 1919, with the given name of Toyosaburo, "*saburo*" meaning "third son." Fred's elementary school friends called him "Toy," as Toyosaburo was more than they could handle. One of Fred's early teachers, who also found his name too hard to pronounce, asked if she could give him another name. She asked, "How would you like to be called 'Fred'"? He had a friend named Fred and liked the name, so he agreed and used that name for the rest of his life.[19]

In school, Fred acquired more than an American name. He learned what it meant to *be* an American, and those lessons resonated deeply with him. The United States was the only country he knew, and he was proud of his country. Years later, he recalled, "When I was in school, we started each day with the pledge of allegiance to the American flag. I studied American history and the Constitution of the United States and believed that persons from in this country were free and had equal rights."[20] He took seriously the commitment he made to America as a citizen, as well as the promise of freedom and equality that the country, in turn, made to him. Both would later be severely tested.

In the Korematsu family home, as in many other immigrant homes, cultural traditions mixed with modern, Western ways. Each Boys' Day, May 5, Kakusaburo was proud to fly four koi streamers above his home, one—ac-

FIGURE 1.3. Fred being held by his mother, Kotsui Korematsu, circa 1919. Courtesy of Karen Korematsu and the Fred T. Korematsu Institute.

cording to Japanese custom—for each son in the family. Fred recalled fondly the times his father took the family to samurai movies at the Oakland Buddhist temple, and Fred loved those movies throughout his later years. While Fred attended a Buddhist church as a young boy, the family converted to Christianity, and Kakusaburo and Kotsui became devoted, active members of the San Lorenzo Japanese Holiness Church, a Protestant congregation founded to serve the spiritual and fellowship needs of its Japanese American parishioners. Fred attended that church every Sunday during his youth, and involvement in church would remain a central part of Fred's life.[21]

Kakusaburo hoped that the boys would learn Japanese and hired a tutor to come to the house weekly to teach them the language. The effort, however, was not wholly successful. While Hi and Harry became fairly proficient in Japanese, the two younger sons showed less ability, or, more likely, less interest, in the language. Fred and Joe were never able to speak more than a broken mix of Japanese and English with their parents.[22]

Kakusaburo ruled his family in the manner of a typical Japanese patriarch. The Issei brought to this country the traditional family values of Meiji Japan, and in that order the father reigned supreme. Every night, Kakusaburo took his bath early and then sat for dinner at the head of the table. He always gave the blessing, usually a long one, asking for protection of everyone's health and prosperity.[23] As the eldest son, Fred's brother, Hi, was next in line in the family hierarchy. Hi enjoyed his privileged position, and Kakusaburo put all of his hopes in him. Hi was, as Fred's wife, Kathryn, would recall, "the king of the jungle."[24]

Fred, as the third son, was near the bottom of the family hierarchy. At an early age, he was acutely aware that he was the misfit. "I was the third son, and the family tradition was my dad always favored the oldest child. The next son was the smartest, and everything he did was wonderful. And the third son, that's me, everything I did was getting into mischief, so they always criticized me. That's the way I felt. I had another brother that was younger, and was the cuter son."[25]

Fred helped in the nursery, but he wasn't much interested in it. The regimen of daily chores was tedious. He was given the most undesirable jobs; his father and older brothers would just tell him what to do. He had a creative, artistic nature and enjoyed making things; he later listed his hobbies as including model boat building and cabinet making. From his mother, he learned to arrange flowers, and he and Joe learned to cook so that their mother could work in the greenhouses. Fred saw no future for himself at the nursery: he was the third son, and Kakusaburo let Fred know his feelings that Fred would never amount to anything. Perhaps Fred and his father clashed because Fred's interests lay beyond the nursery, with his friends and at school. Or perhaps they clashed because he and his father were alike in their independent spirits. Fred would always be grateful that his parents worked hard to provide for him and his brothers, but even in those early years, he lived, in many ways, outside of his family.[26]

Even as aspects of their family life were rooted in Japanese traditions, the Korematsu boys grew up in most ways like any other boys of the time. Fred attended grammar, junior high, and high school, all within a few miles of home. Most all of his friends were white; there were few Japanese Americans who lived close by.[27] Fred met one such friend, Walt Hermann,

FIGURE 1.4. The Korematsu family at their Stonehurst Flower Nursery, 1939.
Left to right: Fred's father, Kakusaburo Korematsu; his mother, Kotsui Korematsu;
Fred; and his brothers Joe, Harry, and Hi. National Portrait Gallery,
Smithsonian Institution. Gift of the Fred T. Korematsu Family.

in Boy Scout Troop 8 while both attended Elmhurst Junior High, and their
friendship lasted the rest of their lives. Years later, at the age of eighty-nine,
Walt recalled, with boyish laughter, the adventures and friendship of their
youth—piling into Walt's car while Walt, at twelve, would drive (illegally) to
the local Hayward plunge; engaging in silly banter during camping trips
in the Oakland hills; and sneaking oranges from neighbors' trees as they
walked home. Walt recalls Fred, with great affection, as a quiet, fun, and
loyal friend.[28]

In high school, Fred liked sports; he was on the school swimming and tennis teams and participated in track, basketball, and football.[29] He also liked girls, but, Walt laughed, he hardly had enough nerve to ask any out. He'd tell Walt, with a sly grin, "That's my new girlfriend," but the girl never knew it. What Fred really loved, as he finished and graduated from high school, was to dance. While Fred was not apt to talk a lot, Walt observed, that didn't mean he was shy, especially when doing something he enjoyed. It was the Big Band era—Glenn Miller, Benny Goodman, Tommy Dorsey, Artie Shaw, and Duke Ellington were all the rage—and the music grabbed Fred.[30]

As he grew up and left the safe environment of his closest friends, however, Fred became painfully aware of the hostility that existed toward Japanese Americans. There, outside, people saw only his Asian face, not his American birthright. "In high school, [I] felt equal, but on the outside, going out in public, after school, people stare at you because I'm different. I'm Asian, so they assumed I'm not an American and that I come from Japan. Restaurants would refuse to serve me, and places would refuse to give you a haircut. I had to go to Chinatown, and that was the only place that would give you a haircut. And when I'd go there, there'd be twenty people waiting, all Asians, to get a haircut."[31] He remembered how Japanese Americans suffered because of American fear of Japan. "The tension and attitude toward Asians, especially Japanese at that time, was not very good, because Japan was very aggressive in Asia. All of this brutality in the news media was more hate than anything else. The JACL [the Japanese American Citizens League] had to be careful about what they said. They feared that harm would come to them."[32]

When the Korematsu boys approached college age, Hi, not surprisingly, was the son who received the best education, first at the University of California, Davis, and then at Cornell.[33] Harry, the second son, studied business, attended floral school, and then he, not Hi, carried on the Korematsu nursery.[34] By the time Fred wanted to go to college, his father told him there wasn't enough money to send him, and if he wanted to go, he would have to work to pay his own way. Fred left to attend Los Angeles City College to study chemistry, but, unable to support himself, he returned to the nursery after just a few months. While he took a few business classes on his return, he never received a degree.[35]

FIGURE 1.5. Fred T. Korematsu, circa 1940, in a photo that now hangs in the National Portrait Gallery's permanent collection exhibition *Struggle for Justice*. National Portrait Gallery, Smithsonian Institution. Gift of the Fred T. Korematsu Family.

As war loomed, Fred, like so many other young men of the time, was anxious to fulfill his patriotic duty and serve his country. He certainly felt he would be more useful helping in the war effort than at the nursery. In 1940, the year Fred turned twenty-one, Congress instituted the first peacetime draft, and Fred registered on the first day.[36] Although he was classified 4-F (disabled because of a gastric ulcer), almost half of those who registered in that first year were rejected for health reasons.[37] He tried, without success, to volunteer for navy radio work. While he was later reclassified as "potential 1-A" in March 1942, by that time, after the bombing of Pearl Harbor, the War Department had stopped taking Japanese Americans into the military. Later in 1942, all persons of Japanese ancestry were classified 4-C, enemy aliens, even those who, like Fred, were American citizens.[38]

Rejected from the military, Fred looked for another way to support the war effort. After getting his father's permission to leave the nursery, he attended welding school and got a job in a shipyard, where his thin frame made it easy for him to slip between the double bottoms of ships to work. That first job, however, was short-lived. He was doing so well in the yard that his superintendent wanted to promote him to foreman. When he reported to work the following Monday, however, instead of a time card in his slot, he found a note telling him to report to his union. There, he was told that he was expelled from the union and could no longer work at the shipyard. When Fred asked why, the agent replied, "I'm sorry, this is wrong. I'm sorry, Fred, I can't help you." He took Fred's card, went in his office, and closed the door. Fred recalled, "That was it, I lost my job. . . . I was very discouraged. I wanted to be in defense work. . . . I'm an American, and I have nothin' to do with Japan, and so it's sort of an insult to me." The same thing happened with his next job. A foreman at Golden Gate Iron Works in San Francisco, Leo Hoffman, who was sympathetic to Fred and knew that Fred would have problems joining the union, offered Fred work on a contract basis. After a few months, however, Fred was fired. All he heard was "Get that man out of here."[39]

Being out of work was surely discouraging, but it would soon be the least of Fred's problems. A week later, the Japanese bombed Pearl Harbor. Fred's life would change in ways he could scarcely imagine.

CHAPTER 2

THE CALL TO GET RID

OF THE "JAPS"

BY 1938, AT THE AGE OF NINETEEN, FRED HAD A GIRLFRIEND, AND he loved her more than most anything else in the world. Ida Boitano, the daughter of Italian immigrant parents, lived in the neighboring town of San Leandro. She and Fred had met on a snow trip, and he initially called on her to learn how to play the piano. Or at least that's what he'd said. Walt remembers Ida as a shy girl. He had taken her out a couple of times before he left to work in Seattle and had the impression that she hadn't dated before. He didn't know that Fred was seeing Ida until Fred wrote him and asked Walt's permission to see her. Walt was amused; it wasn't as if Walt had any claim to her affection.[1]

At the beginning, Fred's and Ida's families seemed to accept their relationship; his parents didn't say much, believing it was just puppy love. Things changed, however, as the young couple became more serious. When Fred's brother Hi started seeing the daughter of an official from Japan, Hi didn't want her family to know that Fred had a white girlfriend. Hi went to Ida's parents to tell them to end the relationship between Fred and Ida. Her parents were insulted, and Fred was upset at his brother's meddling. Fred and Ida started meeting in secret. Walt recalled a visit to Fred's home when one of Fred's older brothers came out, told Walt that Fred was out with Ida, and asked Walt to break up the two. If Fred married Ida, the brother explained, it would devastate their mother. Walt, however, refused to meddle in his friend's love life.[2]

Despite objections from their families, Fred and Ida continued to see each other, and by December 1941 the couple had been together for almost three years. They became engaged, but could not marry, at least not in California. Fred wondered what else he and Ida could do to stay together. He wrote Walt to find out whether a Japanese American could marry a white woman in Washington State, but Walt didn't know.[3]

The morning of December 7, 1941, was sunny in Oakland. Fred and Ida relaxed on a hillside looking down on the expanse of the Bay Area. The Sunday *Oakland Tribune* was spread out in front of them as they listened to music on the car radio. Fred later recalled,

> All of a sudden, the music stopped and they announced that Pearl Harbor was attacked by Japanese airplanes. And I just couldn't believe it. I felt as if my stomach just tightened up and I felt sick to have something like this happen. At first, I thought it was a dream. People never did recognize us as Americans even though how much we tried to be American. So a thing like this, it made it twice as hard to prove you're more American than Japanese. It just burned me up that this happened. I said to Ida, "We better get back home." I better get back home and be with my parents to see what's gonna happen.[4]

For Fred, as well as other Japanese Americans, the attack on Pearl Harbor made worst fears loom large. In the years before the attack, they, along with the rest of the country, had heard the frightening reports of Japanese military aggression in Asia, and they worried about an outbreak of conflict between the United States and Japan. The Nisei knew that a war with Japan would be bad for them: they dreaded that their country—America—might turn on them and their parents if such a war were to come.[5]

After dropping off Ida, Fred went home to the nursery. His parents and brothers were gathered around the kitchen table, glued to the radio. His mother was crying. His father was disgusted. Fred thought, "All that work that my parents did to the nursery; what was going to happen? Why did Japan do such a thing?" He didn't know what the future held for him or his family; there was so much hatred of the Japanese. The family went to church, where other Japanese American nursery families had gathered, and the group agreed that they simply had to try to stay calm and wait to see what would happen next. The next day, they were too scared to go work at the flower market.[6]

Silence fell over the Korematsu home. Fred explained, "Before the war, my parents were very proud people. They'd always talk about Japan and also about the samurai and things like that. Right after Pearl Harbor, they were just real quiet, they kept to themselves, they were afraid to talk about what could happen. I assume they knew that nothing good would come out of it." On December 8, President Franklin D. Roosevelt declared that the nation was at war with Japan.[7]

The force of law fell quickly upon the Japanese American community. Within hours of the Pearl Harbor attack, Roosevelt declared all Japanese immigrants over fourteen years of age "alien enemies." With a stroke of the president's pen, Fred's parents, along with the rest of the Issei who had lived in, and worked to build, this country for decades, became "enemies" of their adopted land. The proclamation further authorized the summary apprehension of "alien enemies" deemed to be dangerous, and in the ensuing days the government began rounding up Nikkei community leaders. Families sat by helplessly as their heads of household were whisked away without notice.[8]

Roosevelt's proclamation also authorized the confiscation of property that might aid espionage or sabotage. In the following months, thousands of homes in which Japanese lived were subject to random search. Fred recalled how the police, without warning, entered his home and took flashlights, cameras, and anything else that could be used for signaling. The foundry next door put spotlights on the nursery and stationed a guard to stand watch near their house. Fred recalled, "One night, I went out to have a cigarette, and someone yelled out at me that I was signaling somebody. Ridiculous, you know."[9]

Japanese Americans up and down the West Coast felt they had to erase from their lives anything that might suggest ties with Japan and, at the same time, prove their loyalty to America.[10] The Japanese American Citizens League, the national organization that sought to speak for the Nikkei community, condemned the attack on Pearl Harbor and pledged its services "unreservedly to the officials and authorities of our country, the United States of America."[11]

While there were some voices of calm that urged the public not to turn on the Nikkei community,[12] those voices fell on the deaf ears of a populace already primed to do so.[13] News reports that appeared in the days after the bombing of Pearl Harbor reflected the hysteria:

> Japanese gardeners were said to be equipped with short-wave transmitters hidden in garden hose[s]; Japanese servants and laborers who failed to appear for work on December 7 (a Sunday) were accused of prior knowledge of the Hawaii attack. Japanese farmers were charged with smuggling poison into vegetables bound for market. . . . A number of anxious Californians, according to one report, went so far as to plow up "a beautiful field of flowers on the property of a Japanese farmer," because "it seems the Jap was a fifth columnist and had grown his flowers in a way that when viewed from a plane formed an arrow pointing the direction to the airport."[14]

Despite reports like these of rampant subversive activity on the part of the West Coast Nikkei, "there was not one demonstrable incident of sabotage committed by a Japanese American, alien or native born, during the entire war."[15]

Violence against persons of Japanese ancestry increased as vigilantes sought to take matters into their own hands. Attorney General Francis Biddle recounted thirty-six instances of criminal activity against Japanese Americans between December 8, 1941, and March 31, 1942, including robberies, extortion, rape, murder, assault, and destruction of property.[16]

In January 1942, demands that the government remove the Nikkei community from the West Coast increased. On January 29, for example, syndicated columnist Henry McLemore called for their banishment in chilling terms: "I am for the removal of every Japanese on the West Coast to a point deep in the interior. I don't mean a nice part of interior either. Herd 'em up, pack 'em off and give 'em the inside room in the badlands. Let 'em be punched, hurt, hungry and dead up against it. . . . Personally, I hate the Japanese. And that goes for all of them." On February 12, influential columnist Walter Lippmann stirred existing fears to an even higher pitch when he warned that "the Pacific Coast is in imminent danger of a combined attacked from within and without. . . . Nobody's constitutional rights include the right to reside and do business on a battlefield." Columnist Westbrook Pegler responded, "What Lippmann says I accept as truth. . . . [T]he Japanese in California should be under armed guard to the last man and woman right now and to hell with habeas corpus until the danger is over."[17]

The exclusionists, who had sought for decades to rid the West Coast of the Japanese, seized the moment. In the words of one official of the Joint Immigration Committee, a group carrying on the cause of the older Asiatic and Japanese Exclusion Leagues, "This is our time to get things done that we have been trying to get done for a quarter of a century."[18]

The calls to remove the Nikkei population from the West Coast resonated in the halls of government and in military war rooms. On January 16, 1942, Congressman Leland Ford of Los Angeles wrote the secretaries of war and navy and FBI Director J. Edgar Hoover that his constituents wanted the Japanese gone. He continued, "[My suggestion is that] all Japanese, whether citizens or not, be placed in inland concentration camps. As justification for this, I submit that if an American born Japanese, who is a citizen, is really patriotic and wishes to make his contribution to the safety and welfare of his country, right here is his opportunity to do so, namely, that by permitting himself to be placed in a concentration camp, he would be making his sacrifice, and he should be willing to do it if he is patriotic and is working for us."[19]

California Attorney General Earl Warren, later to be celebrated as a champion of civil rights during his tenure on the Supreme Court, was a vocal advocate for the expulsion of Japanese from the West Coast. In February 1942, he admitted that there had been no acts of espionage or sabotage on the part of the Japanese community. With strained reasoning, however, he warned that the very absence of subversive activity was powerful proof that it would occur.[20]

From his post at the Presidio Army Base in San Francisco, Lieutenant General John L. DeWitt, head of the Western Defense Command who would oversee the eventual removal of Japanese Americans, heard these West Coast voices loudly. They confirmed his own view that Japanese Americans were inherently treacherous. In January 1942, he stated, for example, "I have little confidence that the enemy aliens are law abiding or loyal in any sense of the word. Some of them, yes; many, no. Particularly the Japanese, I have no confidence in their loyalty whatsoever. I am speaking now of the native born Japanese—117,000—and 42,000 in California alone."[21] In testimony a year later, DeWitt made clear that, while Ida Boitano's Italian-born parents would have caused him very little concern, every member of the Korematsu family was a potential spy: "You needn't worry about the Italians at all except in certain cases. Also, the same for the Germans except in individual cases. But we must worry about the Japanese all the time until he is wiped off the map."[22]

During the early months of 1942, the army—through the particular efforts of DeWitt, Provost Marshal General Allen W. Gullion, and Major (later Colonel) Karl R. Bendetsen—pressed for the authority to rid the West Coast of Japanese Americans.[23] In contrast, civilian authorities, at least early on, sought restraint. On February 7, Attorney General Biddle shared his views with President Roosevelt, stating his belief that a mass removal "at this time [was] inadvisable."[24] FBI Director J. Edgar Hoover was similarly not convinced of the need to expel Japanese Americans from the West Coast. He wrote Biddle, "The necessity for mass evacuation is based primarily upon public and political pressure rather than on factual data."[25] Secretary of War Harry Stimson was also not initially behind wholesale expulsion. He, like the Justice Department, believed it better to create more limited zones around strategic installations from which aliens could be excluded.[26] While confessing distrust of Japanese American citizens, Stimson at least recognized the constitutional issues their mass removal would raise: "The second generation Japanese [Nisei] can only be evacuated either as part of a total evacuation, giving access only by permits, or by frankly trying to put them out on the ground that their racial characteristics are such that we cannot understand or trust even the citizen Japanese. This latter is the fact but I am afraid it will make a tremendous hole in our constitutional system to apply it."[27] Stimson was rightly concerned about the mass removal of such a large number of citizens: out of the 126,947 persons of Japanese ancestry living in the continental United States in 1940, 79,642, or 62.7 percent, of them were, like Fred, American citizens by birth.[28]

By early February, DeWitt decided it was necessary to remove Japanese Americans from the West Coast, but he had nothing to support that decision other than the demands he had heard from West Coast leaders and his own view that the removal was required to prevent sabotage. If he was to gain support from the Justice Department and Stimson, he needed more.

Gullion told DeWitt to write up his position, and DeWitt agreed to provide such a report.[29]

Even without DeWitt's report, discussion about removing Japanese Americans moved forward, with Stimson writing Roosevelt to seek his decision on two key issues. He first asked Roosevelt whether any orders should include Japanese American citizens. He further sought Roosevelt's opinion on the geographic scope of any removal orders: whether they should encompass a broader strip of the West Coast recommended by DeWitt, which would involve "a number of over 100,000 people, if . . . both aliens and Japanese citizens [were included]" or smaller areas, such as cities with large numbers of Japanese Americans or around critical installations.[30] Stimson spoke to Roosevelt by phone; he later wrote in his diary that Roosevelt had told him "to go ahead on the line that I had myself thought best."[31]

After that phone call, the effort to remove Japanese Americans from the West Coast catapulted forward. In a call to Bendetsen, John J. McCloy, Stimson's assistant secretary of war, reported what Roosevelt had said in expansive terms: "[W]e have carte blanche to do what we want to as far as the President's concerned."[32] He explained, "[T]he President, in substance, says go ahead and do anything you think necessary . . . if it involves citizens, we will take care of them, too. He says there will probably be some repercussions, but it has got to be dictated by military necessity, but as he puts it, 'Be as reasonable as you can.'"[33]

On February 14, DeWitt finally sent Stimson his report explaining his justification for removing Japanese Americans from the West Coast. Unable to identify any threatened or actual acts of espionage or sabotage on the part of the Japanese American community to justify their mass removal, DeWitt's report did little more than reiterate racist stereotypes and speculation:

> In the war in which we are now engaged racial affinities are not severed
> by migration. The Japanese race is an enemy race and while many second
> and third generation Japanese born on United States soil, possessed of
> United States citizenship, have become "Americanized," the racial strains
> are undiluted. . . . It, therefore, follows that along the vital Pacific Coast
> over 112,000 potential enemies, of Japanese extraction, are at large today.
> There are indications that these are organized and ready for concerted ac-

tion at a favorable opportunity. The very fact that no sabotage has taken place to date is a disturbing and confirming indication that such action will be taken.[34]

While DeWitt stated that there were "indications" that Nikkei on the West Coast were "organized and ready for concerted action," he did not, and, indeed, could not, explain what those indications were. Lacking any concrete evidence to show that Japanese Americans were poised to strike, DeWitt channeled Earl Warren, explaining that the proximity of Japanese Americans to vital strategic installations proved the danger.[35] DeWitt's report concluded with his recommendation that the president authorize the secretary of war to designate military areas from which he could exclude all Japanese, including U.S. citizens, as well as others deemed enemy aliens or actual or potential saboteurs.[36]

Although devoid of military justification, DeWitt's recommendation won the day. At a meeting of War and Justice Department officials the evening of February 17, 1942, Gullion produced a draft of an executive order granting the army the power to remove both immigrant aliens and citizens as it deemed necessary. Biddle agreed without argument. Assistant Attorney General James Rowe and Justice Department lawyer Edward Ennis were taken aback by Biddle's capitulation. Rowe recounted, "The Attorney General immediately wanted to get to work to polish up the order. His attitude amazed me. Ennis almost wept. I was so mad that I could not speak at all myself and the meeting soon broke up."[37]

On February 19, 1942, President Roosevelt signed Executive Order 9066, delegating sweeping authority to the War Department in terms closely tracking DeWitt's recommendations. The order authorized the secretary of war, and any military commanders he designated, to prescribe military areas "from which any or all persons may be excluded" and within which the right of any person to enter, remain in, or leave may be restricted. Although the order was race-neutral on its face, there was no question that it was intended to authorize military control over the Japanese population on the West Coast.[38]

While Roosevelt's executive order authorized the War Department and military to control and remove the Nikkei population, Congress still needed to pass legislation to make violation of any such military orders a crime. In

March, Congress passed Public Law 503, punishing those who might resist with a fine of up to $500 or imprisonment for up to one year, or both. Nothing in the statute, however, identified the specific conduct criminalized by the law; that conduct would be described by the military orders themselves, which had not yet been issued. Senator Robert Taft of Ohio criticized the bill for its vagueness: "I think this is probably the 'sloppiest' criminal law I have ever read or seen anywhere. . . . I do not want to object, because the purpose of it is understood. . . . I have no doubt that in peacetime no man could ever be convicted under it, because the court would find that it is so indefinite and so uncertain that it could not be enforced under the Constitution." He did not, however, vote against the bill. The bill was signed into law on March 21, 1942.[39]

On February 20, 1942, Stimson delegated to DeWitt the power to implement the executive order within the Western Defense Command. Pursuant to that authority, on March 2, 1942, DeWitt issued Public Proclamation No. 1, creating Military Area No. 1—which encompassed the western halves of Washington and Oregon, the western half of California, and the southern half of Arizona—and announced that all persons of Japanese ancestry, citizen and "alien" resident immigrant alike, would be removed from the area, followed by a more limited removal of German and Italian "aliens." Fred's family, as well as over 110,000 other persons of Japanese ancestry on the West Coast, braced themselves to be taken away on some uncertain future date to some place as yet unknown.[40]

The Nikkei community then became subject to a series of orders issued in quick succession. On March 24, 1942, DeWitt's Public Proclamation No. 3 imposed a curfew on all persons of Japanese ancestry and other "enemy aliens," requiring them to remain in their homes between 8:00 p.m. and 6:00 a.m. It further allowed them to travel only to and from work and within five miles of their homes.[41] Fred could not believe it when he saw the notice: "I thought that American citizens would be excluded, but we weren't." The cloud that had hovered over the Japanese Americans grew even darker. Fred recalled, "During the curfew, whoever went out, the people were watching you. Any Japanese home, there was some person figuring he's a good American citizen by doing their duty and they were watching every move each family were doin'. Or if they went out, they followed them to see where they were goin'."[42]

Three days after the curfew order, on March 27, 1942, DeWitt issued Public Proclamation No. 4, a "freeze order" prohibiting persons of Japanese ancestry from leaving the West Coast military zone unless in a manner specified by the army.[43] While early on DeWitt and other officials had hoped to clear the West Coast of Japanese Americans by simply ordering them to leave, it was soon realized that they had to be removed in a way that prevented their uncontrolled dispersion. Since December 1941, some Nikkei had been leaving their homes in certain strategic areas previously designated by the Justice Department and were able to find new places to stay. Neighboring states, however, did not want Japanese Americans roaming freely. On February 21, 1942, for example, Governor Edward Carville of Nevada sent his state's protest to General DeWitt: "I have made the statement here that enemy aliens would be accepted in the State of Nevada under proper supervision. This would apply to concentration camps as well as to those who might be allowed to farm or do such other things as they could do in helping out. . . . I do not desire that Nevada be made a dumping ground for enemy aliens to be going anywhere they might see fit to travel."[44]

Further, "voluntary" exodus was just not possible for most Nikkei. Many had nowhere else to go. On February 22, 1942, the commandant of the Eleventh Naval District advised Washington of the plight of those who had previously been ordered to move: "Situation of Japanese in Southern California very critical. Many are forced to move with no provision as to subsequent housing or means of livelihood. Many families already destitute. All localities object to movement of evacuees into their areas." A net total of only 4,889 Nikkei left the area as part of the "voluntary" program.[45]

While earlier proclamations applied to German and Italian aliens, as well as persons of Japanese ancestry, Public Proclamation No. 4, the "freeze" order, applied only to the Nikkei community: it prohibited persons of Japanese ancestry in Military Area No. 1, Issei and American citizen Nisei alike, from leaving the area, "to ensure an orderly, supervised, and thoroughly controlled evacuation."[46]

At the end of March, DeWitt issued the first of 108 Civilian Exclusion Orders that would eventually clear the coast of Japanese Americans. Despite their title, however, these orders were about much more than exclusion. They required persons of Japanese ancestry to report for confinement—in most cases, in so-called "assembly centers" where they would be held until more permanent camps could be built. Civilian Exclusion Order No. 1 was issued on March 24, 1942. It ordered the expulsion of all persons of Japanese ancestry, including citizens, from Bainbridge Island, Washington, but prohibited them from moving except to an "approved destination" outside Military Area No. 1. On March 30, 1942, in one long procession, Issei parents and their Nisei sons and daughters walked down the approach to the Eagledale Dock, flanked by soldiers with fixed bayonets. Their two-night trip by ferry, train, and bus ended at the Manzanar concentration camp in the Mojave Desert of California.[47]

In his later dissent in Fred's Supreme Court case, Justice Owen Roberts recognized that, while none of DeWitt's orders expressly ordered indefinite confinement, such confinement was where the orders ultimately led.

> The predicament in which [Fred Korematsu] thus found himself was this: He was forbidden, by Military Order, to leave the zone in which he lived; he was forbidden, by Military Order, after a date fixed, to be found within that zone unless he were in an Assembly Center located in that zone. General DeWitt's report to the Secretary of War concerning the programme of evacuation and relocation of Japanese makes it entirely clear, if it were necessary to refer to that document . . . that an Assembly Center was a euphemism for a prison. No person within such a center was permitted to leave except by Military Order.[48]

There were few voices raised to stop the mass incarceration. On March 28, 1942, Monroe Deutsch, provost of the University of California, sent a telegram to Supreme Court Justice Felix Frankfurter, reacting with alarm to fact that Japanese Americans and Japanese, German, and Italian aliens "will be driven out of their homes." He warned, "The expulsion of an entire group [of] American citizens because of their ancestry is an unprecedented blow to all our American principles. Does the President realize how the Army is acting? If this order goes through, I predict numerous suicides among the refugees. Will you not help[?]"[49] Other brave individuals and organizations, although not many, also spoke out against the incarceration.[50]

The civil liberties community was largely silent, or, at best, conflicted.[51] While the national American Civil Liberties Union (ACLU) wrote Roosevelt to object to Executive Order 9066, the organization seemed to concede that mass removal could occur so long as individual loyalty could be determined "before or after removal."[52] A spring 1942 poll of the ACLU Northern California chapter showed a divided membership. The vote was 144–84 in favor of Roosevelt's executive order, but 188–67 in favor of providing hearings to affected Nisei. One member commented, "The very fact that that you make such an inquiry shows that the Union has completely lost its head. The question you raise is one of military strategy, and the decision of the President and of the Army is definitely none of your business as an organization."[53]

Japanese Americans could do little but prepare to be taken away. The nation had turned on them. Their removal had been demanded by vocal and influential members of the public and the popular press, advocated up the channels of government, and acquiesced to by the president and the Justice Department. Failure to comply would be met with criminal sanctions imposed by Congress, and armed soldiers stood ready should anyone try to resist.

CHAPTER 3

FRED'S DECISION

TO LIVE FREE

JAPANESE AMERICANS REACTED TO THE NEWS OF THEIR IMPEND-ing removal in tens of thousands of different ways—with anger, fear, hurt, shock, resentment, humiliation, shame, disbelief, resignation, quiet acquiescence, and a mix of all of these feelings as well as others. Each reaction was unique and personal; they were, after all, a community of vastly different individuals and different generations. In the end, however, for most, the only choice was compliance. Only a few, like Fred, chose, or could choose, to resist.

General DeWitt's exclusion orders began to appear on telephone poles up and down the West Coast, notifying Japanese Americans in one zone after another to send a representative from each family to report to a civil control station in their area for processing. Each family and family member was assigned a number.[1] They knew that they would be ordered to leave, but they did not know when; the order in which they would be moved was kept secret. They were told that they could take only what they could carry, and once an exclusion notice was posted, families generally had only a week to ten days to decide what to take, how to store what they couldn't take, and how to dispose of the rest.[2]

Fred recalled the anxiety and turmoil at his home: "My folks were so worried about what they were going to do. All they can take was what they could carry with their hands. What they had for twenty-five years of building their business was going to go out the door or they're going to lose it. Many of the neighbors and friends, Caucasian people, came over. Can I have this, you can't take it with you. Could I have this wheelbarrow? You have a bunch of tires over there; you can't take the tires with you."[3]

Many Japanese Americans were able to find friends and business colleagues to take care of their property; some stored their belongings in temples and churches or with generous neighbors. Some of these caretakers were godsends who preserved their belongings until they returned.[4] Most Japanese Americans, however, were not so lucky. Most of the property that was stored was damaged or lost; a postwar survey revealed that 80 percent of goods privately stored were "rifled, stolen, or sold during absence." While the Korematsus were able to lease their nursery, the tenants let it go to waste.[5]

The Japanese American Citizens League (JACL) sought to provide leadership in the midst of the tumult facing the Nikkei community, and it urged both compliance and cooperation. The JACL had been founded in 1930 as a means for the Nisei to assert their identities and rights as American citizens. A year before Pearl Harbor, Mike Masaoka, executive secretary of the JACL, had expressed in the "JACL Creed" the organization's view of gratitude and service to America that would inform its actions in urging Japanese Americans to comply with wartime orders:

I am proud that I am an American citizen of Japanese ancestry, for my very background makes me appreciative more fully of the wonderful advantages of this nation. I believe in her institutions, ideals and traditions; I glory in her heritage; I boast of her history; I trust in her future. . . . Although some individuals may discriminate against me, I shall never become bitter or lose faith, for I know that such persons are not representative of the majority of the American people. True, I shall do all in my power to discourage such practices, but I shall do it in the American way, above board, in the open, through the courts of law, by education, by proving myself worthy of equal treatment and consideration. . . . I pledge myself to do honor to [America] at all times and all places; to support her constitution; to obey her laws; to respect her flag; to defend her against all enemies, foreign and domestic; to actively assume my duties and obligations as a citizen, cheerfully and without reservations whatsoever, in the hope that I may become a better American in a greater America.[6]

In testimony before the Tolan Committee on February 23, 1942, Masaoka stated the JACL's—purportedly the Japanese American community's—pledge to comply with the program of removal:

> Senator Sparkman: . . . Do I understand that it is your attitude that the Japanese-American citizens do not protest necessarily against an evacuation? They simply want to lodge their claims to consideration?
>
> Mr. Masaoka: Yes.
>
> Mr. Sparkman: But in the event that the evacuation is deemed necessary by those having charge of the defenses, as loyal Americans you are willing to prove your loyalty by cooperating? . . . Even at a sacrifice?
>
> Mr. Masaoka: Oh, yes; definitely. I think that all of us are called upon to make sacrifices. I think we will be called to make greater sacrifices than any others. But I think sincerely, if the military says "Move out," we will be glad to move, because we recognize that even behind evacuation there is not just national security but also a thought to our own welfare and security because we may be subject to mob violence and otherwise if we are permitted to remain.
>
> Mr. Sparkman: And it affords you, as a matter of fact, perhaps the best test of your own loyalty?
>
> Mr. Masaoka: Provided that the military or the people charged with the responsibility are cognizant of all the facts.[7]

Masaoka later explained the decision to cooperate: "We were led to believe that if we cooperated with the Army in this mass movement, the government would try to be as helpful and humane as possible to the evacuees." He further explained the fear that any refusal to cooperate would make them appear to be traitors, "forever plac[ing] in jeopardy our future as United States citizens."[8]

Many Japanese Americans did not share the JACL's views. James Omura, for example, who worked in the San Francisco flower industry and published the Nisei magazine *Current Life*, also testified before the Tolan Committee and challenged the JACL position: "I am strongly opposed to mass evacuation of American-born Japanese. It is my honest belief that such an action would not solve the question of Nisei loyalty." He objected to the testimony of other representatives of the community: "I refer specifically to the JACL."[9]

Despite these objections to the JACL position, the organization, through Mike Masaoka and its president, Saburo Kido, would represent the Nikkei community in communications with the government, the military, and the American public, and, in the confusion and stress of early 1942, many Japanese Americans looked to the organization for leadership.[10]

While some Nikkei complied to prove their loyalty, others complied for a myriad of other reasons. Many, like Fred's family, complied simply because they were in shock or overwhelmed with the task of settling their affairs in an exceedingly short period of time. The Korematsu home was stifling with despair. Fred recalled, "They knew that . . . worst gonna come to them. . . . [M]y mother was always in tears all the time. . . . Just worried about, 'What are we gonna do?'" Their business was practically at a standstill, and they barely had enough food to live on. Fred's parents relied on the older two boys; Fred felt that as the third son, his opinion didn't matter much.[11]

Fred needed to be with Ida, the woman he loved and intended to marry, and he could not let the impending removal order separate them. He decided that he had to leave the nursery to make his own way with Ida:

> I decided to leave . . . [a]way from the family because there was so much sadness. . . . [T]hey obeyed the law and did what should be right; they did everything they're supposed to do and whatever they can to help other people; they concentrate on raising their family, just the normal life. And to have this happen, it put them into shame. . . . It was hard to talk to them after that. When the evacuation notice came, they had to worry about what they were going to take and what they could take and what was going to happen to the nursery. . . .
>
> Whatever my problems were, they just didn't have time for me. . . . I was twenty-one then and you know when you're at that age, you have a girlfriend and all just like everyone else. She was more important to me than anything else. In order to think clearly, . . . I had to get away from them. When the evacuation order came, I told them that I would like to leave ahead of them and maybe go out of state before this happened. They said to go ahead, so I decided to leave on my own.[12]

Fred's parents told him that he was old enough to know what he wanted, and if he wanted to leave before the date to report for camp, he should. He hadn't told them that he wanted to stay to be with Ida. Fred thought that he and Ida might be able to escape to Nevada. While they could not marry there, they would at least be outside of the prohibited zone.[13]

In choosing to stay behind with Ida, Fred chose liberty over confinement. That liberty was the freedom to be with the person he loved, to be near her where he pleased, and to enjoy the rights of citizenship guaranteed any other American. Although he may not have initially seen his decision to resist as a matter of principle, in refusing confinement, he was, through his actions, exercising freedom. He couldn't recall exactly when his refusal to report transformed from a choice to stay with Ida to an exercise of his rights, but it did. "I don't remember a conscious moment when it became more than a personal issue. Things were going so fast, and I was so young." He knew, perhaps subconsciously at first and later consciously, that the incarceration violated his rights: "Looking back, I felt it [the removal] was wrong because any person who did wrong, a criminal, would get a fair trial or get a hearing to prove that they're guilty. But to be pushed into evacuation, threatened with punishment, because you look like the enemy is wrong. . . . I felt that I was an American citizen and I had as much rights as anyone else. I don't even have ties with Japan nor have I ever been there. To be accused like this, I just thought it wasn't fair. It was wrong."[14]

He and Ida discussed his decision, but she said she wasn't ready to leave. Fred rented a room in the Fruitvale area of Oakland; perhaps they'd be able to leave once things settled down. He sold his car, a '38 Pontiac— "A very nice car, a sedan. Loved that car." When the dealer offered him only $200 for it, "I said I just paid $800 a year and a half earlier. [He] said that's war. I felt like I was robbed, but I couldn't do anything about it."[15]

Fred and Ida racked their brains to figure out a way to stay in Oakland without being recognized. One Sunday, Ida showed Fred an ad for a plastic surgeon in San Francisco and asked, "Why don't you think of this"? Fred didn't think it was good idea, but Ida said it was one alternative. Fred said he'd look into it; plastic surgery might make it easier if they wanted to travel to Nevada or the Midwest. It might protect him from ostracism, and, as he later told the FBI, "he feared violence should anyone discover that he, a Japanese, was married to an American girl."[16]

On March 4, 1942, Fred went to the office of Dr. B. B. Masten, the doctor who had placed the ad. Fred recalled his uncertainty about the whole idea: "When I was going to the plastic surgeon in San Francisco, it was a regular house, a sort of Victorian, it was white, and I was undecided. There were about ten steps or so to go up to the house. I was going halfway up and then I would finally turn around and go back down. That's how I felt. But I finally went in." Fred explained to the doctor that he was a Japanese American married to an "American girl" and wanted to change his features so that he and wife would not be subject to "comment and harassment." The doctor told Fred that he could "build up his nose and remove the folds from the inner corner of his upper eyelid," but that he could not make Fred look like "an American." The doctor asked for $300 to perform the surgery, but Fred had only $100, which the doctor accepted.[17]

Fred checked into a San Francisco rooming house under the name Henry Lee and had surgery at Dr. Masten's office on March 18 and 24, 1942. Fred later explained that the doctor fixed his nose, which he had broken playing football, but otherwise "[h]e didn't do what he said he'd do; he just took my money." "He didn't do a very good job because even my girlfriend didn't say too much. When I first met my mother in camp, she recognized me right away and so did most of my friends, so I knew there wasn't much of a change." In retrospect, Fred felt the surgery had been a mistake, "I did a stupid thing by doing that." "I just didn't have a broken nose anymore. . . . So it was very foolish of me to do that."[18]

Despite the fact that the plastic surgery was a failure, Fred continued to make plans to leave with Ida. He knew that whenever he and Ida left, they would need money, so he needed to work. He changed his name to Clyde Sarah on his draft card so he'd have some identification to show an employer. He picked Clyde because he wanted to tell people that he was Spanish-Hawaiian, and he thought it sounded like a Spanish name. He picked Sarah because that was Ida's middle name. While welding jobs were plentiful, Fred thought it would be impossible for him to work in the shipyards because there would be guards. At a trailer company in Berkeley he was hired as a welder on the spot and paid cash for his work.[19]

Away from the oppressive environment of home, Fred felt the freedom he sought. He saw Ida almost every other night. He could go about his days just as he had always done. "People going shopping, sitting next to me on the bus, or going to a movie or something like that, they didn't have time to bother to see if I was Japanese or not. It was just like in everyday living. I just felt in the mainstream of American living." His sense of normalcy, however, was interrupted every time he saw a paper. "The only time that I felt uncomfortable was when I happened to glance at a newspaper and it said Jap this and Jap that, all that about the war, and all the bad things about the Japanese. That's the only thing that upset me, and I even refused to buy a paper because of that."[20]

On May 3, 1942, DeWitt issued Civilian Exclusion Order No. 34, requiring the Korematsus and other persons of Japanese ancestry residing in their area of southern Alameda County, California, to register with the army, and proclaiming that they would be banned from the area as of noon, Saturday, May 9, 1942. Now the day had come. Fred recalled seeing the notices: "When the exclusion order was posted on telephone poles in 1942, I felt angry and hurt and confused about my future. I could not understand how the United States Government could do this to American citizens, who were interned while Americans of German and Italian descent were allowed to be free."[21] And for flower growers like the Korematsus, DeWitt's order could not have come at a worse time. Mother's Day would occur on May 10, the day after the Korematsus were required to leave; they would lose their crop and the money and labor the crop represented.[22]

Fred knew from the local papers that his family was being sent away, and his thoughts turned to them: "I happened to overhear at work that the Japanese were all evacuated into camp, so I did buy a paper on the way back from work. I saw the pictures where the Japanese Americans were being marched into camp, and it sort of made me sick to my stomach. . . . I could see my parents going in and my brothers going into camp, and I'm not there. That's the only time that I felt, sort of, all alone."[23]

Headquarters
Western Defense Command
and Fourth Army

Presidio of San Francisco, California

May 3, 1942

Civilian Exclusion Order No. 34

1. Pursuant to the provisions of Public Proclamations Nos. 1 and 2, this Headquarters, dated March 2, 1942, and March 16, 1942, respectively, it is hereby ordered that from and after 12 o'clock noon, P.W.T., of Saturday, May 9, 1942, all persons of Japanese ancestry, both alien and non-alien, be excluded from that portion of Military Area No. 1 described as follows:

> All of that portion of the County of Alameda, State of California, within the boundary beginning at the point where the southerly limits of the City of Oakland meet San Francisco Bay; thence easterly and following the southerly limits of said city to U. S. Highway No. 50; thence southerly and easterly on said Highway No. 50 to its intersection with California State Highway No. 21; thence southerly on said Highway No. 21 to its intersection, at or near Warm Springs, with California State Highway No. 17; thence southerly on said Highway No. 17 to the Alameda-Santa Clara County line; thence westerly and following said county line to San Francisco Bay; thence northerly, and following the shoreline of San Francisco Bay to the point of beginning.

2. A responsible member of each family, and each individual living alone, in the above described area will report between the hours of 8:00 A. M. and 5:00 P. M., Monday, May 4, 1942, or during the same hours on Tuesday, May 5, 1942, to the Civil Control Station located at:

> 920 - "C" Street,
> Hayward, California.

3. Any person subject to this order who fails to comply with any of its provisions or published instructions pertaining hereto or who is found in the above area after 12 o'clock noon, P.W.T., of Saturday, May 9, 1942, will be liable to the criminal penalties provided by Public Law No. 503, 77th Congress, approved March 21, 1942, entitled "An Act to Provide a Penalty for Violation of Restrictions or Orders with Respect to Persons Entering, Remaining in, Leaving or Committing any Act in Military Areas or Zones," and alien Japanese will be subject to immediate apprehension and internment.

4. All persons within the bounds of an established Assembly Center pursuant to instructions from this Headquarters are excepted from the provisions of this order while those persons are in such Assembly Center.

J. L. DeWitt
Lieutenant General, U. S. Army
Commanding

FIGURE 3.1. Fred violated Civilian Exclusion Order No. 34, which ordered persons of Japanese ancestry to leave southern Alameda County, California, and to report for confinement by noon on May 9, 1942. Courtesy of National Archives and Records Administration at San Francisco.

CHAPTER 4

JAIL WAS BETTER THAN CAMP

ON FRIDAY, MAY 8, 1942, FIVE DAYS AFTER RECEIVING NOTICE OF General DeWitt's exclusion order, Fred's family reported to Watkins Street, City Plaza, in Hayward, California, to be taken away. Fred was not with them. The Korematsus became family 21538. Typically, on the date and time set for departure, groups of about five hundred reported to a given spot. Each incarceree was individually tagged: Harry, Kakusaburo, Kotsui, and Joe were designated 21538-A through -D, respectively.[1]

In boarding the buses and trains that took them from their communities, Japanese Americans began journeys they could scarcely anticipate—they did not know where they were going, what would happen to them, or when, if ever, they would return. In the end, they would be gone for years, moved about, and eventually taken far from home.[2]

Most Nikkei found themselves herded into temporary detention centers—euphemistically called "assembly" centers—created to hold them until more permanent facilities for their incarceration were completed. These centers were often racetracks and fairgrounds, places that could be quickly converted to confine large numbers of people; the Korematsus were sent to the Tanforan Racetrack in San Bruno, California.[3]

Years later, Japanese Americans vividly recalled entering camp—while they had committed no crimes, it was clear from what they saw and how they were treated that they were being imprisoned. Armed guards stood at the entrance of compounds surrounded by barbed wire.[4] On arrival, incarcerees were searched for contraband, fingerprinted, interrogated, and inoculated; Miné Okubo, in her account of her arrival at Tanforan, recalled being ordered to strip for a medical exam.[5]

Living quarters were bleak, cramped, and dirty. Many incarcerees found themselves assigned to horse stalls still smelling of fresh manure. Pests such as spiders, mice, and rats abounded. Tiny fleas infested the area. At Tanforan and elsewhere, the first thing incarcerees had to do was to stuff their own mattresses with hay. Eight-person families were placed in twenty-by-twenty-foot rooms, six people in twelve-by-twenty-foot rooms, and four people in eight-by-twenty-foot rooms. Smaller families, including married couples, had to share single rooms with other families. The cramped quarters afforded no privacy. Because partitions between families were only partial, if they existed at all, "[l]oud snores, the grinding of teeth, the wail of babies, [and] the murmur of conversations" could be heard the full length of the barracks or stables.[6]

Life in camp was regimented and difficult. Roll call was held twice a day, at 6:45 a.m. and 6:45 p.m. Showers, bathroom facilities, and dining were communal, and there were endless lines: "'Line-ups here and line-ups there' describes our daily life. We lined up for mail, for checks, for meals, for showers, for washrooms, for laundry tubs, for toilets, for clinic service, for movies. We lined up for everything." Toilets and showers were not partitioned, and "[t]he stench from stagnant sewage was terrible."[7] The food was awful. Sox Kitashima remembered her first meal at Tanforan: two slices of discolored cold cuts, overcooked Swiss chard, and a slice of moldy bread.[8] At its peak, Tanforan housed 7,816 individuals.[9]

The incarceration affected the Nikkei in different and complex ways. The Issei, the older generation, saw their lives, everything they had worked for, their roles as heads-of-household, and their futures turned completely upside down, and many felt adrift.[10] Others found a measure of relief from their former day-to-day struggle for survival.[11] In contrast to the older Issei, the Nisei experienced the incarceration as children or teenagers, or as young adults whose dreams of starting their educations or careers were dashed by confinement. They were American citizens taken from their homes and put behind barbed wire by their own country. Some Nisei, rejecting the Japanese American Citizens League (JACL) view that compliance was a civic duty, felt tremendously betrayed.[12]

Many Nisei recall the profound shifts in family dynamics caused by incarceration. At the same time that Issei parents experienced the loss of their roles as breadwinners and authority figures, many Nisei reveled in their new-found release from parental control.[13] In significant ways, however, the loss of traditional family structures was yet another tragedy of the incarceration. With communal mess halls, children began eating with friends, and family members stopped eating together. "Family life was lacking. Everyone ate wherever he or she pleased. Mothers had lost all control over their children."[14]

Despite these difficult circumstances, the Nikkei endeavored to bring some semblance of normalcy to the unreal environment of camp. They fashioned furniture out of discarded crates and landscaped patches of ground. Scout troops, musical groups, and arts and crafts classes were gradually formed; movies were shown; schools and libraries were opened. While the Nikkei could conduct church services, the services were monitored out of fear that they might spread propaganda. Nikkei in many of the camps started newspapers, although, like all publications in camp, the papers had to be published in English and cleared by the Wartime Civil Control Administration (WCCA), which operated the camps.[15] Although Japanese Americans were not required to work, the WCCA expected that the incarcerees would do most of the camp work. Initially working for no pay, they were later paid, albeit very little: eight dollars per month for unskilled work, twelve dollars for skilled work, and sixteen dollars for professional and technical work.[16]

As of May 8, 1942, the date his family left for Tanforan and he stayed behind, Fred was living in his hometown in Oakland unlawfully. But he didn't feel that he was a criminal. Instead, he felt he was living just as he had always done:

> When I left the nursery and the family, got away from all this problem and everything, I felt that, I'm free. I didn't feel guilty 'cause I don't think I did anything wrong. I'm not like a criminal. I didn't do any criminal act. . . . I was taught in school, you had equal right. You believe in the Constitution and you live by it. And that's what soldiers die for, for freedom. I felt more comfortable on the outside and I felt more comfortable when I went to work. It kept my mind away from all of that. Just concentrate on doing a good job.[17]

It was Memorial Day—the afternoon of May 30, 1942—when an officer stopped Fred and Ida as they walked down Estudillo Avenue in San Leandro. Fred first identified himself as Clyde Sarah but then confessed that he was Japanese and that he had remained behind when his family was sent to Tanforan. He was arrested and booked into the San Leandro Jail—a very small jail, as Fred recalled, with only two cells. He remembered his keepers as being quite nice: "[W]henever I wanted to have food, we went to a restaurant. And they apologized every time they put handcuffs on me to take me out to eat." The captain, however, was not happy about his new charge: "[H]e was all upset because I was still around. He said, 'Fred, you should have gone to internment camp. Now you've caused all this trouble.'" As he lay on his cot, Fred thought about how he had spent Memorial Day in the past; here he was now, looking at the inside of a cell.[18]

Fred was transferred to the Alameda County Jail the next day. The *Oakland Post-Enquirer* headline read, "Oakland Jap Held for FBI" and reported that Fred had been arrested on a tip from two military police officers. The *Oakland Tribune* reported that the tip concerned the presence of a "suspicious character" on Estudillo and quoted Fred as saying simply, "I didn't want to go." The *San Leandro Observer* headline was more charitable to Fred: "Jap Youth No Ancestor Worshipper."[19]

When interviewed by FBI Special Agent Oliver T. Mansfield, Fred explained that he had lived with his family in Oakland all of his life. He acknowledged that he had moved out of his family's home in March, had undergone surgery in an attempt to alter his appearance, and had used an alias. According to Mansfield, Fred said that he knew that remaining in Oakland had been wrong and that he had intended to turn himself in. One might wonder now, over half a century later, why Fred didn't tell Mansfield that he had done nothing wrong—that he, as an American citizen, had a constitutional right to remain free. Maybe he was scared or intimidated or both. Maybe he wanted to protect Ida. Most importantly, however, he, as an American citizen, did not have to invoke his constitutional rights to be able to exercise them. While Fred may not have asserted his rights in words, he had asserted his right to liberty by choosing to stay. As Agent Mansfield reported, Fred "explained his actions in this whole matter as having been prompted by a desire to remain in the San Francisco and East Bay Area until he [could] evacuate voluntarily with his girl . . . to some spot in the Middle

West where they could live as normal people."[20] Fred had stayed behind so that he and Ida could "live as normal people"; while not quoting the Constitution, he was seeking the freedom it promised.

Fred was transferred yet again, this time to the Presidio stockade in San Francisco. Thinking he'd have a hearing at some point, he wondered how he could fight his arrest and worried about the results: "[W]ith everyone against you, the government against you, and no one to help you, I figured that there was slim chance." His answer came when a guard told him he had a visitor. Because everyone he knew was in camp or in the military, he couldn't imagine who it could be, and assumed it was someone with a church group or similar organization. When Fred was escorted to the visiting area, he saw a young man in a gray suit waiting for him.[21] Ernest Besig started with simple pleasantries, just to break the ice: "Hey Fred, how they treating you?" "Well, okay," Fred replied. Besig asked if Fred could use any cigarettes or candy, and Fred said he could. Fred found Besig "a very nice fella, very easy to talk to"; Besig observed Fred to be a shy and reticent young man.[22]

Getting down to business, Besig introduced himself as an attorney with the ACLU. "Oh, my God," Fred thought, "I could not afford an attorney." Besig reassured Fred, "Oh, no, it's on me." Besig said he'd be interested in fighting Fred's case and asked if Fred would like him to help him at his hearing. Fred later related, "I said I had never done this before, so I'll be glad to have someone. I asked him, who do you represent? When he introduced himself as a representative of the American Civil Liberties Union, I didn't even know what that was."[23]

Ernest Besig was the executive director of the San Francisco office of the ACLU. He had been searching for someone willing to bring a test case to challenge the removal orders, to no avail. He had reported to Roger Baldwin, director of the national ACLU, how difficult it was to find someone who would press the case against the military orders in court. The JACL, Besig reported, "had definitely instructed its people not to contest any action by the local, state or federal authorities."[24] He read of Fred's arrest in the papers and went to see him, hoping he would find a willing litigant.

We tried to find a legal challenge to the internment, but, of course, in order to do that, you have to have a test case. You have to find somebody who is willing to have his case carried through the courts way up to the U.S. Supreme Court. . . . It wasn't easy, until I heard of Fred Korematsu's case in the newspapers. And I at once undertook to visit him in the county jail where he was, shall we say, being detained. . . . I was there to persuade Fred, and I was hopeful that he would support a test case, that he would be willing to be the test case—the person who would challenge the government's discrimination against him. And, ultimately, he did.[25]

Besig warned Fred, however, that the chances of winning were slim; it would be an uphill battle, given the prejudice against Japanese Americans and the reluctance of the courts to question military decisions. Further, he warned Fred that he would be subject to the scrutiny of the press, including reporters who would focus on his failed plastic surgery. Despite these warnings from Besig, Fred agreed to challenge his arrest, assuring Besig that he was willing to take his case to the Supreme Court, if necessary.[26] Besig had found his test case.

Although Besig had told Fred that he represented the Northern California chapter of the ACLU, the chapter's membership was deeply fractured. The March 1942 membership poll had resoundingly supported Roosevelt's Executive Order 9066 by a vote of 144 to 84; by a slim majority, however, chapter members opposed DeWitt's orders (113–110). When asked whether the ACLU should test the constitutionality of the orders as they applied to U.S. citizens, a similarily slim majority (120–117) said "no." Nevertheless, the chapter board agreed to pursue the challenge, paving the way for the chapter's support of Fred's case.[27] The division within the Northern California chapter foreshadowed battles Besig would later fight with the national organization.

Meeting Besig gave Fred the means to fight his arrest and made it even clearer to him that he had been wronged: "I didn't have any of these legal experiences behind me. . . . I didn't have any of my friends or my relatives or my family alongside of me to make this decision. So . . . it was quite difficult for me at that time. So it was a slow decision until I met Mr. Besig, and that changed everything."[28]

On June 18, military police took Fred to Tanforan. As Fred approached the camp, he was shocked at what he saw: "As I was going to camp, Tanforan

Racetrack, I can see from the freeway the Japanese people in there and the kids and everything. And you know what they reminded me of? An Indian reservation . . . all the kids were dark and brown from being in the sun and it was dusty and everything. Like people who haven't got very much money and you have to be put into a camp." Fred thought, "All the dust was flying around and it looked terrible. Wow. Am I going there?"[29]

When he arrived, he said he'd prefer his own quarters to give him some time to think before he saw his parents. He described his horse stall:

> And I went over there with the little I had; the FBI took everything, like my clothes and all. And I looked at the number and I opened the door; it had a gap of about six to eight inches from the ground, the dirt floor. And inside they just had a cot and a straw mattress in there. And there's gaping holes on all the walls; the wind just blew in there, and the dust blew in there and everything. As I sat there, as I [lay] there to think it over, I guess I was there for about forty-five minutes and I said, boy, this is really a miserable place, no heat or anything. I mean, this was made for horses, not for human beings. I just wondered how in the world people lived in this for this long.

The cot, its mattress, and a single light bulb hanging from the ceiling comprised his only furnishings. As Fred lay on the cot, he thought, "Gee, jail was a lot better than this. In jail, it's air conditioned, it's heated at night, you have a nice cot with a wash basin."[30]

Fred heard a knock on the door. It was his brother Hi: "Come on, ma and pa want to see you. You better come along." They walked to the family's quarters, on the other side of the camp. When Fred's mother saw him, she cried. Fred said his father "gave me the dickens for getting involved in all this trouble."[31] While Kay Korematsu did not meet the family until later, after she married Hi, she was aware of their reaction to Fred's arrest. Fred's brothers thought his arrest was shameful. Hi was angry: "Why did he do that? It was just solely for that woman." Harry thought Fred was not very intelligent. Kay described Fred's father as very upset: "*[B]akatare dakara, ne*," he said—"dumbbell." "Why did you do this? *Doshite sonnakoto o shitanoka*? Why did you do such a thing?" Fred's mother reacted to Fred's arrest with shame and embarrassment. She did not want to go out, fearful that people were against her. According to Kay, Fred's mother didn't speak of Fred's arrest because it hurt her so much.[32]

Despite their feelings about what Fred had done, Fred's parents insisted that he move in with them. Fred noted how they had fixed up their stall. They had filled the cracks and put newspaper up on the walls. They had hung blankets for partitions. "They made it as homey as possible. They were making the best of it."[33]

The day after Fred arrived at Tanforan, Hi asked him to meet with others to get their views on whether he should fight his arrest, and Fred agreed. At the gathering that night, groups of young people talked among themselves; their backs were turned on Fred, and no one spoke to him. Fred recalled, "[A]ll of a sudden, they disappeared. And then I caught my brother and said, 'What happened?' 'Oh, they think that you're going to make it worse for them. They don't know what's going to happen to them yet, and all you're going to do is make it worse for them. They don't want you to do it.'"[34] A camp official later interviewed by the FBI reported that some Japanese Americans had met with Fred, but that he "did not believe that they would support [him] to any great extent due to the fact that most of them desired to cooperate with the United States government."[35]

Charles Kikuchi, who was at Tanforan at the same time as Fred, recalled the discussion in ways similar to, but also different from, Fred. The group, Kikuchi related, had met in Hi's room to discuss their opinions on Fred's case. Kikuchi knew that Fred had had plastic surgery, but said "he looked quite Japanese to me." Kikuchi explained, "Fred, as far as himself was concerned, is perfectly willing to fight the case as he feels that it may determine a principle. However, he was a little uncertain as to what repercussions it would have on the group if it got wide publicity and he wanted to sound out opinion." Several present warned against a legal challenge. A man named Vic, who Kikuchi described as "legalistically minded," said that Fred should not press his case "because it would only make the pressure groups redouble their efforts." Another man, Mitch, felt that the "evacuation was an established fact and that our prime efforts should be in the direction of the future and make this program a success, which would at the same time prove our loyalty. . . . [H]e thought that it should be fought, but was not sure that this was the proper time." Another, Ernie T., "believed that all Nisei would be hurt by a test case."[36] The group resolved to meet again.

Kikuchi recalled that, at that later meeting, the group said the decision belonged to Fred, as he "would be the only one to suffer in case he lost." However, "we told him that we would all back him as most of us by this time believed that the pressure groups would go ahead with their program regardless of whether we kept quiet or put up a fight." While Kikuchi further stated that Fred's brother Hi supported Fred in fighting his case, nothing Hi ever did or said indicated anything other than disdain for Fred's actions. And while Kikuchi stated in his diary that "many Nisei believe as [Fred] does in regard to this situation," in the end, Fred felt he received no support in fighting his case from the Japanese Americans in camp. Kikuchi's account does show that *he* at least supported Fred, even if privately. Kikuchi wrote, "Fred has the 'guts' to fight this thing. I don't believe that the group would suffer by it. In fact, we have everything to gain. We are not prisoners of war and our civil rights have been taken away without due process of law."[37]

Despite Kikuchi's view that some did support Fred in challenging the government's orders, Fred left the meeting with the belief that he would fight his case alone—not only without the backing of his family or community, but also in the face of their disapproval. Although disappointed, Fred understood the complex and mixed responses that the Nikkei had to their incarceration. He knew that the Nisei were worried for themselves and for their parents. He explained, "Because they were already interned, they feared for their lives. They were also concerned about their parents' safety. They were afraid of what harm would come to them." He knew that many Nisei believed that they would prove their patriotism by complying: "[T]hey wanted to be good Americans by going along with the internment, with what the government wanted, with what America wanted. They didn't like what I was doing."[38]

Fred also understood the community's lack of support because, for some, his actions in challenging the government violated cultural norms.

I assumed that I got myself into this problem and therefore it was my problem and not theirs. . . . If they were in favor of it, I would be much happier that I had them backing me up on this. I just wonder if I was doing wrong or maybe putting them in shame by bringing the issue up again. Because Japanese people, they're peaceful people and they like to leave things alone if they can. They were in enough trouble as it is because of the Pearl Harbor attack. They sorta felt that the country blamed them and they had this sort of guilty complex even though they had nothing to do with it.[39]

The responses of acceptance and compliance had deep roots in the cultural values that the Issei had brought with them from Japan, and while most Nisei had become Americanized, they had of course absorbed the teachings of their Issei parents. Those values had enabled Japanese Americans to endure the discrimination they experienced prior to camp, and now helped them to endure the camps as well. Gordon Nagai, who was four when his family was sent to Amache, Colorado, explained, "There's a saying in Japanese, *shikata ga nai*, means 'it can't be helped.' So any time something bad or tragic happens, that's a saying you'll hear. . . . Regardless of what happens, you have to do the best you can to get the best out of it. So for a lot of Japanese, that's what they did." In addition, *gaman* is a value that requires perseverance in the face of adversity.[40]

Giri requires a sense of duty and obligation, and Japanese Americans had a strong sense of duty to family: *kazuko no tame ni* ("for the sake of the family"). Because of their duties to their families, many Nisei did not, and could not, resist incarceration; they feared what would happen to their parents, and they needed to care for them and do what they could to keep the family together.[41] And this duty required that the Nisei not do anything that would bring their family shame. As Mei Nakano explains:

> To be a "good Japanese" meant bringing pride and honor to the Japanese race. One did that, not surprisingly, by complying with the . . . catalog of Japanese behavioral norms like *gaman* (perseverance) and *enryo* (self-restraint, reserve) and *giri* (sense of duty and obligation). One should also strive to be *majime* (serious, honest) and *sunao* (gentle, obedient), and, by all means, hold *oya koh koh* (filial piety) among the highest of ideals. . . . In addition, parents called forth the specter of *haji* (shame, disgrace) to drive home the injunctions. Errant behavior not only brought *haji* to themselves, Nisei were told, but to their parents, the family, the community, and finally, by extension, to the entire race.[42]

In refusing to comply with the removal orders, leaving his family to be with Ida, and choosing to fight his case, Fred violated these cultural norms. For these acts, others likely saw him as bringing shame to his family and community. For this, he was ostracized. Fred recalled his feeling of isolation: "The other internees knew about me and they kept away from me. They figured I was a troublemaker." He had few friends in camp. When Japanese Americans were put to work to build, maintain, and operate the camp, Fred chose to work the graveyard shift doing maintenance work so that he could sleep during the day and avoid contact with others.[43]

Despite knowing that he would press his case without support from the Nikkei community, Fred was clear in his convictions. In July, when FBI agent G. E. Goodwin visited him at Tanforan for follow-up questioning, Fred told Goodwin that "he did not consider himself a criminal in any way." He believed that "the statute under which he was imprisoned was wrong, and that he [was] guilty of no wrong-doing." In a note to Besig, Fred reflected on camp, as well as on his belief that his case might help address the wrong: "These camps have been definitely . . . an imprisonment under armed guard with orders to shoot to kill. In order to be imprisoned, these people should have been given a fair trial in order that they may defend their loyalty at court in a democratic way, but they were placed in imprisonment without any fair trial! . . . Is this a racial issue? . . . Fred Korematsu's Test Case may help."[44]

Goodwin also interviewed Ida. Perhaps out of fear, Ida had distanced herself from Fred and his actions. She said that Fred had discussed having plastic surgery not only because he wished to stay with her but also because he was ashamed of being Japanese; she said she tried to talk him out of it. She said she knew that Fred was violating the law in refusing to report for detention, and while she had tried to get him to report, he had refused to go. While she acknowledged that she and Fred had been engaged, "she now realized that such a marriage was impossible and that she had made a big mistake, particularly after the law regarding evacuation went into effect." She was "sorry that she did not report him to the proper authorities when he refused to give himself up." Ida did tell Goodwin, however, that she knew Fred "to be perfectly loyal to the United States," that he had never been to Japan, and that he had no relatives there. She said that Fred had written her from Tanforan and that she had written him back, asking that he not write to her anymore.[45]

Ida took a much different tone in writing to Besig. Besig and Fred had begun a steady exchange of letters that reveal not only the warm affection that developed between the two men, but also the trust and confidence Fred placed in Besig. In the earliest of these letters, Fred asked Besig to help him negotiate a number of personal matters that Fred could not otherwise handle from camp. One of those personal matters that Fred reluctantly asked Besig to help with was Ida. Fred wrote Besig,

> What I am going to say in this next line or so in this letter is not in your line of business. But I am helpless here at Tanforan, and as a friend, you are the only one that understands me, and possibly help me. It is about my girl. I must see her personally. I know she is half worried and scared, what's going to happen to both of us. The time I got caught, I didn't have a chance to talk to her. I know that if I see her and talk to her everything will be alright. . . . I hate to ask you for this favor. Because you have done to [sic] much for me already. . . . I must see her. It's important for both of us. In fact very important.[46]

Ida wrote to Besig. She expressed her belief that Fred had not done anything wrong: "I appreciate the fact that you do not think that Fred committed any crime. I don't either. I wish Fred all the luck in this world, and I'd certainly appreciate it if you would tell him that for me." She did, however, ask that Fred not write her "at least for a while 'cause our countries are at war with each other and being that they open all of his letters before they get to me, might prove very dangerous to me." She continued, "I wish I could explain it to Fred, mebbe [sic] you could convince him for me. I know it's very difficult not to be able to write. But until he reaches his destination I would prefer it if he did not write to me. You see I happen to be Italian and this is war, so we must both be careful." She asked Besig to please let her know what was going to happen to Fred. "I am worried as to the outcome of this situation, but I hope everything will turn out all right in the end." She closed, "Please answer this letter as soon as possible, as I am very anxious to know about what happened. Yours Truly, Miss Ida Boitano."[47]

Besig answered Ida's letter on July 7, reporting to her that he had just visited Fred at Tanforan and that Fred "seemed to be in good spirits and getting along fairly well." He told her that he did not anticipate success in the lower courts and that the ACLU intended to appeal to the Court of Appeals and then to the Supreme Court. He encouraged Ida to communicate with Fred and visit him at Tanforan.[48] When Besig called Ida in August to go with him to visit Fred, Ida said she could not; she had, she explained, been advised not to contact Fred.[49] She later told Fred, too, that she could not communicate with him, at least temporarily. On September 3, Fred wrote Besig,

> I have received a letter from my girl friend Ida, and she say's the police force of San Leandro, have adviced her not to contact me nor visit me, because it might get me into trouble or her, But she write's me once in a while to find out how I am getting along. She says she misses me very much, and promise to wait for me, I know if there was a chance to be together again, she would gladly come, But for the moment I think it best to let it go, until I straighten out what's going to happen to me.[50]

While Fred and Ida exchanged letters for a brief period of time during his incarceration, he eventually stopped writing her because he didn't want to create difficulties for her. "I never saw her again. Her family was very friendly with the lieutenant [in San Leandro], so there must have been something funny going on there, but I didn't know. I figured that trying to keep in touch with her would cause her more problems. I'm in trouble already, but I assume that maybe she's not. So if I try to get in touch with her, it may cause her more problems. I decided we might as well just cut it clean."[51]

Formal charges were filed against Fred on June 12, 1942, just before he was sent to Tanforan. The office of the United States Attorney for the Northern District of California in San Francisco alleged that Fred had violated the law by "remain[ing] in that portion of Military Area No. 1 covered by Civilian Exclusion Order no. 34." News of the charges made it as far away as the East Coast: the *New York Times* reported Fred's case, highlighting, of course, his plastic surgery.[52]

Ernest Besig recruited Northern California ACLU chapter board member Clarence Rust to handle Fred's initial arraignment on June 18. The judge set bail at $2,500, and, to Fred's surprise, Besig took out his checkbook without hesitation, wrote out a check for the bail, and gave it to the clerk. What Fred didn't know was that Besig had paid Fred's bail out of the chapter's own, likely meager, reserve funds.[53] Fred recalled how he and Besig marched toward what he thought would be freedom: "Besig said, 'Come on, Fred,' he grabbed ahold of me, and we started walking out. I just couldn't believe this was going on. You could hear our footsteps, clunk, clunk, clunk, all the way down to the door opening to Mission Street and Seventh. And as we opened the door, and I said, 'Wow!' The sun was shining and I just couldn't believe it, here we were going out the door." Despite the fact that Fred had posted bail, which would allow any other person to go free, DeWitt's military orders prohibited Fred, as a Japanese American, from being in the area.

> And then I looked real good, there was four MPs standing there. They already knew this was gonna happen. And Mr. Besig said, "You haven't any authority over him. We paid the bail; he's a civilian. He's not a military man, and he has a right to go. And we're going." And they said "No, he's not. We have orders from my commanding officer that he is not going to step outside this door." And they start pulling out their guns and he said, "Well, I guess we better go in." And they marched us in, the MPs and we all went back to the judge.[54]

What followed seemed a capitulation of the civil authority of the court to the armed authority of the military police. "Then they raised the bail again, higher . . . $10,000 or something. Mr. Besig was going to pull out his check again, and then he laughed and said I wanted to see how far they would go. And he said, 'Fred, you go ahead and go with them. I'll be in touch with you.' So the MPs took me down to the Presidio." As Besig later related, Fred's right to bail had been nullified.[55]

Fred recalled the trip back to confinement. "I sat in the back seat between the two MPs. Going down Mission Street toward the Presidio, I felt like a prisoner of war, like I was being treated like a dangerous person. I felt that I was an American and they were treating me the wrong way. As I was sitting in the back seat of this military car with these MPs, I felt how un-American I could be to be treated like this."[56] From the Presidio, Fred was transported back to Tanforan and waited for his case to make its way through the courts.

In September 1942, the army began to move the incarcerees at Tanforan to the more permanent concentration camp at Topaz, Utah, one of ten "relocation centers" built for the confinement of Japanese Americans "for the duration of the war." Fred was moved to Topaz on September 28. Other camps were in Poston and Gila River in Arizona; Amache near Granada, Colorado; Heart Mountain in Wyoming; Jerome in Utah; Manzanar in the Mojave Desert of California; Minidoka in Idaho; Rohwer in Arkansas; and Tule Lake in California. Like most of the other camps, Topaz had been selected because of its remoteness and its undesirability for other uses. In the end, the Western Defense Command had moved, by its own count, 110,442 "evacuees" into these camps.[57]

From the buses that transported them from the train, incarcerees saw the "Central Utah Relocation Project," the official name of the camp at Topaz.[58] George Hagiwara related his first impressions: "The site of the concentration camp at Topaz was ugly and desolate, barbed wire fencing all around and barren desert, with nothing but sage brush and scorpions. There were military police guards with rifles stationed atop high towers at the four corners of the compound."[59]

In entering these camps, the Nikkei moved into the custody of the War Relocation Authority (WRA), a new civilian agency headed by Milton Eisenhower. Although Eisenhower had resolved "to carry out [the confinement of Japanese Americans] as effectively and humanely as possible,"[60] Topaz ended up being little better than Tanforan. Families were assigned to barracks. Each barrack was divided into four or six rooms, which ranged from twenty-by sixteen to twenty-by-twenty-five feet, and each room housed at least one family. Barracks were organized into living communities, with twelve barracks to a block; each block shared communal facilities, including a mess hall, a recreation hall, a laundry, showers, and toilets.[61] The six adults in the Korematsu family were assigned two small rooms; their new address was Block 28, Building 9, Apartments CD.[62]

As in Tanforan, privacy was impossible to come by. Although each barrack was partitioned into separate rooms, large holes had to be cut in the walls to join the stovepipes from each stove into one of the three flues in the barrack. Because the holes were so large, "everything said and some things whispered were easily heard by people living in the next room."[63]

Weather conditions were harsh. On his arrival at Topaz, Fred wrote Besig of the daytime heat and the dust that was everywhere and that got into everything: "Its terribly dusty here, the top soil here is like flour. Just a little wind and the dust rises like fog all over the Relocation Center. You can't see ten feet in front of you. We all have to wear masks made of cloth. Also inside of the barrack becomes inch think with dust. It seems no use wearing good clothes here. It gets awful hot during the afternoon, and very cold in the morning's. There is no tree's here, just dried up sage brush." In the winter, Fred wrote that things were no better: "It is getting quite cold. It rained quite heavy here. And it gets awful muddy. The ground seems to turn into soft clay."[64]

In these harsh circumstances—difficult for even the healthiest individuals—medical care was inadequate. Equipment and other necessary items, including medicines, were in short supply or totally unavailable. The most critical problem, however, was the lack of medical personnel. Available doctors and nurses were overworked, and, to help, incarcerees were trained as medical aides.[65] One can only wonder about the care that Kotsui received when, after complaining of chronic pain in her side, she was diagnosed with a "huge" fibroid tumor in July 1943. She had surgery at the camp hospital to remove it, and, while they were at it, she also had an appendectomy and subtotal hysterectomy. She was hospitalized for forty-one days.[66]

Again, as they had done in Tanforan, Japanese Americans set out to make their surroundings as hospitable as possible. They made furniture and curtains. They ordered paint and other supplies from catalogues. They created rock gardens and planted flowers, trees, and shrubs. They celebrated Christmas the best they could and made *mochi*, traditional rice cakes, for New Year. They established a community cooperative with a canteen, dry-goods store, beauty parlor, barber shop, cleaning establishment, and shoe repair shop. They showed movies at night. Children attended school. The incarcerees produced art and crafts out of things they could find around the camp, and they organized sports and other forms of recreation. Despite their own circumstances, they found ways to support the needy outside the camp through scrap-metal drives, bond sales, Red Cross drives, and blood donations.[67]

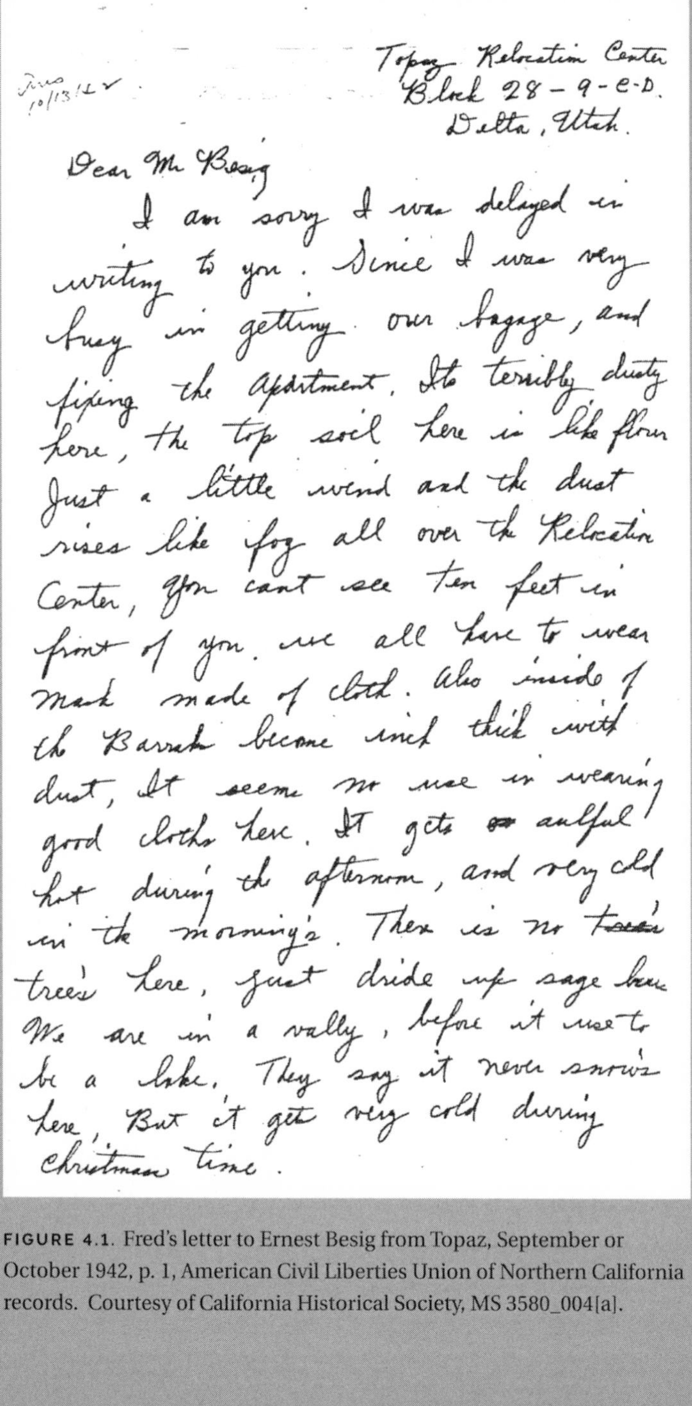

Tues 10/13/42

Topaz Relocation Center
Block 28 - 9 - C-D.
Delta, Utah.

Dear Mr Besig

I am sorry I was delayed in writing to you. Since I was very busy in getting our bagage, and fixing the Apartment. Its terribly dusty here, the top soil here is like flour Just a little wind and the dust rises like fog all over the Relocation Center, You cant see ten feet in front of you. we all have to wear mask made of cloth. Also inside of the Barrak become inch thick with dust, It seem no use in wearing good cloths here. It gets so aulful hot during th afternoon, and very cold in th morning's. There is no trees here, just dride up sage here We are in a vally, before it use to be a lake, They say it never snow's here, But it gets very cold during Christmas time.

FIGURE 4.1. Fred's letter to Ernest Besig from Topaz, September or October 1942, p. 1, American Civil Liberties Union of Northern California records. Courtesy of California Historical Society, MS 3580_004[a].

As they had at Tanforan, most of the younger Nikkei worked in camp—in the mess halls and in construction, health care, sanitation work, security, and community services, such as at the stores. They even engaged in war-related work, such as making camouflage nets. Fred had a series of jobs at Topaz. He wrote to Besig of working in the camp hospital warehouse, moving drywall, and helping to dig the camp well. While the wage scale at Topaz was slightly higher than at Tanforan—$12 per month for unskilled labor, $16 for skilled labor, and $19 for professional employees—many in camp felt that the pay was insultingly low. For example, while a WRA librarian received $167 a month, an incarceree working for her received only $16 a month.[68]

Many Nisei recall good times in the microcosm of camp life. In particular, those who were younger high schoolers at the time replicated, to the extent possible, the trappings of a normal teenage lifestyle. Bruce Kaji was sixteen years old when he attended Manzanar High School in the Mojave Desert—confined behind barbed wire and armed guards. He chuckles when he shares stories of the Jive Bombers, the band he and his friends formed, and of how he and his classmates performed plays and even an operetta in camp. But the reality of their confinement was never far away.[69]

The shooting of James Wakasa at Topaz on April 11, 1943, provided a shattering reminder of that reality. Wakasa, a well-educated sixty-three-year-old Issei, had been in the United States for forty years. He had served in the U.S. Army as a civilian cook instructor during World War I and, although he had received his U.S. citizenship, it was rescinded by the Supreme Court's 1922 *Ozawa* decision. The military police officer who shot and killed Wakasa said that Wakasa had approached the fence and, despite warnings, had continued walking as if to escape. Although the officer said he fired as Wakasa was attempting to crawl through the fence, the military later admitted that Wakasa was forty to sixty-five inches inside the fence when he was shot. The camp community was shocked, frightened, and outraged. Incarceree Tsueko Yamasaki recalled, "We were all scared for our lives."[70]

Many in camp felt frustrated, their lives in limbo. As Miné Okubo relates, "We were tired of the shiftless existence and were restless. A feeling of uncertainty hung over the camp; we were worried about the future. Plans were made and remade, as we tried to decide what to do. Some were ready to risk anything to get away. Others feared to leave the protection of the camp."[71]

Fred was among those who sought a way out. While, of course, he wanted to get away from the wretched conditions in camp, he had other reasons to want to leave, as well. He was an outcast, perhaps even more at Topaz than at Tanforan. By the time he arrived at Topaz, it was public knowledge that he was fighting his case. Sox Kitashima recalled,

> I think . . . after we got to Topaz, Utah, people realized who Fred was. I know that Fred told me that he felt very lonely there at Topaz. He was working digging ditches. They were building a hospital. And the crew was very cold to him. They, some people had this terrible feeling that Fred thought different from the rest of us Japanese Americans, that he was more white than Japanese. And so they thought, sort of shunned him. I know that must have been a terrible feeling for Fred to be treated that way.[72]

Fred was viewed as a criminal. Yuri Yokota's family, which had also run a nursery in the San Francisco Bay Area, lived in the same block as the Korematsus at Topaz. She would see them in the mess hall and remembers seeing Fred in camp. Although she later came to understand and respect his wartime stance, she acknowledged that, at the time, she saw him as others did. She recalled, "I remember what he did. . . . It was the common knowledge with everybody. . . . I felt he broke the law."[73] It could not have helped Fred's family that the camp newspaper, the *Topaz Times*, reported continuing news of his case, letting everyone know that "Korematsu's parents are residents of Topaz."[74]

While Fred languished at Tanforan and Topaz, and over 110,000 other Japanese Americans waited in camps across the U.S. interior, his case, which would decide the constitutionality of their forced expulsion from the West Coast, slowly made its way through the courts.

CHAPTER 5

THE ROCKY, WINDING ROAD

TO THE SUPREME COURT

BECAUSE CLARENCE RUST COULD ASSIST FRED ONLY AT THE INI-tial stages of his case, Besig enlisted attorney Wayne Collins to handle Fred's defense. Besig introduced Fred to Collins at one of his regular meetings with Fred in the visitor's area at the grandstand in Tanforan. Fred considered Collins to be a "very intelligent man" and a "good man"—the kind of person who would stick with a job until it was over.[1] That tenaciousness was evident throughout Collins's representation of Fred.

Rust and Collins quickly set about to seek dismissal of the charges against Fred. On June 20, 1942, they filed a motion to dismiss, termed a "Demurrer to the Information," raising a host of arguments. Collins's briefs were full of extraordinary passion, but his "shotgun" style of argument, seeming to raise everything but the kitchen sink, concerned Besig and national ACLU director Roger Baldwin.[2] Besig, however, stood behind Collins throughout Collins's handling of Fred's case. Among the arguments Collins made in his demurrer were direct attacks on the authority of the president, DeWitt, and Congress, including (1) that Roosevelt's Executive Order 9066 unlawfully usurped the legislative power of Congress and, in any case, exceeded any lawful exercise of presidential power; (2) that DeWitt's Civilian Exclusion Order No. 34, which barred Fred from remaining in Oakland, was also an unlawful exercise of legislative power; (3) that Public Law 503, enacted by Congress to criminalize violations of DeWitt's orders, was an unconstitutional exercise of legislative power and unenforceable because of its vagueness; and (4) that all three—the executive order, the exclusion order, and the public law—deprived Fred of almost the entire range of his constitutional rights, including his rights to be free of unreasonable searches and seizure; to due process; to equal protection; to freedom of movement, travel, expression, and assemblage; to a speedy and public trial; and to be free of cruel and unusual punishment.[3] Furthermore, Rust and Collins, citing the Civil War case of *Ex Parte Milligan*, argued that the constitutional rights of citizens endure, even during times of war, except in a theater of war under martial law.[4] No martial law had been declared on the West Coast at the time of the exclusion orders; thus, the orders were unlawful.

Collins would soon learn that his arguments, or at least some of them, were at odds with national ACLU policy: only days after Collins filed his demurrer, on June 24, 1942, ACLU director Baldwin reported the national board's decision to prohibit test cases from challenging Roosevelt's authority to issue Executive Order 9066.[5] Just a few months earlier, soon after Roosevelt had issued the Executive Order, the organization had taken a much different position. In March, it had sent a letter to Roosevelt expressing concern that Executive Order 9066 was "open to grave question on the constitutional grounds of depriving American citizens of their liberty and use of their property without due process of law."[6] While the national board approved the letter, a faction of Roosevelt loyalists dissented.[7] In May, the board decided to ask the ACLU's national committee for its view on the position the organization should take, providing it a choice between two positions. Resolution 1 opposed any order (meaning Roosevelt's) that, in the absence of martial law, gave military or civil authorities "the power to remove any citizen or group of citizens" from any zone established by those authorities. Resolution 2, in contrast, stated that "the government has the right in the present war to establish military zones and to remove persons, either citizens or aliens, from such zones when their presence may endanger national security, even in the absence of a declaration of martial law."[8] By a 2–1 vote, the national committee chose the latter position, one which, in essence, agreed that the government could remove Japanese Americans from their homes if reasonably related to ensuring national security.[9]

In light of that vote of the national committee, on June 22, Baldwin advised the ACLU's West Coast branches that they could not challenge the government's power to remove citizens from prescribed military zones: "[L]ocal committees are not free to sponsor cases in which the position is taken that the government has no constitutional right to remove citizens from military areas."[10] A later memo made particular mention that Roosevelt's authority was not to be questioned: "The effect of this resolution will be to remove from the test cases in the federal courts a challenge to the constitutional power of the President as Commander-in-Chief."[11] The chapters could only argue that DeWitt's orders were arbitrary because they did not except individuals who were loyal, they covered too wide an area, and they unlawfully discriminated against Japanese Americans.[12] The national office warned, "[s]hould any of the lawyers refuse to bow to the board's dictate, they would be forced to withdraw as ACLU counsel." The board advised defendants in cases already filed to "arrange, if they desire, for counsel who will be free to raise other constitutional issues."[13]

The directive from the national office placed Besig and Collins in an untenable position. If they complied with the national office, they would not be able to make legal arguments they believed essential to challenging the removal orders. Collins was being asked, essentially, to fight for Fred with one hand tied behind his back. Of course, the national office was allowing him to argue that the removal order discriminated against Japanese Americans on the basis of their race, but, under the national office's orders, they could not make the important argument that Roosevelt, Congress, and DeWitt had no constitutional authority to force, en masse, an entire population of citizens from their homes. Fred was being told that he had to find another attorney if he wanted counsel who would challenge the government's authority to issue the exclusion orders.

Besig bristled at the national office's directive. Collins had already sought to dismiss the charges against Fred by arguing that the orders were unconstitutional exercises of government power in the absence of martial law. On July 2, Besig wrote Baldwin, "[W]e feel compelled to proceed as before because we cannot in good conscience withdraw from the case at this late date." When the chapter had agreed to represent Fred, "we were acting in complete accord with the Board's position."[14] "I for one do not intend to be faithless to the commitments we have made with Korematsu. This office just doesn't do business that way. I think the Board has one helluva nerve suddenly to change its opinion and give it retroactive effect."[15] After acting national board chair Walter Frank wrote Besig that Besig had to divest the chapter from Fred's case, Besig dug in his heels: "We don't intend to trim our sails to suit the Board's vacillating policy." "Surely," Besig continued, "the corporation's members could not have intended us to be faithless to our client."[16] The national board wrote Besig to order that Collins drop his "wholly indefensible position" in Fred's case.[17]

Besig ignored the national office's demands; he knew that, by doing so, the chapter might be "heaved out of the Union." But he didn't care; he didn't answer mail from them for more than two months.[18] Because of the policy rift between the national office and the chapter and Besig's view that "he who has the money runs the show," the chapter chose to be financially independent from the national organization. It remained independent the length of Besig's tenure as chapter director and did not restore the affiliation until his retirement in 1971.[19]

While the national ACLU would not challenge Roosevelt's authority to remove the Japanese Americans if deemed a matter of military necessity, it at least recognized that the exercise of that authority was subject to certain constitutional limits, which could and should be raised. In contrast, the Japanese American Citizens League (JACL) condemned any challenge to the constitutionality of the wartime orders. On April 7, 1942, the JACL issued a bulletin, signed by national secretary Mike Masaoka, stating, in unequivocal terms, its opposition to any cases testing the constitutionality of the government's actions. The bulletin was written in response to the case of Minoru (Min) Yasui, a Nisei attorney from Portland who was challenging DeWitt's curfew order and demanding that the national JACL take a stand on the constitutional rights of Japanese Americans. The JACL, in its bulletin, responded in words underlined for emphasis so that there would be no mistake as to the organization's position:

> In regard to this particular case, as well as all other test cases of this nature, . . . this office releases the following statement:
> National Headquarters is unalterably opposed to test cases to determine the constitutionality of military regulations at this time.
> We have reached this decision unanimously after examining all the facts in light of our national policy of: "the greatest good for the greatest number."

The bulletin recognized that individuals like Min—referred to as "self-styled martyrs" willing to be jailed to fight for the rights of citizenship—"capture the headlines and the imaginations of many more persons than our seemingly indifferent stand." The organization, however, explained that it had already pledged cooperation to the president and would not violate that pledge; that cooperation was a sacrifice the Nikkei community needed to make as a contribution to the national war effort; and that a challenge to the orders would further turn public opinion against the community. Citing Attorney General Francis Biddle's belief that the courts would defer to the military's judgment, the organization further doubted that any test case could be won. Masaoka concluded, "In times like these, let us remember that it is much easier to be a martyr than it is to be a quiet, self-suffering good citizen who is vitally interested in the winning of the war."[20]

Masaoka rightly recognized that many did not agree with JACL's stance of cooperation. In his Tanforan diary, Charles Kikuchi commented on the JACL's refusal to challenge the removal orders: "This is an extremely short-sighted approach if there was one."[21] Fred, quite understandably, was not involved in the JACL: "When I refused to cooperate with the military, the JACL did not like what I did. I had to go on my own."[22]

Fred, without any organized support from his community, and Besig and Collins, clashing with the national ACLU on the handling of Fred's case, continued to move forward. On July 8, 1942, Alfonso J. Zirpoli, the assistant U.S. attorney assigned to prosecute Fred, filed his brief opposing Collins's motion to dismiss the charges. Zirpoli, who in later years served as a federal judge known for his commitment to individual rights,[23] had no evidence that Japanese Americans had committed or threatened to commit espionage or sabotage. And he could not argue that Fred was anything other than the loyal American citizen that he was. Lacking any such evidence, Zirpoli argued that President Roosevelt's Executive Order 9066, Congress's Public Law 503, and DeWitt's military orders were constitutional in light of the generalized fear that Japanese Americans posed a threat.

He first characterized the West Coast as a "theater of war":

Thus we find ourselves engaged in a war so vast and so extensive that the field of military operation is no longer confined to the scene of actual physical combat, but includes as well our coastline, our harbors, our industrial and transportation centers, yes even our agricultural centers, in short a war whose success is dependent upon our operations in every state and hamlet of the Union. . . .

Yes, the events in Europe, Asia and Africa prior to our entrance into this war have taught us that modern Twentieth Century War includes not only the actual waging of battle on the field of combat, but also the guarding against sabotage, espionage, and internal disorders, which, under present day conditions of society, could easily be carried on or instituted by persons in any degree of sympathy to the enemy.[24]

He explained that, just a couple of months earlier, on April 15, 1942, a federal court in Washington State had said that the government's orders were necessary and appropriate. In *Ex Parte Ventura*, Nisei Mary Asaba Ventura had filed a petition for a writ of habeas corpus, challenging DeWitt's curfew order. Judge Lloyd Black dismissed her petition on the ground that it was premature; she had not yet been imprisoned. He did, however, feel the need to address the merits of her claim. He believed that both the president and the military had the authority to restrict the movements of civilians, regardless of their loyalty, in military areas essential to the national defense. Black continued that, if Ventura were indeed as loyal as she asserted, she shouldn't be coming to court: "Aside from any rights involved it seems to me that if petitioner is as loyal and devoted as her petition avers she would be glad to conform to the precautions which Congress, the President, the armed forces, deem so requisite to preserve the Constitution, laws and institutions for her and all Americans, born here or naturalized."[25]

Zirpoli then made the argument that would ultimately reach and resonate with the Supreme Court—the frightening argument that the Nikkei possessed "peculiar racial characteristics" that supported the judgment that they were a threat:

Because of the peculiar racial characteristics of these sons and daughters of Nippon, they have not been assimilated into the community life of the population inhabiting this area. Their manners of thought and action, their traditional life patterns and their adherence to the customs and traditions of their oriental origins combined to make of them a people apart despite the provisions of the Nationality Code recognizing those born in this country as citizens. The fact of citizenship, thus conferred, bore little relationship to their status as loyal members of our body politic. . . .

That the presence in this area of this unassimilated group of blood relatives of a nation, with which the people of this country are now engaged in mortal combat, gave ample opportunity for sabotage and fifth column activity, none can gainsay.[26]

According to Zirpoli, and the U.S. government he represented, Fred, who was born and raised in California and educated from birth in American schools, was a "son of Nippon" whose citizenship meant nothing in terms of his loyalty.

Zirpoli concluded by asserting that DeWitt, knowing the foregoing "facts," called on the president for authority to clear the Nikkei from the West Coast, and that the president had issued Executive Order 9066 as a matter of national defense. The "facts, argument, and authorities cited," Zirpoli argued, "clearly sustain the constitutional authority of the President to issue Executive Order 9066, of General DeWitt to issue Civilian Exclusion Order No. 34, and of Congress to pass Public Law 503."[27]

Wanting to ensure that its views in Fred's case were known to the court, the State of California weighed in with an amicus curiae, or friend-of-the-court, brief, filed August 18, 1942. In the brief, Attorney General Earl Warren and his deputies characterized California as a theater of war, "one of the potential battlefields," in which the army occupied the length of the state to prevent invasion, and in which planes, ships, and vital installations stood at the ready as crucial parts of the national defense. The brief argued that in that theater, Japanese Americans posed a real threat, given "the racial consciousness which might assert itself in some persons of Japanese ancestry, . . . the non-assimilability of the Japanese racially and culturally, [and] the concentration of Japanese and their proximity to defense plants and installations." While recognizing the importance of preserving the rights of citizens, the brief argued that "the great constitutional guarantees of personal and property rights are not absolute and must in times of war give way to the fundamental right of the . . . State . . . to preserve itself."[28]

On August 31, 1942, Collins argued his motion to dismiss the charges against Fred before Judge Martin I. Welsh. Judge Welsh, not surprisingly, summarily denied Collins's demurrer without responding to any of the arguments it raised.[29] With the denial of Fred's constitutional challenges to the exclusion orders, the real meat of Fred's defense was lost, at least in this round. The only issue that remained for trial was whether Fred had violated the removal order, that is, whether he was a person of Japanese ancestry found present at a location from which he was excluded.

Fred's trial was repeatedly delayed because of Judge Welsh's schedule. However, in September, the military was poised to start moving Nikkei from Tanforan to Topaz, and Fred would have to leave for Topaz soon. Trial was set for September 8, 1942. Because Judge Welsh was on vacation, the matter was scheduled before the Honorable Adolphus St. Sure. Military police transported Fred from Tanforan to federal district court for the first major stage in his journey through the courts. Collins and attorney Clarence Rust were in court to represent Fred; Zirpoli was present to represent the United States.[30]

Fred pled not guilty to the charges; he felt he hadn't done anything wrong. He waived a jury trial. Zirpoli presented one witness, FBI Special Agent Oliver Mansfield, who testified as to his May 31, 1942, interview with Fred and produced two statements taken from him. Those statements established that Fred was of Japanese ancestry and that, at the time of his arrest, he was present in Oakland when he knew his presence was prohibited. Zirpoli also introduced Fred's altered draft card and birth certificate as exhibits. At the close of the prosecution's case, Collins again argued that the charges should be dismissed based on the constitutional challenges contained in his prior demurrer. Judge St. Sure again denied Collins's request.[31]

Fred testified on his own behalf, explaining that he was a loyal American citizen with no ties to Japan. He told Judge St. Sure that, save for his brief time away to attend school in Los Angeles, he had lived in Oakland all his life. He had never been to Japan; he had never attended, nor cared to attend, any Japanese language school; he spoke Japanese in broken English, and his brother had to translate when he spoke to his mother. He was a registered voter, had registered for the draft, and was willing to serve the United States in any way he could. He expressed his unqualified patriotism to America: "As a citizen of the United States I am ready, willing, and able to bear arms for this country. I am willing to enlist. As a citizen of the United States I am ready to render any service that I may be called upon to render our Government in our war against the Axis nations, including the Empire of Japan. I do not owe any allegiance to any country or nation other than the United States of America." After Fred's testimony, Collins renewed his request that the charges against Fred be dismissed. For a third time, his request was denied.[32]

Judge St. Sure found Fred guilty of the charges and sentenced him to five years' probation, ordering that "pronouncing of judgment be suspended."[33] Ironically, while an order of probation is much preferable to prison time for most people, the order provided Fred no benefit. While an individual placed on probation would normally go free, subject to supervision, Fred would not be free. His order of probation required him to remain in the custody of military authorities until "such time as they order your dismissal from such custody."[34] For Fred, that meant a return to Tanforan. The order of probation further ended up inordinately complicating his case.

Fred wrote Besig from Tanforan the day after his trial. Although Judge St. Sure had found him guilty as charged, Fred thought he was "very nice about the whole situation." Fred understood, however, that this was only round one: "Mr. Besig, I believe it is only the beginning of our fight, and we have a long way's to go yet." He enclosed seventy-fve cents to subscribe to the ACLU monthly newsletter.[35]

Collins wasted no time. Three days after the trial, on September 11, 1942, he filed a notice of appeal on Fred's behalf, asserting that Judge St. Sure was wrong.[36] Fred's case, however, soon became entangled in a procedural nightmare that derailed efforts to have his arguments heard. In December 1942, Zirpoli sought to dismiss Fred's appeal on the ground that Judge St. Sure's order of probation was not a "final" sentence properly subject to appeal. Recent case law had held that a defendant could not appeal where he (as Fred had) received probation and where imposition of sentencing was suspended; instead, an appeal was proper only where sentence had been imposed or at the point in time that the probationary period expired.[37] Under that view, Fred would have to wait for five years, the length of his probation, before he could appeal.

Faced with the government's motion to dismiss the appeal, Collins needed Judge St. Sure to enter a new judgment that could be appealed. Although it is exceedingly odd for a defense attorney to request jail time for his client, Collins needed Judge St. Sure to sentence Fred to do some "time," rather than grant him probation. The judge could impose a sentence and then suspend the sentence *after* imposing it. Jail time didn't matter much to Fred anyway; he'd be in camp if he weren't in jail, and, as Fred knew, jail was better than camp. On December 23, Collins returned to Judge St. Sure, asking that he sentence Fred to, say, five or six days in jail, plus a one dollar fine, and that he then order that the sentence be suspended and Fred be placed on probation.[38] That result would, Collins argued, enable him to appeal Fred's case.

Judge St. Sure balked: "I don't know why I should do that. The judgment rendered was one I thought proper in that case." When Collins explained that the issue was whether an appeal could be taken from the judgment, not whether the judgment was proper, Judge St. Sure said, "I don't care if whether it does or not. That is my judgment . . . I did not wish to send that man to jail." Collins pressed on, arguing that the judgment had to be revised so that Fred's claims could be tested on appeal. The judge asked, "Are there no other cases on which you can test it?" When Collins replied that there were not, the judge shot back, "I am not going to help you make one." Collins pleaded: if Judge St. Sure did not modify his order, he explained, "[t]hat would keep the matter pending here for a period of five years, during which time no appeal could be taken, and this man's rights determined, and we could not attack the constitutionality of the statute."[39]

On December 31, 1942, Judge St. Sure issued his ruling. He refused to modify his order placing Fred on probation on the ground that Collins had not requested the imposition of a sentence at trial.[40] Judge St. Sure's stubbornness, or more likely his desire to avoid appellate review of his order, would significantly delay any hearing on Fred's constitutional challenges to the banishment and incarceration. Fred's conviction, and the constitutionality of the orders that now had over 110,000 Japanese Americans behind barbed wire, would remain in legal limbo.

While Collins fought Fred's case with the government in court, Besig continued to fight for Fred with the ACLU national office. Unable to get Besig to comply with its directives, the national office attempted to go around him with an appeal to the chair of the chapter's board, Bishop Edward Parsons.[41] On November 9, national acting board chair Walter Frank wrote Parsons, "We dislike continuing what may appear to be a controversy concerning the handling of the Korematsu case, but in the interests of a uniform national policy on the issue raised by it we must request the further consideration of your committee." The Northern California committee, Frank suggested, could conform to national policy by a "simple adjustment." It could, he proposed, file an amicus brief "which would not raise the issue of the underlying presidential power and would raise only the points authorized under our national policy. Personal counsel for the defendant can, of course, raise whatever points he may desire." The letter ended with the specter of a public parting of the ways: "It would be very unfortunate if, as the case develops in the higher courts, we were not forced to take a public position at variance with that of the Northern California Committee."[42]

While Frank had suggested that Fred's "personal counsel" could feel free to challenge Roosevelt's order, the Northern California chapter had, in fact, undertaken to represent Fred *as* his personal counsel and could not withdraw or compromise its support of him now. Besig responded to Frank's letter on November 11 that Frank's "simple adjustment" was not possible: "Mr. Korematsu has no counsel other than that furnished by the Union. . . . The practical effect of your suggestion . . . would be no one to carry on directly for Mr. Korematsu. We cannot in good conscience permit such a consequence. We undertook to defend Korematsu and we informed him before he accepted our help that in the event he was convicted, we would undertake an appeal, if necessary, because we regarded his as a test case."[43]

While Besig and Collins worked to clear a path to appeal Judge St. Sure's decision, Fred and his family were moved from Tanforan to Topaz.[44] Soon after arriving at Topaz, Fred wrote Besig that he might be able to obtain a "seasonal leave" permit to get out, even if just temporarily; Fred was excited about the possibility. The leave program had its beginnings when farming operators saw an opportunity to use the incarcerated Nikkei as seasonal labor. What resulted seemed a helpful arrangement for all concerned. On the one hand, the farm operators, desperate for help, obtained a convenient, literally captive, source of workers. On the other hand, although harvesting crops such as sugar beets was back-breaking work, the incarcerated Nikkei would be able to get away from camp. Fred wrote Besig, "Many people here have gone to work in sugar beets. It seems awful hard work. . . . And about 70 people went to a turkey farm to work at 30 cents an hour." By mid-October, ten thousand incarcerees had been given permits to work in the fields. They were credited with saving the sugar beet crop that year.[45]

Given the success of the seasonal leave program, the War Relocation Authority (WRA), now under the leadership of new director Dillon Myer, sought to expand the resettlement of Japanese Americans from the camps into employment outside the prohibited West Coast. That movement, however, would be controlled. On October 1, 1942, the WRA announced that incarcerees could apply for one of three types of leaves. They could apply for short-term leave of up to thirty days for things such as medical procedures. They could apply for work group leave to engage in, for example, seasonal employment. Finally, they could apply for indefinite leave to a location away from the West Coast if they could establish that they had a means of support, that their presence would be acceptable at their intended destination, and that they would not endanger national security. Even if Japanese Americans obtained permission to leave camp under these procedures, they remained in the constructive custody of the WRA and were required to report their movements to it.[46]

Fred wrote Besig about his efforts to leave camp. While he took an odd job here and there in camp—moving drywall one week and digging a well or handling hospital supplies another—what he really wanted to do was get out. He explained, however, that "it seems quite hard. You have to have a job on the outside beforehand in order to get release. I have written to many factories, but they seem to be filled up. . . . [T]he Welders' Union in Salt Lake has not enough work for their own workers. "[47]

Fred's first application sought leave for work at a farming operation in Delta, Colorado. In his application, he was asked if he spoke Japanese; he responded, "poorly." He was asked if he had ever subscribed to a Japanese-language newspaper and whether he had ever belonged to, or was an officer in, a Japanese organization that had contact with Japan or whose activity was conducted primarily in Japanese; he responded, "no." He answered "no" to all of the other questions asking about ties to Japan: he had not worked for a Japanese consulate, had not ever been to Japan, and had not been in the armed forces of Japan. He was asked to list "Caucasian references" who could be called upon for information regarding him, and Fred listed four from back home in the Bay Area: his dentist, his foreman at Golden Gate Iron Works, a printer, and his car dealer in San Leandro, a Mr. M. McKissick.[48]

The chief of the Topaz employment division wrote Mr. McKissick on November 8, seeking his opinion of Fred, "especially with regard to [his] loyalty to this country and the degree of Americanization through education and upbringing." The dealership replied that it had had business dealings with Fred that were always satisfactory, but pointed out Fred's arrest: "[W]hen the Japs were evacuated from here, he tried to remain behind and we read that he was in trouble with the army authorities."[49]

Fred's arrest and conviction did not prevent him from obtaining at least short-term leave. He left to pick sugar beets in Delta in November 1942. In December, he was granted leave to work in Salt Lake City, but when he arrived, he learned that the company had filled his job. Fortunately, Utah Concrete and Pipe had need of a welder to help repair boilers and water heaters.[50] Fred wrote Besig to extend belated Thanksgiving greetings. In his ever-positive way, he wrote, "I hope you had the best Thanksgiving. I hope you didn't get sick eating too much turkey. I didn't have a very good Thanksgiving. But I am thankful I am released again, and no strings attached." Fred neglected to note that he was still required to report to his probation officer, still under WRA jurisdiction, and only on a temporary leave permit, but none of those things, apparently, bothered him too much.

He continued his letter to Besig, explaining his frustration that defense facilities would not hire persons of Japanese ancestry, no matter how skilled or experienced they might be. "I have talked to many a head man of the firms," he said, "But they said, Its [sic] not discrimination. But they are scared there might be trouble with persons who are working alongside of you. And also protection to the factories." Fred could not understand this wrong-headed attitude: "But to my point, if they would think of helping each other and that we were all equal and the main thing is put out more production, to help out in winning this war, and I am just a good American, than any other American. But I can't argue this out to nobody." Besig replied to Fred to congratulate him on his new job and departure from Topaz, but expressed his regret that "a good welder is going to waste."[51]

While Fred was able to leave camp on temporary permits, his application for indefinite leave caused the WRA more concern. Robert Frase of the WRA office in Washington, DC, wrote the regional office in Salt Lake City on February 4, stating that Fred's application was "being held due to necessity of further special investigation of him." He asked that the regional office investigate Fred and submit its recommendation. WRA relocation officer Henry Harris replied back on February 15 with a positive report: "Fred is a tall, nice appearing man who has no trace of Japanese accent. . . . I contacted the Personnel Manager at the Utah Concrete and Pipe Co. and he spoke favorably of Mr. Korematsu, saying that his work is excellent and he has adjusted himself to his fellow workers without any noticeable difficulty."[52] Despite this favorable response, it would be many months before the WRA took any action on Fred's request for indefinite leave.

While Fred welcomed this return to the outside world and the trappings of normal life, he remained the subject of rumor and disparaging talk even in Salt Lake City, miles and miles away from the West Coast and from Topaz. Many of the Japanese Americans who, like Fred, had moved to Salt Lake City to work had heard of him and his case. Kay Korematsu met all four Korematsu brothers at the Japanese Christian Church in Salt Lake City. She perceived Fred to be the gentlest; he talked very softly and was less dynamic than his brothers. She appreciated that he was not "boastful" like some other young men she knew. Despite her positive impression of his manner, Kay knew about Fred's case and saw him as a criminal. He had broken the law, was not a good citizen, and had injured the reputation of, and brought shame to, the Japanese people. Nevertheless, she felt that, because he was already ruined, he had nothing to lose by pressing his case. Her main concern was what he would do if he lost his American citizenship.[53] Fred, however, did receive a lift from a Japanese American couple from Los Angeles. The husband, an accountant by training, worked the only job he could get—making pipes at a concrete company. Fred later related, "They were the ones that told me, 'I'm glad that you did what you did. And I wish there were more like you.'" It was the first time he'd heard someone tell him that.[54]

Besig kept Fred informed of the protracted proceedings in his case. On receiving one of the briefs that Collins had filed on his behalf, Fred said, "It is perfect in every way." Recognizing the difficulty that Collins was having in appealing his case, Fred wrote, "[T]he U.S. attorney seems to block it in every corner . . . I hope luck and leniency will be on our side. . . . I wish there was something I can do to at least help a little."[55]

The government's motion to dismiss Fred's appeal was set for hearing on February 19, 1943, one year to the day after Roosevelt had signed the executive order that Fred sought to challenge. Besig informed Fred that arguments in his case would be heard with those in the cases of Minoru Yasui and Gordon Hirabayashi, two Nisei who had also been convicted of violating DeWitt's orders.[56]

Min Yasui was the Portland attorney the JACL had labeled a "self-styled martyr" in its April 7, 1942, bulletin.[57] He had been twenty-five years old when he had deliberately violated DeWitt's curfew order to test its legality. Born in Hood River, Oregon, Min was a commissioned officer in the army's infantry reserve and a graduate of the University of Oregon School of Law. Unable to find work as a lawyer, he found a job, with his father's assistance, with the Japanese consulate in Chicago. A few days after Pearl Harbor, he received orders from the army to report for duty at Fort Vancouver, Washington, but when he arrived, he was told he was unacceptable for service and ordered off base. When he heard news of DeWitt's impending orders, he resolved to challenge them. On March 28, 1942, the first evening the curfew was in effect, he set about to walk around the streets of Portland until he was arrested. Unable to find an officer to take him in, he finally presented himself at the police station, where a sergeant obliged him.[58]

Judge James Alger Fee delivered Min a judgment that was partially good, although mostly not. He concluded that while the government has expansive powers over alien immigrants during wartime, DeWitt's curfew order could not be constitutionally applied to American citizens: "If Congress attempted to classify citizens based upon color or race and to apply criminal penalties . . . founded upon that distinction, the action is insofar void." However, he determined that Min, by working for the Japanese consulate, had "repudiated his citizenship" in the eyes of the law, and DeWitt's order was valid as it applied to him. He was convicted of violating DeWitt's curfew order and appealed.[59]

Gordon Kiyoshi Hirabayashi was a twenty-four-year-old senior at the University of Washington when Civilian Exclusion Order No. 57 was posted. That order required him to register and report for removal, but Gordon would do neither. On the day he was required to leave, he went to the FBI office in Seattle, accompanied by lawyer and friend Arthur Barnett, and handed FBI Special Agent Francis V. Manson his four-page statement explaining why he could not comply with the order to leave. The statement read, in part,

This order for the mass evacuation of all persons of Japanese descent denies them the right to live. It forces thousands of energetic, law-abiding individuals to exist in a miserable psychological and a horrible physical atmosphere. This order limits to almost full extent the creative expression of those subjected. It kills the desire for a higher life. Hope for the future is exterminated. Human personalities are poisoned. . . .

If I were to register and cooperate under those circumstances, I would be giving helpless consent to the denial of practically all of the things which give me incentive to live. I must maintain my Christian principles. I consider it my duty to maintain democratic standards for which this nation lives. Therefore, I must refuse this order for evacuation.[60]

Gordon was found guilty of violating both the curfew and the exclusion orders. He was sentenced to imprisonment for three months on each count, with the sentences to run concurrently.[61] He appealed.

On February 19, Fred's, Min's, and Gordon's attorneys appeared for argument before the Ninth Circuit Court of Appeals. During the arguments, the court heard the exclusion program "described alternatively . . . as robbing American citizens of their rights and as an expedient necessary to the war effort."[62] On behalf of Fred, Wayne Collins argued, "There is no decision in history upholding the idea that citizenship is a thing of degree. To penalize these American citizens for their ancestry, race and color is contrary to the fundamental concepts."[63] Representing Gordon Hirabayashi, Frank Walters argued that DeWitt's orders, in singling out Japanese Americans, had violated their right to equal protection under the law: "If these things can be done to one minority group, such as the Japanese, they can be done to other minority groups, merely because they happen to be Chinese, or Negroes, or Jews or Catholics."[64]

For the government, Zirpoli quite predictably argued that the orders were necessary because of the government's inability to distinguish loyal Japanese from those who might be disloyal. In a statement that seems equal parts paternalistic and disingenuous, he added that incarcerating citizens together with their immigrant alien parents was "more humane" than interning only Japanese-born immigrant aliens because to do so would separate families. Edward Ennis of the Department of Justice, who had so strongly opposed mass removal, was now required to argue, on behalf of the government, that it was right. However, he could not be less than frank about the facts. When asked whether there had been any cases in which Japanese Americans had been found to be a threat to military security, Ennis had to reply that he knew of none.[65]

Fred awaited word from Besig about the Ninth Circuit proceedings: "Dear Mr. Besig, It is past Feb. 19th and I haven't heard from you as yet. Will you please write to me, since I am very anxious to hear the outcome of our case[?] Even tho it may be bad news, I would like to hear it." He reported that he had started going to night school at the University of Utah to learn to be a machinist. He added a bit of longing for home: "How is it in San Francisco? I sure miss the ocean and the Golden Gate Bridge." Fred didn't know that Besig had written him the same day to fill him in. He cautioned Fred that it might take a while for the court to rule and added his doubts of success before the court. "In any event," he added, "an appeal will be taken to the U.S. Supreme Court. So, what the Circuit Court does will be interesting but not final."[66]

What the Ninth Circuit did after oral argument certainly was interesting, and cause for further delay in Fred's case. Rather than decide the issues raised in each of the three cases, as it would normally do, the Ninth Circuit passed the questions on to the Supreme Court. In Gordon's case, the Ninth Circuit asked the Supreme Court to rule on the constitutionality of Public Law 503 and DeWitt's curfew and exclusion orders. In Min's case, the Ninth Circuit asked the Supreme Court to rule on whether Min had renounced his citizenship as a result of his work with the Japanese consulate. In Fred's case, the Supreme Court was asked whether his probationary sentence was an appealable judgment. In legal terms, the court "certified" these questions to the Supreme Court. In response, the Supreme Court had the option to answer or decline to answer the questions and return the cases to the Ninth Circuit, or to order that the cases be brought to the Supreme Court for full consideration.[67]

The Supreme Court responded to the certified questions by deciding to hear the substantive issues presented by the *Yasui* and *Hirabayashi* cases itself, that is, to determine the whether Min and Gordon had been rightfully convicted.[68] In Fred's case, however, the Court would address only the narrow procedural issue of whether his sentence of probation was appealable.

Collins's brief in Fred's case, filed in the Supreme Court on May 7, 1943, argued that Judge St. Sure's order of probation could be appealed. Fred had been found guilty, Collins argued, and that finding of guilt had "brand[ed him] a convicted criminal."[69] In its opinion of June 1, 1943, the court agreed with Collins. In fact, the government had dropped its opposition to the appeal and, based on "considerations of reason and expediency," had conceded that St. Sure's order was subject to review.[70] Besig wrote Fred that his case would be returned to the Ninth Circuit for its ruling on the question of "whether the military had a right to exclude citizens of Japanese ancestry."[71] Fred's case could move forward again.

CHAPTER 6

THE UGLY ABYSS OF RACISM

FRED FOLLOWED THE CIRCUITOUS COURSE OF HIS CASE WHILE still on temporary leave from Topaz. In March 1943, he wrote Besig, reporting that he had moved from Salt Lake City to Tooele, Utah, to work at a pipe construction company. The pay was better, he said, but the uncertainty of his life was bothering him. Even though he was out of camp, he still had to report back to Topaz and lamented that he was "undecided on everything." Since he couldn't "depend on anything these days," he could neither "get going" nor settle down in one place. "I guess this is war, drives people nuts." In a later letter, responding to Besig's proud news of his victory garden, Fred said how much he missed his own garden. "Right now, I don't even know how it is to have a home. I feel like an orphan or something."[1]

Early 1943 brought a different type of turmoil to Japanese Americans back in camp. Shock, confusion, anxiety, anger, and fear spread through their ranks concerning a questionnaire that asked them to declare their loyalty to the very government that confined them. The questionnaire, which would influence the Supreme Court's later reasoning in Fred's case, had been created in a haphazard fashion, in part because it was conceived to serve distinct and different purposes.

Its initial purpose was to screen young Nisei men for military service. Although in 1942 Nisei had been denied the ability to enlist, since that time, leadership within the Japanese American community, most notably within the Japanese American Citizens League, sought the opportunity to fight: "'[B]eing deprived of right to serve' . . . meant 'being deprived of our biggest chance to prove to those who are skeptical that our loyalty is as great as that of any other group.'"[2] On February 1, 1943, President Franklin D. Roosevelt announced that the War Department would organize a segregated, all-Nisei combat team for those who wished to volunteer.[3] How ironic that Japanese Americans could be trusted enough to bear arms while, at the same time, their families remained imprisoned because of their suspected disloyalty. In the end, however, approximately thirty-three thousand Nisei from the mainland and Hawai'i ended up serving—and serving with extraordinary distinction—during the war (CWRIC, *Personal Justice Denied*, 253).

The loyalty questionnaire also served a second purpose. When the War Relocation Authority (WRA) learned of the War Department's plans, it saw the questionnaire as a means to expedite the screening of incarcerees for clearance to leave camp for work in the interior of the country (190–91). While the questionnaire was drafted for reasons intended to be beneficial to the Nikkei—to allow Nisei men to serve in the military and to screen Japanese Americans for release—the Nikkei were not told how their answers would be used. The program of loyalty review would become "one of the most divisive, wrenching episodes of the captivity" (186).[4]

Questions 27 and 28 were the questions that led to division and conflict. They asked:

27. Are you willing to serve in the armed forces of the United States on combat duty, wherever ordered?
28. Will you swear unqualified allegiance to the United States of America and faithfully defend the United States from any or all attack by foreign or domestic forces, and forswear any form of allegiance or obedience to the Japanese emperor, or any other foreign government, power, or organization?[5]

Because the incarcerees did not know the government's motivations in asking these questions, they did not know the consequences of failing to answer "properly." What was the government asking of them? Would a young man be drafted if he answered "yes" to question 27? If an Issei who was unable to apply for U.S. citizenship renounced loyalty to Japan in response to question 28, would he or she have no citizenship at all? And if an individual renounced allegiance to Japan in answer to question 28, would that be interpreted to mean that he or she once had an allegiance to Japan to renounce? The questionnaire given the Issei, as well as Nisei women, was entitled "Application for Leave Clearance"; in filling it out, would they be forced to leave camp, with no place to go? If an incarceree's answers were "wrong" or different from those given by others family members, would he or she be deported and the family separated?

For many incarcerees who had complied with the government's orders thus far, the questionnaire was the final indignation. The country had taken them from their homes and had imprisoned them; now it was asking if they would be willing to fight for the freedom that they were denied. Fred wrote Besig, "[D]uring that last couple of weeks, the drafting for the army came up. But here are many American citizens in camp that are undecided, since they were treated like enemies of this country and never given a trial to be proven loyal to this country."[6] Albert Nakai later explained his decision to answer "no" to both questions: "I answered both questions 27 and 28 in the negative, not because of disloyalty but due to the disgusting and shabby treatment given us. . . . I[t] is not that I was proud of it, it was just that our legal rights were violated and I wanted to fight back. . . . I didn't want to take this sitting down. I was really angry. It just got me so damned mad."[7] Out of 74,588 Nisei who responded, 6,733, or 9 percent, answered "no" to Question 28, refusing to affirm their unqualified loyalty to the country that had turned on them. Those deemed to be disloyal as a result of their answers were segregated into the concentration camp at Tule Lake, California.[8] In the end, 68,018 incarcerees, or 87 percent of those eligible to register, affirmed their loyalty to the United States by answering "yes-yes" to the questionnaire.[9]

Fred filled out his loyalty questionnaire in May 1943 when he returned briefly to Topaz to visit his parents. So there would be no mistake about his intentions, Fred added exclamation marks to his answers: he answered "Yes!" to question 27 and "Yes!" to question 28. Based on his "unqualified 'yes-yes'" answers to Questions No. 27 and 28, the Topaz Leave Officer recommended to WRA Director Dillon Myer that Fred's application for permanent leave clearance be "given the necessary attention." On May 30, Fred left Topaz again on a short-term leave permit to Salt Lake City.[10]

In the up-and-down proceedings in Fred's case, attorney Wayne Collins prepared a second time for argument before the Ninth Circuit Court of Appeals. His brief reiterated the arguments he had made in his previous demurrer: that Executive Order 9066, Public Law 503, and General John L.

DeWitt's removal orders were unconstitutional. To meet head-on the argument that racial characteristics of Japanese Americans showed their solidarity with Japan, he argued their loyalty and their decency. Many Nisei, like Fred, knew little, if any, Japanese: "The native born," Collins argued, "generally have an acquaintance with colloquial Japanese but a reading and writing knowledge of Japanese is beyond the ken of the vast majority." They were law-abiding: "Whether citizen or aliens, they seldom appear in our criminal and civil courts. They are not litigious. Their criminal element is negligible and probably lower than that of any of our ethnic groups." In a comment that was surely well-intended, even if a bit insulting to some Nikkei, he said, "If they possess any distinguishing characteristics these may well be said to be docility and obedience to the law." He pointed also to the thousands of Nisei in the military fighting to defend their country.

Collins further attacked the argument that Japanese Americans had dual loyalty: "Those who entertain the opinion that these native born citizens owe dual allegiance, one to America and one to Japan, are as ignorant as those who believe that all Americans owe allegiance to their ancestral land across the sea." He posited, for example, the absurdity of the assertion that "all Catholics are subversive because they possess a dual allegiance, one to America and one to the Romish Pope."

Collins asked that the court recognize that Fred's case was not only about exclusion and removal; it was about incarceration. While Executive Order 9066 made no specific mention of confinement, the reality was that Japanese Americans were ordered into camps. He pointed out that, even after posting bail and being released on probation after trial, Fred was sent to Tanforan. Even assuming, for purposes of argument, that it might be lawful to intern the Issei immigrants, Collins argued, there was no lawful authority to intern Nisei citizens.[11]

Collins's job became a good deal more difficult when the Supreme Court decided Gordon Hirabayashi's case on June 1, 1943. Fred wrote Besig that he had read about the decision and believed it was a "show down" for his case, as well.[12] Unfortunately, it turned out he was right in more ways than he knew. In *Hirabayashi*, the Supreme Court upheld DeWitt's curfew order, reasoning that those charged with the country's national defense had a rational basis for imposing it given the circumstances known to them at the time. The Supreme Court, however, made clear that its decision addressed the constitutionality of *only* the curfew order—a much lesser intrusion on liberty than the wholesale removal of Japanese Americans that Fred challenged in his case: "We need not now attempt to define the ultimate boundaries of the war power. We decide only the issue as we have defined it—we decide only that the curfew order as applied, and at the time it was applied, was within the boundaries of the war power." (*Hirabayashi*, 320 U.S. 81, 102). The court dodged having to decide the constitutionality of the removal orders. While Gordon had actually challenged both DeWitt's curfew and the removal orders, the court said that it needed to rule only on the validity of his curfew conviction because the sentences imposed on Gordon for violating the two different orders ran concurrently (85). It would be another year and a half before the court, in Fred's case, addressed the validity of the infinitely more egregious removal orders, and during that time, Japanese Americans would remain banished from the West Coast, most still behind barbed wire.

The Supreme Court's decision in the *Hirabayashi* case set it down a troubling path of judicial abdication and acceptance of racial myth. Chief Justice Harlan Fiske Stone delivered the opinion of the court, and all nine justices joined in concluding that Congress and the president had the constitutional power to prescribe the curfew order. In reaching this decision, the court expressed extreme deference to those bodies in acting in the national defense: where government officials entrusted with the power to wage war are called upon to exercise judgment and discretion, the court explained, "it is not for any court to sit in review of the wisdom of their action or to substitute its judgment for theirs." Despite this stated deference, the court went on to evaluate what it termed "all the facts and circumstances" to determine whether there was any "substantial basis" to conclude that the curfew was necessary to avert sabotage and espionage (93, 95).[13]

What the court deemed "facts and circumstances" could hardly be termed "facts" at all, and it is only through innuendo and groundless assumption that they could support the conclusion that Japanese Americans, as a whole, posed a threat of espionage or sabotage. The court essentially bought the government's argument that the proximity of Japanese Americans to strategic installations and their "racial characteristics" justified action against them to protect national security. The court's "racial characteristics" discussion, in particular, amounted to little more than generalizations and stereotypes. The court explained that "social, economic and political conditions" prevailing since the Japanese began to immigrate had "intensified their solidarity and . . . prevented their assimilation as an integral part of the white population." It observed, for example, that many children of Japanese parentage attended Japanese language schools and, without citation to any evidence, stated that "[s]ome of these schools [were] generally believed to be sources of Japanese nationalistic propaganda, cultivating allegiance to Japan." Further, the court stated that large numbers of Nisei had been sent to Japan for all or part of their education and that Japan maintained a system of dual citizenship. As if being an immigrant itself carried with it a tendency toward subversive behavior, the court related that "large numbers of resident alien Japanese . . . are of mature years and occupy positions of influence in Japanese communities." Further, the court noted that some Nikkei associated with Japanese consulates, which had been deemed "ready means for the dissemination of propaganda." All of these conditions, the court concluded, had resulted in "little social intercourse" between Japanese Americans and the white population, leading to their increased isolation. In summary, the court stated, "Viewing these data in all their aspects, Congress and the Executive could reasonably have concluded that these conditions have encouraged the continued attachment of members of this group to Japan and Japanese institutions" (95–98).

In reasoning that would become significant when Fred, Gordon, and Min later reopened their cases, the court stated that action to control the Nikkei population was necessary because time was of the essence. "Whatever views we may entertain regarding the loyalty to this country of the citizens of Japanese ancestry, we cannot reject as unfounded the judgment of the military authorities and Congress that there were disloyal members of that population, whose numbers and strength could not be precisely and *quickly* ascertained" (99, emphasis added).

Finally, the *Hirabayashi* court summarily rejected the argument that the curfew order unlawfully discriminated against Japanese Americans on the basis of their race. The court granted that "[d]istinctions between citizens solely because of their ancestry are by their very nature odious to a free people whose institutions are founded upon the doctrine of equality." However, the court explained that, in times of war, Congress and the executive branch are not wholly precluded from taking into account those "facts and circumstances" relevant to our national defense, "which may in fact place citizens of one ancestry in a different category from others" (100). The same day that the court affirmed Gordon's conviction, it affirmed Min Yasui's curfew conviction based on its reasoning in *Hirabayashi*.[14]

On December 2, 1943, the Ninth Circuit, not surprisingly, affirmed Fred's conviction in what the *Los Angeles Times* referred to as "the first decision in the country" ruling on the legality of the evacuation of the Japanese.[15] In its brief opinion upholding the constitutionality of the removal orders, the Ninth Circuit relied wholly on the Supreme Court's ruling in *Hirabayashi*. While acknowledging that the *Hirabayashi* case involved the curfew orders, not the exclusion orders at issue in Fred's case, the Ninth Circuit explained that the principle from *Hirabayashi*—that government during wartime can "temporarily" infringe on the rights and liberties of citizens—sustained the validity of the exclusion orders.[16] The court turned a blind eye to the fact that the denial of liberty at issue in Fred's case was not at all "temporary"—by December 1943, it had been over a year and a half since Japanese Americans had been forced to leave their homes. The *New York Times* reported Besig's promise that the decision would be appealed.[17]

Besig told Fred of the Ninth Circuit's ruling and that he and Collins were preparing to ask for review in the Supreme Court. He asked Fred to sign a petition to proceed *in forma pauperis*, that is, to ask for a waiver of court fees to pursue his case before the high court. Besig instructed, "In case you are still as poor as a churchmouse, please return the document, properly notarized, as soon as you can. Best wishes for the holidays."[18]

The Supreme Court would not hear Fred's case as a matter of course. Fred would have to file a request that the court hear his case, referred to as a petition for writ of *certiorari*. The court could agree to hear his case, or decline to review it and let the Ninth Circuit decision stand. Besig wrote Jackson H. Ralston, a member of the Supreme Court bar and board member and honorary chairman of the ACLU chapter, if he would lend his name to Fred's petition.[19]

The ACLU's national office was skeptical about Fred's chances. Baldwin wrote Besig, "I should say to you that [national ACLU board member] Mr. Fraenkel and others are doubtful as to whether the Supreme Court will grant *certiorari* in view of the closeness of the issues to those already decided [in

Hirabayashi]." He further continued to warn Besig that the chapter could not support Collins's arguments in Fred's case in any manner that violated ACLU policy: "What Mr. Collins as attorney of record [for Fred] says is of course his own obligation. Our point is that the Union should not be involved in any issues beyond its declared policy."[20] Besig was firm in reiterating that the chapter was committed to representing Fred, regardless of whether that representation was at odds with national ACLU directives.[21]

The New Year brought Fred some good news. In January 1944, his longstanding application for indefinite leave from Topaz was finally granted. Philip Glick, solicitor for the WRA, himself weighed in to recommend Fred for indefinite leave: "I see no reason for holding this case up any longer and recommend that the project director be notified that the application for leave clearance be approved. [Korematsu] has been out on seasonal leave for over a year."[22] Even while granted "indefinite leave," however, Fred was still prohibited from returning to the West Coast; he was still on probation; and he remained under the supervision of the War Relocation Authority.

Ralston and Collins filed their petition for *certiorari* to the Supreme Court on February 2, 1944, asserting that Fred's case presented issues of national importance that the court needed to decide. The Ninth Circuit decision in Fred's case, the petition argued, had upheld as valid "the whole racial discrimination program . . . under which [Fred] and approximately 70,000 citizens of Japanese ancestry . . . were arrested by military authorities, . . . confined to stockades . . . and . . . thereafter imprisoned in concentration camps . . . where a great number of them are held . . . until [DeWitt] or a higher governmental authority sees fit to release them." The Supreme Court's decision in *Hirabayashi* did not resolve the issues in Fred's case, as that decision had addressed only DeWitt's curfew order: "[T]he question of the validity of the civilian exclusion orders and the whole banishment and imprisonment program of General DeWitt . . . have never been passed upon by this Court."[23] On March 27, 1944, the Supreme Court agreed to hear Fred's case. Oral arguments were set for the beginning of the court's next term, in October 1944. When Fred read that his case would be heading for the Supreme Court, he wrote Besig, "[N]ice going."[24]

As Collins and the government attorneys prepared to appear before the Supreme Court, they had a new and important report to address. On January 19, 1944, after the high court's *Hirabayashi* and *Yasui* decisions,

DeWitt's *Final Report* on the removal of Japanese Americans from the West Coast was made public. The report, which explained DeWitt's justifications for his military orders, had in fact been ready as early as April 1943 but not released. That month, while preparing the government's brief in the *Hirabayashi* case, Justice Department attorney Edward Ennis had asked the War Department for any materials in its possession bearing on the removal of Japanese Americans from the West Coast; he was advised of the report and told that DeWitt's legal staff would determine whether it could be sent. Ennis and the rest of the Justice Department attorneys handling the *Korematsu*, *Hirabayashi*, and *Yasui* cases would not see a copy of the report until over a year and a half later. They received the report on January 7, 1944; it hit newspapers on January 20.[25]

In the report, DeWitt recounted his reasons for seeking to clear Japanese Americans from the coast. Not surprisingly, the report repeated the racial stereotypes and assumptions that had led to DeWitt's orders. His transmittal memo explained, for example, that Japanese Americans were "significantly concentrated" near strategic installations; that hundreds of Japanese organizations on the West Coast had been "actively engaged in advancing Japanese war aims" prior to the bombing of Pearl Harbor; that "thousands of American-born Japanese had gone to Japan to receive their education and indoctrination there and had become rabidly pro-Japanese"; and that "Emperor worshipping ceremonies were commonly held." The report posited that "[t]he continued presence of a large, unassimilated, tightly knit racial group, bound to the enemy by strong ties of race, culture, custom and religion along a frontier vulnerable to attack constituted a menace which had to be dealt with. Their loyalties were unknown and time was of the essence" (DeWitt, *Final Report,* vii).

DeWitt also suggested his belief that Japanese Americans were involved in illegal signaling, although he did not, and could not, cite any evidence to support that belief. He explained, for example, that his requests for tightening West Coast security in December 1941 were based on reports of unauthorized radio transmissions "which had been identified as emanating from certain areas along the coast." He explained that submarine attacks on ships leaving the West Coast "seemed conclusively to point to the existence of hostile shore-to-ship (submarine) communication." He further alleged that "[t]here were hundreds of reports nightly of signal lights visible from the coast, and of intercepts of unidentified radio transmission. Signaling was often observed at premises which could not be entered without a warrant because of mixed occupancy [citizens and aliens of Japanese ancestry residing in the same home]" (ibid., 4, 8). While DeWitt did not state explicitly that it was Japanese Americans who had engaged in any of these alleged illicit signaling and radio transmissions, that was his charge, in that the very purpose of his report was to explain his reasons for removing the Nikkei from the West Coast (vii–viii).

Before taking aim at DeWitt's *Final Report*, Collins's brief, submitted on September 16, 1944, began with Fred's story, explaining his resistance to the removal orders and identifying him to be the loyal American citizen that he was:

> Four weeks before [Korematsu] was scheduled to be confined to a stockade by order of [General DeWitt] he left home to earn enough money to enable him to marry the girl of his choice, a Caucasian girl of Italian extraction. He remained in Alameda County, however. He didn't wish to be ousted from his home or leave his girl and friends. Nobody would. . . .
>
> The appellant has a slight knowledge of the Japanese language. He has never attended a Japanese language school. He has no police record. He has no dual citizenship. He is a loyal American citizen who has exercised the rights and performed the duties of citizenship. He has never been outside the continental limits of the United States. He is and steadily has been ready and willing to render whatever services he may to this nation in our war against the Axis powers. More could not be asked or expected of any citizen.[26]

Collins's brief blasted DeWitt's report for hiding behind euphemism the realities that Japanese Americans faced: "By evacuation the General meant *banishment* and by relocation he meant *detention* so that the whole outrageous program . . . as planned and carried into execution, was *imprisonment* without cause, without justification and without trial in defiance of the very letter and spirit of the Constitution which, by solemn oath, he was bound to defend and preserve." The brief condemned DeWitt as racist, citing his abiding belief that the "racial strains" of Japanese Americans remained "undiluted."[27]

Collins made a host of other arguments. He attacked the Supreme Court's decision in *Hirabayashi*, in particular, its reliance on "racial characteristics" that were said to demonstrate ties between Japanese Americans and Japan. He argued that neither the president's Executive Order 9066 nor Congress's Public Law 503 had specifically authorized the removal of Japanese Americans from the West Coast, and that, in any case, the Executive Order exceeded the president's authority and the Public Law provided no guidelines at all for its implementation. And, as he had done in the trial court, Collins listed the litany of Fred's constitutional rights that had been violated by DeWitt's orders.[28]

As he worked to finish his brief in his San Francisco office, Collins may have heard news of one justice's views that would have heartened him. On September 10, 1944, Supreme Court Justice Frank Murphy delivered an address in San Francisco. While his speech focused on the unjust persecution of Jews, he called for the eradication of hatred against all minorities. In words that foreshadowed the conclusion he would reach in Fred's case three months later, he said, "Our nation has been built on democratic principles. One of these principles is that each among us is to be treated as a human being without regard to the land from which his forefathers came, his racial background, his creed. We should not think of ourselves as Jews or Gentiles. We are American. If any community in our nation betrays the principle of civil and religious liberty a damaging blow will be inflicted on the greatest system of free government known to man."[29] While the printed version of Justice Murphy's remarks does not include any specific references to Japanese Americans, and while judicial rules of conduct normally prohibit judges from commenting on pending cases, the *Rocky Shimpo* quoted Murphy as stating in reference to them: "They are Americans. To say that Japanese blood excludes a man from being an American is to negate our principles. It isn't blood that makes an American. It's what you believe and what you stand for."[30]

In contrast to Collins's wide-ranging brief that covered a stream of issues, the government's brief focused on three main points. First, Executive Order 9066 specifically contemplated removal and so, despite Collins's argument to the contrary, the civilian exclusion order that Fred had violated had been authorized by the president. Second, the exclusion order was a valid exercise of the government's war power and not an unconstitutional delegation of legislative power. The government lawyers pointed the court to its decision in *Hirabayashi*, arguing that the "facts and circumstances" relied on there to justify DeWitt's curfew orders equally justified the exclusion orders at issue in Fred's case. The wholesale removal of Japanese Americans was justified by military necessity, the brief argued, because there was insufficient time to separate those who were disloyal from those who were loyal.[31]

Finally, the government argued that the court should not, in Fred's case, address the constitutionality of the detention of Japanese Americans. The only order validly before the court, the brief asserted, was the exclusion order that Fred had violated; Fred had not been charged with refusing confinement. In making this argument, the government paved the way for the court to artificially separate what, in reality, was inseparable. The removal order and the subsequent confinement of Japanese Americans were two parts of a seamless whole; as the government's own brief pointed out, the exclusion orders themselves informed Japanese Americans that they would be transferred for "temporary residence" in an "Assembly Center."[32] Fred's refusal to comply with exclusion was, in reality, a refusal to submit to incarceration. Just in case the court was inclined to address the detention of Japanese Americans, however, the government's brief argued that detention was nevertheless constitutional because it was designed to ensure the orderly removal of the Nikkei from the West Coast and was within the war powers of the president and Congress.[33]

Three amicus briefs were filed in Fred's case. Two briefs were from familiar players: one brief was filed jointly by the states of California, Oregon, and Washington, of course, in support of the removal orders,[34] and the national ACLU filed a brief opposing them.[35] But there was also a brief from a new and surprising source—the Japanese American Citizens League. The JACL had played no role in the *Korematsu, Hirabayashi*, or *Yasui* cases as the cases made their way up through the courts. After adamantly refusing to support any challenges to the government's orders, however, the league had perhaps realized that its silence had not purchased any reward. JACL leadership, while still not wanting to directly challenge the constitutionality of DeWitt's orders, became increasingly concerned with the "racial characteristics" arguments being advanced by the government and filed amicus briefs when Gordon's, Min's, and Fred's cases reached the Supreme Court.[36]

Executive Secretary Mike Masaoka explained how the JACL's participation wasn't a change in position:

> While we did not participate directly in these cases, it now appears necessary that we submit a brief as a friend of the court which does not challenge the constitutionality of the evacuation orders as such but strongly refuting the government's inferences concerning the loyalty of the Japanese Americans and the other "traits" attributed to the Japanese, citizens and aliens alike. . . .
>
> Should these cases testing the constitutionality of the evacuation orders be carried to the Supreme Court, we believe that the JACL should, and must, appear as "friends of the court" to question the broad constitutional powers involved. While this may seem to be a reversal of our policy, it actually constitutes an affirmation of our policy that we cooperated with the government in the evacuation program but that we did so under protest and without admitting its constitutionality.[37]

JACL president Saburo Kido ignored altogether the JACL's previous "unalterabl[e] oppos[ition] to test cases."[38] He commented that the *Korematsu* and *Endo* cases, which would be heard by the Supreme Court together, were two of the most important cases involving civil rights since the Civil War.[39] After observing the oral arguments in Fred's case, Kido lamented the lack of Japanese American support:

> The question which many Caucasian friends have asked is: Are the Nisei financing these test cases? They are surprised when they are informed that the American Civil Liberties Union and the attorneys interested in the cases have carried the brunt of the cost. Even in the Yasui case, excepting for some help the Minidoka relocation center people gave, there was no contribution. This does not speak too well for persons of Japanese ancestry whose fundamental rights are involved. It is a source of considerable embarrassment because some government officials pointedly asked: Don't the Nisei expect to fight for their rights? Don't they realize that it costs money to carry on test cases?[40]

Besig responded, echoing the absence of Japanese American support for Fred's case:

> I have noted the statement in Saburo Kido's column of October 21 that Wayne Collins spent $2000 of his own money in the Korematsu case and that James Purcell spent about $3,000 of his own money in the Endo case. No mention is made of the time the attorneys have spent on these cases, to the detriment of their own private practices. . . .
>
> I venture to say that if Mr. Collins were compensated for all the work he has done in these Japanese test cases in accordance with usual fees in the legal profession the bill would run into five figures.
>
> Sixty per cent of the money this branch expended on the Japanese test cases came out its reserve funds. While we haven't solicited funds from the Japanese in support of these cases, it is interesting to note that out of our expenditure of $2224.62 not one cent has been contributed by any person of Japanese ancestry.[41]

T. Kako replied to Besig's letter with shock that the Nikkei community had not made any contribution to the cases:

> The Ernest Besig letter as director of the Northern California American Civil Liberties Union . . . astounded me. That the various cases waged on behalf of the civil and citizenship rights of Japanese Americans have been carried on solely without the financial support of those who would derive the most benefit shows an astonishing lack of gratefulness on the part of those of Japanese descent. . . .
>
> Though I am an alien "ineligible for citizenship," I feel strongly that the rights which our boys are fighting for overseas should be preserved intact at home. The maintenance of civil rights is one of the homefront battles. . . .
>
> To start the ball rolling, I am hereby enclosing my check of $50. Please convey this to Mr. Ernest Besig with my apologies on behalf of those who are the recipients of their efforts.[42]

Two years later, the JACL explained its belated participation in the Supreme Court cases. "If the JACL had not appeared as amicus curiae, there would have been the awkward situation of no representation in behalf of Japanese Americans in the cases which vitally concerned their citizenship rights."[43]

The JACL brief filed in Fred's case, prepared by Morris Opler and signed by JACL counsel Al Wirin and president Saburo Kido, was a frontal assault on DeWitt and his *Final Report*. Its two hundred pages challenged DeWitt's claims of military necessity for the removal orders; chastised the *Hira-bayashi* court for accepting the argument that the racial characteristics of Japanese Americans provided a basis for presuming their disloyalty; and charged that DeWitt's racism had motivated his orders. The report's extensive footnotes cited testimony before legislative bodies, articles, books, and government documents to support its argument that there was "no reasonable basis for the military exclusion orders."[44]

One by one, the JACL brief addressed the "considerations" underlying DeWitt's conclusion that Japanese Americans, as an "unassimilated, tightly knit racial group" subject to influence by the government of Japan, posed a threat that required their removal from the West Coast. It challenged, for example, the claims that Japanese Americans were a dangerous element because of their number and concentration near strategic installations; their status as dual citizens (few were); their attendance at allegedly subversive Japanese language schools; and their religious affiliations (thousands, in fact, were Christian). Japanese Americans were instead, the brief argued, highly assimilated, loyal citizens who had contributed greatly to the fabric and life of the country as community members, students, artists, athletes, and scientists. In the end, the brief asserted, the only basis for the exclusion orders was DeWitt's own racist views and his acceptance of the racist views of others who had called for the removal of Japanese Americans from the West Coast.[45]

In September 1944, Fred wrote Besig that he had decided to head further East; his brothers were in Chicago and Detroit, and Fred felt that he might have more opportunities if he left Salt Lake City. By October, he had settled in Detroit, where he found the people "quite friendly" and the city to be a "war boom-town." He had landed a job with a company that made doors, including doors for aircraft hangars, and was living at the YMCA. He believed, or at least hoped, that his case was going smoothly. Besig was glad to hear of Fred's move and wished him success. He advised Fred that Collins had left for Washington to argue Fred's case before the Supreme Court, and he enclosed Collins's brief. And, ever promoting his Northern California ACLU, Besig told Fred that his membership in the chapter had expired and that two dollars would place him again in "good standing."[46]

The nine justices of the Supreme Court entered the courtroom on October 11 to hear arguments in Fred's case. The same day, it would also hear arguments in another case of great import to Japanese Americans, *Ex Parte Endo*, which concerned whether the government could continue to detain a citizen whose loyalty had been established. Kido wrote that the courtroom was packed with attorneys, tourists, and interested spectators, including Nisei.[47] Collins rose to argue on Fred's behalf that DeWitt's removal orders were unconstitutional because they were not based on any military necessity. He shared his argument time with Washington, DC, attorney Charles A. Horsky, who had prepared the National ACLU's amicus brief. Horsky focused on a second critical argument—that the program of exclusion was, in reality, a program of detention. Compliance with the exclusion order, he argued, led inevitably to incarceration, and that incarceration was unlawful.[48]

Solicitor General Charles Fahy then argued on behalf of the United States. The removal orders were military orders, he argued, issued by a military commander, DeWitt, in an area declared a "theater of operations," and made under the authority invested in him by Roosevelt in his capacity as president and commander-in-chief. As military orders, they were "subject to limited review" by the court, as the court had held in *Hirabayashi*.[49] After asserting that the court's review of the exclusion orders was limited, Fahy launched into the meat of his argument. It was clear, he said, that Fred had knowingly violated the order that he leave Oakland: "[Korematsu] desired to remain there, believing that because he was a loyal American native-born citizen, it was beyond the power of the Government to require that he be removed" (*Korematsu* Supreme Court Oral Argument transcript, 5). Given that it was undisputed that Fred had remained when the order required him to leave, the only question was whether the order was constitutional, and Fahy argued that it was.

Fahy pointed the justices to DeWitt's *Final Report*, arguing that nothing in it showed anything other than DeWitt's good faith and honest belief that his actions were necessary. Even while relying on DeWitt's report, however,

Fahy argued that the decision to remove Japanese Americans from the West Coast was not solely DeWitt's; it was a decision by the whole of the United States government: "This is not an instance of a subordinate in some isolated case going beyond the scope laid down by the legislative or executive authority." Justice Felix Frankfurter asked whether the orders should be struck if, as the JACL asserted, DeWitt had issued them based on his own racism. "Suppose," Frankfurter asked, "the commanding general, when he issued Order No. 34, had said, in effect, 'It is my judgment that, as a matter of security, there is no danger from the Japanese operations; but under cover of war, I had authority to take advantage of my hostility and clear the Japanese from this area.' Suppose he had said that, with that kind of crude candor. It would not have been within his authority, would it"? Fahy conceded that it would not (6–7, 10–11, 14–15, 21).

After arguing that the removal orders were valid, Fahy spent most of his argument explaining that Fred's case was only about removal, and not at all about detention. He reiterated that Fred had been charged with violating only the exclusion orders; he had not been charged with refusing detention. And in an argument that should have strained credulity, Fahy argued that Fred's case did not properly raise the issue of detention because nothing showed he refused detention. If Fred had complied with the exclusion orders, Fahy posited, he might have left and refused detention; he might have chosen "to go in another way than that which had been provided by the Government, as all the others went." Fahy argued, "[Korematsu] was not protesting the manner of going. He was protesting the right of the Government to make him go at all" (16–17). Fahy's argument belied the reality that reporting for exclusion led to incarceration. At the time of Fred's arrest, DeWitt's orders prevented him from leaving Oakland except as authorized by the army, and Exclusion Order No. 34 required him to report for confinement at Tanforan.

Fahy continued that, even if the court was inclined to address the issue of detention, it should focus only on the temporary detention camps, the "assembly centers" that, he argued, were necessary incidents to the program of removal. It is doubtful that any of the incarcerated Japanese Americans would have agreed with the picture he painted. Ignoring the barbed wire and armed guards that surrounded the camps, Fahy asserted, "These persons were not prisoners. They were not in concentration camps."

Instead, he characterized the camps as temporary facilities provided by the government when "voluntary" migration had not worked. After the exclusion orders were issued, he explained, neighboring states did not want the Nikkei, and Nikkei who needed to leave were without transportation, shelter, food, and protection. He cast the removal of Japanese Americans to camps as a program adopted out of benevolence: the "stern hand" of the government that required Japanese Americans to move "could turn somewhat, as it did, into a gentle hand, to control this matter in a manner befitting this Government of ours" (21–25).

Further, ignoring the tens of thousands of Japanese Americans who remained in the more permanent camps, such as Topaz, Fahy argued that the validity of those camps was not properly before the court. Fred, he argued, could not challenge his confinement at Topaz because he could have sought leave at Tanforan to avoid being sent to Topaz. Fahy had to concede, however, that there was no formal procedure for requesting leave from Tanforan and that there was no guarantee that Fred would have obtained leave if he had sought it (32–34).

Finally, the justices questioned Fahy regarding the necessary length of confinement. Recognizing that the imprisonment of Japanese Americans had no definite term and lay solely within the government's discretion, Justice Wiley Rutledge asked Fahy, "It is one thing to submit to imprisonment to go through a period of sifting to determine one's loyalty to his country. It may be an entirely different thing to submit to indefinite imprisonment, without any promise or assurance of opportunity for such sifting to take place." Fahy gave the only answer he could: "This whole process took time. . . . It has been the theory of the government, and of all those involved in any responsibility in this case, that these people must be restored to their full liberty of which they are deprived by reason of military necessity. In the face of the difficulties and magnitude of the program, it seems to me that every reasonable method has been devised to accomplish the desired result. No one can help but regret the time it has taken" (36–37). Fahy hoped that Japanese Americans would accept their detention as a necessary sacrifice during a time of war: "It seems to me that those who have been injured— as many have, temporarily—should be asked to view the situation along with the great injuries, losses, sufferings, and hardships of millions of our people in the fight of this nation for its life" (38). In explaining the time it took to determine who was loyal and disloyal, and the "temporary" nature of the program of detention, Fahy noticeably failed to mention that loyalty screening did not begin until well after Japanese Americans had been sent to camp and that, as of the October 1944 day the justices heard Fahy's argument, many Japanese Americans had been in camp for two and half years.

After the oral arguments before the Supreme Court, Fred and the rest of the Japanese American community awaited the court's ruling. Much more was at stake than their freedom; as Nisei journalist Bill Hosokawa put it, what was at stake were basic American principles:

> [If DeWitt's orders are upheld,] [w]hat is to prevent some future use of these precedents against some other minority group when the compelling causes are less urgent than that of war against a treacherous foe?
>
> If anything is to be salvaged out of the tears; the cost, both monetary and to American prestige; the endangering of American principles, then there must be once and for all an unambiguous ruling by the courts which will answer the questions raised by the evacuation. . . .
>
> Despite whatever resentment the evacuees may have felt over this treatment, it is now largely a thing of the past. What matters now is that we must use this tragic episode in the lives of a small fraction of the American population to make sure that similar abridgment of rights cannot take place.[50]

The Supreme Court issued its decision in *Toyosaburo Korematsu v. United States* on December 18, 1944.[51] Six justices upheld the removal orders and affirmed Fred's conviction; three justices dissented. While their decision in the *Hirabayashi* case had been unanimous, the majority and dissenting justices were sharply divided on every point involved in Fred's case. Not only were they divided on the basic issue of whether the removal orders were constitutional, they also fundamentally disagreed in their basic views on the scope and purpose of the military orders; the level of deference due to the military judgment; whether the issue before the court involved detention, as well as removal; and whether the government's actions had been motivated by military necessity or racism.

Justice Hugo L. Black delivered the majority opinion of the court, joined by Chief Justice Harlan Fiske Stone and Justices Stanley Reed, William O.

Douglas, and Wiley Rutledge.[52] The opinion began with two concessions that might normally have foreshadowed a positive result for Fred. First, it made clear that no question had been raised as to Fred's loyalty to the United States. Second, it denounced racism. In terms that would put Fred's case in almost every law student's constitutional law casebook for decades to follow, the opinion explained that courts must strictly scrutinize government actions that treat individuals differently based on their race: "It should be noted, to begin with, that all legal restrictions which curtail the civil rights of a single racial group are immediately suspect. That is not to say that all such restrictions are unconstitutional. It is to say that courts must subject them to the most rigid scrutiny. Pressing public necessity may sometimes justify the existence of such restrictions; racial antagonism never can" (*Korematsu*, 323 U.S. at 216). Despite this ringing language, Black's opinion failed to subject the government's actions to any scrutiny at all, much less the "rigid scrutiny" he described.

The court upheld the removal orders, reasoning, as it had in *Hirabayashi*, that there was no basis for questioning the military judgment that Japanese Americans posed a threat that required quick action. "Here, as in the *Hirabayashi* case, '. . . we cannot reject as unfounded the judgment of the military authorities and of Congress that there were disloyal members of that population, whose number and strength could not be precisely and quickly ascertained.'" Granting that "exclusion from the area where one's home is located is a far greater deprivation" than confinement to the home during curfew hours, the court explained that "exclusion from a threatened area, no less than curfew, has a definite and close relationship to the prevention of espionage and sabotage" (218). Remarkably, the court cited, as proof of the danger, the results of the loyalty questionnaires given to Japanese Americans *after* they had been incarcerated: "That there were members of the group who retained loyalty to Japan has been confirmed by investigations made subsequent to the exclusion. Approximately five thousand American citizens of Japanese ancestry refused to swear unqualified allegiance to the United States and to renounce allegiance to the Japanese emperor, and several thousand evacuees requested repatriation to Japan" (219).

The failure of the court to scrutinize the orders is evident from how it mischaracterized—indeed, how it misrepresented—the program of removal and incarceration. In concluding that the only orders properly before it were the orders excluding Japanese Americans from the West Coast and that it would not and could not address whether the government had the power to put them behind barbed wire, the court separated into phases what was really one inseparable program that culminated in incarceration. According to the court, there were three phases of the program—"(1) depart from the area; (2) report to and temporarily remain in an assembly center; [and] (3) go under military control to a relocation center there to remain for an indefinite time until released conditionally or unconditionally"—and each had separate requirements, imposed distinct duties, and constituted separate offenses if not obeyed (222). The court reasoned that it could not address the issue of detention because the only issue in Fred's case was his failure to depart Oakland; his case did not involve refusing detention (221–22). However, there were no separate detention orders issued—reporting for removal meant reporting for detention. Further, the court said that there was no basis for believing that Fred's entry into temporary detention at an "assembly center" inevitably led to detention in the more permanent "relocation center" (221–22), wholly ignoring that Fred, in fact, had been transferred, as a matter of course, from Tanforan to Topaz.

Contrary to the court's reasoning, DeWitt's orders combined into a seamless program that led to incarceration. After DeWitt's "freeze" order of March 1942, Japanese Americans could not leave the area of their West Coast homes except as directed by military order. Once ordered to leave the area, the only way that they could leave was by submitting to confinement by the army. Once confined, they could not leave unless cleared by the army or the WRA.

While refusing to address whether the government could incarcerate the Japanese Americans, the court acknowledged that some measure of detention was necessary to accomplish exclusion: "The power to exclude includes the power to do it by force if necessary. And any forcible measure must necessarily entail some degree of detention or restraint whatever method of removal is selected" (223). The court said that the constitutionality of detention, beyond that incident to exclusion, could be addressed in a future case: "It will be time enough to decide the serious constitutional issues which petitioner seeks to raise when an assembly or relocation order is applied or is certain to be applied to him, and we have its terms before us" (222). It is difficult, however, to imagine how the court felt that there would be another time to address the constitutionality of the detention of Japanese Americans. Many still remained in camp after two and a half years; did those still there feel that there would be "time enough to decide" the propriety of their confinement? While the court's opinion in the *Endo* case, handed down the same day as opinion in Fred's case, would address the validity of continued confinement, it would not address the question Collins had argued in Fred's case—whether it was lawful for the government to incarcerate Japanese Americans to begin with.

In conclusion, the court explained that the removal orders were not the result of racial discrimination: "Korematsu was not excluded from the Military Area because of hostility to him or his race." Instead, the court said, he was excluded because this country was at war with Japan; because of the fear of invasion; because of the military judgment that it was necessary to "temporarily" segregate Japanese Americans from the West Coast; and because "Congress, reposing its confidence in the time of war in our military leaders—as inevitably it must—determined that they should have the power to do just this" (223).

Justice Felix Frankfurter filed a separate concurring opinion, agreeing that Fred's conviction should be affirmed, but asserting, more explicitly than Black had, that the courts should not second guess Congress or the president in the exercise of their powers to wage war. Reminding that the war power of the government is "the power to wage war successfully,"[53] Frankfurter cautioned that where the bodies of government responsible for the national defense had determined that military necessity required the removal and incarceration of Japanese Americans, it was not for the courts to intervene: "[B]eing an exercise of the war power explicitly granted by the Constitution for safeguarding the national life by prosecuting war effectively, I find nothing in the Constitution which denies to Congress the power to enforce such a valid military order by making its violation an offense triable in civil courts. To find that the Constitution does not forbid the military measures now complained of does not carry with it approval of that which Congress and the Executive did. That is their business, not ours."[54]

Three justices submitted vigorous dissents, condemning the court's decision in resounding terms. Justice Owen Roberts didn't mince words. He began, "I dissent, because I think the indisputable facts exhibit a clear violation of Constitutional rights." The court's majority had failed, Roberts asserted, to see Fred's case for what it was—a case involving resistance to unlawful imprisonment, not the simple refusal to leave a prohibited zone.

> This is not a case of keeping people off the streets at night as was [*Hirabayashi*], nor the case of temporary exclusion of a citizen from an area for his own safety or that of the community, nor a case of offering him an opportunity to go temporarily out of an area where his presence might cause danger to himself or his fellows. On the contrary, it is the case of convicting a citizen as a punishment for not submitting to imprisonment in a concentration camp, based on his ancestry, and solely because of his ancestry, without evidence or inquiry concerning his loyalty and good disposition towards the United States. (*Korematsu*, 323 U.S., Roberts, J., dissenting, 225–26)

The series of orders issued against Japanese Americans, Roberts asserted, had, in their design, the ultimate goal of removing them into incarceration. DeWitt's Public Proclamation No. 4, his "freeze" order, prohibited persons of Japanese ancestry from leaving the West Coast except as directed by further order. DeWitt's subsequent civilian exclusion orders made it unlawful for them to be present on the West Coast, unless within the boundaries of an army detention center. "The obvious purpose of the orders made, taken together, was to drive all citizens of Japanese ancestry into Assembly Centers within the zones of their residence, under pain of criminal prosecution." To cast the exclusion orders as temporary ones that otherwise allowed Japanese Americans to "leave and go elsewhere in their native land outside the boundaries of [the] military area . . . is to shut our eyes to reality" (229, 232).

Furthermore, the orders were conflicting and put Fred in an untenable position. He would be a criminal if he left the zone in which he resided, and a criminal if he did not leave. "In the dilemma that he dare not remain in his home, or voluntarily leave the area, without incurring criminal penalties, and that the only way he could avoid punishment was to go to an Assembly Center ["a euphemism for prison," according to Roberts], and submit himself to military imprisonment, the petitioner did nothing" (230, 232).

Roberts also challenged the majority's view that, if Fred had wanted to protest his confinement in camp, his proper remedy was to submit to army custody and seek release by filing a petition for a writ of habeas corpus from behind barbed wire. Roberts protested, "It is a new doctrine of constitutional law that one indicted for disobedience to an unconstitutional statute may not defend on the ground of [its invalidity] but must obey it though he knows it is no law and, after he has suffered the disgrace of conviction and lost his liberty . . . then, and not before, seek, from within prison walls, to test the validity of the statute" (233). In Roberts's view, Fred need not have suffered an unjust imprisonment in order to challenge it.

Justice Frank Murphy's dissent was no less scathing. "This exclusion of 'all persons of Japanese ancestry, both alien and non-alien,' from the Pacific Coast area on a plea of military necessity in the absence of martial law ought not to be approved. Such exclusion goes over 'the very brink of constitutional power' and falls into the ugly abyss of racism" (*Korematsu*, 323 U.S., 233, Murphy, J., dissenting).

Murphy granted that the decisions of military officials should be given great deference: "In dealing with matters related to the prosecution and progress of a war, we must accord great respect and consideration to the judgments of the military authorities who are on the scene and who have full knowledge of the military facts." Given that level of respect due military decisions, Murphy explained, the courts may uphold an order on a plea of military necessity, even if it denies an individual his constitutional rights, when it is "reasonably related to a public danger that is so 'immediate, imminent, and impending' as not to admit of delay and not to permit the intervention of ordinary constitutional processes to alleviate the danger" (233–34).

In Murphy's view, however, Civilian Exclusion Order No. 34, the order that forced Fred's family from Oakland, did not satisfy even that low level of deferential review. It was, instead, "an obvious racial discrimination, . . . depriving all within its scope of the equal protection of the laws as guaranteed by the Fifth Amendment," the "constitutional rights to live and work where they will, to establish a home where they choose and to move about freely," and their "constitutional rights to procedural due process." Murphy found "no reasonable relation to an 'immediate, imminent, and impending' public danger . . . evident to support this racial restriction, which is one of the most sweeping and complete deprivations of constitutional rights in the history of this nation in the absence of martial law" (235).

That the orders were based on racist assumptions, not military necessity, was clear from DeWitt's *Final Report*. DeWitt's view of Japanese Americans as inherently disloyal was evident in his references "to all persons of Japanese descent as 'subversive,' as belonging to 'an enemy race' whose 'racial strains are undiluted,' and as constituting 'over 112,000 potential enemies . . . at large today' along the Pacific Coast" (235–36). Murphy castigated DeWitt's claims (also argued by the government) that the "racial characteristics" of Japanese Americans showed their purported loyalty to Japan: "Justification for the exclusion is sought . . . mainly upon questionable racial and sociological grounds not ordinarily within the realm of expert military judgment, supplemented by certain semi-military conclusions drawn from an unwarranted use of circumstantial evidence." The claims regarding lack of assimilation, "emperor worshipping ceremonies," Japanese language schools, and allegedly deliberate residence near strategic installations were, Murphy said, "largely an accumulation of half-truths and insinuations that for years have been directed at Japanese Americans by people with racial and economic prejudices—the same people who have been among the foremost advocated of the evacuation" (235–39).

There was, Murphy asserted, no reason that Japanese Americans could not be screened on an individual basis, as was done for persons of German and Italian ancestry. While the government and the majority of the court had said that there was insufficient time to separate the loyal from the disloyal, "nearly four months elapsed after Pearl Harbor before the first exclusion order was issued; nearly eight months went by until the last order was issued; and the last of these 'subversive' persons was not actually removed until almost eleven months had elapsed." Significantly, "not one person of Japanese ancestry was accused or convicted of espionage or sabotage after Pearl Harbor while they were still free" (241). Murphy concluded, "I dissent, therefore, from this legalization of racism. Racial discrimination in any form and in any degree has no justifiable part whatever in our democratic way of life. It is unattractive in any setting but is utterly revolting among a free people who have embraced the principles set forth in the Constitution of the United States" (242).

Justice Robert H. Jackson's dissent echoed Murphy's condemnation of the removal orders as racially based. If Fred had been in the exclusion zone in the company of a German alien, an Italian alien, and a citizen of American-born ancestors who was convicted of treason but out on parole, only Fred would have been arrested. "The difference between their innocence and his crime would result, not from anything he did, said, or thought, different from they, but only in that he was born of a different racial stock." This result, Jackson asserted, flew in the face of the fundamental assumption underlying the legal system that "guilt is personal and not inheritable" (Korematsu, 323 U.S., 243, Jackson, J. dissenting).

Further, contrary to the majority opinion's view, whether the orders were constitutional could not turn simply on whether they were reasonable exercises of military judgment. First, Jackson asserted, it would be unrealistic to expect military authorities, in times of crisis, to conform to norms of legal reasonableness: "When an area is so beset that it must be put under military control at all, the paramount concern is that its measures be successful, rather than legal." (244). In addition, the courts, in hindsight, have no real means to assess the reasonableness of military judgments. In Fred's case, for example, there was no evidence taken on the reasonableness of the removal orders. "So the Court, having no real evidence before it, has no choice but to accept General DeWitt's own unsworn, self-serving statement, untested by any cross-examination, that what he did was reasonable. And thus it will always be when courts try to look into the reasonableness of a military order" (245).

Finally, even if DeWitt's orders were reasonable from a military perspective, as the majority held, that was a wholly separate question from whether they were constitutional. The court's enforcement of a military order that violates constitutional limitations, even if found to be a reasonable exercise of military authority, had far-reaching consequences:

> A judicial construction of the due process clause that will sustain this order is a far more subtle blow to liberty than the promulgation of the order itself. A military order, however unconstitutional, is not apt to last longer than the military emergency. . . . But once a judicial opinion rationalizes such an order to show that it conforms to the Constitution, or rather rationalizes the Constitution to show that the Constitution sanctions such an order, the Court for all time has validated the principle of racial discrimination in criminal procedure and of transplanting American citizens. The principle then lies about like a loaded weapon ready for the hand of any

authority that can bring forward a plausible claim of an urgent need. Every repetition imbeds that principle more deeply in our law and thinking and expands it to new purposes. . . . A military commander may overstep the bounds of constitutionality, and it is an incident. But if we review and approve, that passing incident becomes a doctrine of the Constitution. (245–46)

Jackson would not and could not be asked "to execute a military expedient that has no place in law under the Constitution" (248).

Criticism of the court's decision in Fred's case followed soon after its release, and has continued ever since. The *Washington Post* printed its editorial on December 22, 1944, four days after the decision was announced. Even if the removal of suspicious persons was necessary, the *Post* stated, "the indiscriminate manner of its application, we think, was not. For no attempt was made to distinguish the loyal and the disloyal, although eight months elapsed after Pearl Harbor before the final exclusion order was issued. . . . It is on this ground that we are inclined to take our stand with Mr. Justice Murphy's characterization of the majority opinion as a 'legalization of racism.'"[55] Marjorie McKenzie's editorial of January 6, 1945, was titled "Pursuit of Democracy: Supreme Court's Okay of Removal of Japanese Can Affect Negro Rights." She wrote, "We who are so sensitive to an impairment of our own rights have been singularly dispassionate about the war-time fate of Japanese-Americans. The hot danger of the Supreme Court's Korematsu decision . . . licks pretty close to our skins. We ought to think seriously about Korematsu's case, for, in a way, he is perilously close to being a 20th Century Dred Scott of only different color."[56]

Columnist Westbrook Pegler condemned the court's decision upholding the removal of Japanese Americans he himself had called for in February 1942: "[What the court termed 'temporary segregation' for thousands] has meant three years of imprisonment and the sacrifice of their homes, business interests and property, to say nothing of their rights as loyal, native citizens." He condemned Frankfurter for upholding the removal orders: "Oddly, Felix Frankfurter, himself an immigrant from an enemy country, Austria, concurred with the majority, but in a separate opinion whose reasoning, if any, eludes me. I believe it would have been more to the interest of the United States to snatch Frankfurter from the bench and lock him up, than to intern a thousand Korematsus in the Arizona desert."[57]

Legal commentators have been unanimous in condemning the Supreme Court's decisions in the *Korematsu, Hirabayashi,* and *Yasui* cases. Professor Eugene Rostow's critique appeared in the *Yale Law Journal* only six months after the court's decision in Fred's case:

> All in all, the internment of the West Coast Japanese is the worst blow our liberties have sustained in many years. . . . If the Court had stepped forward in bold heart to vindicate the law and declare the entire program illegal, the episode would have been passed over as a national scandal, but a temporary one altogether capable of reparation. But the Court, after timid and evasive delays, has now upheld the main features of the program. That step converts a piece of war-time folly into political doctrine, and a permanent part of our law. . . . [The court] weakened society's control over military authority—one of the polarizing forces on which the organization of our society depends. And it solemnly accepted and gave the prestige of its support to dangerous racial myths about a minority group, in arguments which can be applied easily to any other minority in society.[58]

In 1945, Nanette Dembitz, one of the Justice Department attorneys who had handled the *Korematsu* case, published her analysis of the court's "dangerous opinion" in the *Columbia Law Review.*[59] In 1954, Jacobus tenBroek and his coauthors concluded that "[i]n the Japanese American cases, the Supreme Court carried judicial self-restraint to the point of judicial abdication."[60] In 1986, Professor Eric Yamamoto sought a clearer, more exacting standard for judicial review of military decisions that curtail civil liberties: "In accepting without close scrutiny the government's claim of necessity, the Court [in *Korematsu*] not only legitimized the dislocation and imprisonment of loyal citizens without trial solely on account of race, but it also weakened a fundamental tenet of American democracy—government accountability for military control over civilians."[61] Critiques of the Supreme Court's *Hirabayashi* and *Korematsu* decisions have continued to the present, especially as the issue of whether civil rights must be compromised in the face of national security concerns has taken on an eerie new relevance in the aftermath of 9/11.[62]

It was not all bad news, however, for the Japanese American community on the December day the *Korematsu* decision was announced. That day, the court also issued its decision in *Ex Parte Endo*, holding that the government could no longer continue to detain citizens whose loyalty had been established.[63] Mitsuye Endo was twenty-two years old when she was confined at the Walarga detention center near Sacramento. On July 13, 1942, represented by attorney James Purcell, she filed a petition for habeas corpus, alleging that she was "a loyal and law-abiding citizen, that no charge [had] been made against her, that she [was] being unlawfully detained, and that she [was] confined in a Relocation Center under armed guard and against her will." A shy young woman, Endo agreed to lend her name to the case because a legal challenge to her continued incarceration "would be for the good of everybody." By the time her case was decided, she had been confined for almost three years, first at Walarga, and then at Tule Lake and Topaz. Although she could have gone through the WRA leave clearance procedures and applied for leave earlier, she remained in camp so that she could test the constitutionality of her incarceration. Her petition was rejected at the district court level, and the Supreme Court agreed to hear her case.[64]

Justice Douglas delivered the unanimous opinion of the court. While the issue in Fred's case was whether the government could constitutionally remove Japanese Americans from the West Coast, the issue in Mitsuye's case was different—it was whether the government could continue to hold a citizen whose loyalty had been established. The government agreed that Mitsuye posed no threat to the "public peace and security." However, it argued that individuals had to prove more than their loyalty to obtain clearance for indefinite leave; they also had to establish additional criteria, including that they had a means of financial support at their proposed destination and favorable public sentiment in the community they would join. This showing was necessary, the government argued, because interior states would not accept the unsupervised, uncontrolled release of Nikkei from camp, and the added screening was required to ensure "a planned and orderly relocation" (*Endo*, 323 U.S., 292–94, 296–97).

The court held that "Mitsuye Endo should be given her liberty." However, it did so on the ground that nothing in the language of Executive Order 9066 or Public Law 503 had specifically authorized her continued detention, not on the ground that her original detention was unconstitutional. Although some measure of detention could be implied as a necessary part of the process of removing Japanese Americans from the West Coast, any further implied power to detain had to be "narrowly confined to the precise purpose of the evacuation program," which was military necessity. Because there was no military necessity in continuing to detain Mitsuye after her loyalty had been established, the court reasoned, she had to be released (Ibid., 296–97, 300–301).

Justices Murphy and Roberts concurred that Mitsuye should be freed. However, they criticized the majority for failing to find the entire program of incarceration unconstitutional from its inception. Justice Roberts argued that the majority's view that Roosevelt's order did not authorize detention "ignore[d] the patent facts." The president, he explained, knew that Japanese Americans would be sent to camps: "It is to hide one's head in the sand to assert that [Mitsuye Endo's] detention . . . resulted from an excess of authority by subordinate officials." The court was instead squarely faced with, and refused to answer, "a serious constitutional question[:] whether [Mitsuye Endo's] detention violated the guarantees of the Bill of Rights." Roberts asserted, "There can be but one answer to that question. An admittedly loyal citizen has been deprived of her liberty for a period of years. Under the Constitution she should be free to come and go as she pleases. . . . She should be discharged" (Ibid., 309–10, Murphy, J., dissenting).

In the end, the Supreme Court never actually addressed whether the government had unconstitutionally incarcerated Japanese Americans. In the *Hirabayashi* and *Yasui* cases, the court upheld DeWitt's curfew orders. In Fred's case, the court upheld the orders removing Japanese Americans from the West Coast. And in the *Endo* case, the court held that the government could not continue to incarcerate concededly loyal citizens. While the court had dodged the fundamental question of the constitutionality of the incarceration, in the end, however, it had, for all intents and purposes, by its silence and all the dancing it did around the issue, given the judicial stamp of approval to all that the government had done.

Not coincidentally, on December 17, 1944, the day before the court issued its decisions in the *Korematsu* and *Endo* cases, the War Department announced that Japanese Americans who had cleared loyalty screenings would be free to leave the camps after January 2, 1945, and "permitted the same freedom of movement throughout the United States as other loyal and law-abiding citizens."[65] In the end, however, the timing of its decision to end incarceration was driven by political concerns, not military judgment. As early as January 1943, with the institution of the loyalty questionnaire program, Secretary of War Harry Stimson and John J. McCloy, his assistant secretary, had become concerned about whether the government had to release Japanese Americans whose loyalty was established.[66] Public sentiment, however, opposed the return of Japanese Americans to the West Coast.[67] Despite that opposition, key factors that had led to their removal and incarceration had changed: DeWitt and Colonel Karl R. Bendetsen had departed from their positions in mid-September 1943, and the tide had turned in the Pacific war in such a way that, on November 1, 1943, the West Coast was declared to no longer be a military theater of operations.[68]

On May 26, 1944, the issue of the continued detention of Japanese Americans reached the cabinet. According to Attorney General Francis Biddle's notes of that meeting, Stimson inquired whether the exclusion orders should be canceled. The War, Interior, and Justice Departments had agreed that it could be done without danger to the national defense, "but doubted the wisdom of doing it at this time before the election."[69] Roosevelt chose to proceed with caution: "The more I think of this problem of suddenly ending the orders excluding Japanese Americans from the West Coast the more I think it would be a mistake to do anything drastic or sudden."[70] On November 10, 1944, the first cabinet meeting after Roosevelt's election, the decision was made to end the exclusion orders, but that decision would not be made public until December 17.[71]

Fred was sorely disappointed to learn that the Supreme Court had upheld his conviction and, in doing so, had approved the mass removal of Japanese Americans. He recalled his reaction in later years:

> In 1944, in Detroit, I received a letter from Mr. Besig and he told me that we lost in the Supreme Court. And I just couldn't believe it. . . . It just seemed like the bottom dropped out. I just felt like, "Am I an American or not?" And how about all those other Japanese Americans; are they Japanese *American*? . . . I thought for sure that we won because it was unconstitutional what they did to the Japanese Americans in putting them into concentration camps. When I found out that I lost my decision, I thought I lost my country.[72]

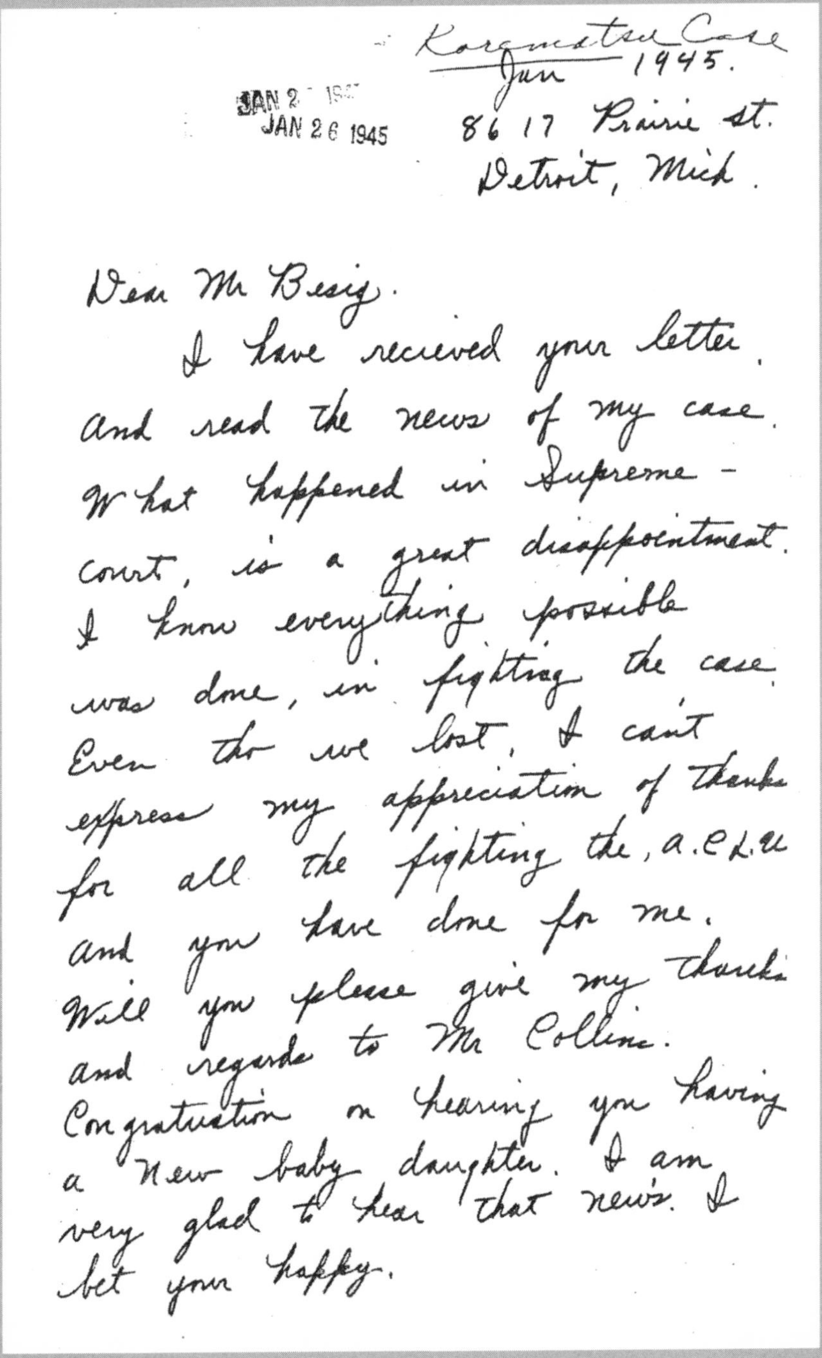

Korematsu Case
~~Jun~~ 1945.

8617 Prairie st.
Detroit, Mich.

Dear Mr Besig,

I have received your letter. And read the news of my case. What happened in Supreme court, is a great disappointment. I know everything possible was done, in fighting the case. Even tho we lost, I cant express my appreciation of thanks for all the fighting the, A.C.L.U and you have done for me. Will you please give my thanks and regards to Mr Collins. Congratuation on hearing you having a new baby daughter. I am very glad to hear that news. I bet your happy.

FIGURE 6.1. Fred's letter to Ernest Besig on learning of his Supreme Court decision, January 1945, American Civil Liberties Union of Northern California records. Courtesy of California Historical Society, MS 3580_005[a].

Fred wrote Besig, expressing both his dismay at the result and gratitude for the work on his behalf: "I have received your letter and read the news of my case. What happened in [the] Supreme Court is a great disappointment. I know everything possible was done in fighting the case. Even though we lost, I can't express my appreciation of thanks for all the fighting the ACLU and you have done for me. Will you please give my thanks to and regards to Mr. Collins."

In a last-ditch effort, Collins petitioned the Supreme Court to reconsider its ruling; his petition for rehearing was denied on February 12, 1945. Despite the news, Fred did not give up hope that one day he'd be able to challenge his conviction and the wrongful incarceration of Japanese Americans again: "[I]n the back of my mind [I thought] this is my country and eventually I'm going to try to reopen it again, if possible.[73]

CHAPTER 7

REBUILDING A LIFE

IN DECEMBER 1944, WHEN THE WEST COAST WAS REOPENED TO
Japanese Americans, tens of thousands still remained in the camps. Kakusaburo and Kotsui were among them. Most of those still there were the older
Issei or Nisei youths. Mainly, it was young, working-age Nisei, like the Korematsu boys, who had departed. Seven out of every ten who left camp in
1943 and 1944 were between fifteen and thirty-five years old. By January
1945, only one of every six Issei had left.[1]

Those young people who had left camp had dispersed far and wide.
Thousands of Nisei, like the Korematsu sons, had left camp to work on
seasonal or indefinite leave, many resettling in Denver, Salt Lake City, and
Chicago. Forty-three hundred Nisei left camp to continue their educations
with the support of a group of private citizens who formed the National
Student Relocation Council.[2]

Approximately thirty-three thousand Nisei served in the armed forces
during World War II; their accomplishments, fighting for their country on
both the European and Pacific fronts, have become legend.[3] The all-Nisei
100th Battalion, 1,432 strong when it first left Hawai'i, fought with enormous sacrifice in the campaign to move Allied forces up the Italian boot.[4]
The 100th joined forces with the 442nd Regimental Combat Team, a unit
comprised of other volunteers from Hawai'i, as well as soldiers from the
mainland, many of whom came from the camps. More than eighteen thousand men served with the unit, which, by the end of the war, suffered some
9,500 casualties, including six hundred killed. It went on to become one
of the most decorated units in history for its size and length of service.[5]

Ironically, Nisei also served with great distinction in the army's Military Intelligence Service (MIS), using their Japanese language skills to translate captured documents and interrogate prisoners. They fought in combat with both army and navy units and were loaned to forces from Australia, New Zealand, England, and China.[6]

Throughout 1945, Japanese Americans returned by the thousands to their former homes in Los Angeles, San Francisco, and Seattle, and in other parts up and down the West Coast. Their homecoming, however, would not be easy. A *Los Angeles Times* editorial, for example, warned the Nikkei to expect a chilly reception:

> As good Americans, the great majority of Pacific Coast residents will ac-
> cept, with the best grace possible to muster, the Army decree permitting
> the return to this seaboard of the evacuated Japanese. But there will not be
> many cheers. In other words, we shall take it, but we shall not pretend to
> like it. . . . However "gradual and well-screened" the process, the return of
> some 100,000 Japanese to communities where their presence will be bit-
> terly if not actively resented will not be good for the communities, for the
> Japs or for anybody or anything else.

The "Japs," the *Times* said, could go elsewhere. There were "quite a number of eastern and middle western farming communities" that had spoken for Japanese Americans and that had condemned the West Coast attitude toward them. "If they like Japs, why not let these communities have them"?[7]

While many officials opposed the return of the Japanese Americans, others, including some who had called for their removal, now asked the public to exercise restraint. Governor Earl Warren, who as attorney general had warned of potential Japanese American treachery, now urged support for the army's decision to allow them to return: "The decision of the commanding general of the Western Defense Command to revoke the mass Japanese evacuation order and to permit the return of those who have established their loyalty to the satisfaction of the Army is based on the military situation as it exists today and is therefore to be respected. . . . I am sure that all Americans will join in protecting constitutional rights of the individuals involved, and will maintain an attitude that will discourage friction and prevent civil disorder."[8]

Despite these appeals for calm, many Japanese Americans were met, as had been predicted, with hostility, discrimination, and even violence on their return. The War Relocation Authority (WRA) reported that in California alone during February–May 1945, "24 cases of violence or open intimidation [had] been directed against the returning Japanese Americans: 15 shooting attacks, one attempted dynamiting, three arson cases, and five threatening visits."[9] "No Japs Wanted" signs began to appear in the windows of shops and stores. Campaigns were organized to boycott Japanese American businesses. American Legion posts all along the Coast refused membership to Nisei servicemen. Employment discrimination was rampant. Although jobs on the West Coast were relatively plentiful, many Japanese Americans were hired to do only menial labor.[10]

Japanese Americans who did not have homes to return to had a nearly impossible time finding a place to live. Fred Ross, who was with the WRA in San Francisco after the war, testified that "the worst thing we were up against was the housing, and I am not talking about housing discrimination. I am just talking about housing—there wasn't any. . . . [W]e had to open a number of what we called hostels in each of the Japanese American churches. . . . [H]undreds of families were having to live under those conditions for months."[11]

Many returning Japanese Americans found that their stored items had been lost or stolen. Homes and businesses had, more often than not, been poorly maintained or ruined. On February 12, 1945, Fred's younger brother, Joe, wrote the WRA asking urgently for permission to return from Detroit to the family nursery in Oakland because the tenant was planning to leave in April and he had to take it back and restart the business. When he returned, he found the nursery in shambles; the greenhouses and most of the glass were broken. The Korematsus would have to take out a loan to start again.[12]

Joe wrote a friend after his return to the nursery, reporting that his reception had not been so bad, but he wished that he had been closer to the neighbors prior to the war: "As far as I can see, there will be some resentment which is natural, but after a while the new neighbors become more than casual acquaintances." He shared news of Shig Nieda, one of his close friends who had also returned from Detroit: "His nursery is being repaired and his neighbors were at first pretty cold but now they are starting to help him." And he put a positive gloss on the work to be done on the Korematsu nursery: "All the property is intact and going as well as can be expected during the war."[13]

Thousands of Japanese Americans who had resettled to the interior states chose to remain where they were and not return to the West Coast at all, resulting in the permanent dispersion of a large segment of the Nikkei community.[14] That dispersion was seen by some as a positive result of the wartime expulsion. The West Coast exclusionists, of course, were glad for every Japanese American who would not return. Some others felt that the permanent resettlement of Japanese Americans away from the Coast was singularly beneficial because it served to end their social isolation and forced them into the mainstream of American society.[15] But that forced dispersion resulted in losses, tangible and intangible, that endure to this day, including the dimming of vibrant Japantowns, Little Tokyos, and other cultural, political, and social centers of the prewar Japanese American community that would never again be as they once were.

Even after they could leave, many Japanese Americans who were still in camp were reluctant to do so. As of August 1945, more than a third of those who had been removed from the West Coast still remained in camp. They had heard of the hostility on the West Coast. They faced the prospect of starting all over again. Most had nowhere to go.[16] While picking up the pieces of their physical lives would be hard enough, perhaps what would be more challenging would be to redefine their place in a society that had banished them. Many would carry a feeling of guilt and shame with them the rest of their lives, despite the fact that they had done nothing wrong.

Over the following months, however, Japanese Americans had to, and did, leave the camps. Kakusaburo and Kotsui returned from Topaz to Oakland on May 28, 1945, with their personal belongings and a government allowance of twenty-five dollars each. Topaz was closed on November 1, 1945; all of the other camps were closed by May 1946. In the end, forty-four thousand had to be forced to leave, each provided with train fare to "the point of the evacuation."[17] While Kakusaburo joined Joe in tending the nursery, Kotsui was less able to work in the greenhouses; camp had been hard on her, and she was not well. She and Kakusaburo, however, found great joy as their house filled with a growing family. Hi and his new wife, the former Kay Tanabe, returned to the nursery from Nebraska, where they had temporarily resettled. Soon the couple welcomed the birth of Kakusaburo and Kotsui's first grandchild, Connie, and the young family stayed at the nursery for a few years until Hi established his own home and business. Joe married Hisaye Watari. They lived at the Korematsu nursery for about five years and there welcomed their firstborns, Joanne and Edie. Two other girls, Alice and Dorothy, followed in later years, and Joanne remembers fondly how she and her sisters played hide-and-seek in the nursery's greenhouses. Harry returned, as well, and took over the management of the nursery. He married the former Bette Nishimura, and they added a boy, Gary, to the Korematsu clan.[18]

Becoming older seemed to have mellowed Kakusaburo. While his limited English made it hard for his grandchildren to communicate with him, they remember him as loving, generous, and caring. Connie recalls traveling with him from Oakland to San Francisco as a child: "I would take the ferry with my grandfather Korematsu and go to the flower market and that's where we'd sell flowers. It was beautiful. . . . [Y]ou could stand on this ferry boat, look out, look all over the place and it was just stupendous . . . smelling the roses, being around other people . . . hanging out with my grandfather."[19]

While life resumed at the Korematsu nursery in Oakland, Fred remained in Detroit. There was, in his mind, no reason to return; there was nothing for him back at the nursery. He took over Joe's room at the local YMCA with roommate Mitz Takayama. In early 1945, Mitz introduced Fred to a gracious, loving, and smart young Southern woman named Kathryn Pearson. She would be his best friend, partner, and wife for the rest of his years—both respecting the stand he took and believing in him as he hoped to someday right the wrong.

Frances Kathryn Pearson had been born in March 1921 in Greenville, South Carolina. Her father was English and German, her mother English and Irish, and both her parents were extraordinary in their open-minded attitudes. While Kathryn grew up in the segregated South and heard plenty of racist talk, her parents taught tolerance. They also supported her in pursuing her education. As a young girl, she'd been fascinated when her father would kill and cut up the family's chickens—she'd poke around them to see their innards—and her curiosity lead her to pursue the life sciences. After high school, Kathryn attended Winthrop College and then the South Carolina State College for Women, where she received her bachelor of science in biology and chemistry. She then moved to Wayne State in Detroit and received a master's degree in medical technology. Her first job was in a bacteriology lab at the Henry Ford Hospital.[20]

In late 1943, the assistant pastor at Kathryn's church invited some young Nisei women to come speak about how they had been taken from the West Coast and confined in camps. Kathryn was dumb-founded. She had seen a newsreel about Japanese Americans who "had made the desert bloom— they took soil that was not productive and made it productive and grew vegetables and things of that sort." She remembered seeing children behind barbed wire, but she didn't know what it was all about. On meeting these Nisei, Kathryn understood that the newsreel had not depicted the true story of the Japanese American incarceration. One of the young women, Elma Amamoto, had been confined at the Santa Anita racetrack and then at Amache in Colorado before moving to Detroit. Through Elma and her friends, Kathryn learned the reality of the camps.

> Here was Elma, she was really quite pretty and very soft-spoken . . . and we just couldn't fathom why they would put people like that in a camp. . . . And we knew . . . somehow we knew it wasn't a delightful-type camp, I mean that came out clear. . . . I couldn't understand how these very gentle people were thought to be a danger to the country.
>
> Of course, I could see that it was wrong what the government had done to them. . . . When I first heard about the camps and what they were like, I was appalled actually to think that they were American citizens like I was an American citizen, yet they had been singled out unfairly just because of their racial characteristics.

Kathryn and Elma became good friends. Kathryn recalls, "Somehow we just clicked."[21]

It was on a Sunday that Mitz called Kathryn to see if she and Elma would like to go for a ride; he had a friend, Fred, who had a car. Fred and Kathryn's first meeting was idyllic. The foursome went to the beautiful park at Belle Isle and walked around for the afternoon. When the day came to an end, Fred walked Kathryn to her apartment door and asked if she'd like to go out that Friday night. She couldn't make it and later kicked herself because Fred ended up taking someone else to hear Tommy Dorsey and his band, but Kathryn agreed to go out with Fred the following Friday.[22]

Kathryn was impressed by Fred. He had a mature, settled air about him; he was pleasant and patient, kind and caring, and very thoughtful. He was creative—he took art lessons and had learned oil painting in Detroit. "Fred was artistic. Artistic people, as the saying goes, they march to the beat of a different drummer, and I think that was [a] reason Fred was able to do what he did." He had lots of interests, and he liked nature. He was different from so many of the other men Kathryn had met: he was comfortable to be around, and he was not full of himself. Fred, Kathryn said, wasn't hypercritical of anything or anybody; he took people for who they were, and if they had flaws, he didn't fret about it. She and Fred, she said, were "perfectly happy when there was just the two of us and doing things just the two of us liked to do. He wasn't perfect, nobody is, but he was actually the best person I ever knew."[23]

She knew that there were some people who didn't approve of an Asian American man dating a white woman, but that didn't bother them. One of Kathryn's colleagues at the hospital told Kathryn that she'd rather Kathryn never married than to marry a Japanese; Kathryn didn't have anything to do with her after that. Kathryn had known about Fred's Supreme Court case before she met him—she had read about it in the Japanese American Citizens League's *Pacific Citizen*, which Elma received—but Kathryn and Fred didn't discuss it, at least not initially. When Kathryn and Elma had heard that Fred was coming to Detroit to visit, they asked Mitz, "Is that Fred Korematsu from the case?" and Mitz said that it was. Kathryn knew that there was talk of his case when the Supreme Court ruled against him; while the younger Nisei had been disappointed by the loss, some of the older Japanese Americans, Kathryn recalls, thought that Fred was "crazy or something."[24]

When Fred later talked to her about his case, Kathryn recalls, he expressed disappointment and thought that the Supreme Court's decision was wrong—"racism, pure and simple"—but he was never bitter. He didn't consider himself a criminal, and neither did Kathryn. She saw him as someone who lived by his own sense of truth: "I think that was another reason that Fred was able to do what he did. He was strong-minded; if he thought he was right, he would not back down—not that you're rigid and can't change your mind—and it actually turned out to be the right thing." While Kathryn knew that Fred had violated the removal orders to be with his girlfriend, she never asked him about Ida: "[H]e didn't ask me about my boyfriends, either!" she laughed. In any case, they didn't spend much time talking about his case—"We were busy living!"[25]

They dated throughout the summer. They went dancing, mainly at Detroit's Eastwood Gardens—he loved to jitterbug, and it didn't seem to bother him that she hated it. They listened to radio broadcasts of their favorite bands. One of their favorites was Russ Morgan, whose program always started, Kathryn recalled, with, "Music from the Morgan Manor, broadcasting live from the Claremont Hotel high atop the Berkeley Hills!" They went to church together—he left the Methodist church he'd been attending to join Kathryn's Presbyterian church.[26]

They both worked. Fred went into drafting—the work he did for the rest of his career—and, when Kathryn was offered the opportunity to do research in a lab at Michigan State, she pursued it. Fred drove back and forth to East Lansing to visit her on weekends, but after about a year, their relationship hit a decision point. Kathryn had thought about pursuing a PhD, the most logical next step in her career. As she later explained, however, in those days, "you chose either a degree or a husband." "Professional women," she said, "just weren't getting married." She loved Fred, and, although he didn't ask her to make a choice, she chose him. The couple became engaged, and Kathryn moved back to Detroit.[27]

Fred and Kathryn married at her church in Detroit on October 12, 1946. Kathryn confirmed that they could marry in Michigan; they could not have married in their home states of California or South Carolina. Mitz was Fred's best man, and Elma was Kathryn's maid of honor. None of Fred's family could attend, but they sent large pom-pom mums, gardenias for Kathryn's hair, and an orchid bouquet. Kathryn's mother, Annie Belle Smith Pearson, made the long flight from South Carolina to be at the wedding and, as Kathryn relates, "accepted Fred as she would have accepted any other husband for her daughter." When Annie Belle went back home to South Carolina, Kathryn explains, "she put out the word that it should never come back to her that anyone said anything disparaging" about her daughter's choice of a Japanese American husband. When Kathryn's father, Fritz Lee Pearson, later met Fred, he liked him right away.[28]

After honeymooning for a blissful week at Niagara Falls, the newlyweds returned to work. Kathryn got a "dream job" teaching microbiology

FIGURE 7.1. Fred and Kathryn Korematsu's wedding, October 12, 1946, at the Woodward Avenue Presbyterian Church, Detroit, Michigan. Courtesy of Karen Korematsu and the Fred T. Korematsu Institute.

to nurses and medical technicians. While they lived relatively undisturbed as a mixed-race couple, they had a hard time finding an apartment; the only person who would rent to them was a Jewish landlord who understood discrimination firsthand.[29]

In 1949, Fred and Kathryn received news that his mother was not well, and they left to see her. When they arrived at the nursery, Kathryn took an immediate liking to Fred's mother. Kotsui was a kind, gentle, and lovely person, and Kathryn saw much of Kotsui in Fred. Kathryn particularly enjoyed Joe and Hisa; they joined in celebrating Fred and Kathryn's anniversary with a night of dinner and dancing. Although Kathryn found Fred's father a bit brusque, he was always pleasant to her.[30]

Fred and Kathryn had intended only to visit; he didn't have good memories of California and didn't want to live there. They figured that they would get to California and then decide where to go next. When Kathryn learned she was pregnant, however, everything changed. Fred now had a family to provide for, and he delighted in impending fatherhood. He needed a place for them to live—they found an apartment. And he needed a job—he was able to help, at least temporarily, preparing for the busy holiday season in Harry's new wholesale flower business. He joined Kathryn in anxious anticipation of the baby's arrival. Together, they attended a Red Cross parenting class to learn to take care of their newborn; Fred's brother Hi could hardly believe that Fred would go to such a class.[31]

On September 3, 1950, Kathryn and Fred welcomed the birth of a daughter, Karen Anne, and Fred was smitten with her. He was the first one up on Sunday mornings to feed her, and he'd feed her when he came home from work. He took her on his errands, including to the hardware store. Fred was an affectionate father to Karen, whom, Kathryn recalls, "was kind of like a Daddy's girl."[32]

The family's joy was shattered on Karen's first birthday, September 3, 1951, when Fred's mother died. She had been diagnosed with a perforated ulcer and had spent a week in the hospital. Fred visited her bedside every day after work. Her death hit him very hard; he had loved her very much.[33] After Kotsui's death, Kay told Fred point-blank, "It's because of you that Okasan [mother] died." Kay explained that Kotsui had developed ulcers in camp and that "we all" thought that she developed ulcers because of Fred's case.[34] Kay's comment no doubt hurt Fred deeply.

In the early years of their marriage, Fred and Kathryn negotiated the typical challenges that faced most young couples. But there were other, different hurdles in their way. In seeking work, Fred not only confronted discrimination based on his race, he also saw doors closed to him because of his criminal conviction. In later years, Fred recalled,

> When I first came back to California after the evacuation was over, . . . I wanted to be a real estate broker like [my brother] was. The application asked if I had a prison record. I knew it was useless to apply, I knew they would turn me down. Also, any state or federal job application had the same thing, so I knew I couldn't get a job in those places. I wanted a job

in a big firm like Bechtel, which has retirement benefits and good profit-sharing and such, but the applications asked if you have a criminal or prison record and I said yes. And I never heard from them.[35]

Unable to get a job with a large company or the government, Fred worked for himself or for small companies. He ended up working two jobs to make ends meet and save enough to buy a home.[36]

Even when Fred and Kathryn eventually had the money to buy a place, however, finding someone willing to sell to them became a whole other matter. No one in San Leandro would sell to them, and all they were shown in Oakland were old ramshackle homes. Kathryn explained, "If they couldn't sell us a piece of junk, they weren't going to sell us anything." Kathryn believed it wasn't coincidence that the people finally willing to sell to them were individuals who, like their landlord in Detroit, understood discrimination. They bought their first house from a German American realtor whose parents had been discriminated against during World War I. They bought their second home from builders who were Italian American. "They understood. . . . Only people who had been discriminated against could understand."[37]

Fred and Kathryn welcomed the birth of a son, Kenneth Toyo, on August 17, 1954, and Fred threw himself into providing his family with as picture-perfect a suburban lifestyle as he could. He couldn't be home much—he wanted Kathryn to be able to stay home with the kids—but he was present for his family as much as he could be and provided for them to the best of his ability.

When Ken was in nursery school and Kathryn got sick, Fred took off work to cover her parent volunteer shift. The teachers thought it was wonderful: "We got a father!" Both of the kids were Scouts, and Fred made sure he was involved in their troops. He took charge of health and safety for Karen's troop under the direction of troop leader Kathryn; when the girls camped out, he stood watch. Karen started tap dance at four, then went on to ballet, and, in high school, became a cheerleader. Ken was the sports guy. When he was in Little League, Fred would work a half a day on Saturdays, then go watch Ken's game, taking treats for the team. In high school, Ken did tennis and track. The kids took music lessons at nearby Mills College: Ken took up the violin, and Karen the clarinet. In retrospect, Karen understands why her

FIGURE 7.2. Fred with Ken and Karen on Ken's first birthday, at home in San Lorenzo, California, August 17, 1955. Courtesy of Karen Korematsu and the Fred T. Korematsu Institute.

father was so upset when she didn't practice; he was working two jobs and overtime to pay for those lessons.[38]

The family's world revolved around Karen and Ken, of course, as well as church and community service. They went for long drives—Fred loved to drive. They put miles and miles on the old Chevy station wagon: driving twice cross-country to visit Kathryn's family in South Carolina; trips down I-5 to Disneyland; and up to see the Space Needle at the Seattle World's Fair. They enjoyed eating out. They were avid Giants fans and loved watching Willie Mays, Willie McCovey, Orlando Cepeda, and Juan Marichel, at first on their huge, wooden, boxlike television—one of the first on their block—and, in later years, with hot dogs and peanuts in hand at Candlestick Park. They spent many an evening watching Ed Sullivan and Lawrence Welk. Karen recalls, "If I saw one Lawrence Welk show, I saw them all!"[39]

Fred and Kathryn became active members of the First Presbyterian Church in Oakland. "He would sing the hymns no matter that he couldn't carry a tune, you know, he would be right there," recalls Kathryn. The kids attended church with them every Sunday, although Ken made no secret of the fact that he attended under duress: "I had to wear a tie every Sunday

FIGURE 7.3. Fred as the event chairman for the San Leandro Lions Club annual crab feed, March 7, 1970. Courtesy of the Lions Club of San Leandro.

till I was eighteen. While everyone else was running around in the streets, I had to go to church." Fred and Kathryn served on the church's mission committee. Fred was baptized in the church, and, in later years, became both a deacon and an elder.[40]

Fred also found camaraderie and fulfillment as part of the San Leandro Lions Club, and he remained a proud Lion for over forty years. He didn't care much for organizations that were purely social. While many of the club's activities were social, there was always a larger, beneficial purpose to meeting; Fred appreciated the club's work to support individuals with disabilities. Fred served twice as club president; he and Kathryn attended the club's conventions; and Fred was in the kitchen at the club's annual crab-and-spaghetti feed and flipped pancakes at its breakfasts. He knew that the money they made would go to help people. When Kathryn couldn't attend the annual installation dinners, Karen would go and dance with her father.[41]

Fred took his responsibilities as a citizen seriously. He always voted. As Kathryn recalls, "He didn't wear his patriotism on his sleeve, but he practiced patriotism in the way he lived. He had a Japanese face, but in his heart he was an American." Neither Fred nor Kathryn ever talked to their children of the importance of public service or civic engagement, but they demonstrated that importance through their example.[42]

As much as Fred worked to meet his family's needs, however, as in most families, there were rough spots. While Fred supported Ken's activities, there was friction at times between father and son. They were not, Ken explained, the "best friends" depicted in the early '70s TV series *The Courtship of Eddie's Father*—"That just didn't happen back then, really." Ken was fiercely independent, perhaps in ways not terribly different from Fred and Fred's father before him, and Ken rebelled against Fred's efforts to keep him in line. "My father and I had a kind of '60s relationship where he was the disciplinarian and I was kind of testing the boundaries of childhood all the time and getting into trouble a lot. . . . He was always telling me what to do, when to come in, and I wanted to go out and hang out with friends and stuff like that. . . . He was just crowding my independence, you know, he was trying to give me a framework of how to live." While Fred was affectionate with Karen, he wasn't with Ken; Karen was, after all, "Daddy's little girl." When Ken turned seventeen, things began to turn around, and he became more forgiving of his father: "He's still my father. I could see that he was trying hard as he could to deal with me and raise a family. . . . They didn't deserve any more grief from me. . . . They didn't deserve a bad kid."[43]

While in most respects Karen and Ken lived the lives of typical American teenagers, they still could not escape the cruel taunts that came with being of Japanese heritage, even decades after the exclusionists' heyday. They grew up in a neighborhood that was largely white, populated with the sons and daughters of veterans who had still-fresh memories of the war. Karen stopped taking the school bus after being called "Jap" and being blamed for Pearl Harbor. She remembers being deeply hurt and going through her school years never feeling that she "fit in." She didn't know if she was Japanese, white, or American; she never knew which box to check on school forms. It was too painful for her to share her feelings with her parents. Ken was constantly harassed while he was growing up; he, too, was blamed for Pearl Harbor—and was called every name in the book: "Chink, Jap, gook, half-breed, Tojo, and a slant-eyed prick." "That was my childhood," he explained. Karen and Ken wished they weren't Japanese American; "Who would want that?" Ken asked.[44]

Karen and Ken had little exposure to the Japanese American community when they were growing up. The church, the Lions Club, and their neighborhood were predominantly white. But Fred and Kathryn made sure that their children remained connected with the rest of the Korematsu clan. They attended family dinners during the holidays and the big Korematsu family picnic that celebrated Kakusaburo's birthday every June at the Oakland Zoo.[45] Joanne Kataoka remembers her Uncle Fred as a sweet man, albeit of few words: "He always readily had a warm smile, always gentle, always very soft-spoken, loved Japanese food. My Auntie Kathryn did most of the talking, as it is now," she recalled with a grin. "So in a sense, I really just remember my Uncle Fred as always being nonverbal. . . . He'd always ask how you were doing, and he would always find a soft, good place where he could smoke his pipe and sit down and talk individually. He was very unassuming." She recalled being fascinated with Fred's work when she'd visit his home: "He would be working, we would talk about what he did. . . . He had this big old drafting board. We would say, 'What's that?' and 'What are you working on?' Especially when he did work for the Zoo, that was really interesting, and he would show us pictures of what he would be working on."[46]

Kakusaburo visited Fred, Kathryn, and their children regularly. Much had changed in Kakusaburo's life after Kotsui's passing. In 1952, Issei became eligible to become naturalized citizens, and on February 17, 1954, at the age of seventy-seven, Kakusaburo officially became an American. With his U.S. passport in hand, he made his first trip back to visit Japan since he had emigrated.[47] When the nursery was sold in 1954, Kakusaburo moved in with Joe, but remained active and fiercely independent. He was a fixture at church Sunday services and prayer meetings; every Memorial Day, he helped coordinate the church's delivery of flowers to local cemeteries. He said grace before every meal, just as he had done in the prewar years for his own family. All of his grandchildren remember how he was always well-dressed, no matter where he went—he wore a suit even at the family picnics. After he suffered a stroke, he used a cane but still took the bus everywhere.[48]

When he'd visit Fred's home, as he did most Saturdays, he'd walk the two blocks uphill from the bus stop to the house and refuse Kathryn's pleas to let her pick him up. He loved Karen and Ken and always brought them gifts—pies or some other small thing he had picked up. He would sit in the living room, often with the kids by his side, and watch westerns all afternoon until dinner, and then the family would take him home. The kids couldn't really communicate with him, but, as Ken recalls, they'd sit together and "kind of like grin and smile at each other." Kakusaburo came to see Fred as a good husband and father.[49]

In October 1969, Kakusaburo fell and broke his hip. He felt that he'd never walk again, and, being such an independent man, he feared being bedridden for the rest of his life. Kathryn believes that he just gave up. He died of pneumonia on November 25 at the age of ninety-one. What Karen remembers most about her grandfather's funeral was that she'd never seen so many flowers before—a fitting tribute from all who had known this Issei pioneer nurseryman.[50]

Fred was not unlike other Nikkei who worked hard to reassemble the pieces of their disrupted lives. Their industry attracted the attention of the popular press. In the decades after Japanese Americans returned to the West Coast, national periodicals like *Newsweek* and the *New York Times* began to marvel at the "model minority" that the Nikkei had become. In 1966, sociologist William Petersen observed that "Barely more than 20 years after the end of the wartime camps, this is a minority that has risen above even prejudiced criticism. . . . Even in a country whose patron saint is the Horatio Alger hero, there is no parallel to this success story."[51] Some Nisei, Professor Harry Kitano explained, responded to their wartime imprisonment by saying, "I'll become an even better American."[52]

Many have rejected the model minority myth, however, as failing to tell the true story. Despite their higher levels of education, Japanese Americans still had difficulty reaching the highest levels of their work and professions, and the higher levels of education did not necessarily translate into higher pay.[53] Further, measures like Japanese American family income, even if similar to that of whites, fail to evidence true social equality or the psychological price paid for assimilation.[54] In any event, Japanese Americans could not be treated as one monolithic group; many never got back on their feet after the war.[55]

In some Nisei, as Michi Weglyn explains, the model minority label "triggered a searching self-examination": "Are we 'good' in the eyes of whites, they began to ask, merely because we 'know our place,' bend over backward not to offend, work hard, and 'don't make waves'? Are we America's 'good niggers?'" Was "success"—if it could be called success—gained only through costly "rigid conformity and accommodation"? What, in the end, Weglyn asks, had Japanese Americans really achieved?

> [T]he Japanese Americans' anguish is the inescapable feeling that success and acceptance are at best tenuous as long as their dilemma in America remains essentially unchanged: the still exasperating inability of the American populace to differentiate between citizenry of Japan and Americans who happen to look Japanese. Thirty years after being held accountable for what Japan had done, and paying an agonizingly high price for the right to be called Americans, the Japanese Americans realize that, like it or not, they are still looked upon as "foreigners" in the land of their birth—linked inextricably to Japan.[56]

Many Sansei, or third-generation Japanese Americans, bristled at both the model minority myth and their Nisei parents' drive for success. Children of the free speech movement and coming of age in the civil rights era and amid antiwar protests, these Sansei watched the black power movement and sought "yellow power"—a movement focused on dismantling the stereotypes that had physically and socially imprisoned their parents and replacing those images with a new identity that was their own. In 1971, Sansei activist Amy Uyematsu wrote that integration and the adoption of white values had robbed Asian Americans of their own identities. She quoted Stokely Carmichael and Charles V. Hamilton: "No person can be healthy, complete, and mature if he must deny a part of himself; this is what 'integration' has required us to do." Further, Uyematsu explained, Asian Americans had been stereotyped as passive, accommodating, and unemotional, and these stereotypes had to be challenged.[57]

As part of reclaiming a Japanese American identity, Sansei demanded that the story of their community be told. Many joined the struggle to establish ethnic studies classes, in particular, Asian American Studies classes, on college campuses.[58] The Nisei, in their quest to put the incarceration behind them and rebuild their lives, had shared next to nothing about the camps with their children. At most, Sansei heard vague references to "camp," never knowing what they were. Sansei Dale Minami, who later represented Fred in reopening his case, related, "You know, until the redress struggle, [the camps] weren't discussed at all. . . . Almost never. It would come up in the context of, 'Oh, that's George Furukawa. We knew him from camp.' Or, 'Oh, yeah, we met them in Santa Anita when we were at camp.' But you never heard 'em talk about conditions."[59]

Like other Nisei, Fred didn't talk to his children about the camps. And he didn't mention his arrest or his case. He explained,

> I was gonna [tell my kids about my case], in the back of my mind, that I was gonna do that. And you know, when they're growing up, when they're teenagers, and Karen was involved in Girl Scouts, involved in being a cheerleader at the high school, and they come in and go out right away, they come in and change clothes and off they go and so forth. And then on top of that, . . . I bought a house . . . and in order to maintain it, I had to have two jobs. So I was busy myself. So before you know it, the time just flew.[60]

Kathryn didn't speak to Karen and Ken about Fred's case, either, believing that Fred would want to be the one to tell them about it. "He didn't think he was a criminal, but thought the kids wouldn't understand until they were older."[61]

It wasn't until Karen was sixteen years old that she learned about her father's case, and she didn't learn about it from Fred. She was a junior at San Lorenzo High School, sitting in her social studies class, when her childhood friend, Maya Okada, rose to give a report on a book about the wartime incarceration. Karen had never heard of the camps before.

> And then [Maya] proceeded to talk about a famous Supreme Court case, *Korematsu v. United States*. Well, I'm thinking, well, what's this about? I knew Korematsu was an unusual Japanese name. . . . And all of a sudden I had, you know, thirty-five pairs of eyes kind of staring at me, and I'm thinking, oh, this has gotta be a black sheep of the family. . . . The thought never even occurred to me that it had anything to do with my father . . . because I thought I would have been told. . . . I could think of everyone else but my father. Because my father just didn't have, to me, that per-

sonality to do something that was against the law. . . . Certainly, if it was a famous Supreme Court case, I would have heard about it, or somebody would have said something by then.[62]

Karen felt flushed and, for some reason, guilty. "Somehow it was a reflection on me that somehow there was some guilt there that I'd been carrying all along since I was a child, you know, because I always felt displaced. . . . So somehow it was a black mark on the family and what I knew about Japanese culture was that everyone was very proud and very honorable and private."[63]

Karen rushed home, burst through the door, and asked Kathryn about the case. Kathryn told her it was her father's. When Karen asked why she hadn't been told about it, Kathryn said Fred had planned to tell Karen and Ken about it later; he was concerned that they might be ashamed and that they might understand better when they were older. She told Karen to talk to her father when he got home. Later that evening, Fred told Karen little: yes, his case had gone to the Supreme Court, and, yes, they had found him guilty and he still had a record. He felt that what he did at the time was right, but it was a long time ago. He didn't give any further details. Karen still chokes up in explaining how painful it seemed for her father to tell her about his conviction; she dropped the conversation.[64]

Ken found out the same way. He was a junior in high school when the class opened its history book to a page about *Korematsu v. United States*. When his teacher asked Ken whether he was any relation to the person in the case, Ken replied that he didn't think so. Maybe it was an uncle. When Ken got home, Kathryn, as she had done with Karen, explained that the case involved Fred. Ken was angry that he hadn't been told about it, but more embarrassed than anything else.[65] Joanne, Fred's niece and Joe's daughter, also didn't learn of Fred's case until she was in high school—a young law student at church camp asked her if she was related to the Korematsu of the Supreme Court case. On learning that she was, he told Joanne that her uncle was famous. Joe told Joanne that he had never told her about her uncle's arrest because "the past is the past." When Joanne was older and pressed her father on what had happened to Fred during the war, Joe told her that Fred had done what he thought he had to do and that it must have been very hard for Fred to be alone when everyone else was in camp. She came to understand that by drawing attention to the family and breaking the law, Fred had placed his family in a negative light, and it was something that they could not talk about.[66]

Fred's niece Connie, Hi's daughter, had a bitter reaction. When her high school history class came to its discussion of Fred's case, Connie's teacher asked her if she was related to Fred. On finding out that she was, the teacher asked her to write a paper on the case. Connie was mortified. She knew nothing about the wartime incarceration and had never known of her uncle's arrest: "What in the world are they even talking about?" Her mother provided little help, so Connie called Fred. Fred said that there wasn't much to tell; he had been in love with an Italian girl and had refused the removal orders to be with her. Connie was disappointed that he had stayed behind for personal reasons, not as a political stand. "I thought he was not strong. I was disappointed to know that somehow a Korematsu didn't stand up." And he left his parents and failed to protect them. "You didn't protect your own mother and father; you were thinking of yourself." To Connie, Gordon Hirabayashi and Min Yasui were the real heroes; they had defied the military orders as acts of civil disobedience. On reflection, however, she acknowledged that Fred did "stand up" in fighting his arrest; she had not given him credit for that.[67]

Don Tamaki, who would later be part of the legal team that reopened Fred's case, came to understand why his Nisei parents didn't care to speak of their years in camp:

> I really didn't understand until after [Fred's] case was over the impact that the internment had on our own families. Of course, we read about it, we talked to our families briefly about it, but I didn't understand really why they didn't want to talk about it. . . . Now, . . . I have a much broader understanding of it. . . . This was an entire population that without evidence, without trial, without due process of any kind, were simply swept into internment camps, many losing their property, some even losing their lives. . . . And when Fred's case went up to the Supreme Court, he, like many other people, probably thought they would get some measure of justice and some measure of vindication. Well, in 1944, to their surprise and to Fred's surprise, he lost. And most people feel that if the court rules against you, well, you must have been doing something wrong, you must be guilty at some level.

And after the war was over, Japanese Americans faced the enormous task in most cases of going back to the very communities that had exiled them in the first place. And the lesson was real clear. And that was anything that made you different, anything that attached you to being a minority, anything that made you connected to Japan or to a foreign country got you in trouble to the point that you could lose your freedom. . . .

So it's no wonder . . . that Japanese Americans did not talk to their children, did not want to pass that bitterness on to their kids, and wanted to protect their children. So frankly speaking, the idea was to become as American as fast as you can, become as white as you can as fast as you can, and put all that ethnic baggage aside. And consequently, Japanese Americans, those who experienced the internment never talked about it, and for many they kept that pain inside them for decades.[68]

Over the years, Fred got lots of calls asking him about his case. Students would want to interview him for papers they were writing; they'd ask whether something like the incarceration could happen again, and Fred would say, "Yes, it could." The Supreme Court had said that you could do that to people, he explained. Professors also called, wanting to talk to the man behind the *Korematsu* case for books or articles they were writing. Fred, however, wasn't much interested in talking to them.[69]

In the spring of 1969, Fred was asked by Professor Paul Takagi to speak to his new "Asian American Studies 100X" ("X" for "experimental") class at UC Berkeley. Takagi told Fred that this kind of class had never been taught before; it had been organized by students, and the students wanted to meet him. Takagi was intrigued by Fred's refusal to comply with the World War II removal orders; he saw Fred as a symbol of resistance. Fred had never spoken in public about his case, and Takagi thought it would be interesting for the students to hear Fred's story.[70]

Takagi's class was held off-campus, in the kitchen of a co-op. The Third World Strike had seized campus—students at Berkeley and San Francisco State sought an end to the marginalization and exploitation of peoples of color and were demanding ethnic studies classes such as Takagi's.[71] Kathryn had to prod Fred to speak. "I sort of talked him into it. He didn't trust his speaking ability, but I was so proud of him. . . . He talked from the heart." Fred spoke to the class, as did a local Nisei nurseryman and Jim Hirabayashi, who was Gordon's brother and a professor at San Francisco State. Fred was far from the most articulate person, Takagi recalled. He couldn't answer everything, and he did more describing than explaining—he talked a lot, for example, about his years in Detroit, but was less comfortable responding to the students' probing questions about politics and principles. He did, however, share a message that he would repeat with students in later years: to get involved, to run for office, to make themselves visible, and to get into jobs that will affect and influence others. Nisei Tom Kitayama had been elected mayor of nearby Union City in 1959, and that had deeply impressed Fred.[72]

The students were very kind and loved Fred, Takagi recalled. There was something very charming about him. Takagi admired him: "[Fred] became an icon of some kind. . . . Despite his lack of presence and lack of sophistication, for a common guy to resist and do what he did was really something special." The students expressed their admiration by giving Fred a standing ovation, the first among hundreds that he would receive during his life.[73]

Although Fred had been warmly received by the students at Berkeley, Karen recalls that it was not a good experience for him. She had gone to watch him speak, and learned for the first time about Ida. To her, Fred seemed uncomfortable; he told her afterward that he didn't want to "do this again." In fact, he would not speak publicly about his case again for another thirteen years.[74]

The Sansei activism that led to classes like Takagi's laid the foundation for some within the Japanese American community to talk of seeking redress for their wartime incarceration. While Congress had passed an Evacuation Claims Act in 1948 that allowed Japanese Americans to seek compensation for losses caused by their wartime removal, the compensation was limited. Under the act, Nikkei could recover only for documented property loss, but few had receipts. In the end, the $37 million paid pursuant to the act was but a fraction of the over $148 million in losses claimed; further, it provided no compensation for the loss of freedom, dignity, education, and careers suffered by Japanese Americans during the war. In 1983, the economic losses caused by the wartime removal and incarceration—counting only lost income and property, and adjusted for inflation and a reasonable rate of return—was estimated to be $2.5 to $6.2 billion.[75]

In 1970, Nisei Edison Uno introduced a resolution at the biennial JACL convention calling for reparations for Japanese Americans who had been incarcerated during World War II. The idea of redress, however, was highly controversial, and over the next decade and a half, the community would struggle with both the form of redress and how best to achieve it. Some activists called for payments directly to individuals; others called for the establishment of a trust fund to educate the public about the incarceration or for the benefit of the Japanese American community. Some asserted the need to seek monetary reparations directly from Congress; the JACL argued that the best route would be to seek a commission to study the issue prior to seeking redress. Many Japanese Americans opposed the idea of compensation altogether, believing that money could not compensate them for the losses they had suffered.[76]

As Japanese Americans began to discuss the issue of redress, other efforts took place to seek official recognition of the wrongs committed against them. In 1976, as a result of the efforts of Nisei activists in Seattle, President Gerald Ford formally rescinded Executive Order 9066: "We now know what we should have then—not only was [the] evacuation wrong but Japanese-Americans were and are loyal Americans. . . . I call upon the American people to affirm with me this 'American Promise' that we have learned from the tragedy of that long-ago experience forever to treasure liberty and justice for each individual American, and resolve that this kind of action shall never again be repeated."[77]

Two years later, in 1978, as the JACL discussed and debated the issue of redress, its president, Clifford Uyeda, called Fred to ask him to appear with Gordon Hirabayashi and Min Yasui to speak at the organization's convention in Salt Lake City. Fred declined. He felt that he had been abandoned by the JACL during the war and was critical of its wartime stance of cooperation. Further, while Fred knew that the JACL had been talking about seeking redress for Japanese Americans, he felt that redress would not go anywhere unless something could be done about the Supreme Court Japanese American incarceration cases, including his.[78] He wasn't going to use vacation time to support the convention.

The Japanese American movement for redress began to move forward in Congress and in the courts. On the judicial front, in late 1980, a group of Nisei leading the National Council for Japanese American Redress (NCJAR) met with attorneys in Washington, DC, to file a class action lawsuit seeking monetary damages on behalf of Japanese Americans unjustly incarcerated during World War II.[79] On the legislative front, in 1980, Japanese Americans secured the establishment of a commission—the Commission on Wartime Relocation and Internment of Civilians (CWRIC)—whose charge was "to review the facts and circumstances surrounding Executive Order [9066] and the impact [it] had on American citizens and permanent resident aliens [and to] recommend appropriate remedies." In pursuing this mandate, the commission reviewed thousands of documents and held twenty days of hearings around the country, taking testimony from hundreds of Japanese Americans who had been subject to the removal and incarceration, from government officials and agencies that had played a role in the wartime tragedy, from academics, and from others who shared their perspectives on the injuries suffered.[80]

In hearing after hearing before the commission, Japanese Americans broke the silence of forty years and told their stories. They were stories of loss–loss of property, loss of family structure, loss of vibrant communities, and loss of freedom. They were, however, also stories of survival and endurance told by so many who had gone on to rebuild and thrive, despite their wartime rejection and imprisonment. The time had finally come to share these stories. Nisei Chizu Iiyama saw Japanese Americans finally empowered to speak: "I think you saw that when they had the redress hearings . . . the feelings people had just repressed because at that time we couldn't deal with it. It [just] came out."[81] Nisei Nikki Bridges felt that it was only after the passage of decades that she could try to come to terms with her wartime experience:

I refused to think about it [the incarceration] as a major moment in my life until maybe thirty years later. I looked back it was like a thirty year double-take. And I said, "My God, I allowed this to happen to me?" And then in my fifties, . . . I was able to look back and say that was a terrible thing. . . . The enormity of what happened to us became clear. And . . . it was then that I was able, having established some sense of security about myself, to speak out and say the things that I did.[82]

Nisei Kiku Funabiki related just one of the many accounts of the human toll of the incarceration in her testimony before the commission in San Francisco. She began, "A few weeks ago I had no intention of testifying. I am a private person. It is not my style to speak before a group and especially to divulge publicly deep personal feelings I have not shared with my closest associates." She spoke of her father, Sojiro Hori, who was handcuffed and taken away after Pearl Harbor. Because their assets were frozen, Kiku, her invalid mother, and her two brothers could barely survive. On their return after the war, they found their home damaged and infested. Their possessions, which had been stored, had been stolen or destroyed. Her father rebuilt, dragging himself to work even after a debilitating stroke. She explained, "My father's story is not unique; nor is it extraordinary. Each of the tens of thousands of Japanese immigrants suffered. Collectively, their story is a heroic one of an invincible human spirit that survived cruel indignities, injustice and the final humiliation of mass exile behind barbed wire for the crime of being Japanese. Still they persevered."[83]

Norm Mineta was one of several Nikkei congressmen who were instrumental in the redress effort; he went on to serve as secretary of transportation under President George W. Bush and as secretary of commerce under President Bill Clinton. When he testified before the House Committee on the Judiciary in support of redress legislation, he spoke not as the distinguished public servant that he was but as one of the Japanese Americans who had been wrongly imprisoned. He spoke of his family:

My father was not a traitor. He sold insurance from a small office in our home on North Fifth Street in San Jose, California. My mother was not a secret agent. She kept house and raised her children to be what she was—a loyal American. Who amongst us was the security risk? Was it my sister Etsu, or perhaps Helen or Aya? Or perhaps it was my brother Al, a sophomore pre-med student at San Jose State.

Or maybe I was the one, a boy of ten-and-a-half who this powerful nation felt was so dangerous I needed to be locked up without a trial, kept behind barbed wire and guarded by troops in high guard towers armed with machine guns.

What was it I had done that made me so terrifying to the government? Murderers, arsonists, even assassins and spies get trials. But not young boys born and raised in San Jose who happen to have odd sounding last names. Is that what this country is about? . . .

I ask on behalf of the 60,000 internees who have died with their honor clouded. I ask on behalf of the 60,000 still alive and seeking justice. I ask on behalf of all Americans who believe that our Constitution really does mean what it says: that we are all created equal.[84]

Fred's case, of course, was also the subject of testimony before the commission. Congressman John K. Burton argued, "The Korematsu decision by the Supreme Court that rules that it was constitutional to do this to American citizens is probably the greatest blot in the history of our great Supreme Court."[85] Noted constitutional law scholar Alan Dershowitz expressed his concern that "many people are still prepared to defend what happened [during World War II] factually and legally." He reminded the commission of Justice Jackson's dissent in Fred's case: if not expressly repudiated, the wartime Supreme Court incarceration cases would stand as a "loaded weapon" that could validate similar injustices in the future—similar detentions or similar policies that might harm racial minorities.[86]

A group organized as Bay Area Attorneys for Redress (BAAR) submitted a brief to the commission outlining the host of constitutional violations caused by the incarceration, and similarly criticized the wartime Supreme Court cases. The group, which consisted mainly of young Sansei lawyers based in San Francisco, wrote that in its *Korematsu*, *Hirabayashi*, and *Endo* decisions, "[t]he Supreme Court approved the concept of guilt by ethnic affiliation ignoring the basic standard of individual guilt essential to our system of legal justice. In brief, the Court abdicated its responsibility by refusing to review military judgments based on half-truths, exaggerations and outright lies."[87]

Numerous groups and entities outside the Japanese American community testified before the commission and before Congress, expressing their support for redress for the survivors of the camps. Among those groups were the NAACP Legal Defense and Education Fund, the Anti-Defamation League of B'Nai Brith, the American Bar Association, the American Jewish

Committee, the San Francisco Board of Supervisors, and the Congressional Black and Hispanic Caucuses.[88]

Bernie Whitebear, executive director of the United Indians of All Tribes Foundation and a member of the Colville Confederated Tribes, explained why such a wide range of groups supported redress for Japanese Americans:

> People may ask why a Native American would be interested in this issue. The answers are simple. . . . [T]he Japanese American redress issue concerns a principle that affects every person in this country. That principle is that in times of peace and in times of stress, all of the people will be governed by a government that recognizes and protects all of our fundamental rights guaranteed by the Constitution. Should this Commission or the Government reject or fail to condemn as repugnant the illegal seizure and imprisonment of racial minorities, then there is little hope that this nation's minorities will fully participate in this country's affairs. . . .
>
> [Further,] as an American citizen I am concerned with the image of this country. Our government, in its international affairs, preaches democracy and condemns the civil rights violations of other people. At the same time the American government committed some of those same acts without even compensating its victims. . . . Our government should take affirmative steps to rectify those wrongs against the victims and take positive measures to insure that this action will never be repeated. Acts such as this would not only restore our faith in our government, it will also enhance this nation's reputation of being a government of the people, by the people and for the people.[89]

Some groups of color, quite understandably, had mixed responses to the Japanese American quest for redress. While the NAACP and the Congressional Black Caucus voiced their support for Japanese American redress, some members of the black community were conflicted about, or opposed, the issue. One African American scholar explained, "The apology [to Japanese Americans] was so appropriate and the payment so justified . . . that the source of my ambivalent reaction was at first difficult to identify. After some introspection, I guiltily discovered that my sentiments were related to a very dark brooding feeling that I had fought long and hard to conquer: . . . 'Why them and not me?'"[90] Nisei Joe Morozumi responded to that question by stating, essentially, "For us, and all of the others, as well." To him, redress was about exposing societal racism, and the quest to bring that racism to the light of day had only just begun: "This is only the beginning. We intend to pursue this long after the Commission has rendered its report. We intend to show that we live in a racist society, that we have not begun to face up to those issues. When [Commissioner] Lungren says that if we give reparations to Japanese Americans, the slaves, or descendants or the slaves and others will follow suit, . . . I say, they ought to."[91]

A number of officials who had played key roles during the wartime removal had passed away but had publicly expressed their regret. Earl Warren, attorney general of California at the time of the incarceration, expressed his remorse: "It was wrong to react so impulsively, without positive evidence of disloyalty, even though we felt we had a good motive in the security of our state. It demonstrates the cruelty of war when fear, get-tough military psychology, propaganda, and racial antagonism combine with one's responsibility for public security to produce such acts." Justice William O. Douglas upheld the removal orders and Fred's conviction during World War II. In his autobiography, he later explained that "[l]ocking up the evacuees after they had been removed had no military justification" and concluded, "[t]he evacuation case . . . was ever on my conscience."[92]

Fred did not testify before the commission. He was not ready to speak; it was not his time yet. But as the commission hearings took place, he could not help but think of his wartime conviction. On and off during the years since his loss before the Supreme Court, Fred would talk with Kathryn about his case. "His big thing," Kathryn relates, "was hoping that there might be some way to go back to court." He never brooded about it and he wasn't ashamed, but he knew that he had been wronged. He said, "Here it was constitutional law, and they just ignored it, somehow, and I couldn't understand it, and it bothered me." But there was no legal basis for challenging his conviction, and reopening his case would cost money. Fred was at a loss to know how he could do it.[93] "So that's the way it went. And for forty years, I was wondering, I'd like to fight it. . . . Can they do this again, send them away? So it bothered me. I got married . . . had two children. . . . [But] I still had in my mind, 'Are we Americans or not? Are they kidding us?'"[94]

CHAPTER 8

"INTENTIONAL FALSEHOODS"

THE PHONE CALL STARTED LIKE OTHERS THAT FRED HAD RE-
ceived over the years. There had been many such calls from people who
wanted to take Fred back to those hard days during World War II and write
about him. But none of the people who called offered a way to *do* something about his case. This phone call to the Korematsu home in January
1982 seemed no different, at least initially. Peter Irons identified himself
as a professor at the University of Massachusetts at Amherst, and when he
explained that he was writing a book about the World War II Supreme Court
Japanese American incarceration cases, Fred thought, "Oh, that figures."
But Peter went on to explain that he had found some documents that might
interest Fred. Fred was wary. When Peter asked if he could visit Fred in San
Leandro, Fred said that Peter should call if he got to the Bay Area and "we'll
see if we can arrange something."[1]

Three months earlier, in late September 1981, Peter had made a Freedom of Information Act (FOIA) request for the Department of Justice files in
the *Hirabayashi*, *Yasui*, *Korematsu*, and *Endo* cases. After much searching,
the files were found—misfiled with records of the Commerce Department.
After learning that the records had been located, Peter headed to Washington, DC. When he got there, he found that the person responsible for FOIA
requests was out sick; her absence may have been a stroke of good luck. She
would normally have reviewed the records before releasing them for review,
but because she was out, Peter was able to look at them—unscreened. "So
I sat down. And there were probably four or five cardboard boxes. . . . And
someone had written in marker the case numbers on the boxes. And they

were all tied together with string. And it was perfectly obvious that nobody had ever opened these boxes since they were initially stored because they were all dusty. . . . So I decided just to sit down and start going through them. And I picked out the box that said *Korematsu v. United States*." Within minutes of opening the box, Peter realized what he had found—evidence proving what appeared to be a government cover-up during Fred's World War II case. One of the first documents he read was a memo from Justice Department lawyer Edward Ennis to Solicitor General Charles Fahy, essentially saying, "We are in possession of information that shows that the War Department's report on the internment is a lie. And we have an ethical obligation not to tell a lie to the Supreme Court." The documents that followed only supported the conclusion that the government had presented the court with a false record. Peter was stunned: "I still remember thinking, 'Oh, my God. This is amazing.'"[2]

Afraid that someone might come over, ask what he was looking at, and remove the boxes, he worked all day, finding more incriminating documents and furiously taking notes. He called Aiko Herzig-Yoshinaga, then chief researcher for the Commission on Wartime Relocation and Internment of Civilians, and told her that she really needed to see the files. Aiko, a feisty Nisei woman, had spent her war years incarcerated, first at Manzanar in the Mojave Desert of California, and then at Jerome, Arkansas. She had transferred to Jerome so that her sick father could see his newborn granddaughter; he died Christmas Day 1943, ten days after their arrival. Decades later, she started to visit the National Archives in Washington, DC, to unearth the history of her imprisonment. "The more I read, the more angry I got. I could clearly see that we were viewed as sub-human, and how politicized the whole internment process had been. I became obsessed." Aiko's husband, Jack Herzig, a former army counterintelligence officer, joined her in her quest, and Aiko became a knowledgeable and skilled archival researcher by the time she started her work with the commission. Peter and Aiko had met in the archives on his first day researching his book, and when they learned of their common work, they agreed to aid each other and share what they found: Aiko could help Peter with her vast knowledge of the archives, and Peter could contribute his understanding of the law. After Peter's call, Aiko collected the Department of Justice files.[3]

Peter believed that the documents he found could help reopen the now-infamous World War II Supreme Court *Korematsu*, *Hirabayashi*, and *Yasui* cases. He had already contacted Gordon and Min, and they'd authorized him to see where that evidence might lead. Now he needed to speak with Fred. On January 12, 1982, Peter arrived in San Francisco and called Fred again. He explained that he had interviewed Ernest Besig, and Fred, perhaps a bit more comfortable on hearing the name of his wartime lawyer, replied, "Well, I might be able to see you tonight if you can come over." Peter was nervous as he took a cab to Fred's house.[4]

Peter found Fred to be friendly, but quiet and reserved. Fred's first impression of Peter was that he looked quite distinguished. Peter put his tape recorder out; Fred put out his. After an exchange of pleasantries, Peter explained to Fred that he had found documents that might enable him to reopen his case. He handed a sampling of the documents to Fred, and for the next thirty minutes or so, Fred puffed on his pipe and read through the stack, saying nothing.[5]

The documents that Peter brought Fred were remarkable and indeed shocking.[6] They, together with other key documents found by Aiko, showed that the government had purposefully suppressed, altered, and destroyed material evidence during World War II to ensure that the Supreme Court upheld the wartime curfew, forced removal, and—if it reached that issue—incarceration. The government had, in sum, engineered a "win" based on a false and fraudulent record and had lied to the court. Among other things, the documents showed that the government had withheld from the court key intelligence reports at odds with its claim that its actions were justified by military necessity. They also showed that when the government learned that General DeWitt's *Final Report* contradicted its arguments in Fred's case, the original report was destroyed and a new, altered version, more consistent with the government's arguments, was given to the court.

The documents showed that the government knew of, and withheld, its own intelligence reports that refuted its claims of military necessity. In Fred's case, the government had argued that Japanese Americans posed a threat that required immediate action. In order to support that argument, the government provided the Supreme Court with DeWitt's *Final Report*, in which DeWitt asserted that the orders were justified because Japanese Americans were prone to disloyalty and because there was evidence suggesting that they were involved in illegal shore-to-ship signaling. Solicitor General Fahy stood behind DeWitt's report in his oral argument before the Supreme Court. He asserted, "[N]ot only the military judgment of the general, but the judgment of the Government of the United States, has always been in justification of the measures taken; and no person in any responsible position has ever taken a contrary position."[7]

In fact, other intelligence agencies *had* taken "a contrary position." At the time the government was arguing the *Hirabayashi, Yasui,* and *Korematsu* cases before the Supreme Court, the government had within its possession reports from the FBI, the Office of Naval Intelligence (ONI), and the Federal Communications Commission (FCC), all bearing on the loyalty of Japanese Americans. The FBI and ONI, in particular, had been given special responsibility on this issue: as early as June 26, 1939, President Franklin D. Roosevelt had declared that all matters concerning suspected espionage and sabotage be handled by the FBI, ONI, and the Military Intelligence Division of the War Department.[8] While intelligence reports from all three of these agencies undermined DeWitt's claims of military necessity, none were presented to the court.

On January 26, 1942, even before Roosevelt had signed Executive Order 9066, Lieutenant Commander Kenneth D. Ringle of the ONI prepared his "Report on the Japanese Question." In that report, Ringle, who had extensive knowledge of the Nikkei community, concluded that the vast majority of Japanese Americans were loyal to the United States. While he did think that perhaps 3 percent of the population might be sympathetic enough to Japan to be of concern, the ones who might be considered most dangerous were, by the date of his report, already in custody or readily identifiable. He concluded, "[I]n short, the entire 'Japanese problem' has been magnified out of its true proportion, largely because of the physical characteristics of the people; that it is no more serious than the problems of the German, Italian, and Communistic portions of the United States population, and, finally that it should be handled on the basis of the *individual*, regardless of citizenship, and *not* on a racial basis."[9] Both the Justice and War Departments were well aware of Ringle's memorandum during early stages of the removal of Japanese Americans from the West Coast. On March 9, 1942, Attorney General Francis Biddle transmitted a copy of Ringle's report to Assistant Secretary of War John J. McCloy, who was "greatly impressed with Commander Ringle's knowledge of the Japanese problem along the Coast.[10]

Edward Ennis became aware of Ringle's report while preparing the government's brief to the Supreme Court in the *Hirabayashi* case, and, on April 30, 1943, greatly concerned that the report should be given to the court, he wrote Solicitor General Fahy. The army, he told Fahy, should be bound by Ringle's opinion because, even before the war, it had "agreed in writing to permit the Navy to conduct its Japanese intelligence work for it." Ennis challenged DeWitt's actions: had the Justice Department "known that the navy thought that 90 percent of the evacuation was unnecessary, we could strongly have urged upon General DeWitt that he could not base a military judgment to the contrary upon Intelligence reports, as he now claims to do."

Ennis reminded Fahy that the government was arguing to the Supreme Court that it was not possible to screen Japanese Americans on an individual basis. Ringle's report directly contradicted that argument:

> [I]n view of the fact that the Department of Justice is now representing the Army in the Supreme Court of the United States and is arguing that a partial, selective evacuation was impracticable, *we must consider most carefully what our obligation to the Court is* in view of the fact that the responsible Intelligence agency regarded a selective evacuation as not only sufficient but preferable. It is my opinion that certainly one of the most difficult questions in the whole case is raised by the fact that the Army did not evacuate people after any hearing or on any individual determination of dangerousness, but evacuated the entire racial group. . . . Thus, *in one of the crucial points of the case the Government is forced to argue that individual, selective evacuation would have been impracticable and insufficient when we have positive knowledge that the only Intelligence agency responsible for advising DeWitt gave him advice directly to the contrary.*

Given his belief that Ringle's report directly undermined the claim that the mass removal of Japanese Americans was necessary, Ennis warned Fahy that the failure to provide the court with the Ringle report would constitute a breach of the government's ethical duties: "In view of this fact, *I think we should consider very carefully whether we do not have a duty to advise the*

Court of the existence of the Ringle memorandum and of the fact that this represents the view of the Office of Naval Intelligence. *It occurs to me that any other course of action might approximate the suppression of evidence.*"[11] Ringle's report, however, was never given to the court.

Without knowledge of Ringle's conclusion that Japanese Americans should be treated on an individual, not group, basis, the court upheld the removal orders in Fred's case, accepting the argument that individual screening was impossible: "We cannot reject as unfounded the judgment that there were disloyal members of [the Japanese American population], whose number and strength could not be precisely and quickly ascertained."[12]

Intelligence reports also refuted DeWitt's claims that Japanese Americans had engaged in illicit signaling and radio transmissions. In his *Final Report*, DeWitt had expressed concern regarding "hundreds of reports nightly of signal lights visible from the coast, and of intercepts of unidentified radio transmission."[13] Reports from the FCC and the FBI, however, discredited those claims, and the Supreme Court was similarly not advised of them. As early as January 1942, George Sterling, chief of the FCC's Radio Intelligence Division, raised serious questions about the reliability of DeWitt's radio monitoring activities. After a meeting with DeWitt and his staff, Sterling wrote,

> Since Gen'l DeWitt seemed concerned and, in fact, seemed to believe that the woods were full of Japs with transmitters, I proceeded to tell him and his staff the organization [of the FCC radio monitoring program]....
>
> Frankly, I have never seen an organization that was so hopeless to cope with radio intelligence requirements.... The personnel is unskilled and untrained.... They know nothing about signal identification, wave propagation and other technical subjects, so essential to radio intelligence procedure. They take bearings with loop equipment on Japanese stations in Tokio ... and report to their commanding officers that they have fixes on Jap agents operating transmitters on the West Coast. These officers, knowing nothing better, pass it on to the General and he takes their word for it. It's pathetic to say the least.[14]

When Attorney General Biddle learned of DeWitt's *Final Report* in January 1944, while the Justice Department was preparing its arguments in

Fred's case, he requested that the FBI and the FCC respond to DeWitt's claims of illegal signaling. The FBI, on February 7, 1944, replied to Biddle that the claims were baseless. FBI Director J. Edgar Hoover summarized: "As indicated in the attached memorandum, there is no information in the possession of this Bureau . . . which would indicate that the attacks made on ships or shores in the area immediately after Pearl Harbor have been associated with any espionage activity ashore or that there has been any illicit shore-to-ship signaling, either by radio or lights."[15] In an April 4, 1944, memo, FCC Commissioner James L. Fly wrote Biddle, explaining that during the period from December 1941 to July 1, 1942, "[t]here were no radio signals reported to the Commission which could not be identified, or which were unlawful." Further, he continued, DeWitt had been directly advised as to the absence of such signaling—he had been "kept continuously informed of the Commission's work, both through occasional conferences and day-to-day liaison."[16]

In February 1944, Ennis wrote to Biddle protesting the government's reliance on DeWitt's report. "I believe it to be a matter of primary and historical importance that we correct on the public record the misstatements in General DeWitt's justification for the Japanese evacuation contained in his Final Report. . . . At present this stands as practically the only record of causes for the evacuation and unless corrected will continue to do so. Its practical importance is indicated by the fact that already it is being cited in the briefs in the *Korematsu* case in the Supreme Court on the constitutionality of the evacuation."[17]

Rebuffed by Fahy, Ennis and fellow Justice Department attorney John L. Burling sought to advise the Supreme Court that the government neither endorsed nor relied on DeWitt's assertions. Burling attempted to insert the following footnote in the government's brief in Fred's case:

The Final Report of General DeWitt (which is dated June 5, 1943, but which was not made public until January, 1944) is relied on in this brief for statistics and other details concerning the actual evacuation and the events that took place subsequent thereto. *The recital of the circumstances justifying the evacuation as a matter of military necessity, however, is in several respects, particularly with reference to the use of illegal shore-to-ship signaling by persons of Japanese ancestry, in conflict with informa-*

tion in possession of the Department of Justice. In view of the contrariety of the reports on this matter we do not ask the Court to take judicial notice of those facts contained in the Report.[18]

Almost immediately, work was begun to water down Burling's disavowal of DeWitt's report. Fahy proposed a revision that suggested only that De-Witt's report was in conflict with "the views of [the Department of Justice]" and deleting specific reference to the "contrariety of the reports." Burling responded to Fahy's revision in a memorandum to Assistant Attorney General Herbert Wechsler:

> You will recall that General DeWitt's report makes flat statements concerning radio transmitters and ship-to-shore signaling which are categorically denied by the FBI and by the Federal Communications Commission. There is no doubt that these statements were *intentional falsehoods*, inasmuch as the Federal Communications Commission reported in detail to General DeWitt on the absence of any illegal radio transmission. . . .
>
> [I]t seems to me that the present bowdlerization of the footnote is unfortunate. There is in fact a contrariety of information and we ought to say so. The statements made by General DeWitt are not only contrary to our views but they are contrary to detailed information in our possession and we ought to say so.

Burling assumed that the War Department would object to his footnote and advised Wechsler that the Justice Department "should resist any further tampering with it with all our force."[19]

Burling was correct about the War Department's response. While the War Department had been given a draft of the government's brief in April 1944, it waited until September 30, when the brief was being sent for final printing, to state its objections to Burling's footnote. McCloy called Fahy, and Fahy "had the printing stopped at about noon."[20] Ennis wrote Wechsler, urging that the department's obligations to the court required that the footnote remain as Burling had drafted it: "The Department has an ethical obligation to the Court to refrain from citing [DeWitt's report] as a source of which the Court may properly take judicial notice if the Department knows that important statements in the source are untrue and if it knows as to other statements that there is such a contrariety of information that judicial notice is improper."

Further, Ennis warned of the injustice to Japanese Americans if De-Witt's claims remain unchallenged: "The report asserts that the Japanese-Americans were engaged in extensive radio signaling and in shore-to-ship signaling. The general tenor of the report is not only to the effect that there was a reason to be apprehensive, but also to the effect that overt acts of treason were being committed. Since this is not so it is highly unfair to this racial minority that these lies, put out in an official publication, go uncorrected. This is the only opportunity which this Department has to correct them." Wechsler forwarded Ennis's memo to Fahy.[21]

Ennis's pleas were ignored. Instead, Wechsler revised the footnote in such a way that the Supreme Court could never know that the government possessed intelligence reports that directly refuted DeWitt's claims. The footnote, as presented to the Supreme Court, stated only the following: "The Final Report of General DeWitt . . . is relied on in this brief for statistics and other details concerning the actual evacuation and the events that took place subsequent thereto. We have specifically recited in this brief the facts relating to the justification for the evacuation, of which we ask the court to take judicial notice; and we rely upon the Final Report only to the extent that it relates to such facts."[22] Wechsler specifically intended that the revision "drop out any specific reference to matters in controversy."[23]

These documents proved that the government suppressed intelligence reports material to Fred's case, and material to every Japanese American who had been put away based on the claim of military necessity. In addition, further documents showed that the version of DeWitt's *Final Report* given to the Supreme Court in Fred's case was not the same as the report DeWitt had first prepared—it had been altered so that it would support, rather than contradict, the government's argument.[24]

In Fred's case, the government had argued that the mass removal was justified because time was of the essence and there was no time to separate the loyal from the disloyal. It relied on DeWitt's *Final Report*, and the version of the report given to the Court had said that the press of time prevented individual screening: "To complicate the situation no ready means existed for determining the loyal and the disloyal with any degree of safety."[25] In fact, DeWitt's view, stated in an original version of his report never given to the court, was that shortness of time was *not* a factor in his decision to order the mass removal of Japanese Americans; rather, he believed that their racial characteristics made it impossible to discern their loyalty. In his original report, discovered by Aiko, DeWitt explained,

> Because of the ties of race, the intense feeling of filial piety and the strong
> bonds of common tradition, culture and customs, this population [of
> Japanese Americans] presented a tightly-knit racial group. . . . While it was
> believed that some were loyal, it was known that many were not. It was
> impossible to establish the identity of the loyal and disloyal with any de-
> gree of safety. *It was not that there was insufficient time in which to make
> such a determination; it was simply a matter of facing the realities that a
> positive determination could not be made, that an exact separation of the
> "sheep from the goats" was unfeasible.*[26]

DeWitt transmitted copies of his bound report to the War Department, in-cluding two to McCloy. He had sent it air express so that it would arrive in time for use in preparing the government's briefs before the Supreme Court.[27]

On reading DeWitt's report, McCloy became greatly concerned that it contradicted the government's argument that there was insufficient time for individualized determinations of loyalty. He immediately contacted Bend-etsen. In response to McCloy's complaint that the report had been printed without first being vetted, Bendetsen assured McCloy that "any change you feel ought to be made, can easily be made." McCloy did not mince words. "I'm distressed about it," he said, referring to the report. "There are a num-ber of things in it now which I feel should not be made public."[28]

DeWitt was indignant when informed of the War Department's objec-tions to his report: "My report to Chief of Staff will not be changed in any respect whatsoever either in substance or form and I will not, repeat not, consent to any, repeat any, revision over my signature." In the face of De-Witt's adamant stand, McCloy was faced with a dilemma. He felt he could not order DeWitt to change his report; yet the public release of the report, as drafted, could seriously undermine the government's entire argument in support of the removal orders. McCloy considered suppressing the report entirely. He told Bendetsen, "I wouldn't want to offend [DeWitt]. I wouldn't want him to think that I was trying to tell him what to say. . . . I would much rather that the report go in to the files and let it go at that."[29]

On May 3, Bendetsen wrote DeWitt to share McCloy's concerns in as diplomatic a tone as possible. Bendetsen conveyed that, while McCloy did not "wish to prescribe what the Commanding General should say or not say in the final report[,] . . . he did say, however, that it might be improved upon." Bendetsen proposed alternative language to DeWitt. "The second objection was to that portion of Chapter II which said in effect that it is absolutely impossible to determine the loyalty of Japanese no matter how much time was taken in the process. He said that he had no objection to saying that time was of the essence and that in view of the military situation and the fact *that there was no known means of making such a determination with any degree of safety* the evacuation was necessary."[30]

DeWitt relented. Captain John Hall of McCloy's staff revised DeWitt's report to delete the language that time was not an issue and replace it: "Page 9, second complete paragraph, substitute for the fifth and sixth sentences the following: 'To complicate the situation, no ready means existed for determining the loyal and the disloyal with any degree of safety. It was necessary to face the realities that a positive determination could not be made.'"[31] That was the language in the version of DeWitt's report ultimately presented to the Supreme Court.

As the 1983 petition to reopen Fred's case later stated, "Hall's revision produced more than a semantic change. It resulted in the complete alteration of DeWitt's original statement and its meaning." The revision explicitly changed DeWitt's rationale for the exclusion orders; instead of stating, as DeWitt truly believed, that time was not an issue in his decision, it stated that he had no "ready" means to separate the loyal from the disloyal. In addition, the revision served to hide the race-based assumptions that lay at the center of DeWitt's thinking. It was DeWitt's true belief that there was no way to tell a loyal Japanese American from a disloyal one, no matter how much time one had. The revision "shifted the argument to the question of practicality and concealed the racist underpinning of DeWitt's . . . claim."[32]

On May 9, 1943, Bendetsen started damage control. In a telegram to General James Barnett, assistant chief of staff of the Western Defense Command, Bendetsen instructed that all copies of the initial version of DeWitt's report be destroyed. "Take action to call in all copies [of the *Final Report*] previously sent to WD [War Department] less inclosures and to have WD destroy all records of receipt of report as when final revision is forwarded letter of transmittal will be redated."[33] On July 29, 1942, Warrant Officer Theodore E. Smith confirmed the destruction of the returned copies of the report. "I certify this date I witnessed the destruction by burning of the galley proofs, galley pages, drafts and memorandums of the original report of the Japanese Evacuation."[34]

Neither the Justice Department nor the court was ever aware that they had received an altered version of DeWitt's report. The result in Fred's case, his later petition would claim, would have been different had the court known DeWitt's true reasons for ordering the mass removal of Japanese Americans. Having only the revised report before it, the court held that DeWitt could reasonably have found mass removal necessary because there was insufficient time to screen the loyal from the disloyal—reasoning that DeWitt would have originally flatly rejected. In Fred's case, the court stated, "Here, as in the Hirabayashi case, we cannot reject as unfounded the judgment of the military authorities and of Congress that there were disloyal members of that population whose number and strength *could not be precisely and quickly ascertained*. We cannot say that the war-making branches of the Government did not have ground for believing that in a critical hour such persons *could not readily be isolated* and separately dealt with, and constituted a menace to the national defense and safety, which demanded that prompt and adequate measures be taken to guard against it."[35]

The documents that Peter and Aiko had found wholly discredited DeWitt's report, as well as the government's claims of military necessity based on that report. Yet Solicitor General Fahy told the court in Fred's case that nothing existed to refute DeWitt's assertions.[36] Fahy, having seen the reports that contradicted DeWitt's claims, knew otherwise.

After looking through the documents, page after page, for what seemed, to Peter, to be an eternity, Fred looked up. "They did me a great wrong," he said.[37] The government had, indeed, wronged Fred. And, in presenting lies and a manipulated record to the Supreme Court, it had wronged over 110,000 Japanese Americans who had been forced from their homes and imprisoned.

Fred asked Peter, "Are you a lawyer"? Peter replied, "Yes, I am." Fred asked, "Would you be my lawyer"? Peter said that he would be delighted to give any help he could. Peter recalls, "At that point, he literally opened up and relaxed. We both did. He had agreed to go ahead with this. And so then I tried to explain to him what might happen, how much work there was to do, how there was no guarantee that this would succeed. It might take a long time." These warnings did not seem to deter Fred; he had heard similar cautionary words forty years earlier, from Besig. Fred said he that needed to check with Kathryn, who readily joined Fred in agreeing to pursue the reopening of his case.[38]

CHAPTER 9

"A LEGAL LONGSHOT"?

Having received the okay to proceed, Peter knew there was much to be done—much more than he could do alone; he was a professor and writer, not a litigator. He needed to find a legal team to join him in the effort to reopen the cases.[1] To his credit, Peter felt strongly that the cases should be brought by Japanese American attorneys. These were cases that affected their community and their families, and the issues were their own. He had heard of Bay Area Attorneys for Redress (BAAR), the group of largely young Sansei attorneys based in San Francisco that had testified before the Commission on Wartime Relocation and Internment of Civilians, and he had high regard for its work.[2]

Peter called Dale Minami, a Sansei attorney in a small private practice in Oakland, California, who had coordinated the work of BAAR and who had been recommended to him because of his work on other Asian American civil rights issues. Dale recalls, "At first, I thought he was crazy." When people call saying they have an interesting case, he explained, "usually they say they have tons of evidence—which Peter said he had—and then they ask if you can do it for free—which Peter asked. But this was different." Peter explained what he hoped for and said he'd like some help. He later wrote Dale that he was familiar with BAAR's efforts in seeking Japanese American redress and that he hoped "to establish the closest possible cooperation with its members on this project." He didn't know at the time that the relationship he would develop with the Bay Area lawyers would indeed become close and would continue for decades. Dale suggested that Peter fly out for a meeting with the BAAR workgroup.[3]

Dale shared the call with Lori Bannai, who worked with him in his office; they were both intrigued at the possibility of working on these cases. As Sansei, the camps were part of their history: their parents, grandparents, aunts, and uncles had been incarcerated during the war—Dale's at Rohwer, Arkansas, and Lori's at Manzanar in the Mojave Desert of California. Like virtually every other lawyer in the country, they had learned of the *Korematsu* case in their constitutional law classes in law school. Fred's case had become standard law school reading, ironically because of its broad pronouncements on the danger of race prejudice. Dale recalled his reaction on first reading the *Korematsu* case as a law student at the University of California, Berkeley, School of Law: "This is bullshit. They're talking about my mom and dad and my brother. My brother [who was a year old when sent to camp] wasn't a threat. My parents were not a threat. . . . We should do something about this. . . . What I came away with is that the rule of law as absolute justice is a myth. . . . [T]he *Korematsu* case was a case about power and it wasn't a case about justice and law." To Dale, Lori, and the other Sansei lawyers who became involved in the coram nobis effort, Fred's case, in so many ways, felt like their case—the opportunity to reopen his case was the opportunity to vindicate their families and community.[4]

On February 22, 1982, Peter wrote to Fred, Dale, and others interested in participating in the cases, summarizing what he had found and outlining the claim he thought could be brought. The legal vehicle that could be used, he suggested, was a petition for writ of error coram nobis, a rarely used proceeding that could be used to attack a criminal conviction. Coram nobis meaning "before us," a petition for a writ of error coram nobis seeks relief for an error committed "before" the court. Unlike a petition for habeas corpus, which seeks an individual's release while he or she is still in custody, a writ of error coram nobis seeks relief from a conviction when the sentence has already been served, based on errors "of the most fundamental nature" that amount to "manifest injustice."[5]

The legal team grew. Joining the team were BAAR members Karen Kai, then in private practice in San Francisco; Dennis Hayashi, a staff attorney at the Asian Law Caucus, an Asian American community legal services office in Oakland; and his law clerk, Marjie Barrows. Karen's husband, Bob Rusky of the San Francisco firm Hanson Bridgett, joined. Dale also involved Don Tamaki, then executive director of the Caucus; Leigh-Ann

Miyasato, then with a firm in San Francisco; and Akira Togasaki, who was associated with Dale's firm. In later months, San Francisco attorney Ed Chen lent his effort to the case. Honolulu attorney Eric Yamamoto, who had just been offered a partnership with his firm, quit his job and moved to San Francisco to work on the case. Peter also quite naturally contacted the Northern California affiliate of the ACLU, no longer a single chapter as it was during World War II, and Executive Director Dorothy Ehrlich enthusiastically offered the affiliate's support.[6] Kathryn Bannai became lead counsel representing Gordon Hirabayashi in Seattle, and Peggy Nagae became lead counsel in representing Min Yasui in Portland, Oregon, and their teams grew, as well.[7]

Kathryn, Fred's wife, was particularly pleased to see the number of women involved in the case. "We were impressed that there were women attorneys. We didn't know any women who had gone to law school. Karen and I were overjoyed, and, you know, Fred wasn't one of those men who thought women had to be at home." In fact, what the Korematsus witnessed in their legal team was, in many ways, the product of fought-for and hard-won admissions policies designed to diversify the legal profession. The 1970s saw an increase in the number of lawyers of color joining the ranks of the bar, and, although their numbers were few, more women of color. Lori later reflected, "It was an extraordinary time. The legal profession held the keys to justice in our society, and there were very few people of color and women in the profession. As more and more became lawyers, we had a means to advocate for the needs of our, and other, communities. . . . Being able to play a significant role in Fred's case helped show that lawyers who were women of color were just as skilled, just as capable, and as effective in terms of leadership, as other lawyers."[8]

Peter flew to the San Francisco Bay Area the weekend of May 8, 1982, sending a first draft of the petition for review before his arrival. The West Coast lawyers wondered what Peter was like—whether he'd be a stodgy, square, reserved, Ivy League professor type. He was nothing of the sort. When Peter asked, "How about getting a beer?" after getting off the plane on that hot May day, Dale knew they'd hit it off.[9]

It soon became clear to the group that the issues raised by the Japanese American incarceration cases resonated powerfully with Peter. Peter recalled, "[T]he one lesson that I remember learning, very explicitly, from my parents was racial tolerance and inclusion." He had a strong sense of justice that had informed his activism prior to law school. He had participated in the Youth March for Integrated Schools, worked within the Student Non-violent Coordinating Committee, organized antidraft activities, protested nuclear testing, supported candidates running on peace platforms, and worked on behalf of unions. He had been arrested several times—the first in a demonstration at a segregated bowling alley. He was, in fact, familiar with coram nobis because he had gone to prison as a draft resister and had filed his own coram nobis case to successfully vacate his conviction.[10]

The legal team met with Peter at Dale's house—the first of many meetings to come—characterized not only by a shared and passionate commitment to a common cause but also by light-hearted ribbing among good friends, Nerf basketball, Pac-Man, food, and beer. Peter fit in well with the high energy and youthful irreverence of the largely Sansei team. When everyone settled down for the two-day-long meeting, however, the discussion was focused and intense. Peter explained the coram nobis vehicle and summarized the evidence he had found. As Dale explained, "It was stunning. . . . We saw this as an incredible opportunity to do something good." At the same time, there were a myriad of issues to confront. What court do we file in—the trial courts, the Courts of Appeal, or the Supreme Court? How do you introduce forty-year-old evidence? As Dale recalls, "It was pretty daunting, [but] we thought we could overcome all of that." Peter was tremendously impressed with the work group: "I felt very quickly that, whatever the outcome was going to be, it was really going to be done very well by really well-trained people."[11]

After Peter left, Dale prepared the first of many long lists of tasks. His first memo, under the heading "Let's Get Going," laid out issues for legal research, documents to be obtained, contacts to call, and strategic decisions to be made. Everyone was assigned his or her tasks. Dale would be lead counsel for Fred's case. Peter and Lori would handle reviewing and organizing the evidence, including the mountains of documents. Dennis and Bob would lead the legal research work. Karen ended up helping with most everything.[12]

The work group was extraordinary. The members of the team were smart, talented, and passionate about the case. They had tremendous chemistry and shared a common vision. Dale later recounted,

I was denominated lead counsel, and my job was to basically coordinate and facilitate. We had such a strong group of people it didn't require leadership that much in some senses because everybody contributed to the leadership of that group. When we started this case, we realized not only the legal significance, but what I liked about this group is that we understood the political significance. . . . People had different skills . . . they brought to the table, and we worked in a really harmonious fashion. . . . This work group that I worked with I think had a sense that we were on a mission. We felt so strongly about the correctness of our cause and, of course, the good evidence we had.[13]

Karen Kai also expressed the passion that the team felt in working on Fred's case: "[You had the feeling] that you're involved in something much bigger than yourself." Leigh-Ann recalls, "We were all so young and idealistic, we didn't know any better. We didn't have families for the most part, so we had a lot of time to spend on it. It was making it up as you went along, that was part of the fun of it, the feeling that you were all blazing this trail here because nobody knew where it was going to lead us, but it was something we all had to do. So it was really cool to be involved in that collective effort like that where everybody was really focused and determined, just really intent on getting justice for Fred."[14]

While seeking justice in court was the core of the team's work, members of the team decided early on that it was just as important to use the case to educate the public.[15] The World War II incarceration had happened, in large part, because the public allowed it to happen by failing to speak up and protect those who could not advocate for themselves. If people could learn and remember what the country did during World War II, perhaps they would speak up when prejudice and fear threaten another group. Lori explained,

The team . . . felt very strongly that the case had to be retried in the court of public opinion, just as much, if not more, than . . . in a court of law. Statutes and court opinions . . . are only pieces of paper that can be changed at any time given enough public pressure or other changes in the political winds. If the goal was to ensure that such an event would never happen again, and truly that was the goal of the community, the public needed to know what happened to Japanese Americans and know that [it] has the power and responsibility to ensure that such an event will not happen again.[16]

The group was also mindful that its work attacking the World War II Supreme Court cases could be important in advancing redress for Japanese Americans, which was before the commission at that time and would soon be moving to Congress.[17] The meeting agendas soon included discussions of not only legal but also political strategies, as well as educational materials and press plans. Don would spearhead the education effort.

So as not to overwhelm Fred's family, Peter and Dale initially met Fred and the rest his family—Kathryn, Karen, and Ken—in May without the rest of the team. Karen, now a successful interior designer, and Ken, now in graphic design, were skeptical and protective of their father. Karen recalls, "My first question was, well, what's in it for you? I mean, why do you want this? I still didn't understand this *pro bono* thing. I could not wrap my head around that one at all. But [they] were gonna work on this case and no one was gonna be charging my father. I mean, how could you do that?" Ken said, "They're not going to do anything without you paying," and he knew that his parents didn't have any money. Don Tamaki's reflections, however, tell what it meant to the team to have the chance to work on Fred's case: "To be able to reopen the case, to be able to vindicate our families, and to rewrite the books on this was a real opportunity. And we weren't paid for it, but, to be honest with you, I would have paid to be on the team. I think most of the lawyers felt the same way. There was no monetary arrangement whatsoever. We were motivated by a sense of injustice of the case. And our desire to right a wrong."[18]

The rest of the team, about ten lawyers in all, crowded into the Korematsus' living room to meet Fred and Kathryn soon thereafter. They were in awe of Fred—he was a legal icon. But they were instantly put at ease. "Fred was just a simple, straightforward straightshooter, a quiet man, quiet dignity, and kind of like our parents," Don recalled. "I mean, he was, he reflected that kind of average Nisei, if there is such a thing, average American. And so we liked him immediately, we identified with him. So we were hoping that he would trust us and go along with us. I look at pictures of ourselves, and I wouldn't have trusted us! 'Cause we were extremely young and green." Fred called Peter over during the meeting and whispered, "Hey, these look like high school kids." Peter assured him, "Oh, no, they're the best." Fred's initial skepticism was fleeting; he later agreed that they were indeed "the best."[19]

Seeing the legal team's commitment to Fred's case and seeing how hard they worked, Fred, Kathryn, and their children soon embraced the team as part of their own family. Kathryn laughed in recounting, "[I]t was a lot of fun to get together with . . . those kids. They were kids to us. . . . [T]hey were . . . people with good senses of humor, and Fred and I just felt very privileged to be with them." Kathryn was always the mother. Leigh-Ann recalls, "Oh, Kathryn was such a wonderful person, just completely supportive of Fred throughout the whole process. And they were truly a team. It is hard to imagine one without the other. She was always so supportive of all of us, too, so appreciative of everything we were doing, a really gracious person. [She was always concerned about] trying to take care of us, being our mother in a way. . . . Oh, just always asking, 'How are you doing, are you getting enough rest? Are you eating well?'" Fred never failed to greet the lawyers on the team with his warm, wide smile, and always had a hug and a kiss on the cheek for the women.[20]

Over the next few months, the legal team met regularly and threw itself into the wide range of work before it. Peter took a position at the University of California at San Diego, making it easier for him to join the meetings. A flurry of memos from Dale, addressed to the "Western Defense Commandos," set out agendas and meeting minutes. The legal research workgroup spent countless hours looking into a host of questions, including the basic requirements for bringing a coram nobis case; which court to file in when the government misconduct had occurred before the Supreme Court; whether the petitions to reopen the *Korematsu, Yasui,* and *Hirabayashi* cases could be consolidated to be heard by one court; whether civil or criminal court rules applied; what rules governed the introduction of evidence; and what type of hearing could be obtained.[21]

The job of compiling and organizing the factual record became huge. Karen Kai undertook the painstaking construction of a chronology of the acts of misconduct in the cases, recording when they had occurred, and who had participated in them. A team of Berkeley undergraduate students prepared a gigantic chart tracking who had participated in the acts of misconduct and how the misconduct had infected the proceedings, both in the parties' briefs and in the Supreme Court decisions.[22]

Peter and Lori began the task of cataloguing thousands of pages of documents that bore on the government's suppression of evidence. Many were from Peter; many were from Aiko; and, later, many were procured from the government pursuant to document requests during the course of the coram nobis litigation. In addition, Aiko and her husband, Jack, enlisted their friends Nick Chen and Phil Nash, who, with a team of about a half a dozen others, engaged in further research in the National Archives in Washington, DC. The documents poured in, from Peter, from Aiko, from the government, and from the "Chen researchers." Together, the efforts resulted in a compelling and irrefutable history of the government's suppression of evidence before the Supreme Court.[23]

Akira Togasaki, a Nisei lawyer-engineer and graduate of MIT who had been incarcerated at Poston in Arizona, lent his computer programming skills to put together a crude dBase III program to catalogue the mountains of documents. His memos, from the "Bilious Backroom Boy" to "Maximal Leader Minami" and others on the team, outlined an elaborate system of document review and data input years before the invention of any of the document control programs that exist in law firms today. Dozens of Bay Area lawyers, law students, and undergraduates spent hours reading documents and cataloguing them by author, date, and topic, looking especially for "hot docs" that had direct bearing on the petition's allegations of governmental misconduct.[24]

Peter's initial draft of the petition was revised, re-revised, and further revised as the group had spirited discussions of how best to frame its allegations. Work began on a memorandum of law that would be filed with the petition. Plans were made to file the petition and its supporting papers in October 1982. As the enormity of the work became clearer, the date was pushed back to December, and then again to January 1983.[25]

While the team members were never deterred, the road to the filing of the petition was not a smooth one. First, the team felt it important to keep the allegations of misconduct confidential until the cases were filed. As Don explained, "We were concerned about people destroying documents in order to save their reputations. We were very much concerned that these documents would start disappearing and we weren't even certain that we had all of them or not."[26]

The inability to publicize the petition's contents, however, made it very hard to address an additional concern—money. The team needed funds, for example, for travel, especially to enable Peter in San Diego and counsel in Seattle and Portland to meet with the San Francisco team. And there were costs for simple things, like postage, telephone bills, and photocopying. Just before the filing of Fred's petition in January 1983, Dale's meeting minutes told of the team's near-empty coffers:

> FUNDING: We have just about exhausted all funds. Zero. Zip. Goose eggs. Circles. Donuts. Tap city.

From early on, Don coordinated the task of raising funds, and the team formed the Committee to Reverse the Japanese American Wartime Cases to support the effort. Everyone was asked to use his or her ingenuity and contacts to find money. Unable to fundraise on a public scale, the team members turned initially to their family and friends. They said, in essence, "We can't tell you what this case is about but it's really, really important." Fifteen, twenty-five, fifty, and one-hundred to two-hundred dollar checks arrived to meet the teams' needs, mainly from Nisei and Sansei friends and relatives.[27]

The team was taken aback when it learned of criticism from an unexpected source. One of Min Yasui's co-counsel, Frank Chuman, had apparently contacted CWRIC commissioner and former Supreme Court Justice Arthur Goldberg, asking his opinion on the prospects for the coram nobis cases. Without any information as to the allegations of governmental misconduct or any of the damaging documents supporting those allegations, Goldberg wrote to fellow CWRIC commissioner Judge William Marutani, offering his view that any attempt to reopen the *Korematsu* case before the Supreme Court would be "fruitless," as well as ill-advised. He said,

> The Supreme Court of the United States has never, to my knowledge, reopened a decided case after such a lengthy interval. There is an obvious and strong public interest in finality of a judgment.
>
> Indeed, any attempt to overturn *Korematsu* at this late date, by seeking its reopening by the Court, runs the danger of legitimizing this bad decision, in public perception, in the virtually certain event of denial by the Court of reopening the case. . . .

> *Korematsu* is a thoroughly discredited decision. . . . [I]t is my consid-
> ered opinion that it not necessary and indeed not procedurally possible to
> mount a legal attack to overrule *Korematsu.*

Marutani forwarded Goldberg's letter to the Japanese American Citizens League's *Pacific Citizen*, which, on October 22, 1982, printed news of it under the headline "Goldberg says writ of coram nobis would be 'fruit-less.'" In the thick of preparations for filing Fred's petition, the legal team was sorely disappointed that a person of Goldberg's stature, as a jurist and CWRIC commissioner, would make a public statement casting doubt on their claims. True, as Goldberg suggested, there was a risk of losing the *Korematsu* case for a second time, but that wasn't something that the team or Fred really thought about.[28]

Finally, Fred and his legal team had to negotiate how they would work with the Japanese American Citizens League (JACL). Forty years earlier, the JACL had, at least at first, refused to oppose the government and sup-port Fred's case; now JACL was one of the key players seeking redress for the wrong that had been done during World War II.[29] Fred and his team wanted to support the redress effort but did not want to be controlled by JACL. During the coram nobis cases, fellow coram nobis petitioner Min Yasui was chair of the JACL Committee for Redress. When he sought to arrange a meeting of the coram nobis attorneys at the JACL convention in Los Angeles in August 1982, Fred felt strongly that his case should remain independent of JACL; he did not have good feelings about the organization's complicity with the government during World War II and its refusal to fight the incarceration. The legal team declined Min's invitation.[30]

Min and John Tateishi, JACL national redress director, were taken aback by the rebuff. John explained that the JACL sought only to facilitate the meeting; he was concerned about the implication that the JACL was not to be trusted and wanted to "take over the proceedings." Min complained, "[It] is apparent here that there is some feeling of proprietary control of an issue that is going to affect not just Nikkei in the United States—but all United States citizens in the future forever more . . . *and it appalls me that an individual is saying, in effect, 'this is my case—keep your hands off!'* JACL is being excluded—and I resent it!" Min had not understood Fred's intentions. Of course, Fred did not view his case as simply his own individual case; he was bringing his case to prove that the Japanese American community had been wronged and to reaffirm the constitutional principles violated by their incarceration. In the end, John agreed that JACL should give its full and public support to the coram nobis efforts, although it should "lay low" in terms of direct involvement, given that such involvement was not welcome.[31]

The JACL did, in fact, publicly support the reopening of Fred's case. Decades after stating its "unalterable" opposition to the *Hirabayashi*, *Yasui*, and *Korematsu* test cases,[32] JACL national president Floyd Shimomura wrote in the *Pacific Citizen*, "Obviously, these cases belong to [Mr. Korematsu, Mr. Hirabayashi, and Mr. Yasui] and not to any group or organization. However, the JACL National Council has recognized that [the implications] of such proceedings are enormous, and if successful, will rectify a major injustice to Japanese Americans and will serve to protect the fundamental rights of all Americans. . . . I urge all JACLers to support these individuals in their fight to clear their names. Their fight is our fight."[33] Fred's case was no longer the embarrassment it was during the war; it was now a cause for his community.

The team prepared for the filing of Fred's petition with intensity. One of the initial questions they grappled with was which court to file in. Dale said, "Initially, when Peter Irons brought us the petition he thought that we might be able to file a case straight in front of the United States Supreme Court. But after we did some research we realized that we would either have to file in the Ninth Circuit Court of Appeals . . . or in the various district courts where the men were convicted. We thought about the advantages and disadvantages of each venue, each forum."[34] With the lawyers from Seattle and Portland, Fred's team decided, for both political and legal reasons, to file three separate petitions: one for Fred in San Francisco, one for Gordon in Seattle, and one for Min in Portland. Dale explained,

> We [decided] upon the idea of filing in three separate courts, which would be conservative legally, [but] would be the best strategy politically because we could gain publicity in each of those areas. Because one of our main missions was to do education around the injustice of the internment experience.
>
> We also thought that if we filed in three different courts, we'd have three bites at the apple. That meant we could lose one, win two. We could lose two, win one. And we would create such a conflict within the district

courts that it would create possibly the chance for appeal and getting to a higher court. That meant that we could not just put all our eggs in one basket so to speak. But we could try three different routes to gain some success.[35]

Given the composition of the district court in San Francisco, it was decided that Fred's case would go first. Dale continued,

> We did an analysis and basically discovered that the most liberal judges were in San Francisco. And the area with the second most liberal judges was Seattle, and Portland came in dead last on that one.
>
> But we thought that if we could file in San Francisco first, we would do so and hopefully get a good judge. If we got a good judge, we would not file in Seattle for a month. We'd give the . . . San Francisco court a head start, so we could use the benefit of a good judge here to lead the way.[36]

In the days leading up to the filing of the papers in Fred's case, the petition and supporting documents were revised and polished. Don worked the phones to inform the press of the historical and legal significance of the case. He said, "I think the most astounding thing to me was how ignorant the American press was about the internment. I would talk to journalists, and they had no background on this." He went on, "I even got questions like, 'Well, the internment—that happened in America?' And 'Isn't that about Japanese prisoners of war?' And I had to inform them we were talking about America imprisoning its own citizens for no other reason than their national origin and racial ancestry."[37]

Don explained to the media that, by his petition, Fred sought to reverse his forty-year-old wartime conviction based on incontrovertible proof that the government had lied to the Supreme Court. Don later recounted, "The national news story was the government cover-up. And this was post-Watergate, where a President had been impeached, and an attorney general had resigned rather than fire the independent investigator on a criminal action. And so the press was teed up, I would say, and they were interested in any type of massive government misconduct like this." Don was in the office every day by 5:30 a.m. to reach the East Coast media. He would call one network, for example, CBS, to tell its desk the power of Fred's story and to convince them that they should look into it. When CBS said it might be interested but made no commitment to cover it, Don called another, for example, ABC, to tell them that CBS was "following the story." ABC then said "we're definitely coming," after which Don would call CBS and NBC "as a courtesy" to let them know.[38] And it went on the same way with the print media. Don's efforts were Herculean.

On the morning of January 31, 1983, Fred's lawyers set out to file his petition, its thick stack of exhibits, and the accompanying memorandum of points and authorities with the clerk for the U.S. District Court for the Northern District of California in San Francisco. Dale drove Peter and Lori across the Bay Bridge from Oakland.

> In the case of selection of federal judges, it's random. So in certain types of cases, the type of judge you get tells you what kind of justice you're going to achieve. And we were crossing the Bay Bridge with a stack of petitions which were three feet high to file on the day of the filing of the Korematsu case. . . . And at the toll plaza, of course, I got into the shortest line to pay my bridge toll and somebody in front was paying in pennies or in some way that just caused a great delay. So even though I was in the short-est line, it took the longest time. I told Peter, "You know, I've really been unlucky about these kinds of things." And Peter goes, "I know what you mean. I get in the shortest grocery lines, I never get done fast, I never have won a lottery, I've never won any kind of raffle." And I said, "Same with me." And we looked at each other realizing at that moment that luck was going to play a role in this case—that we needed good luck to be able to get a good judge.[39]

Dale and Peter decided that, with their kind of luck, they weren't going to be the ones to file Fred's papers. "We then hit upon the idea of . . . Lori Bannai, whose had her share of ups and downs in life, but had some very good luck, as well. [And so we said,] 'Here, Lori, go file these.' And her eyes got really wide, because she knew what it meant. The fate of our case in a sense rested upon her."[40]

Lori handed the stack of documents to the clerk of the court. The filing was unusual. Fred's case had been closed forty years earlier; the petition for writ of error coram nobis was rarely used; and the petition, as required,

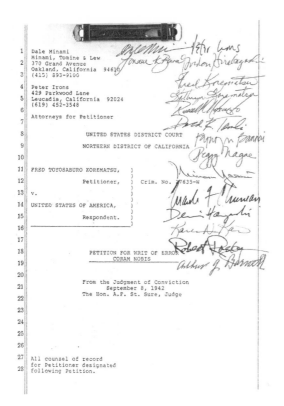

1 Dale Minami
  Minami, Tomine & Lew
2 370 Grand Avenue
  Oakland, California 94610
3 (415) 893-9100

4 Peter Irons
  429 Parkwood Lane
5 Leucadia, California 92024
  (619) 452-3548
6
7 Attorneys for Petitioner

8   UNITED STATES DISTRICT COURT
9   NORTHERN DISTRICT OF CALIFORNIA
10
11 FRED TOYOSABURO KOREMATSU,   )
12   Petitioner,   )   Crim. No. 27635-W
13   v.   )
14 UNITED STATES OF AMERICA,   )
15   Respondent.   )
16 _____)
17
18   PETITION FOR WRIT OF ERROR
                CORAM NOBIS
19
20
21   From the Judgment of Conviction
             September 8, 1942
22   The Hon. A.F. St. Sure, Judge
23
24
25
26
27 All counsel of record
   for Petitioner designated
28 following Petition.

FIGURE 9.1. The petition for writ of error coram nobis filed in *Korematsu v. United States*, signed by Fred, Gordon Hirabayashi, Minoru Yasui, and members of their legal teams on the day it was filed, January 31, 1983.

identified the name of the judge who had convicted Fred, Judge Adolphus St. Sure, who had long since passed away. The clerk at the desk went back to check with the chief clerk as to how to handle the filing. The chief clerk said, "I haven't seen one of these in thirty years."[41]

The clerk punched the docket number into a computer and announced to the team that it had drawn Judge Marilyn Hall Patel. Ecstatic, but not wanting to explode with jubilation in the formal environment of the clerk's office, the team smiled, left, and started the high fives in the elevator. Judge Patel was one of the best judges that they could have drawn. Peter explained, "She'd worked for the National Organization for Women doing legal work for them. She'd been appointed by President Jimmy Carter. She was known as a supporter of civil liberties. Her husband was East Indian by ancestry. She had a lot of experience with racial and ethnic minorities. And we just felt that she would be a really good judge for this case."[42] Patel, the team believed, would understand the injustice wrought upon Fred and the rest of the Japanese American community during World War II.

After filing Fred's papers, the team rushed to the San Francisco Press Club. Don had called a press conference to announce the reopening of Fred's historic World War II case and the proof of governmental misconduct upon which it was based. No one knew if any of the press would attend. No one knew if any would be interested. The team walked into a room packed with reporters and cameras, all jockeying for position. Forty members of the press signed in, representing the wire services, *New York Times, Los Angeles Times, Baltimore Sun, Christian Science Monitor, San Francisco Examiner, USA Today,* other local and Asian American papers, and local television and radio stations. And all three major networks—NBC, ABC, and CBS—showed up.[43]

Fred was not well. Right after Christmas, he had gone to the hospital with bleeding ulcers; he was having trouble swallowing, and he was dehydrated. On New Year's Day, he had surgery to remove a third of his stomach. When Dale, Peter, and Akira had visited Fred in the hospital shortly before his petition was to be filed, Fred didn't look good. They asked Fred if it was okay to file and told him not to jeopardize his health, but Fred said to go ahead.[44] He had waited for this for so long. He had to be present. At the press conference, Fred, appearing frail and weak, sat flanked by Gordon and Min before the roomful of reporters and what seemed to be a sea of cameras. Dale spoke of the import of the day:

> We are filing these petitions for Writ of Error Coram Nobis to reopen cases decided by the Supreme Court [in] landmark cases in 1943 and 1944. The cases upheld the convictions of Min Yasui, Gordon Hirabayashi, and Fred Korematsu. They . . . validated the evacuation and curfew orders which led to the imprisonment of 110,000 Japanese Americans during World War II. The basis of our petitions is recently discovered evidence . . . that indicates that high government officials suppressed, altered and destroyed evidence in order to influence the outcomes of these cases at trial and on appeal, including appeals to the United States Supreme Court. We have here a unique opportunity to correct a wrong. . . . [T]here was a gross violation of civil liberties of Japanese Americans . . . no notice was given, no trials held. . . . There was in fact an enormous toll of human suffering and dev-

astating impact upon the Japanese American community. . . . What we are asking here, however, by filing these petitions [is] not just for sympathy, we are asking for something very simple, and that is the justice that was denied to these men forty years ago.[45]

Fred did not have the powerful and fiery eloquence that Min had. And he did not have the level of education or the developed personal philosophy that Gordon, now a sociology professor at the University of Alberta, possessed. He spoke simply and from the heart, "I was born here in Oakland, here, in the Bay Area, and I went to school here and learned all about the Constitution. I'm just like every other American; I wanted to stay here. And when this evacuation came, I felt that I was not a criminal or enemy alien, which I was classified as. And . . . at the time of the evacuation . . . I stayed. . . . I probably would assume that you, as American citizens, had they told you you had to get out, you'd feel the same way."[46]

News of the filing of Fred's case, soon to be followed by the filing of Gordon's and Min's cases, hit the network news and major newspapers across the country and even internationally. Kathryn recalled, "We didn't quite grasp that this press thing was going to be that big, and we were kind of shocked to go home that night and flip through [and see Fred's case] on all three networks." The press reports shared news of the scandal of the World War II government cover-up. Reaction from official quarters was a mix of surprise and skepticism. When told of the claim that Solicitor General Fahy had lied to the Supreme Court, Rex Lee, solicitor general in the Reagan administration, commented, "I'd be very surprised if that happened. A solicitor general just wouldn't do that." World War II Justice Department lawyer Edward Ennis, although still adamant in his view that the wartime incarceration was wrong, told the *New York Times* that the case faced serious hurdles. Lyle Denniston of the *Baltimore Sun* said that the cases would have to be taken seriously, although, in his opinion, the lawyers' campaign was "a legal longshot." The Justice Department declined to comment, explaining that it had not yet seen the filings.[47]

Fred's legal team continued its work. The *Korematsu*, *Hirabayashi*, and *Yasui* legal teams agreed to move jointly to consolidate the three cases in one court, and there was work to be done on that motion. Legal research continued, especially on the rules of discovery, the process of formal re-

FIGURE 9.2. *Left to right:* Gordon Hirabayashi, Minoru Yasui, and Fred in 1983. Photo by Bob Hsiang. Courtesy of Farallon Films.

quests for further information from the government. Judge Patel scheduled a status conference in Fred's case for March 14.[48]

Now that the petition was filed, the team began to speak publicly about the case. Fundraising became a high priority, and the team reached out to groups in Los Angeles and the San Francisco Bay Area to support the cases. In February, Don reported to Min that the team had so far incurred about $10,000 in costs and was down to its last $500. Pending further fundraising efforts, Don said, the law firms and offices of the attorneys on the teams would continue to front the costs. Don suggested, hopefully, "At some point, when we raise substantial amounts of money, perhaps some of these funds could go to attorney's fees since our private practices are suffering. However, we are so excited about these cases that we will gladly foot the bill and go broke if we have to. . . . Since January 1982 when these cases began, we estimate that the legal team has put in approximately . . . $400,000.00 in attorney time. We view these cases as once-in-a-lifetime experiences, and they are worth the effort without a doubt."[49]

Fred decided that he had to add his voice in support of his legal team. Before the January 1983 news conference, Fred had spoken in public about his case only once—to Paul Takagi's class. When the legal team first met with Fred, he said he'd support the case but didn't want to speak. "That wasn't something he did easily," Kathryn said. "Fred's a very shy person, in lots of ways, and he really was concerned about the attention and his name appearing in the paper." One thing Fred knew for sure was that he didn't want reporters camped out in front of his house. Don assured Fred that he wouldn't have to speak—the team would protect him from the media—and advised Fred to have his telephone number unlisted.[50]

When Fred learned that the team had been going out to raise money to support his case, however, he told Kathryn, "I think we ought to be helping them." He and Kathryn felt that the members of the legal team were putting their careers on the line for him, and he needed to do something to support them. As Dale later recounted,

> I guess [we] lied, because we had them going everywhere. We needed to spread the word about what this case was about. We needed Fred there. And there were times when Fred wasn't in the best of health, but [he showed] the same courage he showed in bringing this case in '44 [in] getting up and going to talk to audiences that he didn't know and explained what his story was about. I think it was as much impressive to us as the fact that he even brought the case, that he would help us spread the word. He became our emissary and our educator for the American public.[51]

Fred traveled to fundraising events in Los Angeles, Sacramento, and around the Bay Area. The Los Angeles event, held in Gardena, California, grossed close to $5,000; organizer Roy Nakano noted, "What is significant . . . is the majority of the money came from working-class and retired Japanese Americans. Some of the Patrons were in fact blue-collar workers. I believe this is indicative of just how much deeply-felt support the [coram nobis] effort has within members of the community."[52]

Fred would later travel the entire country speaking about his case. On May 29, he was interviewed by one of his local papers, the *Oakland Tribune*, which described Fred as "not the kind of man one might expect to be embroiled in historic legal battles. A low-key, shy, slightly built man, he is obviously more at ease talking about his presidency of the San Leandro Lions Club and about his 18 years as mentor of 700 Bay Area Boy Scouts." The article captured Fred's plain-speaking style: "People were saying, 'A Jap is a Jap. You can't trust him.' . . . That was a bunch of baloney. How could you tell by looking at someone whether he is loyal of disloyal?" In 1983, film-maker Steven Okazaki started production on a documentary, *Unfinished Business*, about the coram nobis petitioners. Fred was interviewed for *60 Minutes* by Ed Bradley, and, despite the legal team's earlier promises to Fred, the crew *was* camped out on his front lawn.[53]

Reopening his case, especially in such a public way, was not easy for Fred. He had never told his friends of his wartime criminal conviction. As Kathryn explained, "There was really never any point in bringing it up. So he sort of wondered what the reaction would be." When Fred told his brother Joe that he was going back to court, Joe couldn't figure out why Fred would want to stir everything up again—it had all happened so long ago.[54]

Most significantly, Fred believed that his decision to take the government to court cost him his job. Forty years after being shunned by his community and suffering a criminal conviction, Fred had put himself at risk again. Don recalled, "The day before the press conference, or a couple of days, I got a sense that the coverage was going to be big. . . . And so I said to Fred, 'It's going to be on the front page, Fred, and maybe you ought to talk to your employer and let them know that this is happening?'" When Fred told his boss about the reopening of his case, his boss replied, "Why are you bringing this up now? Why do this now?" Soon thereafter, Kathryn related, "They said, well, they just didn't have enough work and things had slowed down." Fred was laid off. He started to do freelance work at home to help make ends meet.[55]

The legal team didn't hear from the government regarding the petition until the morning of March 2. Victor Stone, counsel for special and appellate matters in the Justice Department's general litigation and special advice section, was assigned to represent the Justice Department in all three cases—Fred, Gordon, and Min's—and he telephoned Dale. The response was a request for delay. Stone explained that his best guess was that the government would ask for an extension of time in which to answer the claims of the misconduct. There was so much material to go through. He needed policy guidance; he couldn't get it in the short time he had; and he didn't want to put anything on paper until he had more direction. On the one hand, to the extent that everybody acknowledged that the incarceration was wrong, he didn't want to argue that it was proper. On the other, to the extent that the petition represented an attack, the government had to defend itself. The severity of the attack, for example, against the solicitor general, might tie the government's hands and preclude a conciliatory approach to the case. Maybe the case would upset some people. He needed more time.[56]

Stone made his formal request for delay before Judge Patel at the first status conference in the case on March 14, 1983. The Commission on Wartime Relocation and Internment of Civilians had issued its long-awaited report in February, and Stone waved his heavily tabbed copy in the air during his argument. He said that, while the report contained the commission's substantive findings, the commission had not yet issued its recommendations. It was necessary, he argued, for the government to delay any response to the petition's allegations of misconduct until after the commission's recommendations so that the government's posture in court would not be perceived to be interfering with the commission's deliberations.[57]

The report did not bode well for the government. Judge Patel asked Stone about its contents. Stone replied, "I won't say that the government comes off looking terribly well." Judge Patel, noting the large, bold print "Personal Justice Denied" on the front cover, replied, "Not from the title, it wouldn't sound as if it does."[58] In fact, after exhaustive study, the commission had unanimously concluded that the incarceration had represented a profound failure of justice. In summarizing its findings, the commission stated, "Executive Order 9066 was not justified by military necessity, and the decisions that followed it—detention, ending detention, and ending exclusion—were not driven by analysis of military conditions. The broad historical causes which shaped these decisions were race prejudice, war hysteria and a failure of political leadership." As a result, the commission continued, "[a] grave injustice was done to American citizens and resident aliens of Japanese ancestry who, without individual review or any probative evidence against them, were excluded, removed and detained by the United States during World War II."[59]

While agreeing to a reasonable delay to await the commission's recommendations, Dale reminded the court that these cases were separate from the commission's work and that the petitioners, who were of advanced age, deserved to see justice done sooner, not later. Judge Patel agreed that the government could defer its response to the petition's allegations until a reasonable time after the commission had issued its recommendations. But she was clear that further delay would not be looked upon favorably. In the meantime, she allowed Fred's counsel to engage in "discovery," that is, to ascertain whether the government had further relevant documents and to obtain them. She ordered the parties to meet and work that out. While Stone objected, Judge Patel was not sympathetic.[60]

Stone had told Dale that the allegations of the petition might upset some people, and he couldn't have been more right. On April 10, 1983, John J. McCloy, who had been assistant secretary of war during World War II and a key player in the Japanese American incarceration, wrote an op ed piece in the *New York Times* decrying the commission's work and the allegations of government misconduct. McCloy was a still-powerful player in Washington politics; in February 1983, *Harper's Magazine* had referred to him as "[t]he most influential private citizen in America." Since the war, he had, among other things, advised nine presidents, been "known and admired by virtually every Western leader of the postwar era," and been chairman of the board of Chase Manhattan Bank.[61]

In his op-ed piece, McCloy complained that the "Japanese-American lobby" was pressing for redress, and asserted, "If we bow to this lobby, we will perpetuate injustice." He defended the mass removal. He asserted, for example, "The consensus of prudent responsible officials, *without rebuttal from any quarter,* was that an attack was possible, accompanied by sabotage by the ethnic Japanese heavily concentrated around vulnerable West Coast defense installations," ignoring the evidence that responsible intelligence agencies had, in fact, rebuted DeWitt's claims of Japanese American espionage and sabotage. He further argued that "[i]t was not feasible to carry out immediate personal evaluation of 120,000 Japanese-Americans and resident aliens," again ignoring the evidence that DeWitt had not based his decision on the shortness of time. McCloy objected to the attack on the integrity of the wartime government officials. "An insufferable element in the Commission's effort to condemn our officials is the imputation of 'racial prejudice' and 'war hysteria' to the deceased statesmen for their support of relocation. The Coast had a record of anti-

Japanese prejudice, but to associate ignorant prejudice with Mr. Stimson and other senior officials is an affront to their memory and a total misconception of the facts and of their characters."[62]

Relations between the legal team and Stone became increasingly strained. Haggling over discovery requests, Stone's struggle to handle the massive number of documents, and his apparent inability to gain coherent guidance from superiors on how to handle the case led to mounting tension and animosity between Fred's lawyers and Stone.[63]

On April 11, 1983, the three legal teams representing Fred, Gordon, and Min jointly asked the Ninth Circuit Court of Appeals to consolidate the cases in one court. Having drawn a good judge, Judge Patel, in Fred's case, the teams felt that consolidation of the cases in front of her would be to their strategic advantage, and, the motion argued, the cases should be heard together, as they presented common questions of law and fact. Consolidation, they argued, "would facilitate the just and efficient litigation of [the] petitions." The motion specifically requested that Judge Patel be allowed to preside over the cases because she had already begun proceedings in Fred's case, while the judges in the other cases had not. Handing the legal teams a disappointing first "loss," Judge James Browning denied the motion.[64] The three cases would proceed independently of each other, although Fred's case was moving forward before the others.

At the next status conference before Judge Patel on May 9, Stone again sought more time to respond to the petition's charges. When Judge Patel asked Stone whether the government could file its response within thirty days after the issuance of the commission's recommendations, Stone said the time frame was unrealistic: "It's a question of me trying to get the wheels of government to—at a lot of different and some very high levels—to review this, and I don't think they work that quickly that within 30 days I can come back and have an answer. . . . This case has waited an awful long time to come here. I don't think that a little bit of time in the front end is going to make much difference." When Stone asked if he could have until October 1 to respond to the petition, Judge Patel said he had until August 29.[65]

The commission issued its recommendations on June 16. Congress, it said, should issue a national apology for the exclusion, removal, and detention of Japanese Americans and provide redress of $20,000 to each living survivor of the camps—approximately 60,000 of the over 110,000 individuals who had been removed from the West Coast. In addition, to the surprise of the Fred and his lawyers, the commission recommended "that the President pardon those who were convicted" of violating the military orders, which, the legal teams assumed, included Fred. In language that was puzzling to the coram nobis legal teams, the commission stated that its pardon recommendation was "made without prejudice to cases currently before the courts."[66] If Fred accepted a pardon, then how could he pursue his case?

The coram nobis legal teams were taken aback by the recommendation of pardons. A pardon, the lawyers believed, would mean that Fred, Gordon, and Min had committed crimes and were being forgiven for them; the men, of course, believed that they hadn't done anything wrong. Dale had earlier informed Angus MacBeth, the commission's counsel, that, while he could not speak for all three of the coram nobis petitioners, he was sure that they would not accept a pardon. In a phone call the day after the commission's recommendations were announced, Stone told Peter that, given the pardon recommendation, the government would seek a further extension of time to answer the petitions. Peter told Stone that the three petitioners "wanted a judicial vacation of their convictions, that their petitions raised serious allegations of misconduct, and that [they] wanted a hearing on [those] allegations." Stone called again, saying that he might be able to offer a "pardon for innocence," a device the lawyers had never heard of, which, Stone explained, would acknowledge that person pardoned was innocent of the charges. Peter told the legal teams, "My feeling is after this second phone call with Stone is that he is desperate for some way to end the cases and dispose of the petitions without going to evidentiary hearings and judicial findings of misconduct."[67]

Fred's lawyers told Fred of the offer of pardon. As Kathryn said, "[The legal team], they treated us just like clients, they asked us our opinions all along the way, if there was a decision to make, they let us make it." When told that the government had offered him a pardon, Fred said "no." Instead, he said, "I think I should be the one pardoning the government. They were wrong."[68]

As expected, Stone sought even more time to respond to the petition. On a phone call on September 26, he said he was in an "unbelievable position." The "number three" man in the Justice Department, he explained, wouldn't let him file his papers until everyone had had their chance to edit and was happy.[69]

On October 4, 1983, the government finally filed its response to Fred's petition. However, instead of admitting or denying the allegations of fraud, misrepresentation, and suppression of evidence alleged in the petition, the government said that the court need not address those allegations at all. The response started out well enough, by acknowledging Fred's wartime stance of resistance: "In 1942, petitioner was one of the few standard bearers who chose to challenge the propriety of World War II military orders which resulted in the mass evacuation of over one-hundred thousand persons of Japanese ancestry from the west coast." But it went on to argue that the government had already taken steps to recognize that the mass removal of Japanese Americans was part of "an unfortunate episode" in our nation's history, citing President Gerald Ford's rescission of Executive Order 9066 and Congress's repeal of Public Law 503 in 1976.

Given that both the executive and legislative branches had acknowledged the wrongfulness of the wartime treatment of Japanese Americans, the government concurred that Fred's conviction should be vacated. However, it argued, in turn, that it was therefore not necessary for the court to address the claims of government fraud:

> In this specific context, the government has concluded—without any intention to disparage those persons who made the decisions in question—that it would not be appropriate to defend this forty year old misdemeanor conviction. Because we believe that it is time to put behind us the controversy which led to the mass evacuation in 1942 and instead reaffirm the inherent right of each person to be treated as an individual, it is singularly appropriate to vacate this conviction for non-violent civil disobedience. . . .
>
> There is, therefore, no continuing reason in this setting for this court to convene hearings or make findings about petitioner's allegations of governmental wrongdoing in the 1940s.

The response concluded with a motion to dismiss not only the original 1942 indictment filed against Fred but also his coram nobis petition and its allegations of misconduct.[70]

The government had crafted a response that purported, at least on its face, to get everyone what they wanted. The government was offering Fred the dismissal of all charges brought against him in 1942 and the vacation of his conviction—in essence, the clearing of his criminal record. The government, in turn, would be able, as it suggested, to "put [this controversy] behind us" by getting Fred's coram nobis petition dismissed. In so doing, it would avoid addressing the charges that it had engineered the presentation of a tainted record to the court and avoid "disparag[ing]" those who had participated in the misrepresentations. The government would be able to do all of this in a spirit of good will: "It's not our intent to keep harassing him. If what he wants is getting his conviction vacated, that's what he can have," said William McGivern, the chief assistant U.S. attorney in San Francisco who served as co-counsel to Stone.[71]

The press praised the government's decision to agree to the vacation of Fred's conviction. The *Washington Post* commented, "Mr. Korematsu's name will always be familiar to legal scholars and historians, teachers and government officials, for his civil disobedience focused attention on the injustice of internment and the suffering of many fellow citizens. He will be honored, as Martin Luther King is honored, for his nonviolent resistance to unjust law. While some might hold that his conviction was a badge of honor, it is fitting that his request for legal as well as historical vindication be granted."[72]

Fred had achieved what he had sought for forty years—the reopening of his case and the clearing of his name. In that respect, he had won. But, in offering to vacate his conviction, the government had not admitted to its lies, its deceit, or its arrogance in arguing before the Supreme Court that the forced removal of over 110,000 Japanese Americans, based solely on their race, was supported by military necessity when it knew otherwise. As Bob Rusky later recalled,

> [Karen and I had] gone on vacation. We came back and had a phone message that, that we had won the case, and I believe it was because the government had actually moved to vacate Fred's conviction rather than responding directly to the petition.
>
> And after getting over the irony of the one vacation we had taken . . . after working on the case for a year, we realized that, I think both Karen and

I realized that we hadn't won yet. That simply getting Fred's conviction set aside, the ultimate relief was not what we were really after. What the case was about was confronting the wrong that had been done, not avoiding it. [T]he government's attempt to avoid confronting the allegations that we had set forth in the petition was itself a wrong, and we needed to contest it very strongly, which we did.[73]

The government's offer to agree to a vacation of Fred's conviction was not enough. It had to admit its wrongdoing or face judgment on its actions before Judge Patel.

While the *Los Angeles Times* agreed that Fred's conviction ought to be vacated, it was curiously "inclined to agree with the government's opposition to further court hearings or findings." It cited the commission's conclusion that "no completely satisfactory answer can be reached about these emotion-laden issues from this vantage point in history."[74] M. J. Mondeau took exception: "[T]he search for truth cannot be postponed. It affects too many of us now. . . . If the government indeed withheld information from the Supreme Court during this case it must be known. To the victims of the internment we are indeed in debt. But our debt goes beyond any monetary value. It encompasses the valuable lessons we . . . must learn in order to prevent another such tragedy. In the future it may be you or me."[75]

Fred's legal team worked fast and furiously to respond to the government's motion to dismiss—time was short, and the stakes were high. Neither Fred nor the team had come this far only to have their claims of governmental fraud dismissed. The team filed its reply to the government's motion on October 31, 1983. They said that Fred's conviction should be vacated, but urged that the court, in addition, specifically rule that the removal and incarceration were not justified by military necessity. The government, Fred's team argued, should not be allowed to avoid the allegations of its misconduct: "Mr. Korematsu's conviction and indictment should be vacated, not because the government now wants to walk away from the issues, but because there was never any legal or factual basis for the internment in the first instance and justice demands that this truth be recognized by a court of law." It was singularly important, the brief asserted, that the judicial branch recognize the wrong that was committed. While the executive and legislative branches had expressed national regret for the wartime military corralling of Japanese Americans, "the court alone, as the third branch of government, has not directly reviewed its role during this sad history." Judge Patel would be the first judge to examine the widely condemned Supreme Court *Korematsu* case, now in light of evidence of the government's misconduct before the court. Fred's brief concluded, "So as to help cleanse this blot on American principles and values, Petitioner respectfully requests that the Court, in the public interest, consider the merits of these important issues and, in its wisdom, resolve them."[76]

Fred submitted his own declaration in support of his lawyers' papers. He told the court that he spoke not only for himself but also for the 110,000 other Japanese Americans who had been imprisoned during World War II:

> For forty years, I have carried with me the remembrance of being treated as a criminal and classified as an enemy alien of the United States even though I was born in Oakland, California. . . . I did *not* do anything wrong. . . .
>
> I want you to know that Japanese Americans are loyal American citizens and obey the laws of the land. They were made to feel shame and suffered by being forced to live in horse racing track stalls and then in concentration camps.
>
> Many Japanese Americans have either told me in person or written letters to me saying that they support me in my fight to clear the record. They feel I am fighting this case for them as well as for myself. It is important for them as well as for me that the United States government admit that it was wrong when Japanese Americans were forced out of their homes and put into concentration camps.[77]

The battle lines were thus drawn for the hearing that would take place before Judge Patel on November 10. While the government wished to avoid the allegations of fraud and misconduct, Fred and his lawyers asserted that justice could be served only if the court recognized, and the public knew, that over 110,000 Japanese Americans had been forcibly taken from their homes on a record of lies.

Numerous organizations sought to file, or co-sign onto, amicus briefs in support of Fred and his petition. The groups were from across the country

A Japanese American's Fight for Justice

'Being a citizen didn't mean a thing — they just put me in prison'

BY EDWARD IWATA

It is May 30, 1942. On a clear, sunny morning in San Leandro, suspicious police arrest Fred Korematsu, a skinny 23-year-old youth walking down the street with his girlfriend.

Korematsu, a shipyard steel welder, is an East Bay native, a Castlemont High graduate and a U.S. citizen of Japanese ancestry. His girlfriend is white. "Jap Spy Arrested in San Leandro!" trumpets a local newspaper headline.

Nearly six months have passed since Pearl Harbor, and two months since the forced "evacuation" of 112,000 Japanese Americans to West Coast racetracks used as temporary jails. Within weeks, they will be removed by the Army to 10 internment camps scattered across the United States.

After Korematsu's arrest for evading the government's evacuation order, FBI agents sharply interrogate him and threaten him with a gun. The shaken young man admits that he is Japanese American and that his family is already being held at the Tanforan racetrack in San Mateo.

Korematsu also confesses that in a desperate scheme to disguise himself as a Hawaiian-Spanish laborer, he underwent plastic surgery on his eyes and nose. A San Francisco doctor had performed the surgery for $100.

"The operation was for the purpose of changing my appearance so that I would not be subject to ostracism when my girl and I went back East," Korematsu says in a statement to the FBI.

Aided by American Civil Liberties Union attorneys, Korematsu decides to test the constitutionality of the Army's "evacuation" order. His case swiftly moves to the U.S. Supreme Court, where the justices rule that evacuation is legal because of "military necessity."

Fred Korematsu 'can still remember what it was like to be put in prison for being a Japanese American.'

challenged the legal might of the White House and the War and Justice Departments.

But Korematsu had immediately decided to tackle the government after his first grim day at Tanforan. Shivering in a horse stall with a dirt floor and straw bed, he swore to himself, "I'm not going to live like this."

"I was scared," he admits. "Here I was, bucking the whole government and military. But I must have had enough confidence as an American citizen to test our democratic system. I was classified as a prisoner-of-war, an enemy alien, so I didn't have anything to lose."

His parents, already humiliated by the stigma of military evacuation, were upset further when their college-age son told them of his legal plans. The concept of "haji," or shame, ran deep among Japanese Americans.

"Before the war, my mother and father were proud people," Korematsu said. "They taught us not to do anything shameful, to always be a good citizen, obey the law, work hard. They couldn't understand why I was doing this.

"After Pearl Harbor, everyone accused us of being traitors. Everything you read and heard was 'Jap this' and 'Jap that.' That really burned me up."

Despite the help of ACLU attorneys Wayne Collins and Ernest Besig, Korematsu was convicted in district court in San Francisco. Seven months later, the U.S. Supreme Court rejected his appeal.

While on probation, Korematsu spent two months at Tanforan and eight months with his family at the Topaz internment camp in Utah.

After the war, his youthful dreams of becoming a real estate agent or an airline pilot were shattered, and he moved to Detroit to study drafting. He then returned to San Leandro and searched long and hard for a job, finally landing work with a small drafting firm.

"I wanted to work for the state, county or a big company with a pension plan, but no one would take a man with a conviction record," he said.

Like most Japanese Americans, Korematsu for decades had erased his bitter World War II memories. He declined to talk about his past with curious students, journalists, historians — and even his own son and daughter. Until last year. That's when lawyer Peter Irons, a San Diego professor and constitutional expert, telephoned Korematsu in hopes of re-opening the Supreme Court "test cases." Irons had discovered Justice Department documents showing that government lawyers had "suppressed and destroyed" key evidence that would have proven the loyalty of Japanese Americans.

"They've done me a great wrong," Korematsu told Irons.

After Korematsu revived his case, Japanese Americans embraced him as a historical hero, seeing in him reflections of their own personal tragedies. Fund-raising dinners and speaking engagements soon netted his legal defense team $25,000.

Early in the appeal, the Justice Department offered to pardon Korematsu rather than pursue further legal action. "The government shouldn't pardon me, I should be pardoning the government!" an angry Korematsu told his San Francisco attorney, Dale Minami.

After his battle in court, the San Leandro man hopes to return his attention to his family and his activities with the local Boy Scouts, the Lions Club and the Oakland First Presbyterian Church.

Until then, he says, "I would like to have completely cleared that this will never happen again to another American citizen, just because he looks a little different than everyone else. If our case still stands (without vacating his conviction), any American who isn't Caucasian can be accused of disloyalty like we were. It can happen again."

BY GARY FONG

FIGURE 9.3. *San Francisco Chronicle*, November 3, 1983. San Francisco Chronicle/Polaris.

FIGURE 9.4. Fred and members of his coram nobis legal team, October 1983. *Front row, left to right:* Dale Minami, Fred, and Peter Irons. *Back row, left to right:* Don Tamaki, Dennis Hayashi, and Lori Bannai. Photo by Crystal Huie. Courtesy of the Korematsu Institute.

and widely diverse, all recognizing that Fred's case had impact far beyond the reversal of his own conviction. Among those who sought to submit briefs supporting Fred's case were the Northern California chapter of the American Civil Liberties Union; the American Friends Service Committee; the Anti-Defamation League of B'nai Brith; the General Assembly of the Presbyterian Church; a consortium of law student groups and lawyers, including the Asian American Law Students Association of Stanford Law School and Rutgers Law School, the national Black American Law Student Association, the Association of Latin American Law Students of Rutgers Law School, the American Jewish Committee, and the National Lawyers

Guild; the Center for Constitutional Rights in New York; the Fellowship of Reconciliation and Jewish Peace Fellowship; and the Society of American Law Teachers. Also offering briefs in support were the National Coalition for Redress/Reparations, the Japanese American Citizens League, the Asian American Legal Defense and Education Fund in New York, the Asian American Bar Association of the Greater Bay Area in San Francisco, the Asian/Pacific Bar of California, and the Japanese American Bar Association of the Greater Los Angeles Area. In the end, there were so many organizations seeking to file briefs that Judge Patel asked them to coordinate their efforts and submit no more than five briefs to the court.[78]

In addition to these organizations, the Japanese American press also expressed its support for Fred's case in the days leading up to his hearing. On November 9, the day before Fred would appear in court, Jim Okutsu of the San Francisco-based *Hokubei Mainichi* wrote,

> Korematsu will finally get his day in court this Thursday. New evidence reveals that the federal government deliberately and willfully suppressed information on the loyalty of Japanese Americans.
>
> While Nov. 10 will be Korematsu's vindication, it will also represent a day of Nikkei liberation, for [the Korematsu] court decision has been a needless collective shame for all Japanese Americans.
>
> Perhaps … the spirit of shiikataganai, better late than never, is one way of philosophizing about the new turn of events, but, damn it, a 40-year-old sentence for being Japanese American because justice was blinded by racism is a little hard to swallow.[79]

Fred, who had stood in court virtually alone forty years earlier, was now not alone at all.

CHAPTER 10

CORRECTING THE RECORD

AS FRED AND HIS ATTORNEYS ARRIVED IN COURT ON NOVEMBER 10, 1983, they did not know what to expect. They had experienced delay after delay, and even though Judge Patel had set this day to hear Fred's case, they feared that the government would request some further way to avoid a ruling on Fred's claims.

In the court's chambers the day before, Judge Patel had met with Fred's and the government's lawyers. She had pressed Stone to state whether the government was conceding or contesting the claims set forth in the petition. Stone replied, "With all due respect, Judge, I don't have authority to make that decision." She said Stone had better be able to state the government's position when everyone came to court.[1] Would Stone say again that he wasn't prepared to answer the allegations of misconduct? Alternatively, would Stone, as he had done before, assert that the court should not rule because the issue of the Japanese American incarceration would be going before Congress? Or would Judge Patel proceed to hear Fred's case, viewing it, properly, as separate from the legislative effort? And, finally, how could she not find the allegations of governmental deceit to be true when they were proved by documents from the government's own files? These, and other questions, swirled in the minds of the members of the legal team as they approached the courthouse on that blustery San Francisco morning.

Judge Patel, aware of the importance of Fred's case to the Japanese American community, had moved the hearing from her own smaller courtroom to the court's ceremonial courtroom so as to accommodate as many observers as could attend. The room was filled mostly by Nisei and

Sansei—so many of their Issei pioneers were now gone. The local Japanese American paper, the *Hokubei Mainichi*, reported the scene, "The courtroom was packed with Japanese Americans, many of whom had waited outside since eight in the morning. Listening to the proceedings were the older Japanese Americans who came as observers in the continuation of a drama in which they played an active, if tragic, role 40 years ago." The Nikkei present, members of the press, and others crowded onto the benches reserved for spectators, in the jury box, and anywhere else there was a seat. Don Tamaki, whose Nisei parents were present at the hearing, recounted what members of Fred's legal team felt: "There was really a sense of electricity in the air. And . . . the reason it was like that was because we were part of that. Our own families were seeking vindication. . . . While certainly it's an important civil liberties principle for all Americans, for us it was more than that, it was very personal." Legal team member Eric Yamamoto recalls, "So it was very intense. . . . No one knew how Patel was going to rule. It really was this sense of anxiety and hope."[2]

After taking the bench, Judge Patel briefly summarized the posture of Fred's case.[3] She had two requests before her: one was the government's motion to dismiss the original indictment against Fred, and the other was Fred's petition to vacate his conviction on the basis of the government's World War II misconduct. She addressed each in turn. The first question was whether the government had the power, procedurally, to seek to dismiss the charges it had filed against Fred in 1942. She concluded that it could not. At any point prior to the time the Supreme Court affirmed Fred's conviction in 1944, she explained, the government could have advised the court of "any information which it believed would render a different decision" and could have terminated its prosecution of Fred. But "[after] the time the judgment has become final, that all appellate proceedings have been exhausted and the sentence imposed, . . . there is no longer any prosecutorial right to [dismiss the proceedings]" (coram nobis hearing transcript, Nov. 10, 1983, 15–16).[4] It was too late, in other words, for the government to decide that it should not have prosecuted Fred.

After concluding that the government could not seek to dismiss the original charges against Fred, Judge Patel turned to the allegations of Fred's coram nobis petition. The government had failed to address the serious allegations of governmental misconduct contained in the petition, and Judge Patel ruled that she would view that failure as a "non-opposition to the petition." Under these circumstances, she explained, it was up to the court, and, indeed, it was its obligation, to weigh the evidence presented and "evaluate independently whether the petition should be granted." In so doing, the court would consider the manner in which the government had responded to the petition—a response she characterized as "tantamount to a confession of error"—as well as the "inherent power of the court . . . to correct its own records . . . in order to undo an injustice" (17–18).

Dale Minami began his argument, framing for the court the significance of Fred's case and the allegations it presented:

> Your Honor, members of the court staff, opposing counsel, co-counsel and members of the audience. We are here today to seek a measure of the justice denied to Fred Korematsu and the Japanese American community 40 years ago. . . .
>
> [I]t must be recognized that we are dealing with an extraordinary case. . . . The allegations we put forth are perhaps unique in legal history, challenging that high government officials suppressed, altered and destroyed information [and] evidence in order to influence the outcome of a Supreme Court decision. . . .
>
> This is not just a 40-year-old misdemeanor conviction, as the government characterizes it. This is a monumental precedent which affected deeply and irrevocably the lives of a hundred thousand Japanese Americans . . . [the] mass banishment of a single racial minority group. The total in lost property, lost opportunities, broken families and human suffering was staggering.
>
> This case also established some of the most criticized and controversial precedents in legal history. First, [it justified] the mass exclusion of an identifiable minority based on race without notice, without hearing, without an attorney. . . . Secondly, [it established that] military judgments in times of crises are virtually unreviewable by the courts, even though the courts are functioning and no martial law has been declared.
>
> *Korematsu v. United States* has never been overruled and has never been reviewed. Today we know that this Supreme Court decision rests on a non-existent factual foundation. (18–21)

Dale then recounted the evidence—including the suppression of the intelligence reports that refuted any necessity for the mass removal of Japanese Americans, and Justice Department attorneys Edward Ennis's and John L. Burling's thwarted efforts to advise the Supreme Court of the existence of those reports—as well as the Commission on Wartime Relocation and Internment of Civilians' conclusion that no military necessity existed for the wartime orders. The incarceration was neither an unfortunate incident nor a mistake; it was "a deliberate and calculated plan to exclude and imprison a single minority group" (26).

Turning toward the Nikkei in the audience who had come that day to court, Dale said, "For the Japanese American community, Fred's fight was their fight. Most knew in their hearts that the exclusion and imprisonment was wrong, but they were too consumed with the business of survival to do anything about it. They, too, have an interest in Fred's case, in Fred's vindication and to validate their own beliefs that they were not criminals in 1942" (26).

Dale then asked if the court would allow Fred to speak. Fred rose and spoke to the hushed courtroom in a voice that, while soft and a bit halting at times, nevertheless resonated powerfully. He spoke for himself and for thousands of others who could, in the future, suffer at the hands of an unchecked government:

> Your Honor, I still remember 40 years ago when I was handcuffed and arrested as a criminal here in San Francisco. . . . It was on Mission Street, that building over there. . . . As an American citizen being put through this shame and embarrassment[, like] all Japanese American citizens who were escorted to concentration camps [and] suffered the same embarrassment, we can never forget this incident as long as we live. The horse stalls that we stayed in were made for horses, not human beings. According to the Supreme Court decision regarding my case, being an American citizen was not enough. They say you have to look like one, otherwise they say you can't tell a difference between a loyal and disloyal American.
>
> I thought that this decision was wrong and I still feel that way. As long as my record stands in federal court, any American citizen can be held in prison or concentration camp without a trial or hearing. That is if they look like the enemy of our country.

Therefore, I would like to see the government admit that they were wrong and do something about it so this will never happen again to any American citizen of any race, creed or color. (30–32)

Victor Stone then rose to address the court. He seemed to assert that there was no reason for Judge Patel to do anything because Fred's case no longer posed a threat to anyone. It was not, as Justice Jackson had feared in his Supreme Court *Korematsu* dissent, a "loaded weapon," ready for use by "any authority that can bring forward a plausible claim of an urgent need." Instead, Stone quoted the commission's statement that "the decision in Korematsu lies overruled in the court of history." Fred's case, however, had never been overruled in a court of law, and many would take issue with the claim that the Supreme Court's decision in Fred's case is no threat. Further, Stone argued that President Roosevelt's Executive Order 9066 and Congress's Public Law 503 had been repealed: "The legislative and executive branches of government have repealed any authority that any underlying statutes might once have had" (33–34). However, the fact that the government had repealed the orders that had led to the World War II Japanese American incarceration did not prevent it from issuing new orders or enacting new statutes that would authorize similar actions against another group in the future.

Judge Patel asked if the attorneys were prepared to submit the issues to the court for decision. Stone seemed surprised and asked if the court was therefore not willing to allow the government to submit further papers. Putting an end to the extensions and back-and-forth of the prior months, Judge Patel said "yes," the government would file no more papers (34). And then she proceeded to explain why.

She had come fully prepared to render her decision from the bench. She later explained why she decided to rule that day:

The day that we were going to have the hearing on the petition, . . . we knew in advance that there was going to be a fair number of people in attendance. . . . And the place was packed. And I decided beforehand that the people would come for a reason and they deserved some kind of response from the court and not just a "Thank you, counsel, and the matter's taken under submission and someday you'll get an opinion from me."

So I gave sort of an abbreviated version of what ultimately I would write. . . . And I knew it meant a lot to the people who were there, that they were there to hear what was going to happen.[5]

Eric Yamamoto recalled the electricity in the air. "Judge Patel shuffled her papers, and then you could tell she was gonna, she had something prepared, so she's gonna rule from the bench. And then it got super quiet again. And I swear I could feel, at that moment, I could feel the intense energy in the room. It felt to me like everything was vibrating, the walls and the air were having this energy like this. And she was quiet, and then she started to read her opinion from the bench."[6]

The government, Patel explained, had not responded at all to the allegations of governmental misconduct contained in Fred's petition, "even though it has had time to do so." Thus, the court had to make its own assessment on those claims. The court need not, she said, "accept the meek acquiescence of the government and merely set aside the order without independently assessing the merits of the petition and the grounds for granting it" (coram nobis hearing transcript, 34, 36).

In reviewing the evidence before her, Patel concluded that the government—in arguing the validity of Executive Order 9066, Public Law 503, and the removal orders before the courts in Fred's World War II case—had relied upon "unsubstantiated facts, distortions and representations of at least one military commander, whose views were seriously infected by racism." There were, she said, numerous facts—known to the government at the time Fred's case was being prosecuted—that "contradicted the military necessity facts set forth by General DeWitt . . . upon which the executive order and the other promulgated orders rely." Among those facts were that "the number of Japanese who were considered to be actually disloyal . . . were minimal, if any" and that it was possible to segregate out any who were disloyal, as with any other community. Further, "the various acts that suggested either the potential for espionage or sabotage that had occurred or could occur in the future, were essentially non-existent or were controverted by evidence that was in the possession of the Navy, the Justice Department, the Federal Communication Commission and the Federal Bureau of Investigation" (38). Patel found that Fred continued to carry the stigma of his conviction even after 40 years, a requirement for the granting of coram nobis relief: "The very nature of this conviction is injurious to a citizen because its implications are such that he is branded as disloyal" (39).

Based on the evidence, Patel concluded, "The public interest and Mr. Korematsu's interest are justly served by vacating his conviction." Therefore, "[t]he conviction that was handed down in this court and affirmed by the Supreme Court in Korematsu v. United States is, by virtue of granting a Writ of Coram Nobis today, vacated and the underlying indictment dismissed" (40–41).

In vacating Fred's conviction, however, Judge Patel took special care to note that she did not, and could not, overrule his infamous Supreme Court case: "I would caution all the parties and the persons in this courtroom that this court cannot, by wiping out the conviction, erase from the books of the Supreme Court's decisions or from history the case of Korematsu v. United States." As a district court judge, she could not overturn a decision of the United States Supreme Court; only the Supreme Court could overrule one of its own decisions. After asserting, perhaps overoptimistically, her view that the case had little, if any, continuing value as precedent, she urged that *Korematsu v. United States* still stood for something very important—as a crucial reminder of the need for vigilance:

Perhaps what [*Korematsu v. United States*] stands for most of all is . . . a caution that in times of war, . . . our institutions must be all the more vigilant of protecting constitutional guarantees. It should stand for the proposition or the caution that in times of distress the shield of military necessity or national security must not be used to protect governmental actions from close scrutiny and accountability, and that in times of international hostility and antagonism our institutions must take the leadership, whether those institutions be the legislative branch, the executive branch or the judicial branch, to protect all citizens from the petty fears and prejudices that are so easily stirred up during those times.

While *Korematsu v. United States* may stand in the Supreme Court reporters of this land . . . the factual underpinnings for it are removed and it stands for the signal of caution . . . I have referred to. (40–41)

Judge Patel then left the bench. Those present had not expected her to announce her ruling that day. Fred turned to Dale to ask what had happened. Kathryn turned to Lori and asked the same thing. They said that Fred had won. Dale told Fred, "Your conviction's been thrown out." Fred, somewhat stunned, said, "That's good, that's really good."[7] It slowly sunk in—Fred's conviction had been vacated. It had been vacated on proof that the government had lied during World War II. The government had lied in arguing that military necessity required the removal of Japanese Americans on the West Coast, and it had engaged in a campaign of cover-ups and intentional falsehoods to gain judicial validation of the mass expulsion of a single racial group.

Smiles, hugs, and celebration filled the courtroom, mixed with tears of remembering and the silent, private release of pain that had been carried for decades. Fred was enveloped by handshakes and words of congratulations. Fred's lawyers exchanged high fives. Legal team member Karen Kai remembered, "The joyous release of emotion in the courtroom after Judge Patel gave her ruling swept all of us up in its current. I remember seeing the judge pause and smile at the scene before leaving the courtroom, and people pressing to reach Fred to thank and congratulate him. He was smiling, of course, and people were crying, laughing, pressing to shake his hand and kiss his cheek. But through all those people, I remember seeing Fred, sharing that extraordinary event with modesty and grace. It was a day on which he completed a journey that had spanned 40 years."[8]

Judge Patel later recalled, "I don't think I was quite prepared for the response to [the hearing] because it really didn't seem to me that there was a dry eye in the courtroom. I mean there was just I think probably a lot of pent up emotion from people, some of them who had worked on these cases, others whose families had gone through similar experiences and identified. And finally something happened. And it was just a very, very emotional experience. And a very heartwarming one, too. And you don't get many of those in court." She said in later years, "I don't think I'll ever forget that case. . . . This was a case everyone reads in law school, and I never dreamed I would have the opportunity to revisit the case."[9] Eric remembers his reaction to Judge Patel's ruling: "This was about Fred, it was about the Japanese American internment, it was about American society and the judiciary's role. It was, couldn't have been better. And at that moment, the room, I could hear people starting to cry in the back. And I could feel my eyes water, I could see everybody on the legal team and we just had that same feeling."[10]

People thanked the team for bringing the case on Fred's behalf. Nisei Amy Eto expressed the feelings of many who attended that day: "There's just joy in my heart, tears in my eyes and gratefulness to what has happened here today. The 40 years have been long and, we owe much to Fred, and as Min has said, certainly to our young Sanseis who have carried it through for us. We say thank you." Kathryn later said, "You all just fulfilled his biggest dream to reopen his case. Who else would've done it but some crazy young people? Who else would've undertaken it?"[11]

Dale recalls, "It was a wonderful moment, not just for Fred and not just for Japanese Americans, but I think for the whole country that a court had finally declared that what happened to Japanese Americans was wrong." Peter reflected on the moment, as well:

> I remember being just flooded with emotion, being really overcome. I wasn't sure in fact that I could even speak to the press or anybody else. And I just felt overjoyed at what had happened. . . . I remember sort of standing back and looking around at this audience, almost all Japanese American, and just seeing how much this affected them. It was sort of like a, a joint, a big collective catharsis. . . . And I also felt, I guess more than I had before ever in my life, that I had been included in a group that was not my own . . . people that I might not otherwise have ever met or gotten to know, and that . . . they had invited me in and included me in this group. And of course, I wouldn't become one of them just as they wouldn't become one of me. But that these artificial boundaries between us had in that experience had sort of dissolved. And that was very important to me.[12]

Fred and his attorneys went to meet the press at a crowded news conference upstairs in the courthouse. "What happened forty years ago involved my family and my personal life, and I had to do some real deep thinking in order to reopen this case again," Fred said. "I am very happy I did, because this is important not only for Japanese American citizens but for all Americans who might get involved in similar conditions." When asked how he felt differently than he did in 1942, Fred replied, "I didn't feel so alone." In later years, he would say that he wished that his mother and father could have known that he had won.[13]

News of Judge Patel's ruling was carried by media across the country, including the *Los Angeles Times*, which ran the headline "Conviction of Man Who Evaded WWII Internment Is Overturned"; the *New York Times'* "Court Overturns a War Internment," and *Time* magazine's "Bad Landmark: Righting a Racial Wrong." Fred also scored what some might consider the ultimate proof of media stardom: a political cartoon depicting him with a ball and chain now severed from his ankle.[14]

The finding that there was, in reality, no basis for their wartime removal or incarceration had profound meaning for the Japanese American community. Judge Robert Takasugi was eleven years old when he and his family were incarcerated at Tule Lake; he went on to become one of the first Japanese Americans appointed to the federal bench. He wrote Dale after reading the transcript of the proceedings before Judge Patel,

> The impotent, condescending posture of the Government was never so evident, never so transparent, never so political as in this proceeding. A simple admission of error would have enhanced its stature. It opted for the serpent's path.
>
> We come away from this experience with mixed feelings of achievement and frustration—achievement for righting a wrong, frustration for knowing that one cannot "unring the bell."
>
> Please permit me to highly commend all counsel, all supporters and, mostly, Mr. Korematsu who braved this historical storm in the tradition of a true human being.[15]

It had been a long, often lonely road from that San Francisco jail cell in 1942 to the Federal courthouse in 1983. Fred had finally cleared his name.

CHAPTER 11

A SYMBOL IN THE CONTINUING

SEARCH FOR JUSTICE

JUDGE PATEL'S RULING IN FRED'S CORAM NOBIS CASE WAS SOME-
what of a beginning for Fred, not an end. He had challenged his conviction
in 1942 and again in 1983 because of his belief that targeting members of
a group based on how they looked was wrong. He knew that while clearing
his name was a great vindication for him, it would not itself prevent similar wrongs from occurring again. The public had to understand what had
happened to Japanese Americans during World War II—if it remembered,
perhaps the vigilance Judge Patel spoke of could be a reality. The struggle
to protect civil liberties, he recognized, was one that had to be continually
fought: "Having this conviction cleared, I am very happy. But there is a lot
more to be done yet, and I would like to have it completely cleared from the
record and that this will never happen again to any American citizen just
because he looks a little different from others. If we go to war with some
other country, and a person looks like [someone from that country] and
[is] put in prison for that, I know that's wrong. So therefore I will still fight,
and my attorneys will fight, until it's completely cleared."[1] Fred's work for
justice was not over.

Fred became involved in the Japanese American quest for redress in
Congress. Even before he went to Capitol Hill himself, however, his name
and case had become significant in the redress effort. In the late 1970s, the
Japanese American Citizens League (JACL) and others had begun educating legislators about what had happened during the wartime incarcera-

tion and the need to acknowledge the wrong.[2] John Tateishi, who had started calling on Congressional offices on the Hill while chair of the JACL National Committee for Redress, explained how critical Fred's reopening of his Supreme Court case was to the redress movement:

> I remember at the 1976 JACL convention, there were some discussions about the [World War II] *Hirabayashi* and *Korematsu* cases . . . that we needed to do something about that . . . how important these cases were in terms of obstacles to achieving anything that we wanted to. . . .
>
> [As] we approached redress, they would always be out there as sort of a dark cloud that was waiting to just pounce on us . . . 'cause the decisions were the law of the land. I did consult with some constitutional law attorneys about this, and they said, . . . it's virtually impossible. . . . The decision was [that] we would approach this through legislation, . . . but that we would return to [the judicial question] if and when we could find a way to open those cases back up. (John Tateishi, interview by author, May 26, 2009)

Tateishi recounted how, time and time again, members of Congress cited the Supreme Court *Korematsu* case to him. The High Court had given its stamp of approval to the wartime removal of Japanese Americans—why should Congress disagree with it? The reopening of the *Korematsu, Hirabayashi,* and *Yasui* cases allowed Tateishi to respond that the Supreme Court cases were being challenged in court because they were based on governmental lies and misrepresentations. He said,

> In those days, 99 percent of the members of Congress were lawyers . . . most very capable lawyers in one way or the other. [Many] would duck behind the Supreme Court cases. . . . I could knock every argument down, but when it came [to] the Supreme Court's decisions in *Korematsu* and *Hirabayashi,* . . . there was no way I could argue that except to say, "but legal scholars for decades have said that those were some of the worst decisions ever rendered by the Court, and you know that's true." . . .
>
> There was still a substantial number who just wouldn't budge. I mean they were opposed to redress, and they were using that as a ra-

tionale. . . . As I went back to Washington and started talking about the cases, when someone would bring it up, I would say, "Well, Congressman, you are familiar with the writ of error coram nobis, aren't you?" They'd say, "Noooo." . . .

It made a difference, just the filing and letting them know. (Ibid.)

Tateishi, who was just a young boy when he was incarcerated with his family, recalls with clarity the moment that he heard of Judge Patel's decision in Fred's case. He was overcome:

When [colleague Carole Hayashino] told me the decision had been handed down[,] I couldn't believe it. I guess that was the first time I was really stunned by the magnitude of it because I was living every day with the decisions and it was such a hard grind to argue against these cases. . . . I started shaking, I think it was the stress of all of this for so long and finally the last barrier had been broken and feeling like, you know this, it was like a cleansing of something really awful. . . . This thing just sat, you know . . . as this dark cloud. . . . It was such a relief for what I was doing. (Ibid.)

Tateishi took out his note cards and, armed with the news of the victory in Fred's case, returned to members of Congress who had not yet decided to support redress. "It changed votes," said Tateishi. But, even more than that, those who were still undecided could no longer claim to be constrained by the now-discredited cases; they were forced to take a stand based on principle.

There [were] members of Congress I went to see and said, "Do you remember the conversation we had once? . . . Well, let me tell you, the *Korematsu* case just got vacated. . . . Now it really comes down to your conscience. . . . If you're gonna vote no, at least do it honestly and don't hide behind these nonsense excuses. And there were, I know, at least ten or fifteen who said well, no, that changes everything. . . . The decision by Patel was huge. Even though it may not have changed some members' minds, it broke down the defense they had and what it did was expose them for who they really were. (Ibid.)

John Ota, a Sansei activist with the National Coalition for Redress/Reparations (NCRR) who came to work closely with Fred, agreed that Judge Patel's decision in Fred's case was a tremendous boost to the redress movement in Congress. "I think it had a really positive impact because it kind of validated what we were seeking. The internment was wrong, should have never happened, the government knew that what it was doing was wrong, and I think it really strengthened the argument for why people should be compensated for what happened. . . . It was kind of . . . like, 'yeah, we knew that [the internment] wasn't necessary, but we did it anyway'" (John Ota, interview by author, Aug. 23, 2010).

Fred and Kathryn became actively involved with NCRR, and with that involvement, they adopted a new set of "kids" into the extended family they had built since the reopening of Fred's case. In addition to their own children and the members of Fred's coram nobis team, they now had the Sansei in NCRR. Fred was always ready with friendly advice whenever Ota would drive him to meetings: "Well, John, you know," Fred would say, "there's a lot of nice young women at NCRR. You know, you ought to really ask them out." "Yeah, you're right, Fred. You're right," Ota would say, not having the heart to tell Fred that he already had (ibid.).

Fred and Kathryn became regulars at meetings and opened their home for gatherings. They stuffed envelopes, sat in booths at street fairs and festivals to distribute materials and collect signatures, and otherwise supported NCRR's efforts any way they could. Fred spoke at workshops for teachers to help them share the lessons of the wartime incarceration with their students. Ota recalls, "They were there to just pitch in, just like everybody else. It wasn't like Fred, although he was a great historical figure, was expecting any special treatment or anything; they just wanted to kind of do their part and help out in the effort just like everybody else was doing. . . . I was impressed by how modest and unassuming they were" (ibid.).

In 1987, H.R. 442—named after the famed all-Nisei 442nd Regimental Combat team that had fought so valiantly during World War II—was introduced in Congress to provide a national apology and monetary reparations to survivors of the camps, as well as a fund to educate the public on the wartime incarceration. When NCRR asked for people willing to go to Washington to lobby for the bill, Fred readily agreed. In the summer of 1987, he and Kathryn joined a delegation of about 120 Nikkei from all over the

FIGURE 11.1. Fred (*left*) with Ted Kojima, lobbying an aide to Representative
Ed Boland, July 1987. Courtesy of John Ota.

country and headed to the Hill. It was a grassroots effort, and the group was
diverse—as Ota explains, there were "students, working people, retirees,
JACL members and anti-JACL people, Nisei, Sansei, Yonsei [fourth generation Japanese Americans], veterans, and draft resisters." Working in teams,
they went from office to office, talking to members of Congress and their
staffers (ibid.).[3]

Ota later recalled the impact of Fred's involvement. "I think just his presence made all of us feel more acutely the historic nature of what we were
doing as well as the historic continuity between what he did and what the
redress movement was about. I know I felt very honored and proud to work
alongside him, and I know others did, too." Fred explained why he had to be
part of the effort. "I hope this [legislation] will further strengthen the Constitution in this country," he later said, "not only for me, but for future generations of Americans, so that this doesn't happen again." Many who received
Fred's lobbying team recognized his name and appreciated what he stood
for; one congressional aide told Fred, "Mr. Korematsu, I wrote a paper about

you in law school!" Fred and Kathryn would return to Washington, DC, two more times to remind Congress of the importance of redressing the wrong.[4]

On August 10, 1988, as a result of the years of effort and combined work of countless individuals and organizations within the Japanese American community, as well as others who understood the need to redress this historic injustice, President Ronald Reagan signed into law the Civil Liberties Act of 1988, which provided a formal apology and redress of $20,000 to each survivor of the wartime removal and incarceration. The act further established a Civil Liberties Public Education Fund to educate the public on the lessons to be learned from that dark chapter in history. In signing the legislation, Reagan stated, "[N]o payment can make up for those lost years. So, what is most important in this bill has less to do with property than with honor. For here we admit a wrong; here we reaffirm our commitment as a nation to equal justice under the law."[5]

Ultimately, 82,219 Japanese Americans who had been forced to leave their West Coast homes because of the wartime orders—among them Fred—received redress checks, enclosed with this letter on behalf of the nation, signed first by President Reagan and then by President George H. W. Bush:

> A monetary sum and words alone cannot restore lost years or erase painful memories; neither can they fully convey our Nation's resolve to rectify injustice and to uphold the rights of individuals. We can never fully right the wrongs of the past. But we can take a clear stand for justice and recognize that serious injustices were done to Japanese Americans during World War II.
>
> In enacting a law calling for restitution and offering a sincere apology, your fellow Americans have, in a very real sense, renewed their traditional commitment to the ideals of freedom, equality, and justice. You and your family have our best wishes for the future.

The redress money was of great help to Fred, who, at that time, was eking out a living off of Social Security and whatever freelance work he could get.[6]

As the redress effort progressed through Congress, there were additional proceedings in the coram nobis cases. A month after Judge Patel's November 1983 oral ruling from the bench, the government filed a notice of its intention to appeal her decision. It asked, however, that it be able to delay the filing of its brief until after she issued her written opinion. She issued that opinion on April 19, 1984, restating her oral ruling, but in more detail. In the opinion, Patel explained that Fred's case was an extraordinary one: "[T]here are few instances in our judicial history when courts have been called upon to undo such profound and publicly acknowledged injustice. Such extraordinary instances require extraordinary relief, and the court is not without power to redress its own errors." She recounted the suppression of the intelligence reports and Edward Ennis's and John L. Burling's warnings regarding the "willful historical inaccuracies and intentional falsehoods" in General DeWitt's *Final Report*. Finding that the courts deciding Fred's case in the early 1940s had before them a selective record, she concluded that the withholding of material evidence provided "ample justification" to vacate Fred's conviction. The government withdrew its appeal in Fred's case on June 21, 1983.[7]

On June 18, 1984, Fred's attorneys filed a motion to recover their attorney's fees and costs from the government. While they had been committed all along to handling Fred's case pro bono, that is, without compensation, federal law allowed the "prevailing party" to recover its fees and costs in certain circumstances. The lawyers were not optimistic about receiving an award, but felt they should at least try; if they were successful, they could perhaps create a community trust fund. Fred submitted a declaration in support of the request: "I know the lawyers on the case worked very long hard hours over these last two years, many times working evenings and weekends. They had to prepare the case, without receiving fees, as well as raise and advance litigation costs and work their own jobs. I believe all of the work they did was necessary and of high quality." In the end, however, the request was denied on the ground that the coram nobis proceeding was a criminal, not civil, case, and so the provisions of the attorneys' fees statute did not apply.[8]

In the months and years following Judge Patel's ruling in his case, Fred and his legal team continued to support Min Yasui's and Gordon Hirabayashi's coram nobis cases. Min's case was set for hearing before Judge Robert C. Belloni on January 16, 1984. Karen Kai flew up to Portland to help Min's attorneys, Peggy Nagae and Don Willner, in preparing their papers; Bob Rusky worked on revisions back in San Francisco. As he had done in Fred's case, Victor Stone of the Justice Department argued that, because the government had agreed to vacate the conviction, it was unnecessary to address the charges of government misconduct. Ten days after the hearing, Judge Belloni issued his order, agreeing with Stone. Min appealed Belloni's decision, but passed away while his case was pending. His widow, True, sought to fulfill Min's deathbed wish that his case continue, but in November 1986 his appeal was dismissed.[9]

Gordon's case was the next to proceed, and Stone took a more aggressive stance. Kathryn Bannai served as initial lead counsel, followed by Rod Kawakami. Fred's attorneys lent their support in any way they could; Bob and Karen flew up to Seattle several times to help. When Stone moved to dismiss Gordon's petition, Judge Donald Voorhees denied the motion and scheduled a full-scale hearing on the claims of misconduct. Rod, joined by Camden Hall, handled the two-week hearing for Gordon, with Edward Ennis, the Justice Department attorney who had valiantly sought to do right during World War II, as their star witness. Stone, remarkably, put on a case that sought to establish that military necessity existed for the wartime orders, calling four military and FBI officials to testify as to the fear of espionage and sabotage. On February 10, 1986, Judge Voorhees vacated Gordon's conviction for violating the removal order but did not vacate his curfew conviction; he reasoned that, because the curfew was a relatively mild intrusion on liberty, the Supreme Court would likely have upheld the curfew conviction even if not lied to. Both the government and Gordon appealed. On September 24, 1987, Judge Mary Schroeder of the Ninth Circuit Court of Appeals ruled that both Gordon's curfew and removal convictions should be vacated.[10] Fred made it to Seattle to join the celebration.

As the redress effort continued in Congress and as the other coram nobis proceedings worked their way through the courts, Fred began to speak extensively about his case. He had promised to work to ensure that people remembered the incarceration to prevent similar injustices, and he kept that promise the rest of his days. Once shy and reluctant to enter the public view, Fred was now glad when he was asked to tell his story; if he did, perhaps others would speak up to defend those who might fall victim to future, similar acts.

He was not a polished speaker. He had a quiet presence—in its profile of Fred, *Biography* magazine described him well as "a slender 5'8" man with a 'modest manner' and 'shy smile.'" At times his talks were a bit disjointed, and audiences followed him into side stories—but, in some ways, all that made him much more an "everyman" that people could relate to. Fred's son, Ken, who inherited Fred's dry sense of humor, said that Fred developed a folksy "'Will Rogers' style, sort of like, 'A funny thing happened to me on the way. . . .'" Fred didn't speak from a script; there was never anything written. He had tried to use written notes, but that just didn't work. Regardless of his lack of oratory skills, however, Fred was always warmly received, and his message was clear. Fred said, "Whenever I am asked to make an appearance, I do because I feel that there are so many people who don't know what happened. I want them to know. . . . I hope this could never happen again. But it could."[11]

Fred traveled the country—often accompanied by members of his legal team, and always with Kathryn. He spoke to students—from grade and high schools to colleges and universities—and before civic organizations, bar associations, and numerous other groups. His audiences were extremely diverse, from every background and walk of life, and the gatherings ranged from large and grand to intimate and personal.

Fred took every opportunity he could to be part of, and support, the Japanese American community from which he had previously felt so isolated. His daughter, Karen, said, "To be accepted by the Asian American community was something he'd always wanted, but he never felt like he could be a part of it [before]." Fred became a regular participant at annual Day of Remembrance events, held on February 19 each year in Nikkei communities across the country, to commemorate the signing of Executive Order 9066. At one such remembrance in March 1998, Fred joined the 150 participants, most former incarcerees and their families, as they carried candles and walked through the streets of San Jose's Japantown.[12]

In November of 1983, Fred visited New York to speak at the celebration of the tenth anniversary of the Asian American Legal Defense and Education Fund (AALDEF) at Lincoln Center and to attend the New York premiere of *Unfinished Business*, Steven Okazaki's Academy Award–nominated documentary on the coram nobis cases. Fred was wowed by New York. AALDEF board member Phil Nash recalls taking Fred and Kathryn to Macy's or some other big department store and being touched by Fred's amazement at the selection of things. He was so well-known, but still such a "small town" guy. The AALDEF event was huge; among the four hundred people present were foreign diplomats, judges (including Nanette Dembitz, who had worked on Fred's case during World War II as a Justice Department attorney with Edward Ennis), other dignitaries, and community members. Fred appealed to the audience: "Let America know what happened, . . . let them know that this should never happen again." He was greeted, as he usually was, with a warm standing ovation both before and after his remarks.[13]

Fred spoke to groups outside of the Japanese American community, as well—not only those who already knew of the incarceration and were partners in fighting injustice, but also to those who did not yet know the story. In May 1986, he spoke at San Francisco's Temple Emanu-El to an audience of six hundred. Rabbi Robert Kirschner addressed the crowd: "The forcible removal of innocent people solely on the basis of their ancestry is an injustice we Jews recognize only too well. We know what it is to be considered alien, to watch backs turn, to hear words of hatred. But we are not the only ones who know these things." Understanding what Fred could teach about citizenship, Judge Patel asked Fred to speak to newly sworn Americans at naturalization ceremonies. At those ceremonies, Judge Patel explained, Fred spoke of the value of citizenship but also reminded those present that "you always have to watch out about protecting your rights."[14]

Fred traveled to schools across the country: the University of Hawai'i, UCLA, Stanford, Berkeley, Seattle University, Western Washington University, Princeton, NYU, Boston College, Amherst, Smith, the University of Chicago, and dozens of others. Of all of the students Fred addressed, he particularly felt it important to speak to students studying law. They would be the lawyers of the future, and Fred believed that they, more than anyone else, would be in positions to protect the civil rights of those who might not be able to protect themselves. In 1988, for example, he visited the American heartland at the University of Iowa School of Law and was overwhelmed by the reception he received from both faculty and students there. Leroy Gee, president of the law school's Asian American Law Student Association, was one of the hundreds of law students Fred would meet in his travels who hosted him with generosity and great affection and admiration.[15]

Everywhere Fred went, law students would tell him how he, his story, and his case had inspired them. Those sentiments were echoed powerfully at the University of Washington School of Law in May 1996—a moment that Fred and Kathryn always remembered fondly. In the middle of a full day of speaking to undergraduate and law students and faculty, Fred was asked to meet over lunch with about a dozen Asian Pacific American law students. So that Fred would have a chance to eat, Associate Dean Tom Andrews asked the students in the conference room if there was anything they would like to say to Fred. One by one, around the room, student after student told Fred that he was the reason they were in law school and that he and what his case had taught them about both the failures and promise of the law carried them through their arduous studies. Kathryn recalls, "They all so seemed to have been touched by his case, and by the time they were finished, I was almost in tears, I really was."[16]

Fred gave the same message whenever he spoke to students: that they needed to do their part to prevent injustice. "I hope this could never happen again. But it could and some [people] think that what the government did was right. They don't understand what happened. . . . Even though it was unconstitutional; you still have to tell them. You have to stay on your toes and be strong. That's what I want all of you kids to do."[17] And, as part of that message, he always encouraged students to enter public service. He had learned many things during his trips to Capitol Hill, but the most important thing was the importance of having diverse voices in positions of power. "The message is that we need more people in public office, in Congress, and in the Senate in Washington. . . . [E]ven judges and so forth, lot of times you have difficult times with judges. They have their own ideas, too, and maybe sometimes it's against the Constitution. They may ignore it, so we gotta be aware of that, too, to get good judges up there. So I say, one thing is, education is very important, and two, not to fool around and really study and get up and get a good position to help out."[18] Kathryn's message to students was similar. Choking back tears, she said she told students to remember "that one person can make a difference, even if it takes forty years."[19]

Fred's message was about so much more than the wartime treatment of Japanese Americans. It was about preventing this country from again compromising civil rights and fundamental freedoms based on fear and ignorance—a message that resonated, and continues to resonate, widely. During the early years of the AIDS crisis, for example, individuals living with AIDS or who were HIV-positive were outcast, and gays were demonized. Conservative political commentator Patrick Buchanan described AIDS as nature's retribution on gays.[20] Presidential candidate Pat Rob-

FIGURE 11.2. Fred addressed students at NYU Law School in April 2000. Kathryn and Fred are on a bench dedicated to John F. Kennedy, Jr., in a courtyard adjacent to the school. Courtesy of Lia Chang.

ertson and Senator Jesse Helms suggested quarantining individuals who were HIV positive.[21] In his essay "AIDS and Mr. Korematsu: Minorities at Times of Crisis," Professor Mark Barnes recalled the Japanese American incarceration and called for care in addressing AIDS so as not to similarly trample on the rights of gays and others facing the disease: "The internments of innocent Japanese Americans demonstrate that governmental powers, being nearly unlimited in perceived or real emergencies and largely insulated from judicial review, ought to be exercised with extreme care and caution, especially when exercised over disadvantaged and heavily stigmatized minorities."[22]

During the Iranian hostage crisis, Iranians living in the United States became targets of public anger and hostility. There was violence against them; some states passed measures to bar Iranian students from their universities; a bumper sticker sold in Texas read, "Let's Play Cowboys and Iranians." In 1980, California Senator S. I. Hayakawa, a Japanese Canadian who was not incarcerated during the war, proposed that the president intern Iranian nationals: "We interned 110,000 Japanese during World War II and we managed that all right."[23]

During the Gulf War, after Iraq invaded Kuwait and the United States intervened, anti-Arab sentiment grew to a fevered pitch.[24] Fred's case was again a cautionary tale. Professor Jamin Raskin wrote in his essay "Remembering Korematsu,"

> The Arabs are the Japanese of 1991. Never mind that Arab-Americans are American citizens and that they are more likely to be the victims than the perpetrators of racial violence. Never mind that most of their leaders have denounced Saddam Hussein and support the demand that Iraqi forces withdraw from Kuwait. There is great uneasiness in the Arab-American community and whiff of a witch hunt in the F.B.I.'s curious "interviews" with Arab-Americans.
>
> Would the Supreme Court today find a violation of the equal protection clause if the government rounded up Arab-Americans or Palestinian-Americans as potential traitors and saboteurs? It is hard to know. . . . But wartime is wartime, and the Rehnquist Court accords much deference to the military's power.
>
> And then there is the strange fact that Korematsu is no dead letter.

The decision is generally condemned, but it has not been overruled. It is a dismal precedent.[25]

Then-congressman Norm Mineta pled, "The U.S. Constitution must not become a casualty of our conflict with Saddam Hussein."[26]

With ominous premonition of what more was to come to Muslims, Arab Americans, other persons of Middle Eastern descent, and individuals who just looked like them, Fred said, "There are Arab Americans today who are going through what Japanese Americans experienced years ago, and we can't let that happen again. I met someone years ago who had never heard of the roundup of Japanese Americans. It's been sixty years since this [arrest] happened, and it's happening again, and that's why I continue to talk about what happened to me."[27]

The terrorist attacks of September 11, 2001, were shattering. This country was attacked on its own soil with tremendous loss of life. As it was after the bombing of Pearl Harbor in 1942, the country was frightened, angry, and desperate to protect itself. Unfortunately, also as it did after Pearl Harbor, the country turned its fright, anger, and desperation on groups already subject to stereotype and suspicion—this time, Muslims, Arab Americans, and anyone else who, it was believed, looked like the enemy. Hate crimes against Arab Americans and Muslims increased dramatically.[28] A majority of the public thought that Arab Americans should be watched more closely, and a sizeable number even felt that the government ought to intern legal immigrants from countries believed to have terrorist ties.[29] Law enforcement began targeting Arab Americans and Muslims. FBI agents sought to enter mosques to conduct interviews and recorded the license plate numbers of cars parked there. Hundreds of individuals were either arrested or detained, and thousands of resident aliens, almost all of them of Middle Eastern descent, were asked to submit to "random questioning."[30] As of November 2001, more than 1,100 people had been detained in the nationwide hunt for terrorists, most of them young men of Middle Eastern descent.[31]

Fred's case was in the news again. While many cited the case as a caution against the targeting of minorities, it was resurrected by at least one conservative group as support for the government's actions. The *New York Times* reported,

After nearly two months of criticism by civil liberties groups about the Bush Administration's antiterrorism crackdown, supporters of the measures have begun to outline a legal defense of the actions, saying that the president has broad powers to protect national security in wartime and that accusations of rights violations have been overblown. . . .

Lawyers supporting the administration say the critics have ignored Supreme Court precedents that approved such extreme wartime actions as the internment of Japanese-Americans in World War II. "The precedents are overwhelmingly in favor of what the president is doing," says Richard A. Samp, chief counsel of the conservative Washington Legal Foundation.[32]

In February 2003, Congressman Howard Coble, chairman of the Judiciary Subcommittee on Crime, Terrorism, and Homeland Security, stated that he agreed with President Franklin D. Roosevelt's decision to intern Japanese Americans during WWII. "Some were probably intent on doing harm to us, just as some of these Arab Americans are probably intent on doing harm to us."[33] Furthermore, despite an enormous body of authority to the contrary, some conservative commentators even attempted to rewrite the historical record, arguing both that the incarceration was justified and that we cannot protect civil rights to the sacrifice of national security.[34] Again, sixty years after the incarceration of Japanese Americans, the country was vilifying, and the government was detaining, individuals based on their ethnic affiliations. Again, suspicion was cast on individuals who "looked like" the enemy.[35]

Fred's efforts to educate the public took on new urgency. People needed to remember that the country had gone down this path before and had come to regret how it had sacrificed its values. Just two months before the 9/11 attacks, filmmaker Eric Fournier's documentary about Fred's life and cases, *Of Civil Wrongs and Rights*, premiered on PBS, and after 9/11, requests that Fred accompany the film and speak about his case increased. Fred, Kathryn, and Eric—and often Karen and son-in-law Donald Haigh—traveled from city to city across the country to share Fred's story.[36] Among those talks was an address in 2002 at the invitation of the Robert H. Jackson Center in New York, a center dedicated to preserving the legacy of the justice who had written one of the scathing dissents in Fred's World War II case.[37]

Fred contributed his voice to the public debate on the extent to which civil liberties should be compromised in the name of national security. In 2004, conservative commentator Michelle Malkin argued that the Japanese American incarceration had been justified and that using the incarceration to criticize the government's actions in the war on terror jeopardized homeland security. Fred responded,

> It is painful to see reopened for serious debate the question of whether the government was justified in imprisoning Japanese Americans during World War II. It was my hope that my case and the cases of other Japanese American internees would be remembered for the dangers of racial and ethnic scapegoating.
>
> Fears and prejudices directed against minority communities are too easy to evoke and exaggerate, often to serve the political agendas of those who promote those fears. I know what it is like to be at the other end of such scapegoating and how difficult it is to clear one's name after unjustified suspicions are endorsed as fact by the government. If someone is a spy or terrorist they should be prosecuted for their actions. But no one should ever be locked away simply because they share the same race, ethnicity, or religion as a spy or terrorist. If that principle was not learned from the internment of Japanese Americans, then these are very dangerous times for our democracy.[38]

Also in 2004, Fred appeared as an amicus, or a "friend of the court," in two briefs filed before the U.S. Supreme Court arguing the danger of sacrificing individual rights in the name of national security. In *Rasul v. Bush*, detainees at Guantanamo Bay were held incommunicado, without charges or access to counsel, and with no opportunity to contest their confinement. When they sued, the government argued that the courts had no power to hear their claims. Reflecting on his own experience, Fred's brief—in which two of his coram nobis lawyers, Eric Yamamoto and Dale Minami, participated—urged that the courts hear those claims to prevent the government from having carte blanche to compromise basic rights. "History teaches that, in time of war, we have often sacrificed fundamental freedoms *unnecessarily*. The executive and legislative branches, reflecting public opinion formed in the heat of the moment, frequently have overestimated the need to restrict civil liberties and failed to consider alternative ways to protect the national security. Courts, which are not immune to the demands of public opinion, have too often deferred to exaggerated claims of military necessity and failed to insist that measures curtailing constitutional rights be carefully justified and narrowly tailored."[39] The United States Supreme Court held that the government could not shield its actions from court review; the Guantanamo detainees did, indeed, have the right to have their claims heard.[40] In another case that year, *Rumsfeld v. Padilla*, Fred joined others in arguing that Jose Padilla, an American citizen arrested on U.S. soil, could not be subject to indefinite military detention and was entitled to due process guaranteed him on account of his citizenship.[41]

For his work seeking to advance justice and for what he had come to symbolize, Fred received countless recognitions and honors. In 1983, in great twist of irony, the Northern California ACLU asked Fred if he would accept its Earl Warren Civil Liberties Award, to be given to him, Gordon, and Min for their courageous stands during World War II. Fred at first felt that he could not accept an award named for Warren, who had advocated for the wartime removal of Japanese Americans. In its letter asking Fred to accept the award, the affiliate itself noted, "P.S. We are most aware that the title of our Award may appear to be a misnomer. However, at the time the Award was established, it was (and is) our intent to name it after the great Chief Justice of the U.S. Supreme Court—not the earlier, lesser, Attorney General and Governor of the State of California. We hope you can appreciate the irony." Fred agreed to accept the award.[42]

The day before Fred received the honor, he went to visit Ernest Besig. It had been over forty years since they had last met, but they greeted each other like old friends—with deep affection and great mutual respect. Fred asked Besig what he should say about Besig in accepting the ACLU award. Besig, then seventy-nine years old and still spry enough to be working on his tennis game, replied, "You can tell them I thought it was unconstitutional then, and I still think it's unconstitutional." In addressing the crowd and accepting the award the following night, Fred said, "I will never forget the ACLU of Northern California, for you were the only organization which stood by me forty-one years ago. . . . Words alone cannot express the deep appreciation I feel for the support which the ACLU has given me."[43]

Fred was recognized by other organizations representing a diverse range

FIGURE 11.3. Fred and his WWII attorney, Ernest Besig, January 7, 1989. Photo by Shirley Nakao. Courtesy of Karen Korematsu and the Fred T. Korematsu Institute.

of constituencies and interests—his fights were their fights, as well. On June 30, 1998, for example, he received the Pearlstein Civil Rights Award from the central Pacific region of the Anti-Defamation League.[44] In 1999, at a star-studded event in Beverly Hills celebrating Jesse Jackson's birthday, Fred received a Rainbow PUSH Coalition Trailblazer Award, which honors movers and shakers committed to social justice.[45] In addition, Fred, who was never able to finish college as a young man, donned a cap and gown as he received each of four honorary degrees.[46]

On January 15, 1998, Fred received the Presidential Medal of Freedom— the nation's highest civilian honor—from President Bill Clinton. Fred, of course, appreciated the acknowledgement of his efforts on behalf of causes he believed in, but the medal meant more than that to him. It was further a tribute to the strength and endurance of all Japanese Americans who had,

FIGURE 11.4. Fred and civil rights icon Rosa Parks, meeting as Parks was honored by the Northern California ACLU, December 1988. Photo by Shirley Nakao. Courtesy of Karen Korematsu and the Fred T. Korematsu Institute.

along with Fred, experienced the camps and gone on to rebuild their lives. And it was another way for the country, from the highest office in government, to pledge that it would not forget what it had done.

The day was extraordinary. Fred was one of fifteen individuals receiving the Medal of Freedom that day. Prior to the ceremony, the Korematsus, assigned a member of the military who served as a White House attaché, waited with other groups in the Blue Room of the White House. When Donna Shalala, then secretary of health and human services, came in to visit, she extended her hand to Ken, who was so sick he refused to shake it. "I've got the flu," he said, "I can't shake anybody's hand, and I don't want to kill the president." She said, "Don't worry, President Clinton has all his shots." When President and Mrs. Clinton approached, the president extended his hand to Fred and said, "Mr. Korematsu, It's an honor to meet you. It was a very brave thing that you did to stand up against the government."[47]

The gathering moved to the East Room for the ceremony. The Marine Corps band played "Pomp and Circumstance" in the foyer. Three or four rows of press were in the back. As the ceremony began, President Clinton explained the significance of the day and the singular distinction of the individuals being honored. Fred was in remarkable company.

> It is fitting that today this ceremony occurs on the birthday of Dr. Martin Luther King, Jr., who 21 years ago was granted the award by President Carter posthumously. . . . Humanity makes progress through decades of sweat and toil by dedicated individuals who give freely of themselves and who inspire others to do the same, the kind of heroic men and women we honor today. All of our honorees have helped America to widen the circle of democracy by fighting for human rights, by righting social wrongs, by empowering others to achieve, by preserving our precious environment, by extending peace around the world. Every person here has done so by rising in remarkable ways to American's highest calling, the calling . . . of active citizenship.[48]

Clinton then called and introduced each honoree. When Fred's name was called and he stepped forward, the president paid him this tribute:

> In 1942 an ordinary American took an extraordinary stand. Fred Korematsu boldly opposed the forced internment of Japanese-Americans during World War II. After being convicted for failing to report for relocation, Mr. Korematsu took his case all the way to the Supreme Court. The high court ruled against him. But 39 years later, he had his conviction overturned in Federal court, empowering tens of thousands of Japanese-Americans and giving him what he said he wanted most of all, the chance to feel like an American once again. In the long history of our country's constant search for justice, some names of ordinary citizens stand for millions of souls . . . Plessy, Brown, Parks. . . . To that distinguished list, today we add the name of Fred Korematsu.[49]

FIGURE 11.5. Fred receiving the Presidential Medal of Freedom from President Bill Clinton, January 15, 1998. Courtesy of William J. Clinton Presidential Library.

The citation Fred received read, "An American who wanted only to be treated like every other American, Fred Korematsu challenged our nation's conscience, reminding us that we must uphold the rights of our own citizens even as we fight tyranny in other lands. . . . A man of quiet bravery, Fred Korematsu deserves our respect and thanks for his patient pursuit to preserve the civil liberties we hold dear." Fred received a standing ovation. Even the press corps stood.[50]

Fred told Karen that he accepted the medal for everyone who had been incarcerated. And he wished his parents could have been there that day.[51] Dale remarked, "It's a beautiful irony. He is being honored for what he was in prison for 56 years ago." The *San Francisco Examiner* was glad to see Fred's wartime stance officially acknowledged: "The U.S. government waited too

FIGURE 11.6. Fred and his daughter, Karen, after receiving the Presidential Medal of Freedom. Photo by Shirley Nakao. Courtesy of Karen Korematsu and the Fred T. Korematsu Institute.

long to do full justice to the courage of Fred Korematsu, who as a 22-year-old Oakland native stood in lonely defiance of the order sending 120,000 Japanese Americans into internment during World War II."[52]

While most members of the Japanese American community celebrated the recognition of Fred, some, sadly, did not. Japanese American columnist Bill Hosokawa asked, "Why is the president honoring Korematsu?" Hosokawa complained that Fred had not resisted as an act of civil disobedience, like Gordon and Min; Fred's motives for resisting removal were simply "personal."[53] In later years, John Tateishi shared his response when he heard similar criticisms of Fred: "You don't criticize someone for something that he or she does trying to maintain what they know is right in their life. . . . Sometimes love is as good or maybe a better reason. . . . [When I heard members of Congress] talk about Fred in personal ways like that . . ., the denigration of the man was to me an insult of the community. . . . Who the hell do you think you are to insult this guy like that, to denigrate what he did?"[54]

But others within the Japanese American community joined in the tribute to Fred. JACL national director Herbert Yamanishi remarked, "Out of [Fred's] case, it became evident that the camp experience was because of racism, not because of military necessity." Nikkei Congressman Bob Matsui said that Fred had "animated a national conscience to redress an injustice perpetrated upon citizens by their own government. . . . Every American today and in the future owes Fred a debt of gratitude for his efforts to guarantee that no citizen, regardless of their ancestry, can be denied due process and the basic liberties guaranteed by our Constitution."[55]

Fred's life had changed in many ways since that first phone call from Peter Irons in 1982. Once reluctant to speak in public, Fred spoke all over the country, meeting new people and inspiring students. And, after the stain of his conviction had been erased, Fred became more extroverted and seemed more content. His brother Joe saw that Fred became more animated. Fred's niece Joanne also noticed the change. "He was more engaged and able to talk about his case and he laughed more. I could see that he had real purpose . . . he could see why it was important for him to be able to speak up." The relationship between Fred and his son Ken, which had once been somewhat tumultuous, mellowed. In the late 1980s, Fred took up golf; Ken recalls the times he and Fred walked the fairways and Fred would tell him stories of his days in camp and his early years in Oakland—and he'd laugh when he thought his stories were funny. "The best time I had with my father was when we played golf towards the end, before he hurt his back and couldn't play anymore. Those are good times for me, and it was like, you know . . . that was more of a friendlier and happy time that we did something together. . . . That was a good father and son thing for me."[56]

Although Fred had changed in some ways, in the most important ways, he had not changed at all. For all the people he met, famous and not famous, and all the things he did, from traveling to the White House to stuffing envelopes in the campaign for redress, Fred remained the same person he had always been. People seemed struck by his "ordinariness," Kathryn recalled. "In other words, he never was an egotist . . . he's not pompous, he's just Fred. Lots of people, you know, [were] kind of mystified, I think, when they met him. He never pretended to be anything that he wasn't. And of all the honors that were heaped upon him, he never once thought he was the cat's meow or anything of that sort. . . . He took it all in stride." Karen related that "Everyone was always so honored to meet him and they wanted his autograph and to have their picture taken with him. And he just, he was very humble about the whole thing." As legal team member Leigh-Ann Miyasato observed, "People [could] really relate to him because he is an 'every man,' you know, who somehow found the strength to stand up for what he believed was right. I think people really respect that kind of courage."[57]

Indeed, Fred's belief that he was, and should be treated, just like everyone else was what had driven his original decision to refuse the removal orders. He did not view himself as a hero or exceptional person. He simply did what he felt was right. Attorney Holly English wrote of her interview with Fred, "In the course of his interview, Korematsu waived away words of admiration as if physically shielding his face from the limelight. He is clearly uneasy with the 'hero' label, and not merely because of modesty. . . . [H]e seems to resist glorification because, in his view, he never should have been a hero merely for conducting his life as did every other American citizen. His larger point, which he repeated quietly over and over, is that he is 'just like anybody else,' and should have been treated that way."[58]

Fred asked for little for himself. Most everything he did was for others. He rarely took vacations; most all of the traveling he did in his later years was to speak about his case. When Karen told him that she and her husband Donald wanted to take Fred and Kathryn to Japan in 2000, it was the first time Karen saw him tear up. Although he was concerned about going because he didn't speak the language, he was curious about his parents' homeland. He was the only member of his family who had never been there, and he never thought he'd be able to go. While there, Karen was able to locate Fred's cousin, Yoshiaki Korematsu, Kakusaburo's nephew, who, to Fred's surprise, knew about his case. When the families met in Fukuoka, Kakusaburo and Kotsui's home province, Yoshiaki showed Fred a news seg-

Fred Korematsu

FIGURE 11.7. Fred in one of his last public appearances, speaking at a commemoration of the sixtieth anniversary of the Japanese American wartime cases, November 2004. Courtesy of the Japanese American National Museum.

ment about Fred's case that he had recorded.[59] As Kathryn recalled, there was a lot of sign language during the meeting, but it was a special time filled with warm hospitality. Fred loved Japan; there were happy connections. Donald took him to see a samurai movie, just like the ones Fred had enjoyed growing up in Oakland. And the food reminded him of the food that his mother cooked.

Fred's health began to wane in the last years of his life. He continued, however, to travel as much as he could to speak about his case, accompanied by Karen, Donald, or Eric Fournier, who attended to Fred's and Kathryn's needs. In one of his last talks, in November 2004, Fred spoke at a commemoration of the sixtieth anniversary of the wartime Supreme Court Japanese American incarceration cases at the Japanese American National Museum in Los Angeles. He was frail and thin. As he sat with legal team member Lori Bannai on the dais before they both spoke, Lori became worried that he was not well and sought eye contact with Karen, who was in the audience. Fred started his remarks slowly and tentatively, but within minutes of starting, he seemed to rise in both stature and energy, nourished by the audience, their welcome, and the ovation they gave him.[60]

On March 30, 2005, at the age of eighty-six, Fred slipped away peacefully at Karen's home. He had developed pneumonia, and as much as he fought to get better, he couldn't fight any more. Letters and e-mails of condolence and official commendations poured in from across the country from public officials, organizations, and friends. News of his passing, accompanied by remembrances of him and tributes, were carried far and wide. There were about seven hundred in attendance at his service; people flew in from everywhere. Kathryn, Karen, and Ken were particularly grateful that the members of the extended Korematsu clan were there. Fred was the last remaining Korematsu brother, and now he was gone. Judge Patel was among the dignitaries present, and Fred's legal team was there. The audience joined together in singing "America the Beautiful," which Kathryn had selected as the final hymn:

> It was really because of what it said about brotherhood. . . . Going to school in Charlotte, North Carolina, at assembly, we were singing that song, and I often wondered what brotherhood was. I didn't know anybody that was a different race from me. . . . After I met Japanese Americans who had come out of camp from the war, [I read Carey McWilliams's book] *Brothers Under the Skin*, and then I understood what brotherhood really was. . . . I knew it from the song that it was something bigger than the people I knew. . . . [Japanese Americans] who were really brothers under the skin . . . were treated as non-citizens. . . . "And crown thy good with brotherhood from sea to shining sea." Each verse had something in it that spoke about Fred.

Legal team member Ed Chen, now a federal judge, was moved to tears. After the service he told Kathryn that he would never hear the song in quite the same way again. He was moved, in part, because the song described the America he knew Fred envisioned—an America whose promised beauty he sought to fulfill, one true to its founding principles. For the postlude, played as the service ended, the minister, so appropriately, selected "Tribute to the Common Man" by Aaron Copeland.[61]

Fred is buried at Mountain View Cemetery high up in the Oakland Hills in a beautiful, peaceful spot under a pine tree. Standing there, looking over the San Francisco Bay, one can almost imagine it all: the ferry Kakusaburo took each dawn to transport his flowers to market; Fred and Walt camping nearby as teenage boys; Japanese Americans gathered at street corners waiting to be taken away to San Bruno, visible just across the bay, and then so far away; Fred being handcuffed and arrested in 1942; and then, forty years later, returning home after his hearing before Judge Patel, his community grateful and his name cleared. Fred had seen and led a remarkable and good life.

EPILOGUE

SINCE FRED'S PASSING, THE RELEVANCE OF HIS LIFE AND CASE
has only grown. His story has remained important as the nation has continued to try to heal the wounds of the wartime incarceration. On May 20, 2011,
for example, Acting Solicitor General Neal Katyal publicly acknowledged
the improper actions of his World War II predecessor, Charles Fahy, when
arguing Fred's case before the Supreme Court. In his blog post "Confession
of Error: The Solicitor General's Mistakes during the Japanese-American Internment Cases," Katyal explained that while solicitor generals have played
important roles throughout history in advancing civil rights, "it is also important to remember the mistakes."

Citing the evidence presented in Fred Korematsu's and Gordon Hirabayashi's coram nobis cases, Katyal related that Fahy was aware of "key
intelligence reports that undermined the rationale behind the internment" but failed to disclose those reports to the Court. "And to make matters worse," Katyal continued, "[Fahy] relied on gross generalizations about
Japanese Americans, such as they were disloyal and motivated by 'racial
solidarity.'" He concluded, "Today, our Office takes this history as an important reminder that the 'special credence' the Solicitor General enjoys
before the Supreme Court requires great responsibility and a duty of absolute candor in our representations to the Court. Only then can we fulfill
our responsibility to defend the United States and its Constitution, and to
protect the rights of all Americans." Peter Irons commented that he thought

the statement was "good and very long overdue." "This was a deliberate, knowing lie by Fahy to the Supreme Court. For the nation's highest counsel to make that statement now is quite noteworthy and admirable."[1]

Fred's words have further echoed hauntingly as the country has continued to grapple with issues of race, profiling, and the protection of civil liberties during times of crisis. For example, provisions of the National Defense Authorization Act (NDAA) again raise the specter of indefinite military detention without charges or trial, and Fred's name and case have been invoked to warn of the danger of compromising due process guarantees. Section 1021 of the NDAA of 2012, still in effect, affirms the authority of the military to indefinitely detain individuals who, in the judgment of military authorities, are considered to have "substantially supported" terrorist organizations. Many criticize that this language is so vague it would allow the indefinite detention of innocent individuals, including American citizens, if the military believed them to be "supporting" terrorism, without charges or trial or other judicial review.[2]

In support of legislation to require due process protections, Senator Dianne Feinstein recalled before the Senate Judiciary Committee how her father had taken her to see the wartime detention center at Tanforan when she was a young girl. There, she saw the throng of Japanese Americans held in confinement "for no reason other than that we were at war with Japan." She said, "I think I didn't really realize the impact of that until many years later. It remains in my view as a dark stain on our history and our values and also something we should never repeat." She reminded the committee of Fred, to warn of the need to check the exercise of military discretion:

> I want to be very clear about what this bill is and what it's not about. It's not about whether [those] who would do us harm should be captured, interrogated, incarcerated, and severely punished. They should be.
>
> But what about an innocent American like Fred Korematsu or other Japanese Americans during World War II? What about someone in the wrong place at that wrong time, who gets picked up and held without charge or trial until the end of hostilities—and who knows when these hostilities will end? The Federal government experimented with the indefinite detention of United States citizens during World War II—a mistake that we now recognize as a betrayal of our core values.

Lori Bannai, a member of Fred's legal team, testified at the same hearing, asking that the country not forget the camps of World War II.

The lessons of the Japanese American incarceration are many. . . . First, of course, is the real, tangible meaning of the guarantee of Due Process. . . . During World War II, persons of Japanese ancestry were incarcerated without any due process. . . . There were no charges brought against them; they had no hearings [and] the rule of law was suspended. We are now confronted with new fears against new peoples, and, while we do need to ferret out and prosecute criminal conduct, we need to do so in a way that preserves our system of laws.

Second, the Japanese American incarceration teaches us about the danger of unfettered discretion. Seventy years ago this month, on February 19, 1942, President . . . Roosevelt essentially issued the War Department and military authorities a blank check, delegating to them the authority to take whatever actions they deemed necessary against whomever they saw fit. Pursuant to this authority, General John L. DeWitt . . . issued orders subjecting Japanese Americans to curfew and then removal from the West Coast and into indefinite detention. . . .

Finally, the wartime incarceration of Japanese Americans teaches us about human frailty during times of crisis. Those who played roles in the incarceration were smart and educated, and saw themselves as devoted public servants who thought that they were doing what was in the best interests of the country. Many came to later regret their decisions. . . . In this regard, we are warned to ensure that executive and military decisions are checked by the civil branches of government and constitutional limits. This is particularly true in times of crisis when fear and racism can infect responsible judgment.[3]

When the NDAA was challenged in court in *Hedges v. Obama*, Fred's children, Karen and Ken (in a brief drafted by Fred's legal team members Eric Yamamoto, Lori Bannai, and Bob Rusky) joined Gordon's and Min's children in asking that the courts remember their fathers' cases and not again allow military detention without due process.[4]

Karen has carried on her father's work, educating others about the lessons to be learned from his case and seeking to preserve his legacy. As executive director of the Fred T. Korematsu Institute in San Francisco, she speaks out against threats to civil rights such as the indefinite detention provisions of the NDAA. She is involved in recognitions of her father, such as the installation of his photographs in the National Portrait Gallery. She has seen four schools named for him. One of those schools is the Fred T. Korematsu Discovery Academy, a K–5 school focused on math and science opened on the site of Stonehurst Elementary School, the school that Fred and his brothers attended as children. Karen travels the country providing trainings and curriculum packets to teachers to help them educate their students on the wartime incarceration.[5]

Karen has further been involved in efforts to recognize Fred's birthday, January 30, as a day for public reflection on the constitutional rights he fought so hard to protect. On September 23, 2010, Governor Arnold Schwarzenegger signed legislation recognizing Fred's birthday as Fred Korematsu Day of Civil Liberties and the Constitution in California, the first time in U.S. history that a day has been named for an Asian American. Six other states have also recognized Fred's birthday as a day to remember the wartime incarceration. The U.S. Commission on Civil Rights has urged that the president and Congress create a national holiday in Fred's honor.[6]

Two other endeavors also work in Fred's name to advance the causes he stood for—equal rights and healing historic injustice—extending his fight for social justice to other contexts, on behalf of other communities, both nationally and internationally.[7] In 2009, the Fred T. Korematsu Center for Law and Equality was founded at Seattle University School of Law. The Korematsu Center, under the leadership of center executive director Bob Chang and director (and Korematsu legal team member) Lori Bannai, seeks to advance Fred's legacy through civil rights litigation, including the filing of amicus briefs; policy work; research; and other programs. In Fred's name, the center has, among other projects, fought an Arizona statute used to dismantle Tucson's successful Mexican American Studies program, criticized the use of national origin profiles, and addressed issues of racial bias in the criminal justice system.[8]

In addition, in 2012, the University of Hawai'i School of Law named Korematsu legal team member Eric Yamamoto its inaugural Fred T. Korematsu Professor of Law and Social Justice. In his work, Eric contributes to amicus briefs and political initiatives calling for judicial vigilance in the delicate balance of national security and civil liberties, and advocates for the support of reconciliation and reparation efforts abroad. Most recently, he has worked on redress with officials and communities in Jeju, South Korea, to heal persisting wounds of U.S.-related injustice.[9] Both the center and professorship seek to train law students in social justice advocacy, making education central to their missions, just as it was central to Fred's.

Fred's journey and message continue to be important in many ways. His call for vigilance is as relevant now as it ever was and will remain so as long as individuals are targeted based on stereotypes and fear. As recently as February 3, 2014, at a session with students at the University of Hawai'i School of Law, Supreme Court Justice Antonin Scalia stated his belief that something like the wartime Japanese American incarceration could happen again. When asked about Fred's World War II case, he replied, "Of course *Korematsu* was wrong. . . . But you are kidding yourself if you think the same thing will not happen again. . . . That's what was going on—the panic about the war and the invasion of the Pacific and whatnot. That's what happens. It was wrong, but I would not be surprised to see it happen again, in time of war. It's no justification, but it is the reality."[10] Scalia's words would have been chilling to Fred, who was always fearful that history would repeat itself.

But Fred's story remains important not only for the warning it provides. It also reminds us of what we, each of us, can do to advance justice. Fred didn't have lots of money, an advanced education, or great political influence; what he had was a power and grace that grew from a commitment to live by his principles, to refuse unfairness and injustice, and to stand up for others. His story reminds us that we, each of us, have the ability to make those same commitments, and if we do, our communities and country will be all the better for it.

FIGURE E.1. Fred Korematsu, January 30, 1919–March 30, 2005. Courtesy of Lia Chang.

NOTES

The following abbreviations and shortened forms denote the following sources:

CWRIC   U.S. Commission on Wartime Relocation and Internment of Civilians. Citations are made to testimony received by the commission by indicating the witness, the date, and the city in which the testimony was received. Documents collected and held in the commission's records are cited by CWRIC document number. Also cited are the commission's report *Personal Justice Denied*, and the short addendum that contains the commission's recommendations.

Densho   Interviews conducted by Densho: The Japanese American Legacy Project. Available at http://www.densho.org/.

Korematsu **Coram Nobis Litigation Collection.**   Documents of the legal team that successfully reopened Fred Korematsu's case in 1982, catalogued as Collection No. 545 and located in the Dept. of Special Collections, Charles E. Young Research Library, UCLA.

NARA–SF   National Archives and Records Administration at San Francisco, 1000 Commodore Drive, San Bruno, CA 94066.

NCCLU, CHS   Records of the Northern California Civil Liberties Union, located at the California Historical Society, San Francisco, CA.

Personal Justice Denied   Report of the U.S. Commission on Wartime Relocation and Internment of Civilians (CWRIC), Congress of 1980, originally published in 1982 by the Government Printing Office and republished in 1997 by the Civil Liberties Public Education Fund & University of Washington Press.

Transcript of record to WWII Supreme Court.   A thirty-one-page compilation of trial and appellate court documents constituting the record before the Supreme

Court in the World War II *Korematsu v. United States* case, including the record of the trial proceedings, microformed on United States Supreme Court Records and Briefs, 323 U.S. 214, 1944 (Microform, Inc.). Many of the separate documents contained in this record can also be found in the *Korematsu v. United States* court files at the National Archives–Pacific Region (NARA-SF), ARC Criminal Case Files, 1935–1951, Case No. 27635, *Korematsu v. United States*, 9NS-21-91-008, U.S. District Courts for the San Francisco Division of the Northern District of California, Record Group 21, Records of the District Court of the United States.

PREFACE

1   Gordon Hirabayashi refused to comply with the curfew and removal orders, Hirabayashi v. United States, 320 U.S. 81 (1943), *conviction vacated*, 828 F.2d 591 (9th Cir. 1987), and Minoru Yasui refused to comply with the curfew orders, Yasui v. United States, 320 U.S. 115 (1943), *conviction vacated as noted in* Yasui v. United States, 772 F.2d 1496, 1498 (9th Cir. 1985). Others challenged the wartime orders in other ways. Mitsuye Endo and Ernest and Toki Wakayama filed petitions for writs of habeas corpus seeking release from their wrongful incarceration. See Ex Parte Endo, 323 U.S. 283 (1944); Elaine Elinson and Stan Yogi, *Wherever There's a Fight* (Berkeley, CA: Heyday Books, 2009), 428–30 (discussing Wakayama case). And some objected by refusing to swear loyalty to, or to serve in, the armed forces of the country that had imprisoned them. See *infra*, chapter 6.

CHAPTER 1. THE SON OF IMMIGRANTS, BUT ALL-AMERICAN

1   "Individual Record," Kakusaburo Korematsu WRA records, Nov. 9, 1942, National Archives and Records Administration, Washington, DC; Kay Korematsu, interview by author, May 26, 2008; passenger list of the *USS Doric* for Oct. 17, 1904, microfiche, A 3422, Roll 6, "Passenger Lists of Vessels Arriving at Honolulu, HI, 1900–1953," NARA-SF. Kakusaburo's father was Shinzaburo Korematsu of Kataya-Mura, Itshima-Gun, Fukuoka, Japan. Kotsui Korematsu immigration records, File 13177/15-1, "Immigration Arrival Investigation Case Files, 1884–1944," San Francisco District Office, RG 85, records of the Immigration and Naturalization Service, NARA-SF (hereafter cited as Kotsui Korematsu immigration file). For a discussion of the emigration of young Japanese men to work in the sugar plantations of Hawai'i, see Sucheng Chan, *Asian Americans: An Interpretive History* (Boston: Twayne Publishers, 1991), 9–12, 38; Ronald Takaki, *Strangers from a Different Shore: A History of Asian Americans* (Boston: Little, Brown and Company, 1989), 42–45, 132. Hawai'i was a territory of the United States from 1900 to 1959. Chan, *Asian Americans*, 3.

2   Kay Korematsu, interview by author, May 26, 2008. Passenger list of the *SS Alameda*, sailing Apr. 26, 1905, from Honolulu, Hawai'i, to San Francisco, California,

National Archives Microfilm Publication M1494, Roll 1, "Passenger Lists of Vessels Arriving at San Francisco From Honolulu, 1902–1907," records of the Immigration and Naturalization Service, RG 85, NARA-SF; Petition for Naturalization of Kakusaburo Korematsu, no. 104846, "Petitions for Naturalization, 1903–1991" (ARC ID # 605234), NARA-SF (hereafter cited as Kakusaburo Korematsu naturalization petition). For a discussion of working conditions in the plantation camps and the emigration of Japanese from Hawai'i to the West Coast, see Gary Y. Okihiro, *Cane Fires: The Anti-Japanese Movement in Hawaii, 1865–1945* (Philadelphia: Temple University Press, 1991), 33–35; Takaki, *Strangers*, 26–27, 133–42, 147–48 (by early 1907, forty thousand Japanese had left Hawai'i for the West Coast); Chan, *Asian Americans*, 36–37; Yukiko Kimura, *Issei: Japanese Immigrants in Hawaii* (Honolulu: University of Hawai'i Press, 1988), 89.

3 For a general discussion of the early history of anti-Asian and anti-Japanese agitation in the mainland United States, see Roger Daniels, *The Politics of Prejudice*, 2nd ed. (Berkeley: University of California Press, 1962); Takagi, *Strangers*, 179–82, 197–212; Chan, *Asian Americans*, 45–61. For personal accounts of the discrimination that Issei encountered on the mainland, see, e.g., Eileen Sunada Sarasohn, *The Issei: Portrait of a Pioneer, An Oral History* (Palo Alto, CA: Pacific Books, 1983). Nisuke Mitsumori, for example, recalls being pelted by horse dung and called a "Jap" on his arrival in San Francisco in 1905. Ibid., 59.

4 Daniels, *Politics*, 21, quoting *San Francisco Examiner*, May 8, 1900; *San Francisco Chronicle*, May 8, 1900. Phelan's words were later echoed in 1943 when the Supreme Court noted the failure of Japanese Americans to assimilate as supporting the argument that they had strong ties with Japan. *Hirabayashi*, 320 U.S. 81, 96–98. See further discussion of the *Hirabayashi* decision, *infra*, chapter 6.

5 For an excellent overview of key court decisions that served to exclude Japanese Americans and other Asian Americans from civic life, see Eric Yamamoto et al., *Race, Rights, and Reparation: Law and the Japanese American Internment*, 2nd ed. (New York: Wolters Kluwer Law & Business, 2013), 23–81.

6 Daniels recounts headlines from the *San Francisco Chronicle* in 1905 depicting the Issei as a scourge on society: for example, "Crime and Poverty Go Hand in Hand with Asiatic Labor," "Japanese a Menace to American Women," and "The Yellow Peril How Japanese Crowd Out the White Race." *San Francisco Chronicle* headlines, in Daniels, *Politics*, 25, quoting *San Francisco Chronicle*, Feb. 23–Mar. 13, 1905.

7 Daniels, *Politics*, 27–28, quoting Asiatic Exclusion League, "Proceedings" (San Francisco, 1907–1912), Mar. 1910, pp. 13–14.

8 For a history of the events leading up to the "Gentlemen's Agreement," see Daniels, *Politics*, 31–45; Frank Chuman, *The Bamboo People: The Law and Japanese-Americans* (Del Mar, CA: Publisher's Inc., 1976), 18–27.

9 Kay Korematsu, interview by author, May 25, 2008. "Self-employment was not an Asian 'cultural trait' or an occupation peculiar to 'strangers' but a means of survival, a response to racial discrimination and exclusion in the labor market." Takaki, *Strangers*, 13.

10 Fred Korematsu, interview by Lorraine Bannai and Tetsuden Kashima, Seattle, May 14, 1996, Densho Visual Histories, http://archive.densho.org/main.aspx. After arriving in San Francisco, Kakusaburo had gotten work with an Italian American nurseryman in San Leandro and saved until he could start his own business. Kathryn Korematsu, interview by author, May 22, 2008. For an account of prewar life within the San Francisco Bay Area Japanese American flower nursery community, see Gary Kawaguchi, *Living with Flowers: The California Flower Market History* (San Francisco: California Flower Market, 1993); Yoshimi Shibata, *Across Two Worlds: Memoirs of a Nisei Flower Grower* (San Jose, CA: Mt. Eden Floral Company, 2006).

11 Although property records do not exist for 1913, other records suggest that Kakusaburo purchased his property that year. "K. Korematsu" was not assessed in 1912 for the nursery's property at 10800 Edes Avenue in Oakland, California, but he was assessed in 1914. Kathleen DiGiovanni (Oakland History Room at the Oakland Public Library), e-mail to author, July 15, 2008. Many Issei circumvented the Alien Land Law, at least temporarily, by placing property in the names of their American-born children. In 1920, exclusionists won a state-wide initiative to "plug the loopholes" in the 1913 law. Daniels, *Politics*, 88–90. For commentary on the Alien Land Law, Chapter 113, California Statutes 206, 1913, see Daniels, *Politics*, 63; and Edwin E. Ferguson, "The California Alien Land Law and the Fourteenth Amendment," *California Law Review* 35 (1947): 67.

Japanese immigrants were deemed not eligible for naturalization in the 1922 Supreme Court case *Ozawa v. United States*, which reasoned that the original framers in 1790 intended to confer the privileges of citizenship only on persons they knew as white. Ozawa v. United States, 260 U.S. 178, 197 (1922); see also Devon W. Carbado, "Yellow by Law," *California Law Review* 97 (2009): 633–91, which addresses how Ozawa was "made" yellow by the courts. Japanese immigrants would not be eligible for naturalization until 1952, with the passage of the McCarran-Walter Act, Public Law No. 82-414, 66 Stat. 163 (1952). As Professor Yuji Ichioka explains, the inability to become citizens denied the Issei not only the ability to own land; it denied them the ability to become full participants in American society. Although beleaguered, European immigrants, with the right to naturalization, were able to enter the political arena and fight for their rights; Japanese immigrants, however, could not. Yuji Ichioka, *The Issei: The World of the First Generation Japanese Immigrants, 1885–1924* (New York: Free Press, 1988), 1–2.

12 Japanese women began to arrive in the United States in significant numbers between 1900 and 1920, and many, though not all, were picture brides. In 1900, there were only 985 women in the total Japanese immigrant population of 24,236. By 1910, the population of Japanese women rose to 9,087, and by 1920, there were 22,193 women out of a total Japanese population in the United States of 111,010. Emma Gee, "Issei: The First Women," in *Asian Women's Journal* (Berkeley: University of California Press, 1971; repr., LA: Asian American Studies Center, UCLA, 1975), 8–9. For a discussion of the arrival of the Japanese picture

brides, see Chan, *Asian Americans*, 107; Gee, "Issei: The First Women," 8–9, 24–26; Yuji Ichioka, "Amerika Nadeshiko: Japanese Immigrant Women in the United States, 1900–1924," *Pacific Historical Review* 49, no. 2 (May 1980): 340–43; Mei T. Nakano, *Japanese American Women: Three Generations, 1890–1990* (Berkeley: Mina Press Publishing, 1990), 24–26.

13 Kay Korematsu, interview by author, May 25 and 26, 2008; Kakusaburo naturalization petition; Kotsui Korematsu immigration file.

14 Meeting records of the Board of Special Inquiry, Angel Island Station, Jan. 15, 1914; letter from Yasutaro Numano, acting consul general of Japan, Jan. 12, 1914; and marriage certificate, Jan. 15, 1914, Kotsui Korematsu immigration file.

15 Daniels, *Politics*, 84–85, citing the letterhead of the California Oriental Exclusion League; Native Sons of the Golden West, *Grizzly Bear*, Dec. 1919. Daniels notes that the membership of these various bodies drew "chiefly from four organized groups within the state: the Native Sons of the Golden West and its distaff counterpart, the Native Daughters; the newly organized American Legion; the California State Federation of Labor; and various farm bodies, chiefly the California State Grange." Daniels, *Politics*, 85.

16 V. S. McClatchy, testimony, *Hearings before the U.S. Senate Committee on Immigration on S. 2576*, 68th Cong., 1st sess. (Washington: U.S. Government Printing Office, 1924), 5–6, 34, quoted in Daniels, *Politics*, 99.

17 Daniels, *Politics*, 1.

18 Immigration Act of 1924, 43 Stat. 153, § 13(c) (1923); Daniels, *Politics*, 100–105. Secretary of State Charles Evans Hughes noted that "the practical effect . . . is to single out Japanese immigrants for exclusion," and President Calvin Coolidge, in signing the bill, expressed regret that its provisions "affects especially the Japanese." Chuman, *Bamboo People*, 98, 101–2.

19 Kay Korematsu, interview by author, May 26 and June 26, 2008; Fred Korematsu, unedited interview for *Unfinished Business: The Japanese American Internment Cases*, Nov. 15, 1983, documentary, produced by Steven Okazaki (Berkeley, CA: Farallon Films, 1985), DVD; Fred Korematsu, unedited transcript, interview for *Of Civil Wrongs and Rights: The Fred Korematsu Story*, 1991, documentary, produced by Eric Paul Fournier and Ken Korematsu (New York: Docurama, 2006), DVD; Karen Korematsu, interview by author, May 23, 2008.

20 Declaration of Fred Korematsu in Support of Reply to Government's Response and Motion under L.R. 220-6, Oct. 30, 1983, *Korematsu v. United States*, *coram nobis* litigation federal court files, NARA-SF, 9NS-21-91-008: 27635, Fred Toyosaburo Korematsu Folder 2 [6 of 7], Docket Nos. 48–65 (hereafter cited as Fred Korematsu declaration, Oct. 30, 1983).

21 Kathryn Korematsu, interview by author, May 23, 2008; Fred Korematsu, unedited transcript, address to Asian Pacific Islander Law Student Association Group, filmed for *Of Civil Wrongs and Rights*; Kay Korematsu, interview by author, June 25, 2008; Joanne Kataoka, interview by author, Jan. 8, 2011.

22 Kay Korematsu, interview by author, June 25, 2008.

23 Kay Korematsu, interview by author, May 25, 2008. "Absolute authority lay vested

in the eldest male, the patriarch, at least in theory. . . . All family members were required to obey him and accord him preferential treatment. He sat at the head of the table, was served first the choicest part of the meal, and went first to bathe." Nakano, *Japanese American Women*, 34.

24 "[T]he eldest Nisei son usually received special treatment. . . . In many families, the eldest son was the second to be served at meals, after his father, and he was generally indulged by his mother. Younger siblings were instructed to follow his directions, and even older sisters were expected to defer to him." Sylvia Junko Yanagisako, *Transforming the Past: Tradition and Kinship Among Japanese Americans* (Stanford, CA: Stanford University Press, 1985), 146–47, 171–72. See also Nakano, *Japanese American Women*, 34. Kathryn Korematsu, interview by author, May 23, 2008.

25 Fred Korematsu, unedited interview for *Unfinished Business*.

26 Kay Korematsu, interview by author, May 25, 2008; Kathryn Korematsu, interview by author, May 22 and 23, 2008; "Statement of United States Citizen of Japanese Ancestry," Fred Korematsu WRA records, May 25, 1943, National Archives and Records Administration, Washington, DC, p. 3 (hereafter cited as Fred Korematsu, "Statement of U.S. Citizen," May 25, 1943); Karen Korematsu, interview by author, May 23, 2009; Fred Korematsu, unedited interview for *Of Civil Wrongs and Rights*.

27 Fred Korematsu, unedited interview for *Unfinished Business*; Kay Korematsu, interview by author, May 25, 2008. The nursery was isolated; an open field for farming sat on one side, and a foundry on the other.

28 Walt Hermann, interview by author, May 27, 2008; Fred Korematsu, "Statement of U.S. Citizen," May 25, 1943, p. 2.

29 Castlemont High School Falconet, 1937; Kathryn Korematsu, interview by author, May 23, 2008. Nisei Tom Oishi recalled how his team from Richmond, California, played basketball against Fred's San Leandro team. Tom Oishi, interview by Donna Graves and David Washburn, in *Tom Oishi: Rosie the Riveter World War II American Homefront Oral History Project* (Berkeley: University of California, 2007), 126, accessed Apr. 12, 2015, http://digitalassets.lib.berkeley.edu/roho/ucb/text/oishi_tom.pdf. While Fred dreamed of being on his school's football team, his slight build made it just that—a dream. Jane Meredith Adams, "To Clear His Name," *Biography* 2, no. 9 (Sept. 1998): 66.

30 Walt Hermann, interview by author, May 27, 2008. Chizu Iiyama, a co-ed at UC Berkeley when she first met Fred, recalled him as a happy-go-lucky guy and good dancer who seemed to be at every dance in the Bay Area. Chizu Iiyama, interview by author, May 27, 2008, and Mar. 2, 2011.

31 Fred Korematsu, address to public school, transcribed for *Of Civil Wrongs and Rights*.

32 Larry W. Yackle, "Japanese American Internment: An Interview with Fred Korematsu," *Boston University Public Interest Law Journal* 3 (1993): 99.

33 Fred Korematsu, unedited interview for *Unfinished Business*; Kay Korematsu, interview by author, May 25, 2008.

34 Harry Korematsu WRA records, National Archives and Records Adminstration, Washington, DC. Harry Korematsu is pictured in Kawaguchi, *Living with Flowers*, as a member of the Junior Floriculture Society of Northern California, a society created to bring the next generation of flower growers into the business; Kawaguchi, *Living with Flowers*, 47–48. He is also pictured at a California flower market picnic (49) and in one of the family's greenhouses (59).

35 Fred Korematsu, unedited interview for *Unfinished Business*; William A. Marmolejo (dean of student enrollment, Los Angeles Community College), e-mail to author, Nov. 10, 2010; Fred Korematsu, "Statement of U.S. Citizen," 2; testimony of Fred Korematsu, Sept. 8, 1942, record on appeal to World War II Supreme Court, 39, *Korematsu v. United States*, microformed on United States Supreme Court records and briefs, 323 U.S. 214 (1944), Microform, Inc. (hereafter cited as transcript of record to WWII Supreme Court).

36 Report of Special Agent O. T. Mansfield, FBI, June 4, 1942, pp. 2–3, *Korematsu Coram Nobis Litigation Collection*, Collection Number 545, UCLA, Box 21, Folder 12 (hereafter cited as Mansfield FBI report); Arthur A. Hansen, "The 1944 Nisei Draft at Heart Mountain, Wyoming: Its Relationship to the Historical Representation of the World War II Japanese American Evacuation," *OAH Magazine of History* 10, no. 4 (Summer 1996): 54.

37 Mansfield FBI report, 2; Marcus S. Goldstein, "Physical Status of Men Examined through Selective Service in World War II," *Public Health Reports* 66, no. 19 (1951): 597, table 3, available at http://www.jstor.org/stable/4587719.

38 Mansfield FBI report; Commission on Wartime Relocation and Internment of Civilians (CWRIC), *Personal Justice Denied* (Washington, DC: U.S. Government Printing Office, 1982), 187, 253.

39 Fred Korematsu, remarks at the conference "Judgments Judged and Wrongs Remembered: Examining the Japanese American Civil Liberties Cases of World War II on Their 60th Anniversary," Japanese American National Museum, Los Angeles, Nov. 5–6, 2004 (hereafter cited as "Fred Korematsu JANM remarks"); Adams, "To Clear His Name," 67; Fred Korematsu, unedited interview for *Of Civil Wrongs and Rights*.

CHAPTER 2. THE CALL TO GET RID OF THE "JAPS"

1 Fred Korematsu, unedited interview for *Unfinished Business*; report of FBI Special Agent G. E. Goodwin, FBI, July 11, 1942, pp. 2–4, *Korematsu Coram Nobis Litigation Collection*, UCLA, Collection Number 545, Box 21, Folder 12 (hereafter cited as Goodwin FBI report); Walt Hermann, interview by author, May 27, 2008.

2 Fred Korematsu, unedited interview for *Of Civil Wrongs and Rights*; Fred Korematsu, unedited interview for *Unfinished Business*; Walt Hermann, interview by author, May 27, 2008.

3 Goodwin FBI report; Walt Hermann, interview by author, May 27, 2008. At various points, as many as thirty-eight states had antimiscegenation statutes prohibiting interracial marriage. See Peggy Pascoe, *What Comes Naturally:*

Miscegenation Law and the Making of Race in America (New York: Oxford University Press, 2009), 92, map. Cal. Civ. Code § 60 (1905) (enacted by 1872 based on Stats. 1850, p. 424, §3; amendment by Stats. 1901, p. 335, declared unconstitutional; amendment reenacted by Stats. 1905, p. 554). As Professor Rachel Moran explains, antimiscegenation statutes "confirmed [the] status [of Asians] as unassimilable foreigners" and grew out of fear that Asian men would covet white women. Rachel F. Moran, *Interracial Intimacy: The Regulation of Race and Romance* (Chicago: University of Chicago Press, 2001), 17, 18, 36; see also Hrishi Karthikeyan and Gabriel J. Chin, "Preserving Racial Identity: Population Patterns and the Application of Anti-Miscegenation Statutes to Asian Americans, 1910–1950," *Asian Law Journal* 9 (2002): 14–16. The California Supreme Court invalidated the state's antimiscegenation statute in 1948. Perez v. Sharp, 198 P.2d 17 (Cal. 1948). It was not until the 1967 case of Loving v. Virginia, 388 U.S. 1 (1967), that the Supreme Court struck down antimiscegenation statutes as invalid under the federal Constitution.

4 Fred Korematsu, unedited interview for *Of Civil Wrongs and Rights*; Fred Korematsu, unedited interview for *Unfinished Business*.

5 In 1937, one Nisei student at UC Berkeley asked, "What are we going to do if war does break out between United States and Japan? . . . In common language we can say 'we're sunk.' . . . [O]ur properties would be confiscated and most likely [we would be] herded into prison camps perhaps we would be slaughtered on the spot." Roger Daniels, *Concentration Camps USA: The Japanese Americans and World War II* (New York: Holt, Rinehart, and Winston, 1972), 26, quoting statement in the Berkeley *Campanile Review* (Fall 1937).

6 Fred Korematsu, unedited interview for *Of Civil Wrongs and Rights*; Fred Korematsu, unedited interview for *Unfinished Business*.

7 Fred Korematsu, unedited interview for *Of Civil Wrongs and Rights*; CWRIC, *Personal Justice Denied*, 47.

8 Presidential Proclamation 2525, Dec. 7, 1941, reprinted in Roger Daniels, *The Decision to Relocate the Japanese Americans* (Philadelphia: J. B. Lippincott Co., 1975), 61. For an excellent examination of Roosevelt's knowledge about, and attitude toward, Japanese Americans in the months leading up to the war, see Greg Robinson, *By Order of the President: FDR and the Internment of Japanese Americans* (Cambridge, MA: Harvard University Press, 2001). Intelligence agencies had already prepared lists of Japanese they deemed to be "dangerous." Unable to identify members of the resident Japanese community connected with subversive activity, the agencies focused their lists instead on community leaders and individuals who might merely have the opportunity to commit sabotage, such as fishermen, Shinto and Buddhist priests, farmers, Japanese language teachers, martial arts instructors, travel agents, and newspaper editors. Peter Irons, *Justice at War: The Story of the Japanese American Internment Cases* (New York: Oxford University Press, 1983), 21–22, citing Bob Kumamoto, "The Search for Spies: American Counterintelligence and the Japanese American Community 1931–1942," *Amerasia Journal*, 6, no. 2 (Fall 1979): 58. By the evening of Decem-

ber 7, 1941, 736 mainland Japanese aliens had been taken into custody. Within four days, the total grew to 1,370. Jacobus tenBroek, Edward N. Barnhart, and Floyd W. Matson, *Prejudice, War, and the Constitution* (Berkeley: University of California Press, 1954), 101, citing Department of Justice press releases, Dec. 8 and 13, 1941. See also Daniels, *Concentration Camps*, 34–35; and CWRIC, *Personal Justice Denied*, 54–55.

9   Fred Korematsu, unedited interview for *Unfinished Business*; Fred Korematsu, unedited interview for *Of Civil Wrongs and Rights*. Upon pressure from the army, the Department of Justice dispensed with any need to show probable cause for a search; instead, spot raids were allowed on any home in which an Issei resided. Summary, Assistant Attorney General James Rowe to Lt. General John L. DeWitt, Jan. 4, 1942, NARS, RG 228, CWRIC, pp. 1258–59, excerpted in part in CWRIC, *Personal Justice Denied*, 373n81. Items considered to be contraband included anything that might be used as weapons, explosives, radio transmitters and radios, and certain cameras. Daniels, *Concentration Camps*, 43.

10 Minoru Tamaki, who was the same age as Fred and in his last year of pharmacy school at the time of Pearl Harbor, later testified, "I recall how, in great fear, my mother and sisters meticulously went through all our belongings looking for anything 'Japanese.' I remember them yanking our pictures from our family album and burning them. We removed all Japanese calligraphy hangings from our walls, even though we could not read them. In short, we tried to deny our very culture and origins." Minoru Tamaki, testimony, hearing before the Commission on Wartime Relocation and Internment of Civilians (hereafter cited as CWRIC hearing), San Francisco, Aug. 13, 1981, p. 185. Minoru's son, Don Tamaki, would be part of the legal team that sought justice for Fred forty years later.

11 "National C. L. Pledges Support to America," *Rafu Shimpo*, Dec. 9, 1941.

12 For example, the night of the Pearl Harbor attack, naturalist Donald Culross Peattie broadcast a radio message in Santa Barbara, seeking restraint: "[Our citizens of Japanese descent] must not be penalized for the treachery of the government of Japan. . . . To make them the victims of the Japanese government's cruelty would be to begin our part in this war by committing a grave injustice. To do so would be the first defeat to our cause." Broadcast by Donald Culross Peattie, reprinted in "We Must Prove Our Loyalty to U.S.," *Rafu Shimpo*, Dec. 15, 1941.

13 "The Japanese stereotype was not created at Pearl Harbor; the basic ingredients had been mixed years before. . . . For half a century [Americans] had heard of the treachery and deceitfulness of resident Japanese." tenBroek et al., *Prejudice, War, and the Constitution*, 68, 70.

14 Ibid., 70, citing *Los Angeles Herald*, Dec. 9, 1941; *Sacramento Bee*, Dec. 17, 1941; *San Francisco Examiner*, Dec. 29, 1941; see also Daniels, *Concentration Camps*, 32–34, for news reports of purported Japanese espionage and sabotage in the aftermath of Pearl Harbor.

15 Daniels, *Concentration Camps*, 33.

16 Francis Biddle, *In Brief Authority* (Westport, CT: Greenwood Press, 1962), 224.

17 tenBroek et al., *Prejudice, War, and the Constitution*, 73–74; Henry McLemore,

"Why Treat the Japs Well Here?" *San Francisco Examiner*, Jan. 19, 1942; Walter Lippmann, "The Fifth Column on the Coast," *New York Tribune*, Feb. 12, 1942, quoted in Daniels, *Concentration Camps*, 68; Westbrook Pegler, "Fair Enough," *Los Angeles Times*, Feb. 16, 1942, I2.

18 tenBroek et al., *Prejudice, War, and the Constitution*, 78, quoting minutes of the California Joint Immigration Committee, Feb. 7, 1942, p. 6. For a discussion of the exclusionist movement from the early Asiatic Exclusion League to the Japanese Exclusion League and the California Joint Immigration Committee, see Daniels, *Politics*, 27–75, 91–105. In his dissent in *Korematsu v. United States*, Justice Frank Murphy quoted Austin E. Anson, managing secretary of the Salinas Vegetable Grower-Shipper Association: "We're charged with wanting to get rid of the Japs for selfish reasons. We do. It's a question of whether the white man lives on the Pacific Coast or the brown men. They came into this valley to work, and they stayed to take over. . . . If all the Japs were removed tomorrow, we'd never miss them in two weeks, because the white farmers can take over and produce everything the Jap grows. And we don't want them back when the war ends, either." Korematsu v. United States, 323 U.S. 214, 240 n.12 (1944) (Murphy J., dissenting), quoting from Frank J. Taylor, "The People Nobody Wants," *Saturday Evening Post*, May 9, 1942, 66.

19 CWRIC, *Personal Justice Denied*, 70, quoting Leland M. Ford to Stimson, Jan. 16, 1942, NARS, RG 107, CWRIC, p. 4376; Morton Grodzins, *Americans Betrayed: Politics and the Japanese Evacuation* (Chicago: University of Chicago Press, 1949), 64–65. On January 30, the Pacific Coast members of the House of Representatives called on the War Department to immediately remove from "critical areas . . . all aliens and their families, including children under 21, whether aliens or not," and provide for their "[t]emporary internment . . . pending completion of long-range resettlement or internment program." Recommendations by Pacific Coast Delegation (U.S. House of Representatives), "Suggested Program," to the president following delegation meeting, Jan. 30, 1942, Bancroft Library, A12.06, CWRIC, p. 11334, reprinted in Daniels, *Decision to Relocate*, 77–78.

20 Daniels, *Concentration Camps*, 76; Earl Warren, testimony, *Hearings before the Select Committee Investigating National Defense Migration*, 77th Cong., 2d Sess. (Washington, DC: U.S. Government Printing Office, 1942), 11011–12 (hereafter cited as Tolan Committee hearings). As purported proof of the threat posed by Japanese Americans, Warren offered maps plotting the location of Japanese American homes and farms to argue that their location near strategic installations had to "manifest something more than mere coincidence." CWRIC, *Personal Justice Denied*, 96–97, quoting Tolan Committee hearings, 10974. For a discussion of Warren's role in the World War II incarceration, examined in reference to his later contributions while on the Supreme Court, see Sumi Cho, "Redeeming Whiteness in the Shadow of Internment: Earl Warren, Brown, and a Theory of Racial Redemption," *Boston College Law Review* 40 (1998): 73–170.

21 Transcript of meeting in DeWitt's office, Jan 4, 1942, RG #220 of the Fiscal,

Judicial, and Social Division of the National Archives and Records Center, Washington, DC, available on microfilm in the papers of the CWRIC, Reel 2, Box 2 (CWRIC 1250–57).

22 CWRIC, *Personal Justice Denied*, 66, quoting DeWitt, testimony before House Naval Affairs Subcommittee, Apr. 13, 1943, NARS, RG 338, CWRIC, pp. 1725–28). As Professor Roger Daniels relates, proposals to remove Italian alien immigrants were viewed unsympathetically. Congressman John Tolan, chair of the Tolan Committee, asked an Italian American attorney to "tell us about the DiMaggios," whose son, Joe DiMaggio, had just set a record for getting a base hit in fifty-six straight games. The attorney explained that, although DiMaggio's parents were not citizens, it would not be good policy to force such honest, law-abiding persons to move. However, many Italian and German aliens were forced to move from sensitive areas, and the elder DiMaggio could not continue fishing from San Francisco's Fisherman's Wharf. Roger Daniels, *Prisoners Without Trial* (New York: Hill and Wang, 1993, 8th printing, 2000), 51.

23 For a discussion of the army's campaign for the removal of Japanese Americans, see, e.g., Daniels, *Concentration Camps*, 38–73; Alice Yang Murray, *Historical Memories of the Japanese American Internment and the Struggle for Redress* (Stanford, CA: Stanford University Press, 2008), 15–51. DeWitt had first rejected the mass removal of the Nikkei community: "[W]hile they may not be loyal, I think we can weed the disloyal out of the loyal and lock them up if necessary." Stetson Conn, Rose C. Engelman, and Byron Fairchild, *United States Army in World War II: The Western Hemisphere: Guarding the United States and Its Outposts* (Washington, DC: Office of the Chief of Military History, Department of the Army, 1964), 117. DeWitt later took the position that it was impossible to determine the loyalty of a Japanese American. When that position was found to contradict the government's argument before the Supreme Court, DeWitt flip-flopped again and took a third position, that Japanese Americans were removed because there was insufficient time to separate the loyal from the disloyal. See discussion of the alteration of DeWitt's report, *infra*, chapter 8. Bendetsen was described by James Rowe, assistant attorney general at the time of the incarceration, as "mainly responsible for [the evacuation] as any man." Rowe went so far as to characterize Bendetsen as a "bad, bad fellow." James Rowe, interview by Amelia Fry (Earl Warren Oral History Project), *Japanese-American Relocation Reviewed*, vol. 2 (Berkeley: Regents of the University of California, 1976), 8–9.

24 CWRIC, *Personal Justice Denied*, 78, quoting memo, Biddle, "Luncheon Conference with the President," Feb. 7, 1942, Franklin Delano Roosevelt Library, Biddle Papers (CWRIC 5750). Earlier, on January 24, Attorney General Biddle wrote Representative Ford that "[u]nless the writ of habeas corpus is suspended, I do not know any way in which Japanese born in this country, and therefore American citizens, could be interned." Biddle, *In Brief Authority*, 215.

25 Memorandum, J. Edgar Hoover to Attorney General, Feb. 2, 1942, CWRIC Reel 5, Box 5, CWRIC 5794–5803, quoted in CWRIC, *Personal Justice Denied*, 72–73.

26 In his diary on February 11, 1942, Stimson wrote, "General DeWitt is asking for

some very drastic steps: to wit: the moving and relocating of some 120,000 people including citizens of Japanese descent. . . . I directed them to pick out and begin with the most vital places of army and navy production and take them on in that order as quickly as possible." CWRIC, *Personal Justice Denied*, 79, quoting Stimson diary, Feb. 11, 1942, Sterling Library, Yale University (CWRIC 19649).

27 CWRIC, *Personal Justice Denied*, 79, quoting Stimson diary, Feb. 10, 1942, Sterling Library, Yale University (CWRIC 19649). The argument that Stimson found suspect, that the "racial characteristics" of Japanese Americans made them untrustworthy, was precisely the argument that the government later made successfully before the Supreme Court. See discussion of the racial characteristics argument in *Hirabayashi*, 320 U.S. 81, 96, *infra*, chapter 6.

28 Daniels, *Concentration Camps*, 21.

29 CWRIC, *Personal Justice Denied*, 75, quoting telephone conversation, DeWitt, Gullion, and Bendetsen, Feb 1, 1942, NARS, RG 389, CWRIC, pp. 4314–18), reprinted in Daniels, *Decision to Relocate*, 84.

30 War Department Memo for Record (unsigned), Feb. 11, 1942, ASW 014.311 EASC, quoted in Conn, Engelman, and Fairchild, *United States Army*, 131; Robinson, *By Order of the President*, 105.

31 Conn, Engelman, and Fairchild, *United States Army*, 131–32, quoting Stimson diary, Feb. 10, 1942, Sterling Library, Yale University (CWRIC 19649); Robinson, *By Order of the President*, 105–6. For a comprehensive discussion of Roosevelt's role with regard to the removal Japanese Americans on the West Coast, see Robinson, *By Order of the President*.

32 Conn, Engelman, and Fairchild, *United States Army*, 132, quoting telephone conversation, McCloy and Bendetsen, Feb. 11, 1942, WDC-CAD 311.3 "Tel Convs." (Bendetsen, Feb.–Mar. 1942).

33 Daniels, *Concentration Camps*, 65.

34 DeWitt, "Final Recommendation of the Commanding General, Western Defense Command and Fourth Army, submitted to the Secretary of War," Feb. 14, 1942, included in DeWitt, *Final Report: Japanese Evacuation from the West Coast 1942* (Washington, DC: United States Government Printing Office, 1943), available at https://archive.org/stream/japaneseevacuati00dewi#page/8/mode/2up (hereafter DeWitt, *Final Report*), appendix to chapter III, 34.

35 For example, DeWitt noted that Japanese farms in Washington State were located near the Boeing Aircraft facility and that communication, power, and water lines to the facility ran through areas populated by Japanese. He pointed out that large numbers of Japanese operated vegetable markets along waterfronts near naval installations; that others engaged in fishing along waterways; and that many were within easy reach of forests, mills, and stockpiles of lumber, which could easily be set afire during dry seasons. DeWitt, Final Recommendation, 34–35.

36 Ibid., 36, reprinted in part in Daniels, *Decision to Relocate*, 109–11.

37 James H. Rowe, Jr., interview, Oct. 15, 1942, quoted in tenBroek et al., *Prejudice, War, and the Constitution*, 111. Years later, Biddle explained why he ceded to the army: "[T]he decision had been made by the President. It was, he said, a mat-

ter of military judgment. I did not think I should oppose it any further. . . . The military might be wrong. But they are fighting the war. . . . [T]he Constitution has never greatly bothered any wartime President. That was a question of law, which ultimately the Supreme Court must decide. And meanwhile—probably a long meanwhile—we must get on with the war." Biddle, *In Brief Authority*, 219. Biddle explained with regret, "[I]f, instead of dealing almost exclusively with McCloy and Bendetsen, I had urged [Stimson] to resist the pressure of his subordinates, the result might have been different. But I was new to the Cabinet, and disinclined to insist on my view to an elder statesman whose wisdom and integrity I greatly respected." Ibid., 226.

38 Executive Order No. 9066, 7 Fed. Reg. 1407, Feb. 19, 1942, reprinted in Daniels, *Decision to Relocate*, 113–14. In April 17, 1943, Biddle wrote the president, "You signed the original Executive Order permitting the exclusions so that Army could handle the Japs. It was never intended to apply to Italians and Germans." Biddle, memorandum for the president, Apr. 17, 1943.

39 Pub. L. No. 77-503, 56 Stat. 173 (1942); Congressional Record, Mar. 19, 1942, p. 2726, quoted in CWRIC, *Personal Justice Denied*, 99; CWRIC, *Personal Justice Denied*, 99.

40 CWRIC, *Personal Justice Denied*, 100–101, citing Public Proclamation No. 1, and accompanying material, Mar. 2, 1942, NARS, RG 107 (CWRIC 255–59). Figures on the number of Japanese Americans incarcerated during World War II vary. In its brief to the U.S. Supreme Court in Fred's case, the government stated that 110,219 Japanese Americans were sent to the temporary detention centers, and 108,503 of them were sent to the more permanent "relocation" centers. Brief of the United States, *Korematsu v. United States,* available at 1944 WL 42850, 9, Oct. 5, 1944. The Commission on Wartime Relocation and Internment of Civilians states that, by November 1, 1942, 106,770 Japanese Americans were in the "relocation" centers. CWRIC, *Personal Justice Denied*, 149–50. Neither set of figures, however, include individuals in the Department of Justice internment camps, where immigrant alien Japanese had been sent. I will use the figure of 110,000.

41 Public Proclamation No. 3, Mar. 24, 1942, reprinted in Daniels, *Decision to Relocate*, 124–25.

42 Fred Korematsu, unedited interview for *Of Civil Wrongs and Rights*; Fred Korematsu, unedited interview for *Unfinished Business*.

43 Public Proclamation No. 4, Mar. 27, 1942, records of the Northern California Chapter of the ACLU MS 3580, Series 111, Box 56, Folder ACLU 1385 Korematsu, Fred, Calif. courts 1942–44, California Historical Society, San Francisco, CA (hereafter cited as NCCLU, CHS).

44 CWRIC, *Personal Justice Denied*, 101–2, quoting letter Carville to DeWitt, Feb. 21, 1942 (CWRIC 767). Governor Sidney Osborn of Arizona expressed a similar view: "We not only vigorously protest but will not permit the evacuation of Japanese, German or Italian aliens to any point in Arizona." tenBroek et al., *Prejudice, War, and the Constitution*, 89, quoting Osborn to Tolan, Feb. 28, 1942, printed in Tolan Committee, "Preliminary Report . . . on Evacuation of Military Areas," House

Report No. 1911, Mar. 19, 1942, p. 27. For a discussion of the basis for DeWitt's freeze order, see Greg Robinson, *A Tragedy of Democracy: Japanese Confinement in North America* (New York: Columbia University Press, 2009), 124–25.

45 CWRIC, *Personal Justice Denied*, 103. Conn, Engelman, and Fairchild, *United States Army*, 138 (quoting Secretary of the Navy to Attorney General, Feb. 22, 1942, ASW 014.311 EAWC). The army did little to aid Japanese Americans in resettling. On February 21, 1942, Bendetsen told the State Department that, while the army was prepared to provide food, shelter, and transportation to those Japanese Americans already forced to move from strategic areas, it "did not, however, desire to advertise [the fact] for fear that there might be a rush on the part of numerous aliens to take advantage of free living." Memorandum of telephone conversation between Bendetsen and Bernard Gufler, Feb. 21, 1942, RG 220 of the Fiscal, Judicial, and Social Division of the National Archives and Record Center, Washington, DC, available on microfilm in the papers of the Commission on Wartime Relocation and Internment of Civilians, Reel 3, CWRIC 2806–07.

46 Public Proclamation No. 4, Mar. 27, 1942, NCCLU, CHS.

47 Fred Beck, executive of the Historical Services Division, United States Army, Center of Military History, testimony, CWRIC hearing, Washington, DC, July 14, 1981, p. 163. While Nikkei families on Terminal Island in San Pedro, California, had been forced to leave by the navy a month earlier, the Bainbridge Island removal order was the first issued by DeWitt. Daniels, *Concentration Camps*, 85–86; CWRIC, *Personal Justice Denied*, 108–9. For a further discussion of the removal of Bainbridge Islanders, see Mary Woodward, *In Defense of Our Neighbors: The Walt and Milly Woodward Story* (Bainbridge Island, WA: Fenwick Publishing, 2008), 68, 75–76.

48 *Korematsu*, 323 U.S. 214, 230 (Roberts, J., dissenting).

49 CWRIC, *Personal Justice Denied*, 113, citing telegram, Deutsch to Frankfurter, Mar. 28, 1942, NARS, RG 107, CWRIC, p. 3077. Two Issei did choose suicide over removal. When Hideo Murata, a World War I veteran living in Pismo Beach, California, was found, he was grasping an Honorary Citizenship certificate in his hand. The certificate, which he'd received at an Independence Day celebration the year before, read, "Monterey County presents this testimony of heartfelt gratitude, of honor and respect for your loyal and splendid service to the country in the Great World War. Our flag was assaulted and you gallantly took up its defense." Carey McWilliams, *Prejudice: Japanese Americans: Symbol of Racial Intolerance* (Boston: Little Brown & Co., 1944), 133, cited in Michi Weglyn, *Years of Infamy* (New York: Morrow Quill Paperbacks, 1976), 78.

50 Walt and Milly Woodward were two journalists who stood up for their Japanese American neighbors from the small office of their *Bainbridge Review*. Woodward, *In Defense of Our Neighbors*, 57. See also Edw. Ayers Taylor (professor of English, University of Washington) to Biddle, Feb. 20, 1942, CWRIC 13336, stating that handling of the so-called "Japanese problem" could not be regarded "as any thing [sic] more than another manifestation of economic greed and meanness."

51 CWRIC, *Personal Justice Denied*, 69.

52 American Civil Liberties Union to Roosevelt, Mar. 20, 1942, JACL Redress Collection, 1936–1992, Series 1, Box 1, declassified documents requested by John Tateishi 1981, 2 of 2, Japanese American National Library, San Francisco, CA.

53 William Petersen, *Japanese Americans: Oppression and Success* (New York: Random House, 1971), 77–78, citing *ACLU News*, San Francisco, Apr. 1942.

CHAPTER 3. FRED'S DECISION TO LIVE FREE

1 Betty Matsuo described the dehumanizing experience: "I lost my identity. At that time, I didn't even have a Social Security number, but the WRA gave me an ID number. That was my identification. I lost my privacy and dignity." CWRIC, *Personal Justice Denied*, 135, quoting testimony, Betty Matsuo, San Francisco, Aug. 11, 1981, p. 273.

2 CWRIC, *Personal Justice Denied*, 107. For a description of the chaos created as families sought to dispose of their belongings and salvage what cash they could, see, e.g., Weglyn, *Years of Infamy*, 77. For a discussion of the removal of Japanese Americans, see, e.g., Robinson, *Tragedy of Democracy*, 126–28.

3 Fred Korematsu, unedited transcript, address to Asian Pacific Islander Law Student Association.

4 Weglyn, *Years of Infamy*, 77. For example, Bob Fletcher was a state agricultural inspector who quit his job so he could work to save farms owned by Nikkei families in Florin, California. Gerald Yamada, letter to the editor, *Pacific Citizen*, June 7–20, 2013, p. 2; William Yardley, "Bob Fletcher Dies at 101; Helped Japanese-Americans," *New York Times*, June 6, 2013. See also Sarasohn, *Issei*, 254–55, which relates the story of Mrs. Kane Kozono, whose family ranch was cared for by a Mexican American family who worked for them and whose neighbor kept her valuables for her until after the war.

5 Weglyn, *Years of Infamy*, 77; Kathryn Korematsu, interview by author, May 22, 2008; Fred Korematsu, interview by Lorraine Bannai and Tetsuden Kashima, Seattle, May 14, 1996.

6 JACL Creed, written by Mike Masaoka in 1940, published in the Congressional Record for May 9, 1941, p. A2205, quoted in Daniels, *Concentration Camps*, 24–25. Numerous sources recount the role of the National Japanese American Citizens League in cooperating with the wartime incarceration. See, e.g., Daniels, *Concentration Camps*, 79–81; Murray, *Historical Memories*, 103–39; Bill Hosokawa, *JACL in Quest of Justice* (New York: William Morrow, 1982), 18–32.

7 Mike Masaoka, testimony, Tolan Committee Hearings, 11148, quoted in David K. Yoo, *Growing Up Nisei* (Urbana: University of Illinois Press, 2000), 143.

8 Hosokawa, *JACL in Quest of Justice*, 151, quoting Mike Masaoka.

9 James Omura, testimony, Tolan Committee hearings, 11229, quoted in Yoo, *Growing Up Nisei*, 144; *Densho Encyclopedia*, s.v. "James Omura," last updated Jan. 4, 2014, http://encyclopedia.densho.org/James_Omura/. A group of Nisei from San Francisco, living in New York, similarly objected to the JACL's testimony: "[B]oy, that Tolan Committee Hearings testimony of the JACL burns everybody

up. . . . [T]he answer to the question whether the nisei were willing to be evacuated was almost a categorical 'yes.'" Yoo, *Growing Up Nisei*, 143–44, quoting Japanese [American] Evacuation and Resettlement Study (JERS), B12.41, Bancroft Library, University of California at Berkeley.

10 In March 1942, for example, the Gardena, California, JACL chapter asked Japanese Americans "to have confidence in the Citizens League and in its effort to aid them." "Gardena C. L. Mass Meeting," *Kashu Mainichi* (Los Angeles, CA), Mar. 18, 1942. The JACL stance of compliance was echoed by others within the community. On March 21, 1942, in its last issue before leaving its offices and suspending publication, the *Kashu Mainichi*, a Japanese American community newspaper in Los Angeles, closed with these words: "Let us join the evacuation movement, which is of vital necessity to our country, cheerfully and without rancor, for this is the supreme test of our loyalty and worth as an integral part of the American nation." "Notice," *Kashu Mainichi*, Mar. 21, 1942.

11 Fred Korematsu, unedited interview for *Unfinished Business*; Fred Korematsu, interview by Bannai and Kashima, May 14, 1996.

12 Mansfield FBI report, 2; Fred Korematsu, unedited interview for *Unfinished Business*.

13 Fred Korematsu, unedited interview for *Of Civil Wrongs and Rights*. Nevada's antimiscegenation statute prohibited marriage between "any person of the Caucasian or white race" and "any person of the Ethiopian or black race, Malay or brown race, Mongolian or yellow race, or the American Indian or red race." The statute was not repealed until 1959. Pascoe, *What Comes Naturally*, 91, 242.

14 Fred Korematsu, unedited interview for *Unfinished Business*. As Elaine Elinson and Stan Yogi have observed, "Korematsu's romantically inspired civil disobedience transformed into a quiet but steadfast belief that the government had violated his fundamental rights as an American." Elaine Elinson and Stan Yogi, *Wherever There's a Fight* (Berkeley, CA: Heydey Books, 2009), 418.

15 Fred Korematsu, unedited interview for *Unfinished Business*; Fred Korematsu, unedited interview for *Of Civil Wrongs and Rights*.

16 Goodwin FBI report, 2; Fred Korematsu, unedited interview for *Unfinished Business*; Fred Korematsu, unedited interview for *Of Civil Wrongs and Rights*.

17 Goodwin FBI report, 2, 5–6; Fred Korematsu, unedited interview for *Of Civil Wrongs and Rights*.

18 Fred Korematsu, unedited interview for *Of Civil Wrongs and Rights*; Mansfield FBI report, 3, and Goodwin FBI report, 6; Fred Korematsu, unedited interview for *Unfinished Business*. Charles Kikuchi, a Nisei who chronicled his experiences during and after World War II, also considered plastic surgery. Charles Kikuchi, *The Kikuchi Diary: Chronicle from an American Concentration Camp*, ed. John Modell (Urbana: University of Illinois Press, 1973). In his examination of Charles Kikuchi's writings in *Jim and Jap Crow: A Cultural History of 1940's Interracial America*, Professor Matthew Briones quotes Kikuchi: "It wasn't because of any shame in my background, but I felt that economically, I would be better off if I did not have a Japanese face." Matthew Briones, *Jim and Jap Crow: A Cultural*

History of 1940's Interracial America (Princeton, NJ: Princeton University Press, 2012), 24, quoting Kikuchi to D. Thomas, June 28, 1945. In addressing Fred's plastic surgery, Briones focuses on the adversity that Fred faced: "This particular case demonstrates that to an American of Japanese ancestry at this specific historical moment, a procedure as terrifying as invasive plastic surgery was a *reasonable* way to cope with an atmosphere of systemic repression and terror[,] . . . an act of desperate self-preservation." Briones, *Jim and Jap Crow*, 24–25.

19 Fred Korematsu, unedited interview for *Of Civil Wrongs and Rights*; Yackle, "Japanese American Internment," 100; Goodwin FBI report, 2; Fred Korematsu, unedited interview for *Unfinished Business*.

20 Fred Korematsu, unedited interview for *Of Civil Wrongs and Rights*.

21 Civilian Exclusion Order No. 34, Federal Register, May 28, 1942; Fred Korematsu declaration, Oct. 30, 1983.

22 "The hardest thing to lose was the full 1942 Mother's Day crop of flowers, which [had been] in process from Christmas time." CWRIC, *Personal Justice Denied*, 125, quoting testimony, Vernon Yoshioka, Los Angeles, Aug. 6, 1981, p. 111. See also Kawaguchi, *Living with Flowers*, 57. "All of the Japanese growers, citizens and aliens alike, were in a state of frenzy. . . . [W]e had to sell everything that would bring in cash so we could support ourselves. Most of our money was tied up in land and greenhouses." Shibata, *Across Two Worlds*, 60.

23 Fred Korematsu, unedited interview for *Unfinished Business*.

CHAPTER 4. JAIL WAS BETTER THAN CAMP

1 Family folders of the Korematsu family, Tanforan Assembly Center, records of Japanese-American Assembly Centers, 1942–1946 (ARC ID # 2679430), Wartime Civil Control Administration, Western Defense Command, U.S. Army Defense Commands (RG 499), National Archives at San Francisco (NARA-SF) (hereafter cited as Korematsu Family Tanforan records). Hi had arrived at Tanforan on April 28 and was assigned a separate family number, 14761.

2 CWRIC, *Personal Justice Denied*, 135–36. While many Americans celebrated the exodus, some watched sadly as their Japanese American friends and neighbors left. "As children, we were shocked when these fellow Americans, our friends, were almost instantaneously removed from the area in the dark of night, as if they had committed some heinous crime. We found this very hard to understand. They were with us one day, the next day, they were gone and we never heard from them again." James McEtee, director of the Santa Clara County Human Relations Council, testimony, CWRIC hearing, San Francisco, Aug. 13, 1981. For many Japanese Americans, the trip to camp was difficult. Grace Nakamura recalled, "On May 16, 1942, at 9:30 a.m., we departed for an unknown destination. To this day, I can remember vividly the plight of the elderly, some on stretchers, orphans herded onto the train by caretakers, and especially a young couple with four pre-school children. . . . The shades were drawn on the train for our entire trip. Military police patrolled the aisles." CWRIC, *Personal Justice Denied*, 136,

quoting testimony, Grace Nakamura, Los Angeles, Aug. 6, 1981, p. 252.

3   Korematsu Family Tanforan records. There were sixteen of these temporary confinement centers in all—one each in Washington, Oregon, and Arizona, and the rest in California. CWRIC, *Personal Justice Denied*, 104–6, 137.

4   William Kochiyama recounted his arrival at Tanforan: "At the entrance . . . stood two lines of troops with rifles and fixed bayonets pointed at the evacuees as they walked between the soldiers to the prison compound. Overwhelmed with bitterness and blind with rage, I screamed every obscenity I knew at the armed guards daring them to shoot me." CWRIC, *Personal Justice Denied*, 136, quoting testimony, William Kochiyama, New York, Nov. 23, 1981, p. 97. For other accounts of Tanforan, see Susan B. Richardson, ed., *I Call to Remembrance: Toyo Suyemoto's Years of Internment* (New Brunswick, NJ: Rutgers University Press, 2007), 37–61; Miné Okubo, *Citizen 13660* (New York: Columbia University Press, 1946; repr., Seattle: University of Washington Press, 1983); Kikuchi, *The Kikuchi Diary*; and Sandra C. Taylor, *Jewel of the Desert: Japanese American Internment at Topaz* (Berkeley: University of California Press, 1993), 62–88.

5   CWRIC, *Personal Justice Denied*, 137; Okubo, *Citizen 13660*, 30–31.

6   Okubo, *Citizen 13660*, 44–45, 47, 66, 68; Kikuchi, *Diary*, 60–61, entry for May 7, 1942; CWRIC, *Personal Justice Denied*, 140. Sox Kitashima recalled that when she, her mother, and three adult brothers arrived in their horse stall at Tanforan, there was manure on the floor and horse tail hair stuck on the rough walls. Sox Kitashima, testimony, CWRIC hearing, San Francisco, Aug. 13, 1981, p. 168. Haruyo Saito was assigned a room in a barrack for herself, her husband, and their two young children: "The floor had cracks and the wind coming in which made it very cold at night. I cried many, many nights from fear." Haruyo Saito, testimony, CWRIC hearing, San Francisco, Aug. 13, 1981. Many sources describe conditions in both the temporary detention centers and the later concentration camps. See, e.g., CWRIC, *Personal Justice Denied*, 137–84; Robinson, *Tragedy of Democracy*, 129–32, 154–71; John Tateishi's oral histories of former internees in *And Justice for All: An Oral History of the Japanese-American Detention Camps* (Seattle: University of Washington Press,1984); and the visual histories of former incarcerees at "Densho: Japanese American Legacy Project," Densho, accessed Dec. 27, 2014, http://www.densho.org.

7   Okubo, *Citizen 13660*, 59, 72–76, 78, 86.

8   CWRIC, *Personal Justice Denied*, 141, quoting testimony, Tsuyako Kitashima, San Francisco, Aug. 13, 1981, p. 167.

9   Tanforan was occupied from April 28 to October 13, 1942, when most of its inmates were moved to the more permanent camp at Topaz, Utah. CWRIC, *Personal Justice Denied*, 138.

10 Some, like Osuke Takizawa, fell into despair: "I felt miserable, but I couldn't do anything. . . . We really worried about our future. I just gave up." Sarasohn, *Issei*, 183–84, quoting Osuke Takizawa. Charles Kikuchi described his Issei father, a barber, as despondent when they first arrived at Tanforan: "Made me feel sort of sorry for Pop tonight. . . . He probably realized that he no longer controls the

family group and rarely exerts himself so that there is little family conflict as far as he is concerned. What a difference from about fifteen years ago when I was a kid. He used to be a perfect terror and dictator." As Kikuchi observed, "The role of the Issei father in the family life has become less dominant because he no longer holds the purse strings." Kikuchi, *Diary*, 62, 82, entries for May 7 and 17, 1942.

11 Kikuchi observed, for example, "This evacuation is making a new life for Mom. For twenty-eight years she has been restricted at home in Vallejo, raising children and doing housework. Her social contacts have been extremely limited.... Now she finds herself here with a lot of Japanese, and it has given her a great deal of pleasure to make all of these new social contacts." Kikuchi, *Diary*, 122, entry for June 11, 1942.

12 When Nisei Hiroshi Kajiwara sat down on his cot in his family's horse stall, he thought, "Why us? We are Americans. . . . [W]hat have I done to deserve this treatment"? Hiroshi Kajiwara, testimony, CWRIC hearing, San Francisco, Aug. 11, 1981, p. 234.

13 See Weglyn, *Years of Infamy*, 83, who comments that "the adolescent Nisei . . . experienced their first exhilarating sense of release—from the severe parental restraint placed upon them."

14 Okubo, *Citizen 13660*, 89. For some Nisei, the loss of family meals times marked the loss of something special and important. Minoru Tamaki explained, "Prior to the war, my family got together three times a day at mealtime. Because my father had died years earlier, my mother was the authority figure at home and responsible for providing for us. All this, however, was suddenly altered. Meals were served at the central mess hall. . . . We never had meals together in our quarters. We often could not even sit at the same table. . . . Mealtime ceased to be a time for family conversations. Our family became fragmented. I began to sit not with my mother, brother or sisters, but with friends of my own age. My mother was no longer the authority figure or the provider, and I became more estranged from my family." Minoru Tamaki, testimony, CWRIC hearing, San Francisco, Aug. 13, 1981, pp. 185–86. For discussion of the loss of traditional family structures in camp, see, e.g., Anne Umemoto, "Crisis in the Japanese American Family," in *Asian Women's Journal*, 31–34.

15 CWRIC, *Personal Justice Denied*, 139–40, 145–46; Okubo, *Citizen 13660*, 97–99, 102–5. DeWitt named Karl R. Bendetsen to head the WCCA. Fred Beck, executive of the Historical Services Division, United States Army, Center of Military History, testimony, CWRIC hearing, Washington DC, July 14, 1981, p. 163.

16 CWRIC, *Personal Justice Denied*, 146. Miné Okubo, for example, became an art instructor, eventually teaching forty-four hours a week for sixteen dollars a month. Okubo, *Citizen 13660*, 92. Other incarcerees provided a range of other needs, serving, for example, as doctors, dentists, mess hall workers, garbage collectors, stenographers, clerks, block wardens, and sign painters. Weglyn, *Years of Infamy*, 83.

17 Fred Korematsu, unedited interview for *Unfinished Business*. Fred told the FBI

that he moved three times in the span of a few months, to different rooming houses in Oakland, all the while working as a welder. Mansfield FBI report, 2, 3.

18 Mansfield FBI report; Fred Korematsu JANM remarks; Fred Korematsu, unedited interview for *Unfinished Business*; Fred Korematsu, unedited interview for *Of Civil Wrongs and Rights*. The San Leandro History Museum has the 1942 jail register for the San Leandro Police Department, in which Fred carefully printed his name on booking.

19 San Leandro Police Department jail register, San Leandro History Museum, San Leandro, California. "Oakland Jap Held for FBI," *Oakland Post-Enquirer*, June 1, 1942; "Two Bay Japs Evade Evacuation; Captured," *Oakland Tribune*, June 1, 1942, 1; "Jap Youth No Ancestor Worshipper," *San Leandro News Observer*, June 5, 1942.

20 Mansfield FBI report. Following the interview, FBI agents searched the room that Fred had been staying in and found, among other things, a photo of his friend Walt Hermann and a letter from Ida.

21 Fred Korematsu, unedited interview for *Unfinished Business*; Fred Korematsu, unedited interview for *Of Civil Wrongs and Rights*; Fred Korematsu JANM remarks.

22 Fred Korematsu JANM remarks; Fred Korematsu, unedited interview for *Unfinished Business*; Irons, *Justice at War*, 97, citing interview with Ernest Besig.

23 Fred Korematsu, unedited interview for *Unfinished Business*; Fred Korematsu JANM remarks. While Besig had received his law degree from Cornell University, he never became licensed in California. *Densho Encyclopedia*, s.v. "Ernest Besig," last updated Aug. 28, 2014, http://encyclopedia.densho.org/Ernest%20Besig/; Julie Kutulas, "In Quest of Autonomy: The Northern California Affiliate of the American Civil Liberties Union and World War II," *Pacific Historical Review*, vol. 67, no. 2, May 1998, p. 204. Although Besig advocated for Fred and stood by his side throughout Fred's case, he arranged for Clarence Rust and Wayne Collins to represent Fred in the legal proceedings. See *infra*, this chapter and chapter 5.

24 Irons, *Justice at War*, 112, quoting Besig to Baldwin, Mar. 13, 1942, NCCLU, CHS, Box 4, Folder ACLU 82.

25 Ernest Besig, unedited interview for *Of Civil Wrongs and Rights*. See also "One 'Test Case' Endures as an Advocate's Cause," *San Francisco Daily Journal*, Feb. 19, 1992.

26 Irons, *Justice at War*, 97, citing interview with Ernest Besig. Besig had approached two other Nisei at the jail, who, like Fred, had been arrested for violating the removal orders. Ibid., citing *San Francisco Examiner*, June 2, and June 14, 1942. Both met with Besig but declined his offer of representation. Both pled guilty to violating Public Law 503 and were sentenced to short terms in federal prison camp. Ibid., citing interview with Ernest Besig.

27 William Petersen, *Japanese Americans* (NY: Random House, 1971), 78, citing *ACLU News*, San Francisco, Apr. 1942. "One 'Test Case' Endures as an Advocate's Cause," *San Francisco Daily Journal*, Feb. 19, 1992.

28 Fred Korematsu, interview by Bannai and Kashima, May 14, 1996.

29 Fred Korematsu address to Asian Pacific Islander Law Student Association, unedited transcript for *Of Civil Wrongs and Rights*. "Social Data Registration," Fred Korematsu, Korematsu family Tanforan records; Fred Korematsu, unedited interview for *Unfinished Business*.

30 Fred Korematsu, unedited interview for *Unfinished Business*; Yackle, "Japanese American Internment," 102; Fred Korematsu, unedited interview for *Of Civil Wrongs and Rights*.

31 Fred Korematsu, unedited interview for *Of Civil Wrongs and Rights*; Fred Korematsu, unedited interview for *Unfinished Business*.

32 Kay Korematsu, interview by author, May 25, 2008. Yuri Yokota, who knew the Korematsu family in camp, similarly believed that Fred's mother suffered because of Fred's arrest. Yuri Yokota, interview by author, May 23, 2008.

33 Fred Korematsu, unedited interview for *Of Civil Wrongs and Rights*; Fred Korematsu, unedited interview for *Unfinished Business*.

34 Fred Korematsu, JANM remarks; Fred Korematsu, unedited interview for *Unfinished Business*; Fred Korematsu, unedited interview for *Of Civil Wrongs and Rights*.

35 Goodwin FBI report, 3, relating the report of William Kilpatrick, supervisor of education at Tanforan.

36 Kikuchi, *Diary*, 136–37, entry for June 19, 1942.

37 Ibid., 133–38. In later years, other Nisei have said they agreed with Fred's resistance to incarceration. Nisei Tom Oishi, for example, explained, "[W]e thought Fred was different. But Fred turned out to be a hero. He has enough guts to say, 'I'm an American citizen. I'm entitled to stay here. You have no business putting me into camp.' He refused to go. . . . I thought Fred had a lot of courage." Tom Oishi, interview by Graves and Washburn, 126.

38 Yackle, "Japanese American Internment," 102.

39 Fred Korematsu, unedited interview for *Unfinished Business*.

40 Nakano, *Japanese American Women*, 37, 105. Lauren Lee, "I don't think we can forget what happened. We have to remember," *KVAL News*, Dec. 7, 2011, http://www.kval.com/news/local/I-dont-think-we-can-forget-what-happened-I-think-we-have-to-remember-135142253.html (interview with Gordon Nagai).

41 Nakano, *Japanese American Women*, 37–38. Fred's wife, Kathryn, observed that because Fred was not the main support for his parents, he had the ability to challenge the removal orders that other Nisei did not have. "[T]he Nisei had to be protective of their parents. Fred, having three brothers, was freer than a lot of Nisei. A lot of them wish now that they could have refused, but who would have helped them?" Kathryn Korematsu, interview by Bannai and Kashima, May 14, 1996, Densho Visual Histories, http://archive.densho.org/main.aspx.

42 Nakano, *Japanese American Women*, 105.

43 Yackle, "Japanese American Internment," 102; Kathryn Korematsu, interview by author, May 23, 2008.

44 Goodwin FBI report. Statement, Fred Korematsu to Ernest Besig, NCCLU, CHS,

MS 3580, Series 111, Box 56, Folder ACLU 1386, also quoted in Irons, *Justice at War*, 99.

45 Goodwin FBI report.

46 Fred Korematsu to Ernest Besig, undated, NCCLU, CHS, MS 3580, Series 111, Box 56, Folder ACLU 1387.

47 Ida Boitano to Besig, undated, NCCLU, CHS, MS 3580, Series 111, Box 56, Folder ACLU 1387

48 Besig to Boitano, July 7, 1942, NCCLU, CHS, MS 3580, Series 111, Box 56, Folder ACLU 1387.

49 Besig to Fred Korematsu, Aug. 4, 1942, NCCLU, CHS, MS 3580, Series 111, Box 56, Folder ACLU 1387.

50 Fred Korematsu to Besig, Sept. 3, 1942, NCCLU, CHS, MS 3580, Series 111, Box 56, Folder ACLU 138.

51 Fred Korematsu, unedited interview for *Of Civil Wrongs and Rights*.

52 Information, June 12, 1941, in transcript of record to WWII Supreme Court, 1; "3 Japanese Defy Curbs: Army Says One Tried to Become 'Spaniard' by Plastic Surgery," *New York Times*, June 13, 1942, 8.

53 Irons, *Justice at War*, 117; Besig to Thomas, July 10, 1942, NCCLU, CHS, MS 3580, Series II, Box 28, Folder ACLU 592; Fred Korematsu, unedited interview for *Of Civil Wrongs and Rights*.

54 Fred Korematsu, unedited interview for *Of Civil Wrongs and Rights*.

55 Fred Korematsu, unedited interview for *Of Civil Wrongs and Rights*; Besig to Thomas, July 10, 1942, p. 2, NCCLU, CHS, MS 3580, Series II, Box 28, Folder ACLU 592.

56 Fred Korematsu, unedited interview for *Of Civil Wrongs and Rights*.

57 Fred Beck, executive of the Historical Services Division, United States Army, Center of Military History, testimony, CWRIC hearing, Washington, DC, July 14, 1981, pp. 163–64; Okubo, *Citizen 13660*, 111; "Individual Record," Nov. 10, 1942, Fred Korematsu WRA records; CWRIC, *Personal Justice Denied*, 157.

58 Miné Okubo described the train trip to Topaz as "a nightmare that lasted two nights and a day. . . . All the shades were drawn and we were not allowed to look out of the windows. . . . Many became train sick and vomited. The children cried from restlessness. At one point on the way, a brick was thrown into one of the cars." Okubo, *Citizen 13660*, 117–18; see also CWRIC, *Personal Justice Denied*, 149–50. For a further account of the Japanese American incarceration at Topaz, see Taylor, *Jewel of the Desert*, 89–285; and Richardson, *I Call to Remembrance*, 68–205.

59 George Hagiwara, testimony, CWRIC hearing, San Francisco, Aug. 11, 1981.

60 Soon after Roosevelt asked Eisenhower to head the agency, Eisenhower wrote, "I feel most deeply that when the war is over and we consider calmly this unprecedented migration of 120,000 people, we as Americans are going to regret the avoidable injustice that may have been done." Milton S. Eisenhower, *The President Is Calling* (Garden City, NY: Doubleday & Co., 1974), 96–98; Daniels, *Concen-*

tration Camps, 91, quoting Eisenhower to Wickard, Apr. 1, 1942, Correspondence of the Secretary of Agriculture, Foreign Relations, 2-1, Aliens-Refugees, RG 16, National Archives.

61 Okubo, *Citizen 13660*, 124; CWRIC, *Personal Justice Denied*, 158, citing report of the WRA, Mar. 18–June 30, 1942, p. 7.

62 Charles F. Ernst (Topaz project director) to Mr. E. M. Rowalt (acting regional director, WRA, San Francisco), Oct. 13, 1942, Fred Korematsu WRA records. Tom Misawa recalled his family's quarters: "My family was assigned to a room; the only furnishing being a coal-burning stove. Cots were brought in by truck and dumped outside, with everyone scrambling to get a better one. Foraging for bits of wallboard and wood, anything salvageable to perhaps build shelves or partitions in the rooms. This was our introduction to Topaz." Tom Misawa, testimony, CWRIC hearing, San Francisco, Aug. 13, 1981.

63 CWRIC, *Personal Justice Denied*, 160, quoting Gladys Bell, "Memories of Topaz," unpublished manuscript.

64 Fred Korematsu to Besig, undated, NCCLU, CHS, MS 3580, Series 111, Box 56, Folder ACLU 1385. Hiroshi Kajiwara recalled "facing the cold wintry days when you left the shower with your hair still damp [and] by the time you got to the barracks, the water on your head would turn to ice." Hiroshi Kajiwara, testimony, CWRIC hearing, San Francisco, Aug. 11, 1981, p. 237.

65 CWRIC, *Personal Justice Denied*, 163–64, citing report of the WRA, Oct. 1–Dec. 31, 1942, p. 8; report of the WRA, July 1–Sept. 30, 1942, p. 32; Dillon Myer, *Uprooted Americans: The Japanese Americans and the War Relocation Authority During World War II* (Tucson: University of Arizona Press 1971), 52–53; Ruth E. McKee, "History of WRA: Pearl Harbor to June 30, 1944," unpublished manuscript, 1944, 120. Sachi Kajiwara testified that she became a nurse's aide at Topaz after three weeks of instruction: "I didn't even know the names of the instruments—I felt terribly inadequate to take care of some very sick people." CWRIC, *Personal Justice Denied*, 165, quoting unsolicited testimony, Sachi Kajiwara.

66 Kotsui Korematsu WRA records, National Archives and Records Administration, Washington, DC.

67 CWRIC, *Personal Justice Denied*, 161; Okubo, *Citizen 13660*, 156–57, 164–67, 169–74.

68 CWRIC, *Personal Justice Denied*, 165–69; Ruth Colburn, testimony, CWRIC hearing, San Francisco, Aug. 11, 1981, 277, cited in CWRIC, *Personal Justice Denied*, 167; Fred Korematsu to Besig, undated, NCCLU, CHS, MS 3580, Series 111, Box 56, Folder ACLU 1385.

69 Kaji recalls that the Manzanar High School yearbook staff wanted to include a photo of a camp guard tower in its yearbook. "When we made this yearbook, it became not only pictures of graduation, but pictures of all kinds of activities in camp. . . . So we called it 'Our World,' the world we lived in. Not just high school. But it was a big controversy, because it was our world, and our world was a concentration camp, and that we were behind barbed wires and had a tower with

soldiers guarding it. We wanted that symbol of [our incarceration], the guard tower and the barbed wire." Camp director Ralph P. Merritt initially refused but later relented. Bruce Kaji, interview by author, Sept. 11, 2008. See also Bruce Kaji, *Jive Bomber: A Sentimental Journey* (Los Angeles: Kaji & Associates, 2010).

70 Taylor, *Jewel of the Desert*, 136–37, citing Russell A. Bankston, "The Wakasa Incident," May 10, 1943, Topaz files, WRA, RG 210, and minutes of the Community Council, Apr. 15, 1943, JERS; Tsueko Yamasaki, testimony, CWRIC hearing, San Francisco, Aug. 12, 1981, p. 493.

71 Okubo, *Citizen 13660*, 139.

72 Sox Kitashima, unedited interview for *Of Civil Wrongs and Rights*.

73 Yuri Yokota, interview by author, May 23, 2008.

74 "Korematsu Case: Eviction Order Declared Legal," *Topaz Times*, Dec. 9, 1943. News of the proceedings in Fred's case was also published in other camp newspapers, including the *Heart Mountain Sentinel*, the *Manzanar Free Press*, the *Minidoka Irrigator*, and the *Rohwer Outpost*.

CHAPTER 5. THE ROCKY, WINDING ROAD TO THE SUPREME COURT

1 Fred Korematsu, interview by Bannai and Kashima, May 14, 1996; Irons, *Justice at War*, 117.

2 Irons, *Justice at War*, 117.

3 Demurrer to Information, June 20, 1942, in transcript of record to WWII Supreme Court, 2–11.

4 Points and Authorities in Support of Demurrer to Information, June 20, 1942, in transcript of record to WWII Supreme Court, 11–13. In *Ex Parte Milligan*, the court stated that martial law could not arise "from a *threatened* invasion. . . . The necessity must be actual and present; the invasion real, such as effectually closes the courts and deposes the civil administration." Ex Parte Milligan, 71 U.S. 2, 127 (1866).

5 Memo, Baldwin to members of the National Committee, June 24, 1942, NCCLU, CHS, MS 3580, Series II, Box 28, Folder ACLU 592. For a discussion of the national ACLU's position and actions with regard to the orders that led to the Japanese American incarceration, see Irons, *Justice at War*, 106–18, 128–34, 168–75, 186–95, 254–61, 267–68, 303–5; Judy Kutulas, *The American Civil Liberties Union and the Making of Modern Liberalism, 1930–1960* (Chapel Hill: University of North Carolina Press, 2006), 97–103, 113–25; Kutulas, "In Quest of Autonomy," 201–31; Roger Daniels, *The Japanese American Cases: The Rule of Law in Time of War* (Lawrence: University Press of Kansas, 2013), 47–50, 63; and Samuel Walker, *In Defense of American Liberties: A History of the ACLU*, 2nd ed. (Carbondale: Southern Illinois University Press, 1990), 136–49.

6 Walker, *In Defense of American Liberties*, 137–38, quoting Edward Alsworth Ross (national chairman), Edward L. Parsons (vice-chair, national committee), John Haynes Holmes (chairman, board of directors), and Roger Baldwin (director), et al. to Roosevelt, Mar. 20, 1942.

7   Irons, *Justice at War*, 109, citing ACLU board minutes, Mar. 23 and 30, 1942.

8   Walker, *In Defense of American Liberties*, 140, quoting ACLU, memo, May 22, 1942.

9   Irons, *Justice at War*, 129, citing ACLU board minutes, May 18, 1942, Reel 9, ACLU Microfilms and Memo, "To Active Members of the Corporation," May 22, 1942, vol. 2444, ACLU, Princeton University Library, and List, "Ballot on Removal of Civilians from Military Area," June 16, 1942, Vol. 2444, ACLU, Princeton Univ. Library; memo, Baldwin to members of the national committee, June 24, 1942, NCCLU, CHS, MS 3580, Series II, Box 28, Folder ACLU 592. See also Elinson and Yogi, *Wherever There's a Fight*, 430–31.

10 Irons, *Justice at War*, 130, citing ACLU board minutes, June 22, 1942, Reel 9, ACLU Microfilms.

11 Memo, Baldwin to members of the national committee, June 24, 1942, NCCLU, CHS, MS 3580, Series II, Box 28, Folder ACLU 592.

12 Walter Frank et al. to A. L. Wirin, July 2, 1942, NCCLU, CHS, MS 3580, Series II, Box 28, Folder ACLU 592.

13 Irons, *Justice at War*, 130, citing ACLU board minutes, June 22, 1942, Reel 9, ACLU Microfilms.

14 Irons, *Justice at War*, 131, quoting Besig to Baldwin, July 2, 1942, vol. 2397, ACLU, Princeton University Library. For a discussion of the clash between the Northern California ACLU chapter and the national ACLU over Fred's case, see Kutulas, "In Quest of Autonomy," 213–16.

15 Elinson and Yogi, *Wherever There's a Fight*, 431.

16 Irons, *Justice at War*, 132, citing telegram, Frank to Besig, July 8, 1942, vol. 2397, ACLU, Princeton University Library; telegram, Besig to Forster, July 9, 1942, NC-CLU, CHS, MS 3580, Series 111, Box 56, Folder ACLU 1386.

17 Irons, *Justice at War*, 132, citing ACLU board minutes, July 20, 1942, Reel 9, ACLU Microfilms; Milner to Besig, July 22, 1942, NCCLU, CHS, Box 4, Folder 83.

18 Besig to Thomas, July 10, 1942, p. 2, NCCLU, CHS, MS 3580, Series 111, Box 56, Folder ACLU 1386; Irons, *Justice at War*, 132.

19 "One 'Test Case' Ensures as an Advocate's Cause," *San Francisco Daily Journal*, Feb. 19, 1992.

20 Bulletin 142, Japanese American Citizens League, Office of the National Secretary, 1–2, Apr. 7, 1942, NCCLU, CHS, MS 3580, Series II, Box 28, Folder ACLU 592.

21 Kikuchi, *Diary*, 88, entry for May 25, 1942.

22 Yackle, "Japanese American Internment," 99–100.

23 "Alfonso Zirpoli, Federal Judge, Is Dead at 90," *New York Times*, July 13, 1995.

24 Brief of Plaintiff in Opposition to Demurrer, p. 6, July 8, 1942, NCCLU, CHS, MS 3580, Series 111, Box 56, Folder ACLU 1385.

25 Ex Parte Ventura, 44 F. Supp. 520, 523 (W. D. Wash. 1942). See also discussion of the *Ventura* case in Irons, *Justice at War*, 112–13.

26 Brief of Plaintiff in Opposition to Demurrer, p. 11, July 8, 1942, NCCLU, CHS, MS 3580, Series 111, Box 56, Folder ACLU 1385.

27 Ibid., 11–12.

28 Brief of the State of California as Amicus Curiae, 12, 19–20, 36–37, Aug. 18, 1942,

Korematsu Coram Nobis Litigation Collection, Collection Number 545, Box 25, Folder 3.

29 Order Overruling Demurrer, in transcript of record to WWII Supreme Court, 14; Irons, *Justice at War*, 152.

30 Yackle, "Japanese American Internment," 103; Irons, *Justice at War*, 152; letter, Frank E. Davis (Tanforan Manager), Sept. 8, 1942, Fred Korematsu WRA records; Judgment, Sept. 8, 1942, in transcript of record to WWII Supreme Court, 15.

31 Judgment, Sept. 8, 1942, testimony of Oliver T. Mansfield, and Motion to Dismiss, in transcript of record to WWII Supreme Court, pp. 15, 19–23; Irons, *Justice at War*, 152–53.

32 Testimony of Fred Korematsu and Motion to Dismiss, in transcript of record to WWII Supreme Court, 23–25.

33 Judgment, Sept. 8, 1942, in transcript of record to WWII Supreme Court, 15–16.

34 Conditions of Probation, Fournier court documents, Folder 12, Korematsu Institute, San Francisco, Cal.

35 Fred Korematsu to Besig, Sept. 9, 1942, NCCLU, CHS, MS 3580, Series 111, Box 56, Folder ACLU 1385.

36 Notice of Appeal, Sept. 11, 1942, and grounds of appeal, Sept. 10, 1942, in transcript of record to WWII Supreme Court, 16–17.

37 Reporter's Transcript, 1–3, Dec. 23, 1942, *Korematsu* Coram Nobis Litigation Collection, UCLA, Collection Number 545, Box 25, Folder 3; Irons, *Justice at War*, 162.

38 Reporter's Transcript, 1–2, Dec. 23, 1942, *Korematsu* Coram Nobis Litigation Collection, UCLA, Collection Number 545, Box 25, Folder 3.

39 Ibid.

40 Memorandum and Order, Dec. 31, 1942, quoted in "Appellant's Memorandum of Points and Authorities in Opposition to Appellee's Motion to Dismiss Appeal," 5–6, NCCLU, CHS, MS 3580, Series 111, Box 56, Folder ACLU 1385.

41 Irons, *Justice at War*, 168.

42 Frank to Parsons, Nov. 9, 1942, NCCLU, CHS, MS 3580, Series 111, Box 56, Folder ACLU 1385.

43 Besig to Frank, Nov. 11, 1942, NCCLU, CHS, MS 3580, Series 111, Box 56, Folder ACLU 1385.

44 Charles F. Ernst (Topaz project director) to E. M. Rowalt (WRA acting regional director), Oct. 13, 1942, Fred Korematsu WRA records.

45 Walter Funabiki later recounted, "It was an opportunity for the farmers and *hakujins* [white folk] out there because they were looking for cheap labor. Here was this source, in this camp, for cheap labor and they said why not? We saw it as an opportunity to get to go to the store and to buy stuff to bring back to the family." Walter Funabiki, written testimony, CWRIC hearing, San Francisco, Sept. 29, 1981, quoted in CWRIC, *Personal Justice Denied*, 180. Fred Korematsu to Besig, undated, NCCLU, CHS, MS 3580, Series 111, Box 56, Folder ACLU 1385. CWRIC, *Personal Justice Denied*, 181–82.

46 CWRIC, *Personal Justice Denied*, 182–83.

47 Fred Korematsu to Besig, undated, NCCLU, CHS, MS 3580, Series 111, Box 56, Folder ACLU 1385; "Individual Record," Fred Korematsu WRA records.

48 "Application for Permit to Leave a Relocation Center for Private Employment," undated, Fred Korematsu WRA records.

49 Claude Cornwall, chief, employment division, to Mr. M. McKisih [*sic*], Nov. 18, 1942, and McKissick Motor Co. to Mr. Cornwall, marked "received" Dec. 6, 1942, Fred Korematsu WRA records.

50 "Individual Record," Fred Korematsu WRA records; Harris to Frase, Feb. 15, 1943, Fred Korematsu WRA records; Yackle, "Japanese American Internment," 103.

51 Fred Korematsu to Besig, undated, and Besig to Fred Korematsu, Dec. 2, 1942, NCCLU, CHS, MS 3580, Series 111, Box 56, Folder ACLU 1385.

52 Frase to Harris, Feb. 4, 1943, and Harris to Frase, Feb. 15, 1943, Fred Korematsu WRA records.

53 Kay Korematsu, interview by author, May 25, 2008.

54 Yackle, "Japanese American Internment," 103–4.

55 Fred Korematsu to Besig, undated, NCCLU, CHS, MS 3580, Series 111, Box 56, Folder ACLU 1385.

56 Besig to Fred Korematsu, Jan. 29, 1943, NCCLU, CHS, MS 3580, Series 111, Box 56, Folder ACLU 1385.

57 Bulletin 142, Japanese American Citizens League, Office of the National Secretary, p. 1, Apr. 7, 1942, NCCLU, CHS, MS 3580, Series II, Box 28, Folder ACLU 592.

58 Irons, *Justice at War*, 84, quoting Irons, interview with Minoru Yasui.

59 United States v. Yasui, 48 F. Supp. 40, 53, 55 (D. Ore. 1942); United States v. Yasui, 51 F. Supp. 234, 235 (D. Ore. 1943).

60 Irons, *Justice at War*, 87–88, quoting memo, special agent in charge, Seattle, to director, FBI, May 23, 1942, File 146-42-20, DOJ. For insight into Gordon's background and what motivated him to resist through the lens of his wartime journals, see Gordon K. Hirabayashi, with James A. Hirabayashi and Lane Ryo Hirabayashi, *A Principled Stand: The Story of* Hirabayashi v. United States (Seattle: University of Washington Press, 2013); Jeanne Sakata, *Hold These Truths*, play directed by Lisa Rothe, performed July 31–Aug. 3, 2014, at the ACT Theater, Seattle.

61 *Hirabayashi*, 320 U.S. 81, 84.

62 "Exclusion Program Debated in Court," *Los Angeles Times*, Feb. 20, 1943, A.

63 "Attack on Order Evacuating Japs Before 7 Judges," *Chicago Daily Tribune*, Feb. 20, 1943, 7.

64 Irons, *Justice at War*, 178, quoting *San Francisco Examiner*, Feb. 20, 1943, p. 4.

65 Irons, *Justice at War*, 178–79, quoting *San Francisco Examiner*, Feb. 20, 1943, p. 4, and *New York Times*, Feb. 21, 1943, p. 23; "Attack on Order Evacuating Japs Before 7 Judges," *Chicago Daily Tribune*, Feb. 20, 1943, p. 7.

66 Fred Korematsu to Besig, Mar. 3, 1943, and Besig to Fred Korematsu, Mar. 3, 1943, NCCLU, CHS, MS 3580, Series 111, Box 56, Folder ACLU 1385.

67 Irons, *Justice at War*, 182–83. As Irons explains, neither the defense counsel nor the Supreme Court knew that Attorney General Biddle was behind the request for certification. Ibid., 182, citing interview with Edward Ennis.

68 *Hirabayashi*, 320 U.S. 81, 85; *Yasui*, 320 U.S. 115, 116.

69 Brief for Appellant, Korematsu v. United States, 319 U.S. 432 (1943) (No. 912) 1943 WL 54793, 9 (May 7, 1943).

70 Korematsu v. United States, 319 U.S. 432, 433, 436 (1943); "Court to Hear Japanese: High Tribunal Orders Appeals Body to Consider Case," *New York Times*, June 2, 1943; Ennis to Zirpoli, May 12, 1943, CWRIC 10034, CWRIC Reel 9, Box 9, DOJ correspondence, briefs, and materials in *Korematsu v. United States*.

71 Besig to Fred Korematsu, June 9, 1943, NCCLU, CHS, MS 3580, Series 111, Box 56, Folder ACLU 1385.

CHAPTER 6. THE UGLY ABYSS OF RACISM

1 Fred Korematsu to Besig, Mar. 27, 1943, and July 23, 1943, NCCLU, CHS, MS 3580, Series 111, Box 56, Folder ACLU 1386.

2 Eric L. Muller, *Free to Die for Their Country: The Story of the Japanese American Draft Resisters in World War II* (Chicago: University of Chicago Press, 2003), 42, quoting minutes of the Special Emergency National Conference, Japanese American Citizens League, 36-17-24, Nov. 1942, Salt Lake City, on file with the UCLA Library, Department of Special Collections, Collection 2010, Box 296.

3 See Muller, *Free to Die*, 41, 43–49; Robinson, *By Order of the President*, 163–70.

4 For a discussion of the turmoil and confusion caused by the loyalty oaths, see, e.g., ibid., 191–97; Weglyn, *Years of Infamy*, 134–51; Muller, *Free to Die*, 50–58; and, discussing resistance to the registration program at Topaz, Cherstin M. Lyon, *Prisons and Patriots: Japanese American Wartime Citizenship, Civil Disobedience, and Historical Memory* (Philadelphia: Temple University Press, 2012), 80–104. For a discussion of the government's ill-founded, failed attempts to judge the loyalty of Japanese Americans, see Eric Muller, *American Inquisition: The Hunt for Japanese American Disloyalty in World War II* (Chapel Hill: University of North Carolina Press, 2007), 31–38.

5 See CWRIC, *Personal Justice Denied*, 191–92; "Statement of United States Citizen of Japanese Ancestry," Selective Service Form 304A, Jan. 23, 1943.

6 Fred Korematsu to Besig, Mar. 27, 1943, NCCLU, CHS, MS 3580, Series 111, Box 56, Folder ACLU 1386.

7 Albert Nakai, testimony, CWRIC hearing, San Francisco, Aug. 12, 1981, pp. 140–41, quoted in CWRIC, *Personal Justice Denied*, 196. For John Okada's experience as one of the "no-no" boys, see his seminal work *No-No Boy* (Tokyo: Charles E. Tuttle Co., 1957; repr., Seattle: University of Washington Press, 2014). For accounts of the Japanese American draft resisters during World War II, see Eric Muller, *Free to Die*; *Conscience and the Constitution*, produced by Frank Abe (Hohokus, NJ: Transit Media, 2000), DVD. For another account of resistance, that of Japanese Americans in the military who refused to serve in combat while

their families were incarcerated, see Shirley Castelnuovo, *Soldiers of Conscience: Japanese American Military Resisters in World War II* (Westport, CT: Praeger Publishers, 2008).

8   Muller, *American Inquisition*, 38; Weglyn, *Years of Infamy*, 154–55.

9   CWRIC, *Personal Justice Denied*, 195, 253.

10   "Special Travel Permit," May 21, 1943; "Statement of United States Citizen of Japanese Ancestry," May 25, 1943; Frank Twohey, leave officer, to Dillon Myer, WRA director, May 27, 1943; and "Citizen's Leave Permit for Work Group," Fred Korematsu WRA records.

11   Appellant's Opening Brief, *Korematsu* Coram Nobis Litigation Collection, UCLA, Collection Number 545, Box 25, Folder 2.

12   Fred Korematsu to Besig, June 26, 1943, NCCLU, CHS, MS 3580, Series 111, Box 56, Folder ACLU 1387.

13   For a discussion of the *Hirabayashi* case, see, e.g., Irons, *Justice at War*; and Yamamoto et al., *Race, Rights and Reparation*, 91–114. In addition, Eric Muller writes that the wartime government lied in arguing, in *Hirabayashi*, that the curfew was necessary to meet a serious threat of a Japanese invasion of the West Coast when they foresaw no such invasion. Eric L. Muller, "Hirabayashi and the Invasion Evasion," *North Carolina Law Review* 88 (May 2010): 1333–87.

14   *Yasui*, 320 U.S. 115, 116. For a discussion of the *Yasui* case, see, e.g., Irons, *Justice at War*; and Yamamoto et al., *Race, Rights and Reparation*, 114–20.

15   Korematsu v. United States, 140 F.2d 289, 290 (9th Cir. 1943); "Federal Court Upholds Jap Evacuation Order," *Los Angeles Times*, Dec. 3, 1943, pg. A.

16   *Korematsu*, 140 F.2d, 290.

17   "Upholds DeWitt on Evacuation," *New York Times*, Dec. 3, 1943.

18   Besig to Fred Korematsu, Dec. 11, 1943, and Dec. 16, 1943, NCCLU, CHS, MS 3580, Series 111, Box 56, Folder ACLU 1386.

19   Besig to Ralston, Dec. 11, 1943, NCCLU, CHS, MS 3580, Series 111, Box 56, Folder ACLU 1386; Daniel F. Tritter, "In the Defense of Fred Korematsu: Vox Clamantis in Deserto Curiarum," *Thomas Jefferson Law Review* 27 (2005): 279; "Ralston, Labor Attorney, Dies," *Los Angeles Times*, Oct. 14, 1945, p. 8. Ralston had also been counsel on Fred's brief during Fred's first appeal to the Supreme Court in 1943. Brief for Appellant, Korematsu v. United States, 319 U.S. 432 (1943) (No. 912), 1943 WL 54793 (May 7, 1943).

20   Baldwin to Besig, Dec. 13, 1943, and Dec. 20, 1943, NCCLU, CHS, MS 3580, Series 111, Box 56, Folder ACLU 1386.

21   On December 16, 1943, Besig wrote Fraenkel, standing behind Collins as representing both the chapter and Fred, "I think it ought to be recognized that Mr. Collins is attorney of record for Korematsu by virtue of his being counsel for the Civil Liberties Union." Besig to Fraenkel, Dec. 16, 1943, NCCLU, CHS, MS 3580, Series 111, Box 56, Folder ACLU 1386. In a later letter to Professor Harrop S. Freeman, Besig made the chapter's disagreement with the national office clear: "I am frank to confess that we do not share the sentiments of our national office with reference to this case. This branch is opposed to the Executive Order and

is opposed on principle to any exclusion by the Military unless martial law is operative." Besig to Freeman, Mar. 23, 1944, NCCLU, CHS, MS 3580, Series 111, Box 56, Folder ACLU 1386.

22 Memo from Glick, Jan. 1, 1944, Fred Korematsu WRA records.

23 Petition for Writ of *Certiorari* to the United States Circuit Court of Appeals for the Ninth Circuit and brief in support thereof, Feb. 2, 1944, pp. 9–10; "Jap-American Appeals Army Ouster Order," *Los Angeles Times*, Feb. 10, 1943; "Evacuation Test Case Is Filed in Supreme Court," *Rocky Shimpo*, Feb. 16, 1944.

24 Korematsu v. United States, 321 U.S. 760 (1944); "Supreme Court Will Review Exclusion Case," *Rocky Shimpo*, Mar. 31, 1944; Irons, *Justice at War*, 268; Fred Korematsu to Besig, undated, NCCLU, CHS, MS 3580, Series 111, Box 56, Folder ACLU 1385.

25 Irons, *Justice at War*, 206, 278–79, citing, e.g., "DeWitt Raps Biddle Failure to Check Japs" and "DeWitt Shows Plenty of Reasons for Removing Japs," *Los Angeles Times*, Jan. 20, 1944, pp. 2, 4; DeWitt, *Final Report*.

26 Brief for Appellant, *Korematsu*, 323 U.S. 214 (No. 22), 1944 WL 42849, 4–6 (Sept. 16, 1944).

27 Ibid., 6–7, 63–64.

28 Ibid., 35–50, 87–95.

29 Remarks by Frank Murphy, "The American Way of Life Can It Survive?" Sept. 10, 1944, published by the National Committee Against Persecution of Jews, Washington, DC.

30 "Negation of Idea Hit by Justice Murphy," *Rocky Shimpo*, Sept. 13, 1944.

31 Brief for the United States, *Korematsu*, 323 U.S. 214 (No. 22), 1944 WL 42850, 18–21, 24 (Oct. 5, 1944).

32 Ibid., 28–33.

33 Ibid., 40–59.

34 Brief of the States of California, Oregon, and Washington as Amici Curiae, on Behalf of Appellee, *Korematsu*, 323 U.S. 214 (No. 22), 1944 WL 42851 (Oct. 7, 1944).

35 Brief for the American Civil Liberties Union, Amicus Curiae, *Korematsu*, 323 U.S. 214 (No. 22), 1944 WL 42853 (Oct. 10, 1944).

36 Brief for the Japanese American Citizens League, Amicus Curiae, *Hirabayashi*, 320 U.S. 81 (No. 870); *Yasui*, 320 U.S. 115 (No. 871), 1943 WL 54782 (May 10, 1943). Brief of Japanese American Citizens League, Amicus Curiae, *Korematsu*, 323 U.S. 214 (No. 22), 1944 WL 42852 (Oct. 9, 1944).

37 JACL Bulletin No. 7, Mar. 4, 1943, JACL Archives.

38 Bulletin 142, Japanese American Citizens League, Office of the National Secretary, 1–2, Apr. 7, 1942, NCCLU, CHS, MS 3580, Series II, Box 28, Folder ACLU 592.

39 "Case Important," *Rocky Shimpo*, Oct. 11, 1944.

40 Saburo Kido, "Timely Topics," *Pacific Citizen*, Oct. 21, 1944.

41 Besig to Pacific Citizen, *Pacific Citizen*, Nov. 4, 1944.

42 "Say Japanese Should Help Attorneys Defray Court Test Legal Costs," *Rocky Shimpo*, Nov. 15, 1944.

43 "Official minutes," Ninth Bienniel National Convention, Japanese American Citizens League, Feb. 26–Mar. 4, 1946, Denver, Colorado, pp. 9–10, JACL History Collection, 1923–95, Series 14, Box 46, Japanese American National Library, San Francisco.

44 Brief of Japanese American Citizens League, amicus curiae, *Korematsu*, 323 U.S. 214 (1944) (No. 22), 1944 WL 42852, 3 (Oct. 9, 1944).

45 Ibid., 13, 16–49, 151–78, 197–200.

46 Fred Korematsu to Besig, Sept. 2, 1944, and Oct. 1, 1944; and Besig to Fred Korematsu, Oct. 9, 1044, NCCLU, CHS, MS 3580, Series 111, Box 56, Folder ACLU 1387.

47 Saburo Kido, "Timely Topics," *Pacific Citizen*, Oct. 21, 1944.

48 Irons, *Justice at War*, 313–15. No transcript is available for Collins's or Horsky's arguments; all that exists are notes taken by an observer. Ibid., 312.

49 Transcript of proceedings before the Supreme Court, Oct. 12, 1944, pp. 1–3, *Korematsu* Coram Nobis Litigation Collection, UCLA, Collection Number 545, Box 25, Folder 5 (hereafter cited as *Korematsu* Supreme Court Oral Argument transcript).

50 Bill Hosokawa, "Principle Involved in Court Test Cases," *Pacific Citizen*, Oct. 21, 1944.

51 *Korematsu*, 323 U.S. 214; "Court Upholds Army Moving of Japanese," *Atlanta Constitution*, Dec. 19, 1944, 7.

52 For an excellent discussion of the justices' deliberations in the *Korematsu* case, see Irons, *Justice at War*, 319–41.

53 *Korematsu*, 323 U.S., 224 (Frankfurter, J., concurring), quoting Charles Evans Hughes, "War Powers under the Constitution," *Marquette Law Review* 2 (1917): 9.

54 *Korematsu*, 323 U.S., 225 (Frankfurter, J., concurring).

55 Editorial, "Legalization of Racism," *Washington Post*, Dec. 22, 1944, 8. "[T]his blow to civil liberties concerns every one of us, without respect for difference in the color of skin." Merlo Pusey, "War and Civil Rights," *Washington Post*, Dec. 26, 1944, 7.

56 Marjorie McKenzie, "Pursuit of Democracy," *Pittsburgh Courier*, Jan. 6, 1945, 6.

57 Westbrook Pegler, "Is Korematsu Case Opinion Truly American?" *Deseret News*, Mar. 15, 1945, 4.

58 Eugene Rostow, "The Japanese American Cases—A Disaster," *Yale Law Journal* 54 (1945): 490–91, 503–4.

59 Nanette Dembitz, "Racial Discrimination and the Military Judgment: The Supreme Court's Korematsu and Endo Decisions," *Columbia Law Review* 45 (1945): 183.

60 tenBroek et al., *Prejudice, War, and the Constitution*, 220.

61 Eric Yamamoto, "Korematsu Revisited—Correcting the Injustice of Extraordinary Government Excess and Lax Judicial Review: Time for a Better Accommodation of National Security Concerns and Civil Liberties," *Santa Clara Law Review* 26 (1986): 3.

62 For other critiques of the World War II decision in *Korematsu v. United States*, see e.g., Eric Yamamoto et al., *Race, Rights, and Reparation*; Liam Braber, "Korematsu's Ghost: A Post–September 11th Analysis of Race and National Security," *Villanova Law Review* 47 (2002): 451–90; Jerry Kang, "Thinking Through Internment, 12/7 and 9/11," *Amerasia Journal* 28 (2001): 42–50; Lorraine K. Bannai and Dale Minami, "Internment during World War II and Litigations," in *Asian Americans and the Supreme Court: A Documentary History*, ed. H. Kim (Westport, CT: Greenwood Press, 1992); and Erwin Chemerinsky, "*Korematsu v. United States*: A Tragedy Hopefully Never to Be Repeated," *Pepperdine Law Review* 39 (2011): 163–72.

63 *Ex Parte Endo*, 323 U.S. 283 (1944); Warren Francis, "Supreme Court Rules Loyal Nips Held Illegally," *Los Angeles Times*, Dec. 19, 1944, 1; Joseph H. Short, "Court Rules Jap-Americans Loyal to U.S. Can't Be Held," *Sun*, Dec. 19, 1944, 11.

64 *Endo*, 323 U.S., 284, 288–89; see also Irons, *Justice at War*, 102–3, 143–51, 255–58, 265–68; Tateishi, *And Justice for All*, 60–61; Eric Muller, "This Week at IsThatLegal: An Online Mini-symposium Commemorating the Life of Mitsuye Endo, A Quiet Civil Rights Hero," June 5, 2006, http://ericmuller.org/archives/2006/06/.

65 Irons, *Justice at War*, 345.

66 CWRIC, *Personal Justice Denied*, 215–24.

67 In a December 1943 *Los Angeles Times* poll, 9,855 readers responded that they would "permanently exclude all Japanese from the Pacific Coast States"; 999 said that they would not. 10,598 said they would favor a constitutional amendment to deport all Japanese and forbid further immigration; 732 said they did not. "Public Demands New Policy on Japs in U.S.," *Los Angeles Times*, Dec. 6, 1943. In an editorial of April 22, 1943, the *Los Angeles Times* expressed outrage at talk of returning Japanese Americans to the West Coast: "As a race, the Japanese have made for themselves a record for conscienceless treachery unsurpassed in history. Whatever small theoretical advantages there might be in releasing those under restraint in this country would be enormously outweighed by the risks involved." Editorial, "Stupid and Dangerous," *Los Angeles Times*, Apr. 22, 1943.

68 Robinson, *By Order of the President*, 198–99.

69 CWRIC, *Personal Justice Denied*, 228, quoting "Summary of Cabinet Meeting of May 26, 1944," Francis Biddle Papers: Cabinet Meetings, Jan. 1944–May 1945, FDRL (CWRIC 3794).

70 CWRIC, *Personal Justice Denied*, 229, quoting memorandum, "FDR to the Acting Secretary of State and the Secretary of the Interior," June 12, 1944, FDRL. OF 4849 (CWRIC 3717-18).

71 CWRIC, *Personal Justice Denied*, 233; "Army Will Permit Approved Evacuees to Return to the Pacific Coast," *Rocky Shimpo*, Dec. 18, 1944. Japanese American reaction to the news that they could return to the West Coast was mixed. While some were hesitant to return because they feared their reception or because they were bitter about their treatment, many came to understand a sense of freedom that only those who have lost freedom could understand: "Whether the evacuees will return to the West Coast in droves, essentially, is an immaterial issue. . . . The

important fact is, that, once again we may travel through the length and breadth of our own country. The essence of this simple truth lies not in the fact all of us shall leave for any point in the country at any determined time, but that we may do so whenever we wish." Roy M. Takeno, "On the Other Hand: To Move Freely," *Rocky Shimpo*, Dec. 20, 1944.

72 Fred Korematsu, unedited interview for *Of Civil Wrongs and Rights*.

73 Korematsu v. United States, 324 U.S. 885 (1945). See Petition for Rehearing, *Korematsu v. United States*, Feb. 5, 1945, in *Landmark Briefs and Arguments of the Supreme Court of the United States*, Constitutional Law, vol. 42, p. 565; Fred Korematsu, unedited interview for *Of Civil Wrongs and Rights*.

CHAPTER 7. REBUILDING A LIFE

1 CWRIC, *Personal Justice Denied*, 204, 241. As of April 12, 1945, there were approximately 18,000 Japanese Americans remaining at Tule Lake, as well as approximately 55,000 in the eight remaining camps. Robinson, *By Order of the President*, 250.

2 CWRIC, *Personal Justice Denied*, 181, 206.

3 CWRIC, *Personal Justice Denied*, 253, citing Selective Service System, Special Groups, Special Monograph no. 10, vol. 1, 142 (Washington, DC: U.S. Department of the Army) (CWRIC 29640). For the stories of one group of Nisei soldiers, from Hood River, Oregon, see Linda Tamura, *Nisei Soldiers Break Their Silence: Coming Home to Hood River* (Seattle: University of Washington Press, 2012).

4 By the end of the campaign, the 100th was down to 521 men; its 900 Purple Hearts earned it the nickname "Purple Heart Battalion." CWRIC, *Personal Justice Denied*, 256, citing McKee, "History of the WRA," 168; Chester Tanaka, *Go For Broke: A Pictorial History of the Japanese American 100th Infantry Battalion and 442nd Regimental Combat Team* (Richmond, CA: Go For Broke, 1982), 49; Thomas D. Murphy, *Ambassador in Arms: The Story of Hawaii's 100th Battalion* (Honolulu: University of Hawai'i Press, 1954), 58, 69, 123–76.

5 CWRIC, *Personal Justice Denied*, 257–59, citing Tanaka, *Go For Broke*, 47–51; Bill Hosokawa, *Nisei: The Quiet Americans* (New York: William Morrow & Co., 1969), 409–10; Selective Service System, Special Groups, Special Monograph no. 10, vol. 1, pp. 141–42 (Washington, DC: U.S. Department of the Army) (CWRIC 29640). All told, during the war and as a result of subsequent investigation after the war, the unit earned seven Distinguished Unit Citations, as well as thousands of individual decorations, including 21 Congressional Medals of Honor, 29 Distinguished Service Crosses, 588 Silver Stars, more than 4,000 Bronze Stars, and more than 4,000 Purple Hearts. *Densho Encyclopedia*, s.v. "442nd Regimental Combat Team," accessed Jan. 3, 2015, http://encyclopedia.densho.org/442nd_Regimental_Combat_Team/#Aftermath_and_Legacy. On awarding the unit one of its Distinguished Unit Citations, President Harry Truman said, on July 15, 1946, that it had fought "not only the enemy, but you fought prejudice." Robert Asahina, *Just Americans: How Japanese Americans Won a War at Home and*

Abroad (New York: Gotham Books, 2006), 234–35, quoting Truman's remarks of July 15, 1946.

6 CWRIC, *Personal Justice Denied*, 254–56; *Densho Encyclopedia*, s.v. "Military Intelligence Service," last updated July 12, 2013, http://encyclopedia.densho.org/Military%20Intelligence%20Service/.

7 "We Shan't Pretend to Like It," *Los Angeles Times*, Dec. 19, 1944, A4.

8 "Warren Urges People Support Army Decision," *Los Angeles Times*, Dec. 18, 1944, 1.

9 "Are Japs Wanted?," 33. Daniels tells of the experience of the Doi family, the first Nikkei family to return to Placer County, California. In January 1945, the night of a mass meeting to protest the return of Japanese Americans, someone attempted to burn down a packing shed on the Dois' Newcastle ranch; two days later, shots were fired into their home. Two AWOL soldiers and a bartender were charged but were acquitted and regarded as heroes. Daniels, *Concentration Camps*, 159.

10 Daniels, *Concentration Camps*, 160–61; see also CWRIC, *Personal Justice Denied*, 241–42; Hiroshi Kajiwara described how he could get only housecleaning jobs when he returned to San Francisco from Detroit. Hiroshi Kajiwara, testimony, CWRIC hearing, San Francisco, Aug. 11, 1981, 235. White workers refused to work alongside Japanese Americans. Fred Ross, who was employed by the WRA in San Francisco in 1945–46, related the experience of Takeo Minemoto, a highly qualified mechanic, who had, with the agency's assistance, obtained work at the municipal transit station. Seventy-five muni workers sat down and refused to work if Minemoto was there. Ross boarded a bus with three leaders of the revolt, negotiating as the bus ran its route around the city. Fred Ross, testimony, CWRIC hearing, San Francisco, Aug. 11, 1981, 202.

11 Ross, testimony, CWRIC hearing, 204; CWRIC, *Personal Justice Denied*, 241.

12 Joe Korematsu to WRA, Feb. 12, 1945, Joe Korematsu WRA records; Fred Korematsu, interview by Bannai and Kashima, May 14, 1996; Kay Korematsu, interview by author, May 25, 2008. "The evacuation and internment represented an enormous setback for the Issei generation, particularly self-employed farmers and entrepreneurs like the flower growers. The loss of career and income potential, and property was incalculable, but what hurt the most were the losses of what had been built through long hours and sacrifice." Kawaguchi, *Living with Flowers*, 60.

13 Joe Korematsu to Mr. Gee, Apr. 2, 1945, Joe Korematsu WRA records.

14 For a discussion of the WRA's strategy to disperse the Japanese American community, see Daniels, *Concentration Camps*, 166–67.

15 See discussion in CWRIC, *Personal Justice Denied*, 296. In December 1944, columnist Selden Menefee wrote, "Now that the evacuation order has been reversed, some Nisei state that the whole affair, discriminatory though it was, had one good effect. Some 34,000 of the younger generation, nearly all American citizens, have been forced to strike out for themselves. They have settled in places where prejudice was less acute than on the West Coast, and most of them will probably stay there. Best of all, they have been induced by circumstances

to break away from the control of their Japanese-born elders—which will help them become assimilated into the Nation's economic and social life." Selden Menefee, "America at War: Japanese-Americans Return," *Washington Post*, Dec. 21, 1944, p. 11.

16 Daniels, *Concentration Camps*, 167; "Maintain Reserve at Topaz Center," *Rocky Shimpo*, Dec. 29, 1944; CWRIC, *Personal Justice Denied*, 241.

17 "Alien's Travel Permit," May 28, 1945, Kotsui and Kakusaburo Korematsu WRA records; CWRIC, *Personal Justice Denied*, 241; Taylor, *Jewel of the Desert*, 202; Department of Interior, quoted in Daniels, *Concentration Camps*, 167.

18 Kathryn Korematsu, interview by author, May 22, 2008; Kay Korematsu, interview by author, May 25, 2008; Joanne Kataoka, interview by author, Jan. 8, 2011.

19 Connie Wirtz, interview by author, Aug. 24, 2010; see also Joanne Kataoka, interview by author, Jan. 8, 2011.

20 Kathryn Korematsu, interview by author, May 22, 2008.

21 Ibid.; Kathryn Korematsu, unedited interview for *Of Civil Wrongs and Rights*.

22 Kathryn Korematsu, interview by author, May 22, 2008.

23 Kathryn Korematsu, interview by author, May 22 and 23, 2008; Kathryn Korematsu, unedited interview for *Of Civil Wrongs and Rights*; Kathryn Korematsu, interview by Bannai and Kashima, May 14, 1996.

24 Kathryn Korematsu, interview by author, May 22, 2008; Kathryn Korematsu, interview by Bannai and Kashima, May 14, 1996.

25 Kathryn Korematsu, interview by author, May 22 and 23, 2008; Kathryn Korematsu, unedited interview for *Of Civil Wrongs and Rights*.

26 Kathryn Korematsu, interview by author, May 22 and 24, 2008.

27 Kathryn Korematsu, interview by author, May 22, 2008.

28 Kathryn Korematsu, interview by author, May 23, 2008; Kathryn Korematsu, unedited interview for *Of Civil Wrongs and Rights*.

29 Kathryn Korematsu, interview by author, May 22 and 23, 2008; Kathryn Korematsu, unedited interview for *Of Civil Wrongs and Rights*.

30 Kathryn Korematsu, interview by author, May 22, 2008.

31 Kathryn Korematsu, unedited interview for *Of Civil Wrongs and Rights*; Kathryn Korematsu, interview by author, May 23, 2008.

32 Kathryn Korematsu, interview by author, May 23, 2008.

33 Ibid.

34 Kay Korematsu, interview by author, May 25, 2008.

35 Fred Korematsu, unedited interview for *Unfinished Business*; see also Fred Korematsu declaration, Oct. 30, 1983.

36 Kathryn Korematsu, interview by author, May 23, 2008; Kathryn Korematsu, unedited interview for *Of Civil Wrongs and Rights*.

37 Kathryn Korematsu, interview by author, May 22 and 23, 2008.

38 Kathryn Korematsu, interview by author, May 23, 2008; Karen Korematsu, interview by author, May 23, 2009; Ken Korematsu, interview by author, Jan. 7, 2011.

39 Karen Korematsu, interview by author, May 23, 2009.

40 Kathryn Korematsu, interview by author, May 23 and 25, 2008; Ken Korematsu,

interview by author, Jan. 7, 2011; Karen Korematsu, interview by author, May 23, 2009.

41 Karen Korematsu, interview by author, May 23, 2009; Kathryn Korematsu, interview by author, May 23, 2008.

42 Kathryn Korematsu, interview by author, May 23, 2009; Karen Korematsu, interview by author, May 23, 2008.

43 Ken Korematsu, interview by author, Jan. 7, 2011.

44 Karen Korematsu, interview by author, May 23, 2008; Ken Korematsu, interview by author, Jan. 7, 2011.

45 Karen Korematsu, interview by author, May 23, 2008; Kathryn Korematsu, interview by author, May 23, 2008; Joanne Kataoka, interview by author, Jan. 8, 2011.

46 Joanne Kataoka, interview by author, Jan. 8, 2011.

47 McCarran-Walter Act, Public Law No. 82-414, 66 Statutes 163 (1952); see Yamamoto et al., *Race, Rights and Reparation*, 201–2; Kakusaburo naturalization petition; Karen Korematsu, interview by author, May 23, 2008.

48 Kathryn Korematsu, interview by author, May 22, 2008; Kay Korematsu, telephone interview by author, June 25, 2008; Joanne Kataoka, interview by author, Jan. 8, 2011.

49 Kathryn Korematsu, interview by author, May 22 and 23, 2008; Karen Korematsu, interview by author, May 23, 2008; Ken Korematsu, interview by author, Jan. 7, 2011.

50 Kathryn Korematsu, telephone interview by author, Apr. 28, 2011; Joanne Kataoka, interview by author, Jan. 8, 2011; Karen Korematsu, interview by author, May 23, 2008.

51 William Petersen, "Success Story, Japanese American Style," *New York Times Magazine*, Jan. 9, 1966, 21.

52 Harry Kitano, quoted in "Success Story: Outwhiting the Whites," *Newsweek*, June 21, 1971, 25.

53 Petersen, "Success Story," 43; see also Chan, *Asian Americans*, 167–68. A 1979 study of comparative incomes in four major cities found that the income of ethnic Japanese males with four or more years of college averaged only 83 percent, and Japanese females 53 percent, of that of white males with comparable educations. CWRIC, *Personal Justice Denied*, 296–97, citing U.S. Commission on Civil Rights, *Success of Asian Americans: Fact or Fiction?* (Washington, DC: Clearinghouse Publication 64, Sept. 1980).

54 See, e.g., Sucheng Chan, *Asian Americans*, 171; "An Interview with Harry Kitano," in *Roots: An Asian American Reader* (Los Angeles: University of California Press, 1971), 8, 9.

55 In 1971, *Time* magazine quoted Nisei attorney Kenji Ito as saying, "Poor, what poor?" while sitting in his office a block away from the dismal rooming houses of Little Tokyo, Los Angeles, home to elderly Issei men still struggling to make ends meet. Kenji Ito quoted in "Outwhiting the Whites," 25. For further critique of the Model Minority Myth, see Robert S. Chang, "Toward an Asian American Legal Scholarship: Critical Race Theory, Post-Structuralism, and Narrative Space," *California Law Review* 81 (1993): 1258–64.

56 Weglyn, *Years of Infamy*, 270.

57 Amy Uyematsu, "The Emergence of Yellow Power in America," in *Roots: An Asian American Reader* (Los Angeles: Regents of the University of California, 1971), 8, 9; see also Daniel Okimoto, "The Intolerance of Success," in *Roots: An Asian American Reader* (Los Angeles: Regents of the University of California, 1971), 14. Many have discussed the emergence of Sansei political activism. See, e.g., William Wei, *The Asian American Movement* (Philadelphia: Temple University Press, 1993).

58 "In step with their peers in other minority groups many young Japanese-Americans are concerned not simply with assimilating but with unraveling the mysteries of their cultural heritage." "Outwhiting the Whites," 24; see also Murray, *Historical Memories*, 200–13, discussing early Sansei activism seeking to have the history of the incarceration told.

59 Dale Minami, interview by Tom Ikeda and Margaret Chon, Seattle, Feb. 8, 2003, Densho Visual Histories, http://archive.densho.org/main.aspx. It took years before Yuri Yokota could discuss her World War II incarceration with her daughters: "I found out that a lot of people didn't talk about it for a long time. . . . I just didn't feel like talking [to my children] about it I guess. . . . They say soldiers don't talk about what they went through in the war. It's like that, I guess." Yuri Yokota, interview by author, May 23, 2008. Judy Kajiwara further described the effect of the wartime incarceration on the Sansei: "The psychological impact of the camps and history of racism perpetrated upon the Issei and Nisei influenced how they would raise the future generation of Sansei. Many of us, as Sansei, were brought up in a very Americanized way, not understanding the full implications of what happened to our parents and grandparents during the war. Through this process, we lost much of our language and culture and, more importantly, an understanding of our history as Japanese Americans." Judy Kajiwara, testimony, CWRIC hearing, San Francisco, Aug. 31, 1981, pp. 131–32.

60 Fred Korematsu, interview by Bannai and Kashima, May 14, 1996.

61 Kathryn Korematsu, interview by author, May 23, 2008.

62 Karen Korematsu, interview by author, May 23, 2009.

63 Ibid.

64 Ibid.

65 Ken Korematsu, interview by author, Jan. 7, 2011.

66 Joanne Kataoka, interview by author, Jan. 8, 2011.

67 Connie Wirtz, interview by author, Aug. 24, 2010.

68 Don Tamaki, unedited interview for *Of Civil Wrongs and Rights*.

69 Kathryn Korematsu, interview by author, May 23, 2008; Kathryn Korematsu, interview by Bannai and Kashima, May 14, 1996.

70 Paul Takagi, e-mail to author, July 4, 2008. Takagi's incarceration at Manzanar left him with terrible memories. In December 1942, during a confrontation between inmates and camp guards, two incarcerees were killed, and nine were wounded. CWRIC, *Personal Justice Denied*, 179. Takagi, an orderly in the camp hospital, was left alone to care for a dying young man who had been shot in the back and who, like Takagi, was only nineteen years old. Takagi sat

at his bedside the whole night. Sixty-six years later, Takagi could not relate the story without crying: "It did something to me for the rest of my life. . . . I guess I really wanted to teach what this country is really, is really, all about. . . . And that's what I used to teach is the Manzanar experience of what happened to the Japanese. It really shaped my life, you know." Paul Takagi, interview by author, Aug. 8, 2008.

71 Paul Takagi, interview by author, Aug. 8, 2008; Wei, *Asian American Movement*, 15.

72 Kathryn Korematsu, interview by author, May 23, 2008; Paul Takagi, interview by author, Aug. 8, 2008; Kathryn Korematsu, interview by Bannai and Kashima, May 14, 1996.

73 Paul Takagi, interview by author, Aug. 8, 2008.

74 Karen Korematsu, interview by author, May 23, 2008.

75 CWRIC, *Personal Justice Denied*, 118–21; Daniels, *Prisoners Without Trial*, 89; Fred Barbash, "Losses to Japanese From Internment Put at $2.5 Billion," *Washington Post*, June 16, 1983, A17.

76 Fred Barbash, "League's Aid in Internment Still Debated," *Washington Post*, Dec. 9, 1982. For a discussion of the movement for Japanese American redress, see, e.g., Mitchell Maki et al., *Achieving the Impossible Dream: How Japanese Americans Obtained Redress* (Urbana: University of Illinois Press, 1999); Murray, *Historical Memories*, 289–332; Daniels, *Japanese American Cases*, 136–63.

77 Maki, *Achieving the Impossible Dream*, 70; Proclamation No. 4417, 41 Fed. Reg. 7741, Feb. 19, 1976.

78 Kathryn Korematsu, interview by author, May 23, 2008.

79 For a discussion of the NCJAR class action lawsuit, see Maki, *Achieving the Impossible Dream*, 121–28. The class action suit was later dismissed on several grounds, including that it was barred by the statute of limitations.

80 CWRIC, *Personal Justice Denied*, 1. For a listing of the witnesses appearing before the commission at its public hearings, see Aiko Herzig-Yoshinaga and Marjorie Lee, eds., *Speaking Out for Personal Justice: Site Summaries of Testimonies and Witness Registry from the U.S. Commission on Wartime Relocation and Internment of Civilians Hearings (CWRIC), 1981* (Los Angeles: UCLA Asian American Studies Center Press, 2011).

81 Chizu Iiyama, unedited interview for *Unfinished Business*.

82 Nikki Bridges, unedited interview for *Unfinished Business*.

83 Kiku Hori Funabiki, testimony, CWRIC hearing, San Francisco, Aug. 12, 1981, p. 59.

84 Testimony, Norman Mineta, House Committee on the Judiciary, Subcommittee on Administrative Law and Governmental Relations, Washington, DC, June 20, 1984. Other Nikkei members of Congress who testified included Senator Dan Inouye, Senator Spark Matsunaga, and Congressman Bob Matsui.

85 Congressman John L. Burton, testimony, CWRIC hearing, San Francisco, Aug. 13, 1981, pp. 88–91.

86 Alan Dershowitz, testimony, CWRIC hearing, Boston, Dec. 9, 1981, pp. 63–67.

87 "Brief by Bay Area Attorneys for Redress on Selected Constitutional Issues," July 7, 1981, *Korematsu* Coram Nobis Litigation Collection, UCLA, Collection 545, Box 35, Folder 2; see also Dennis Hayashi, testimony, CWRIC hearing, Washington, DC, July 16, 1981; Lorraine K. Bannai, testimony, CWRIC hearing, San Francisco, Aug. 11, 1981; Jon Kawamoto, "Challenging their parents' evacuation," *San Francisco Examiner*, Mar. 18, 1981.

88 Jack Greenberg, director-counsel, NAACP Legal Defense and Education Fund, testimony, CWRIC hearing, Washington, DC, July 16, 1981, pp. 402, 408–9; Rhonda Abrams, Anti-Defamation League of B'Nai Brith, testimony, CWRIC hearing, San Francisco, Aug. 11, 1981, pp. 167, 170–73; Jonathan Bridge, chairperson of the Social Action Committee of Temple de Hirsch-Sinai, testimony, CWRIC hearing, Seattle, Sept. 11, 1981, pp. 36–37; testimony of Ruth Lansner, vice-chair, National Committee on Discrimination, Anti-Defamation League of B'Nai Brith, House Committee on the Judiciary, Subcommittee on Administrative Law and Governmental Relations, 99th Cong. 2nd Sess. on HR 442 and HR 2415, Civil Liberties Act of 1985 and the Aleutian and Pribilof Islands Restitution Act, Apr. 28 and July 23, 1986, Part 1, Serial No. 69, pp. 759, 760, U.S. Government Printing Office, Washington, DC; statement of William L. Robinson on behalf of the American Bar Association, Subcommittee on Administrative Law and Governmental Relations of the Committee on the Judiciary, U.S. House of Representatives, Apr. 28, 1986, p. 9; statement of the American Jewish Committee on HR 442, Civil Liberties Act of 1985, Subcommittee on Administrative Law and Governmental Relations of the Committee on the Judiciary, U.S. House of Representatives, May 12, 1986; statement of John Molinari, president of the San Francisco Board of Supervisors, CWRIC hearing, San Francisco, Aug. 12, 1981, p. 42; "Black and Hispanic Caucuses Endorse Nikkei Reparations Bill," *East West*, June 13, 1984.

89 Statement of Bernie Whitebear, CWRIC hearing, Seattle, Sept. 11, 1981, pp. 47–51.

90 Vincene Verdun, "If the Shoe Fits, Wear It: An Analysis of Reparations to African Americans," *Tulane Law Review* 67 (1993): 647, quoted in Eric K. Yamamoto, "Beyond Redress: Japanese Americans' Unfinished Business," *Asian Law Journal* 7 (2000): 132.

91 Joseph Morozumi, testimony, CWRIC hearing, San Francisco, Aug. 13, 1981, p. 25.

92 Earl Warren, *The Memoirs of Earl Warren* (New York: Doubleday & Company, 1977), 149; William O. Douglas, *The Court Years: 1939–1975* (New York: Random House, 1980), 280.

93 Kathryn Korematsu, interview by author, May 23, 2008; Fred Korematsu, interview by Bannai and Kashima, May 14, 1996; Kathryn Korematsu, interview by Bannai and Kashima, May 14, 1996.

94 Fred Korematsu JANM remarks.

CHAPTER 8. "INTENTIONAL FALSEHOODS"

1 Fred Korematsu JANM remarks; Peter Irons, ed., *Justice Delayed: The Record of the Japanese American Internment Cases* (Middletown, CT: Wesleyan University Press, 1989), 4–5.

2 Peter Irons, interview by Alice Ito and Lorraine Bannai, Seattle, Oct. 27, 2000, Densho Visual Histories, http://archive.densho.org/main.aspx.

3 Aiko Herzig-Yoshinaga, interview by Emiko Omori and Chizu Omori, San Francisco, Mar. 20, 1994, Densho Visual Histories, http://archive.densho.org/main.aspx.; "It Was Bigger Than All of Us," *Nikkei Heritage* 11, no. 2 (Spring 1999), 6–7, National Japanese American Historical Society; Peter Irons, interview by Ito and Bannai, Oct. 27, 2000; Aiko Herzig-Yoshinaga, interview by author, Sept. 13, 2008; Josh Getlin, "Redress: One Made a Difference," *Los Angeles Times*, June 2, 1988.

4 Peter Irons, interview by Ito and Bannai, Oct. 27, 2000; memorandum, Peter Irons to Gordon Hirabayashi, Fred Korematsu, Minoru Yasui, and others, Feb. 22, 1982, *Korematsu* Coram Nobis Litigation Collection, UCLA, Collection 545, Box 9, Folder 8.

5 Peter Irons, interview by author, Apr. 30, 2009; Fred Korematsu, JAMN remarks.

6 For further discussion of the evidence that formed the basis for reopening the *Korematsu, Hirabayashi*, and *Yasui* cases, see Irons, *Justice at War*; Irons, *Justice Delayed*; Yamamoto et al., *Race, Rights and Reparation*, 221–46; Bannai and Minami, "Internment during World War II," 775–80; Yamamoto, "Korematsu Revisited," 8–19; Jerry Kang, "Denying Prejudice," *UCLA Law Review* 51 (2004): 976–84. For copies of the exhibits to the coram nobis petition, as well as other documents related to the *Korematsu, Hirabayashi*, and *Yasui* cases, see the companion website to Yamamoto et al., *Race, Rights, and Reparation*, accessed Apr. 13, 2015, http://jerrykang.net/racerightsreparation/resources/coram-nobis/.

7 DeWitt, *Final Report,* 3, 4, 8–9; *Korematsu* Supreme Court Oral Argument transcript, Oct. 12, 1944, p. 7.

8 United States, Navy, Office of Naval Intelligence, "United States Naval Administration in World War II," pp. 67–69, included as Ex. M, exhibits to petition for writ of error coram nobis (hereafter cited as exhibits to coram nobis petition).

9 Memorandum, "Japanese Question, Report on," Lt. Commdr. K. D. Ringle to Chief of Naval Operations, Jan. 26, 1942, p. 3, File BIO/ND 11BF37/A8-5, records of the United States Navy, included as Ex. N, exhibits to coram nobis petition (emphasis in original). For a discussion of Ringle's report and Ennis's efforts to advise the Supreme Court of its findings, see Irons, *Justice at War*, 202–6.

10 Biddle to McCloy, Mar. 9, 1942, File ASW014.311 [Eastern Defense Command, Exclusion Order reports], Entry 47, Box 6, RG 107, records of the assistant secretary of war, National Archives and Records Service, Washington, DC, included as Ex. O, exhibits to coram nobis petition; McCloy to Biddle, Mar. 21, 1942, included as Ex. P, exhibits to coram nobis petition.

11 Memorandum for the solicitor general, Apr. 30, 1943, included as Ex. Q, exhibits to coram nobis petition (emphasis added); see also Irons, *Justice at War*, 202–6.

12 *Korematsu*, 323 U.S., 218.

13 DeWitt, *Final Report*, 4, 8.

14 Memorandum, "Conference with General DeWitt at San Francisco, Friday, January 9 [1942]," Files of the Radio Intelligence Division, RG 173, records of the Federal Communications Commission, National Archives and Records Service, Washington, DC, included as Ex. U, exhibits to coram nobis petition. For a discussion of FCC and FBI reports and their suppression, see Irons, *Justice at War*, 280–92.

15 Memorandum, J. Edgar Hoover to attorney general, Feb. 7, 1944, Folder Japanese Relocation Cases III, Box 37, Fahy Papers Franklin D. Roosevelt Library, Hyde Park, NY, included as Ex. W, exhibits to coram nobis petition.

16 Fly to Biddle, Apr. 4, 1944, Folder 3, Box, 37, Fahy Papers, FDRL, included as Ex. V, exhibits to coram nobis petition; see also memorandum, Fly to Biddle, Apr. 1, 1944, JACL Redress Collection, 1936–92, Series 1, Box 1, declassified documents requested by John Tateishi, 1981, 1 of 2, Japanese American National Library, San Francisco.

17 Edward Ennis, "Memorandum for the Attorney General re: General DeWitt's *Final Report* on Japanese Evacuation," Feb. 26, 1944, Box 27, Folder 3, Charles Fahy Papers, Franklin Delano Roosevelt Library, Hyde Park, New York, included as Ex. Z, exhibits to coram nobis petition.

18 Memorandum, John L. Burling to assistant attorney general Herbert Wechsler, Sept. 11, 1944, File 146-42-7, records of the Department of Justice, included as Ex. AA, exhibits to coram nobis petition (emphasis added). A party may ask a court to take judicial notice of facts "not subject to reasonable dispute." Federal Rules of Evidence 201. For a critique of the use of judicial notice in the Japanese American incarceration cases, see Bannai and Minami, "Internment during World War II," 769–70; Nanette Dembitz, *Racial Discrimination and the Military Judgment: The Supreme Court's* Korematsu *and* Endo *Decisions, Columbia Law Review* 45 (1945): 185–87.

19 Memorandum, John L. Burling to Assistant Attorney General Herbert Wechsler, Sept. 11, 1944, File 146-42-7, records of the Department of Justice, included as Ex. AA, exhibits to coram nobis petition (emphasis added).

20 Memorandum, Burling to Ennis, Oct. 2, 1944, included as Ex. BB, exhibits to coram nobis petition.

21 Memorandum, Edward Ennis to Herbert Wechsler, Sept. 30, 1944, Folder 3, Box 37, Fahy Papers, included as Ex. B, exhibits to coram nobis petition; memorandum, Burling to Ennis, Oct. 2, 1944, included as Ex. BB, exhibits to coram nobis petition.

22 Brief for the United States, *Korematsu*, 323 U.S. 214 (No. 22) 1944 WL 42850, 11 n.2 (Oct. 5, 1944); memorandum, Captain Fisher to McCloy, Oct. 2, 1944, File 014.311, Western Defense Command Exclusion Orders (Korematsu), Box 9, RG 107, National Archives, included as Ex. CC, exhibits to coram nobis petition.

23 Transcript of telephone conversation, Fisher and Wechsler, Oct. 2, 1944, File

014.311, Western Defense Command Exclusion Orders (Korematsu), Box 9, RG 107, National Archives, included as Ex. DD, exhibits to coram nobis petition.

24 For a discussion of the suppression, alteration, and destruction of DeWitt's original report, see Irons, *Justice at War*, 206–12; Aiko Herzig-Yoshinaga, interview by Larry Hashima and Glen Kitayama, Los Angeles, Sept. 11, 1997, Densho Visual Histories, http://archive.densho.org/main.aspx.

25 Brief for the United States, *Korematsu*, 323 U.S. 214 (No. 22) 1944 WL 42850, 12 (Oct. 5, 1944); DeWitt, *Final Report*, 9.

26 DeWitt, *Final Report*, "Japanese Evacuation from the West Coast," 1942 [initial version], p. 9, included as Ex. D, exhibits to coram nobis petition (emphasis added).

27 DeWitt to McCloy, Apr. 15, 1943, included as Ex. C, exhibits to coram nobis petition.

28 Transcript of telephone conversation, Bendetsen and McCloy, Apr. 19. 1943, File 319.1, Section 1, RG 338, National Archives, quoted in Irons, *Justice at War*, 209.

29 Radiogram, Barnett to DeWitt, Apr. 26, 1943, File 319.1, Section 1, RG 338, National Archives, cited in Irons, *Justice at War*, 209; radiogram, DeWitt to Barnett, Apr. 27, 1943, File 319.1, Section 1, RG 338, National Archives, and transcript of telephone conversation, Bendetsen and McCloy, Apr. 19, 1943, File 319.1, Section 1, RG 338, National Archives, quoted in Irons, *Justice at War*, 209.

30 Bendetsen to DeWitt, May 3, 1943, included as Ex. F, exhibits to coram nobis petition (emphasis in original).

31 Memorandum, "Suggested Changes by Capt. Hall in Final Report: Japanese Evacuation from West Coast 1942," p. 3, included as Ex. G, exhibits to coram nobis petition. Emphasis in original.

32 Petition for writ of error coram nobis, 28, Korematsu v. United States, 584 F. Supp. 1406 (N.D. Cal. 1984).

33 Telegram, Bendetsen to Barnett, May 29, 1943, included as Ex. H, exhibits to coram nobis petition.

34 Theodore E. Smith, Memo, June 29, 1943, included as Ex. K, exhibits to coram nobis petition.

35 *Korematsu*, 323 U.S. 214, 218 (emphasis added).

36 Korematsu Supreme Court Oral Argument transcript, Oct. 12, 1944, p. 7.

37 Irons, *Justice Delayed*, 5.

38 Peter Irons, interview by Ito and Bannai, Oct. 27, 2000; Irons, *Justice Delayed*, 5–6.

CHAPTER 9. "A LEGAL LONGSHOT"?

1 For an account of the preparation for, and proceedings in, the coram nobis cases, see Irons, *Justice Delayed*, 1–46; Yamamoto, *Race, Rights and Reparation*, 221–310; Maki, *Achieving the Impossible Dream*, 128–36.

2 Dale Minami, interview by Ikeda and Chon, Feb. 8, 2003; Irons, *Justice Delayed*, 9–10.

3   Dale Minami, interview by Ikeda and Chon, Feb. 8, 2003; Irons, *Justice Delayed*, 9; Irons to Minami, Feb. 22, 1982, *Korematsu* Coram Nobis Litigation Collection, UCLA, Collection 545, Box 42, Folder 4.

4   Dale Minami, interview by Ikeda and Chon, Feb. 8, 2003.

5   Irons to Minami, Feb. 22, 1982, and memorandum, Irons to Minami, Hira-bayashi, Korematsu, Yasui, and others, Feb. 22, 1982, *Korematsu* Coram Nobis Litigation Collection, UCLA, Collection 545, Box 35, Folder 2. For a discussion of the writ of error coram nobis, see Margaret Chon, "Remembering and Repairing: The Error Before Us, in Our Presence," *Seattle Journal for Social Justice* 8 (Spring/ Summer 2010): 645.

6   Present during the early stages of the case were BAAR members Russell Matsu-moto and Mike Wong. Donna Komure communicated with organizations seek-ing to file amicus briefs. Numerous other lawyers and undergraduate and law students worked on Fred's case, as well as Gordon and Min's cases, doing legal research, reviewing documents, and contributing in other ways. Law partners of legal team members contributed by supporting their colleagues' involvement in the work. It is unfortunately not possible to list all of the individuals who worked on the cases, and no complete list is attempted for fear of omitting someone. But each one was critical to the effort.

7   The *Korematsu, Hirabayashi*, and *Yasui* coram nobis legal teams supported each others' cases, and they have continued to work together to advance Fred, Gordon, and Min's legacies to this day.

8   Statement, Lorraine Bannai, July 26, 2014; Kathryn Korematsu, interview by au-thor, May 25, 2008.

9   Irons to Minami, May 1, 1982, *Korematsu* Coram Nobis Litigation Collection, UCLA, Collection 545, Box 42, Folder 4; Dale Minami, interview by Ikeda and Chon, Feb. 8, 2003.

10 Peter Irons, interview by Ito and Bannai, Oct. 25, 2000, Densho Visual Histories, http://archive.densho.org/main.aspx.

11 Dale Minami, interview by Ikeda and Chon, Feb. 8, 2003; Peter Irons, interview by Ito and Bannai, Oct. 27, 2000.

12 Memo, Minami to BAAR, May 10, 1982, *Korematsu* Coram Nobis Litigation Col-lection, UCLA, Collection 545, Box 10, Folder 1; Peter Irons, interview by Ito and Bannai, Oct. 27, 2000.

13 Dale Minami, unedited interview for *Of Civil Wrongs and Rights*.

14 "Bigger Than All of Us," *Nikkei Heritage*, National Japanese American Histori-cal Society 11, no. 2 (Spring 1999): 16, quoting Karen Kai; Leigh-Ann Miyasato, interview by author, Dec. 14, 2010.

15 Irons, *Justice Delayed*, 12.

16 Lorraine K. Bannai, interview by Margaret Chon and Alice Ito, Seattle, Mar. 23 and 24, 2000, Densho Visual Histories, http://archive.densho.org/main.aspx.

17 Lori Bannai described the coram nobis lawyers' awareness of being part of a broader movement: "The biggest significance of the case for me is that it was re-ally not just one legal case . . . but it really was one part of a much larger political

effort. It was our case being brought at the same time redress was being sought before Congress at the same time NCJAR . . . was bringing its class action, at the same time there was media . . . covering the story, plays being written. . . . The issue of redress and the experience of Japanese Americans was a whole movement brought by and pushed by numerous different segments within the community itself." Lorraine K. Bannai, interview by Chon and Ito, Mar. 23 and 24, 2000.

18 Ken Korematsu, interview by author, Jan. 7, 2011; Karen Korematsu, interview by author, May 23, 2009; Kathryn Korematsu, interview by author, May 23, 2008; Donald K. Tamaki, unedited interview for *Of Civil Wrongs and Rights*.

19 Fred Korematsu, unedited interview for *Of Civil Wrongs and Rights*; Donald K. Tamaki, interview by Tom Ikeda and Lorraine Bannai, Seattle, Apr. 17, 2009, Densho Visual Histories, http://archive.densho.org/main.aspx.

20 Fred Korematsu JANM remarks; Kathryn Korematsu, interview by Bannai and Kashima, May 14, 1996; Leigh-Ann Miyasato, interview by author, Dec. 14, 2010.

21 See, e.g., memo, Minami to "Western Defense Commandos," Nov. 21, 1982, *Korematsu* Coram Nobis Litigation Collection, UCLA, Collection 545, Box 9, Folder 7; Rusky to Minami and Bannai, May 27, 1982, *Korematsu* Coram Nobis Litigation Collection, UCLA, Collection 545, Box 10, Folder 1.

22 Irons, *Justice Delayed*, 13.

23 Aiko Herzig-Yoshinaga, interview by author, Sept. 13, 2008; e-mail from Phil Nash to author, June 9, 2011.

24 Irons, *Justice Delayed*, 13; memo, L. Bannai to Korematsu theory group, Sept. 26, 1983, *Korematsu* Coram Nobis Litigation Collection, UCLA, Collection 545, Box 19, Folder 9.

25 Irons, *Justice Delayed*, 13–14.

26 Memo, Minami to Korematsu defense team, Oct. 4, 1982, *Korematsu* Coram Nobis Litigation Collection, Collection 545, Box 10, Folder 2; Tamaki, unedited interview for *Of Civil Wrongs and Rights*.

27 Meeting minutes, Jan. 27, 1983, *Korematsu* Coram Nobis Litigation Collection, Collection 545; Irons, *Justice Delayed*, 12; Tamaki, unedited interview for *Of Civil Wrongs and Rights*; "Bigger Than All of Us," *Nikkei Heritage*; Tamaki to Chuman and attachment, Nov. 16, 1982, *Korematsu* Coram Nobis Litigation Collection, UCLA, Collection 545, Box 10, Folder 2, and list of contributors, Box 19, Folder 8.

28 Tamaki, unedited interview for *Of Civil Wrongs and Rights*; Goldberg to Marutani, Oct. 1, 1982; Irons, *Justice Delayed*, 13–14. A few days after the publication of Goldberg's remarks, Fred Barbash of the Washington Post went forward with a story about the reopening of the *Korematsu, Hirabayashi*, and *Yasui* cases, reporting the allegations of governmental misconduct, as well as Goldberg's statements questioning the wisdom of the coram nobis effort. William Barbash, "Japanese Americans Plan to Ask High Court to Reopen '40s Cases," *Washington Post*, Oct. 25, 1982; Irons, *Justice Delayed*, 14.

29 At the time the coram nobis cases were being prepared, there were three main groups seeking monetary compensation for Japanese Americans: the JACL; the National Coalition for Redress/Reparations (NCRR), a grassroots coalition of

Japanese American community groups; and the National Council for Japanese American Redress (NCJAR), which brought a class action suit seeking money damages from the United States. Maki, *Achieving the Impossible Dream*, 89–90.

30 Memo, Yasui to Tateishi, June 28, 1982, JACL Redress Collection, 1936–92, Series 2, Box 9, Yasui Correspondence, June 1982, Japanese American National Library, San Francisco, Cal.; Minami to Yasui, July 14, 1982, *Korematsu* Coram Nobis Litigation Collection, UCLA, Collection 545, Box 10, Folder 2. Kathryn Bannai similarly communicated that Gordon Hirabayashi's lawyers would not participate in an attorneys' meeting at the JACL convention.

31 Tateishi to Yasui, July 21, 1982; Yasui to Tateishi, July 18, 1982, emphasis in original; memo, Tateishi to Yasui, Oct. 27, 1982, JACL Redress Collection, 1936– 92, Series 2, Box 9, Yasui Correspondence, Jan. –Feb. 1982, Japanese American National Library, San Francisco; Chuman to Minami and K. Bannai, July 21, 1982, *Korematsu* Coram Nobis Litigation Collection, Collection 545, Box 10, Folder 2.

32 Bulletin 142, Japanese American Citizens League, Office of the National Secretary, p. 1, Apr. 7, 1942, NCCLU, CHS, MS 3580, Series II, Box 28, Folder ACLU 592.

33 Floyd Shimomura, "Coram Nobis," *Pacific Citizen*, Oct. 29, 1982.

34 Minami, unedited interview for *Of Civil Wrongs and Rights*.

35 Ibid.

36 Ibid.

37 Donald K. Tamaki, interview by Ikeda and Bannai, Apr. 17, 2009; Tamaki, unedited interview for *Of Civil Wrongs and Rights*.

38 Tamaki, interview by Ikeda and Bannai, Apr. 17, 2009; Tamaki to Lampell, Oct. 27, 1987, *Korematsu* Coram Nobis Litigation Collection, UCLA, Collection 545, Box 17, Folder 5.

39 Minami, unedited interview for *Of Civil Wrongs and Rights*.

40 Ibid.

41 Minami, interview by Ikeda and Chon, Feb. 8, 2003.

42 Peter Irons, interview by Ito and Bannai, Oct. 27, 2000.

43 "Press Sign-Up," Jan. 19, 1983, *Korematsu* Coram Nobis Litigation Collection, UCLA, Collection 545, Box 10, Folder 2.

44 Kathryn Korematsu, telephone interviews by author, May 24 and July 3, 2008; Peter Irons, interview by author, Apr. 30, 2009.

45 Press conference, San Francisco Press Club, Jan. 19, 1983, p. 2.

46 Remarks, Fred Korematsu, press conference, San Francisco Press Club, Jan. 19, 1983, p. 7.

47 Yasui to Tamaki, Jan. 30, 1983, *Korematsu* Coram Nobis Litigation Collection, UCLA, Collection 545, Box 10, Folder 3; Kathryn Korematsu, interview by author, May 23, 2008; "Suppression of Internment Data Charged," *Los Angeles Times*, Jan. 19, 1983, 1; "3 Japanese-Americans Ask Court to Overturn Wartime Convictions," *New York Times*, Jan. 31, 1983, A14; Lyle Denniston, "A Fight to Restore Blighted Feelings," *Baltimore Sun*, Jan. 23, 1983.

48 Meeting minutes, Feb. 10, 1983, *Korematsu* Coram Nobis Litigation Collection, UCLA, Collection 545, Box 9, Folder 7.

49 Ibid., and Tamaki to Yasui, Feb. 10, 1983, Box 16, Folder 1, *Korematsu* Coram Nobis Litigation Collection, UCLA, Collection 545.

50 Kathryn Korematsu, interview by Bannai and Kashima, May 14, 1996; Kathryn Korematsu, press conference, Oct. 4, 1983, San Francisco Press Club; Irons, *Justice Delayed*, 14.

51 Kathryn Korematsu, interview by Bannai and Kashima, May 14, 1996; Kathryn Korematsu, interview by author, May 23, 2008; Minami, unedited interview for *Of Civil Wrongs and Rights*.

52 Roy Nakano to Don Tamaki, Nov. 7, 1983, *Korematsu* Coram Nobis Litigation Collection, UCLA, Collection 545, Box 10, Folder 7.

53 Raul Ramirez, "Man Who Defied Relocation Sues to Clear Name," *Oakland Tribune*, May 29, 1983; Steven Okazaki, *Unfinished Business*, accessed Apr. 11, 2015, http://www.farfilm.com/films/unfinished-business.html.

54 Kathryn Korematsu, press conference, Oct. 4, 1983, San Francisco Press Club; Kay Korematsu, interview by author, May 25, 2008; Karen Korematsu, interview by author, May 23, 2008.

55 Donald K. Tamaki, interview by Ikeda and Bannai, Apr. 17, 2009; Kathryn Korematsu, interview by author, May 22, 2008; Karen Korematsu, interview by author, May 23, 2009.

56 Minami notes of telephone conversation with Victor Stone, Mar. 2, 1983, *Korematsu* Coram Nobis Litigation Collection, UCLA, Collection 545, Box 41, Folder 15.

57 Reporter's transcript, Mar. 14, 1983, p. 7, *Korematsu v. United States*, coram nobis action, Crim. No. 27635-W, *Korematsu* Coram Nobis Litigation Collection, UCLA, Collection 545, Box 2, Folder 6.

58 Ibid., 10–11.

59 *Personal Justice Denied*, 18; Judith Miller, "Wartime Internment of Japanese Was 'Grave Injustice,' Panel Says," *New York Times*, Feb. 25, 1983; John Fogarty, "Japanese Internment Called Needless, Racist," *San Francisco Chronicle*, Feb. 25, 1983; "A Grim Conclusion," editorial, *Oakland Tribune*, Feb. 25, 1983. Professor Natsu Taylor Saito challenges the conclusion that the wartime incarceration resulted from "wartime hysteria." The evidence instead demonstrates that it was the result of "economically motivated racial animus." Natsu Taylor Saito, *From Chinese Exclusion to Guananamo Bay: Plenary Power and the Prerogative State* (Boulder: University Press of Colorado, 2007), 68–78.

60 Reporter's transcript, Mar. 14, 1983, *Korematsu v. United States*, coram nobis action, Crim. No. 27635-W, *Korematsu* Coram Nobis Litigation Collection, UCLA, Collection 545, Box 2, Folder 6.

61 Alan Brinkley, "Minister Without Portfolio," *Harper's Magazine*, Feb. 1983, 31.

62 John J. McCloy, "Repay U.S. Japanese?" *New York Times*, Apr. 10, 1983, A21 (emphasis added); "McCloy Charges Reparations Campaign Perpetrates Injustice," *New York Nichibei*, Apr. 14, 1983.

63 The team's April 19 meeting minutes reflected the strain: "Dale and Peter recounted the arduous and frustrating conversations with Stone who appears to be . . . in a panic over the cases." Meeting minutes of Apr. 16, 1983, dated Apr. 19, 1983, *Korematsu* Coram Nobis Litigation Collection, UCLA, Collection 545, Box 41, Folder 15.

64 Request for Designation of District Judge Under 28 U.S.C. Section 292(b), filed Apr. 11, 1983, and order, Apr. 29, 1983, In re Coram Nobis Petitions of: Fred Korematsu, Gordon Hirabayashi, and Minoru Yasui vs. United States of America, United States Court of Appeals for the Ninth Circuit, Misc. # 83-8085. *Korematsu* Coram Nobis Litigation Collection, UCLA, Collection 545, Box 1, Folder 4.

65 Reporter's transcript, May 9, 1983, *Korematsu* Coram Nobis Litigation Collection, UCLA, Collection 545, Box 2, Folder 6.

66 CWRIC, *Personal Justice Denied*, "Part 2: Recommendations," 8–9.

67 Irons, *Justice Delayed*, 19–21; memo, Irons to Hirabayashi-Yasui-Korematsu legal teams, June 20, 1983, *Korematsu* Coram Nobis Litigation Collection, UCLA, Collection 545, Box 10, Folder 4. "[A] pardon . . . carries an imputation of guilt; acceptance a confession of it." Burdick v. United States, 236 U.S. 79, 94 (1915). See Ashley M. Steiner, "Remission of Guilt or Removal of Punishment? The Effects of a Presidential Pardon," *Emory Law Journal* 46 (1997): 959–1003.

68 Kathryn Korematsu, interview by Bannai and Kashima, May 14, 1996; Kathryn Korematsu, interview by author, May 24, 2008. The New York *Nichibei* concurred: "This recommendation must be rejected because it not only confuses the victim with the perpetrator, but also leaves intact the legal authority for the imprisonment of American citizens on the basis of race during a national emergency." Marc H. Iyeki, "Korematsu Decision in 1944: A 'Loaded Weapon,'" *Nichibei* (New York), Sept. 1, 1983.

69 Notes of telephone conversation, Bannai and Stone, Sept. 23, 1983.

70 "Government's Response and Motion Under L.R. 220.6," Oct. 4, 1983, File 27635; Criminal Case Files, 1851–1982; U.S. District Courts for the San Francisco Division of the Northern District of California, RG 21, records of the District Courts of the United States, NARA-SF (hereafter cited as "Government's Response"); Philip Hager, "U.S. Conceded on WWII Internment Cases," *Los Angeles Times*, Oct. 5, 1983.

71 Maitland Zane, "U.S. War Camp Resister Cleared," *San Francisco Chronicle*, Oct. 5, 1983.

72 "An Old Wrong Redressed," editorial, *Washington Post*, Oct. 9, 1983.

73 Bob Rusky, unedited interview for *Of Civil Wrongs and Rights*.

74 "We Are in Debt," *Los Angeles Times*, Oct. 17, 1983.

75 M. J. Mondeau, letter to the editor, *Los Angeles Times*, Oct. 24, 1983.

76 Reply to Government's Response and Motion under L.R. 220-6, Oct. 31, 1983, *Korematsu v. United States* coram nobis case.

77 Fred Korematsu declaration, Oct. 30, 1983.

78 List of Organizations Requesting Consent to File Amicus Curiae Brief, Aug. 22,

1983, and "Order re: Amicus Briefs," Sept. 27, 1983, *Korematsu* Coram Nobis Litigation Collection, UCLA, Collection 545, Box 1, Folder 6.

79 Jim Okutsu, "Korematsu: A Look Back," *Hokubei Mainichi*, Nov. 9, 1983.

CHAPTER 10. CORRECTING THE RECORD

1 Minami, unedited interview for *Of Civil Wrongs and Rights*.

2 Marilyn Hall Patel, unedited interview for *Of Civil Wrongs and Rights*; Douglas Rice, "Korematsu vs. United States A Total Victory," *Hokubei Mainichi*, Nov. 12, 1983; "Court Overturns a War Internment," *New York Times*, Nov. 11, 1983; Donald K. Tamaki, unedited interview for *Of Civil Wrongs and Rights*; Eric K. Yamamoto, interview by Lorraine Bannai, Seattle, Apr. 17, 2009, Densho Visual Histories, http://archive.densho.org/main.aspx.

3 For an account of the November 10, 1983, hearing in Fred's case, see Irons, *Justice Delayed*, 24–27.

4 Transcript, Motion to Vacate Conviction and Dismiss Indictment of Fred T. Korematsu, 15–16, Nov. 10, 1983, File 27635, Criminal Case Files, 1851–1982, U.S. District Courts for the San Francisco Division of the Northern District of California, RG 21, records of the District Courts of the United States, NARA-SF (cited as coram nobis hearing transcript, Nov. 10, 1983).

5 Patel, unedited interview for *Of Civil Wrongs and Rights*.

6 Eric K. Yamamoto, interview by Lorraine Bannai, Apr. 17, 2009.

7 Kathryn Korematsu, interview by Lorraine Bannai and Tetsuden Kashima, May 14, 1996; Minami, unedited interview for *Of Civil Wrongs and Rights*.

8 Karen Kai, "A Special Case," *Recorder*, Apr. 8, 2005.

9 Patel, unedited interview for *Of Civil Wrongs and Rights*; Jonathan Gladstone, "Patel Takes Pride in Creating Role Models," *Recorder*, Dec. 18, 1987.

10 Eric K. Yamamoto, interview by Lorraine Bannai, Apr. 17, 2009.

11 Amy Eto, *Unfinished Business*; Kathryn Korematsu, telephone interview by author, Jan. 11, 2011.

12 Peter Irons, interview by Ito and Bannai, Oct. 27, 2000; Minami, unedited interview for *Of Civil Wrongs and Rights*.

13 "Conviction of Man Who Evaded WWII Internment Is Overturned," *Los Angeles Times*, Nov. 11, 1983; Kathryn Korematsu, telephone interview by author, Apr. 28, 2011; Kathryn Korematsu, interview by author, May 25, 2008.

14 "Conviction of Man Who Evaded WWII Internment Is Overturned," *Los Angeles Times*, Nov. 11, 1983; "Court Overturns a War Internment," *New York Times*, Nov. 11, 1983; "Bad Landmark: Righting a Racial Wrong," *Time*, Nov. 21, 1982; Jack Matsuoka, "Fred Korematsu," cartoon, *Hokubei Mainichi*, Nov. 15, 1983.

15 Robert Takasugi to Dale Minami, Dec. 23, 1983, *Korematsu* Coram Nobis Litigation Collection, UCLA, Collection 545, Box 10, Folder 7.

CHAPTER 11. A SYMBOL IN THE CONTINUING SEARCH FOR JUSTICE

1   Fred Korematsu, press conference, San Francisco Press Club, San Francisco, Oct. 4, 1983, recorded in *Unfinished Business*.

2   The issue of Japanese American redress was controversial. A *San Francisco Examiner* poll showed that 51 percent of its readers opposed monetary reparations to Japanese Americans. George Snyder, "Close Vote on Reparations to U.S. Japanese," *San Francisco Chronicle*, June 23, 1983. See also Mike Feinsilber, "Angry Americans Oppose Apology to WWII Internees," *Oakland Tribune*, June 30, 1983. Conservative columnist James J. Kilpatrick opposed the payment of redress, citing Justice Hugo L. Black's majority opinion in Fred's case to say that five thousand Japanese Americans had refused to swear allegiance to the United States. James J. Kilpatrick, "$1.2 Billion Worth of Hindsight," *Washington Post*, Mar. 5, 1988. Like Justice Black, however, Kilpatrick failed to note that these Japanese Americans had been asked about their loyalty *after* they were imprisoned.

3   Maki, *Achieving the Impossible Dream*, 172–73.

4   John Ota, interview by author, Aug. 23, 2010; John Ota, e-mail to author, Oct. 9, 2008; Gerald Davis, "Big Push Slated for WWII Internment Reparations," *Oakland Tribune*, July 26, 1987, A12; Kathryn Korematsu, interview by author, May 24, 2008.

5   Ronald Reagan, *Public Papers of the Presidents of the United States: Ronald Reagan, 1988–1989*, Aug. 10, 1998, p. 1054; Civil Liberties Act, Pub. L. No. 100-383, 102 Stat. 903 (1988) (codified as amended at 50 U.S.C. App. §§ 1989–1989(d) [1988]); Julie Johnson, "President Signs Law to Redress Wartime Wrong," *New York Times*, Aug. 11, 1988; Larry Liebert, "Reagan Signs Reparations Bill," *San Francisco Chronicle*, Aug. 11, 1988.

6   Maki, *Achieving the Impossible Dream*, 214, 225; Karen Korematsu, interview by author, May 24, 2009.

7   Korematsu v. United States, 583 F. Supp. 1406, 1413, 1418, 1419 (N.D. Cal. 1984); Motion to Suspend the Current Briefing Schedule and Withdrawal of Notice of Appeal, *Korematsu* Coram Nobis Litigation Collection, UCLA, Collection 545, Box 2, Folder 9.

8   Equal Access to Justice Act, 28 U.S.C. § 2412(d)(1)(A), (d)(2)(B); Memorandum of Points and Authorities in Support of Motion for Attorneys' Fees and Costs, June 18, 1984, *Korematsu* Coram Nobis Litigation Collection, UCLA, Collection 545, Box 2, Folder 9; Declaration of Fred Korematsu in Support of Application for Attorneys' Fees and Costs, June 12, 1984, and Order Denying Petitioner's Motion for Attorneys' Fees and Costs, Aug. 1, 1984, File 27635, Criminal Case Files, 1851–1982, U.S. District Courts for the San Francisco Division of the Northern District of California, RG 21, Records of the District Courts of the United States, NARA-SF. Members of the team estimated that they had put in a combined total of approximately 4,378 hours into the case and, if billed, their fees and costs would have run about $378,671, using extremely conservative

billing rates of seventy-five dollars per hour for its most experienced litigators. "Korematsu Appeal Withdrawn," *Hokubei Mainichi*, June 26, 1984.

9   For a discussion of Min Yasui's coram nobis case, see Irons, *Justice Delayed*, 27–30; L. A. Chung, "Dead Man Seeks His Day in Court," *San Francisco Chronicle*, Jan. 8, 1987; *Yasui*, 772 F.2d 1496, 1498.

10 Hirabayashi v. United States, 627 F. Supp. 1445 (W.D. Wash. 1986), *judgment aff'd in part, rev'd in part*, 828 F.2d 591 (9th Cir. 1987). For a discussion of Gordon Hirabayashi's coram nobis case in general, see Irons, *Justice Delayed*, 30–46; Mary M. Schroeder, "What Gordon Hirabayashi Taught Me About Courage," *Seattle Journal for Social Justice* 11 (2012): 65–75; Kathryn A. Bannai, "*Gordon Hirabayashi v. United States*: 'This Is an American Case,'" *Seattle Journal for Social Justice* 11 (2012): 41–51; and Gordon K. Hirabayashi, with James A. Hirabayashi and Lane Ryo Hirabayashi, *A Principled Stand: The Story of Hirabayashi v. United States* (Seattle: University of Washington Press, 2013), 181–90.

11 Adams, "To Clear His Name," 64, 66; Ken Korematsu, interview by author, Jan. 7, 2011; Karen Korematsu, interview by author, May 25, 2009; Yackle, "Japanese American Internment," 104; Elizabeth Navas Finley, "The Man Who Won Justice for Japanese," *San Francisco Chronicle*, Apr. 16, 1987.

12 Karen Korematsu, interview by author, May 25, 2009; "Korematsu, Mineta, Honda among Speakers at S. J. Day of Remembrance," *Hokubei Mainichi*, Mar. 14, 1998.

13 E-mail, Phil Nash to author, June 5, 2011; David Margolick, "Legal Legend Urges Victims to Speak Out," *New York Times*, Nov. 24, 1984; "Korematsu Greeted by Standing Ovations on New York Visit," *New York Nichibei*, Nov. 22, 1984.

14 Don Plansky, "600 Asians, Jews Join for Emanu-El Program on Internment," *Northern California Jewish Bulletin*, May 9, 1986; "Man Who Fought Internment Gets Nation's Highest Award," *Rafu Shimpo*, Jan. 17, 1998.

15 See, e.g., Kathryn Korematsu, interview by author, May 24, 2008; Kathryn Korematsu, interview by Bannai and Kashima, May 14, 1996; Elizabeth Navas Finley, "The Man Who Won Justice for Japanese," *San Francisco Chronicle*, Apr. 16, 1987.

16 Kathryn Korematsu, interview by author, May 24, 2008. Scores of students have made similar comments. For example, Josephine Yeh told Fred, while she was a first-year law student, "Mr. Korematsu, I just wanted to tell you that I saw you speak to my class two years ago at U. C. Berkeley, and you are the reason that I went to law school." Eric Yamamoto, Dale Minami, and May Lee Heye, "One Man Seeks Justice from a Nation: *Korematsu v. United States*," quoting Josephine Yeh, Mar. 1999, in *Untold Civil Rights Stories*, eds. Stewart Kwoh and Russell C. Leong (Los Angeles: UCLA Asian American Studies Center, 2009), 77.

17 Fred Korematsu, quoted in Yamamoto, Minami, and Heye, "One Man Seeks Justice," 84.

18 Fred Korematsu, interview by Bannai and Kashima, May 14, 1996.

19 Kathryn Korematsu, interview by Bannai and Kashima, May 14, 1996.

20 Thomas B. Edsall, "Pat Buchanan's New Home—Conservative Crusader Embraces the Reform Party, But It's Not a Perfect Fit," *Seattle Times*, Jan. 9, 2000.

21   David Shribman, "Candidates Craft Positions on AIDS Carefully," *Wall St. Journal*, May 13, 1987, 70, col. 1; "Bennett Would Detain Some Carriers of AIDS," *New York Times*, June 15, 1987, A13, co. 1.

22   Mark Barnes, "AIDS and Mr. Korematsu: Minorities at Times of Crisis," *St. Louis University Public Law Review* 7 (1988): 38.

23   Larry Stammer, "Intern Iranians, Hayakawa Urges: Cranston Call for Global 'Quarantine,'" *Los Angeles Times*, Mar. 12, 1980, OC1.

24   "Racist stereotypes of Arabs as terrorists, as oil profiteers, as desert warriors who place less value on human life than Westerners do pervade the United States even in times of peace. Since the Iraqi invasion of Kuwait and the immediate U.S. military response in early August, hatred and discrimination directed at Arab-Americans have intensified." Jennie Anderson, "Blame the Arabs: Tensions in the Gulf Bring Bigotry Home," *Progressive*, Feb. 1991, 28–29.

25   Jamin B. Raskin, "Remembering Korematsu: A Precedent for Arab-Americans?" *Nation*, Feb. 4, 1991, 117–18.

26   Nancy Gibbs, "Walking a Tightrope," *Time*, Feb. 4, 1991, 43.

27   Fred Korematsu, *Of Civil Wrongs and Rights*.

28   Portions of this discussion of the relevance of Fred's case post-9/11 are taken substantially from Lorraine K. Bannai, "Taking the Stand: The Lessons of Three Men Who Took the Japanese American Internment to Court," *Seattle Journal for Social Justice* 4, no. 1 (Fall 2005): 1–38. The FBI reported 481 incidents of hate crimes motivated by bias against the Islamic religion in 2001, an increase of 1600 percent over the previous year. Federal Bureau of Investigation, "Hate Crimes Statistics, 2001," Federal Bureau of Investigation, accessed Dec. 30, 2014, http://www.fbi.gov/about-us/cjis/ucr/hate-crime/2001/hatecrime01.pdf. See also American-Arab Anti-Discrimination Committee, *Report on Hate Crimes and Discrimination against Arab Americans: The Post–September 11 Backlash, September 11, 2001–October 11, 2002* (Washington, DC: American-Arab Anti-Discrimination Committee Research Institute, 2003).

29   According to a CNN/USA Today/Gallup poll taken a few days after the September 11 attacks, 58 percent of persons polled favored requiring all Arabs, including U.S. citizens, to undergo more intense security screening before boarding planes to help prevent terrorist attacks; 49 percent felt that Arabs and Arab Americans should carry some form of special identification; and 32 percent backed "special surveillance" of Arabs and Arab Americans. See Mark Memmott et al., "Poll Finds a United Nation," *USA Today*, Sept. 17, 2001, 4A; Sam Howe Verhovek, "A Nation Challenged: Civil Liberties; Americans Give in to Racial Profiling," *New York Times*, Sept. 23, 2001, 1A. In another survey conducted immediately after September 11, twelve hundred adults nationwide were asked whether they would favor "[a]llowing the U.S. government to take legal immigrants from unfriendly countries to internment camps to curb terrorism during times of tension or crisis." Twenty-nine percent of respondents were in favor, and 57 percent were not. "Overwhelming Support for Bush, Military Response, But . . . American Psyche Reeling from Terror Attacks," Pew Research Center for the People and the Press,

Sept. 19, 2001, http://www.people-press.org/2001/09/19/american-psyche-reeling-from-terror-attacks/, cited in Chisun Lee, "Rounding Up the 'Enemy': Sixty Years after It Jailed Japanese Americans, Would the U.S. Consider Another Ethnic Internment?" *Village Voice*, July 30, 2002, http://www.villagevoice.com/news/0231,lee,37003,1.html.

30 "Many in Seattle's Muslim and Arab American communities said their fear arises not so much from their neighbors or employers, but from the government's war on terrorism, with its secretive dragnets and surveillance of religious institutions." Vanessa Ho and Daikha Dridi, "For Some, the Fear Persists: American Arabs and Muslims Still Feel Threatened a Year after the Attacks," *Seattle Post-Intelligencer*, Sept. 10, 2002, A12; Jackie Koszckuk and Sumama Chatterjee, "Muslims, Arabs Assert FBI Abuse," *Pittsburgh Post-Gazette*, Sept. 24, 2001, A8.

Numerous scholars have criticized the manner in which the government's actions in the war on terrorism have infringed on civil liberties and have drawn parallels between the treatment of Japanese Americans during World War II and the treatment of Arab Americans and Muslims. See, e.g., Yamamoto et al., *Race, Rights, and Reparation*, 389–419; Natsu Taylor Saito, "Symbolism Under Siege: Japanese American Redress and the 'Racing' of Arab Americans as 'Terrorists,'" *Asian Law Journal* 8 (2001): 12; Frank H. Wu, "Profiling in the Wake of September 11: The Precedent of the Japanese American Internment," *Criminal Justice* 17 (2002): 52–58; Liam Braber, "Korematsu's Ghost," 452–53; Farah Brelvi, "Un-American Activities: Racial Profiling and the Backlash after Sept. 11," *Federal Lawyer* 48 (Nov.–Dec. 2001): 70–72; Jerry Kang, "Thinking Through Internment: 12/7 and 9/11." Many have underscored that the enduring danger of the Korematsu case is its expansive view of government power during times of war, whether or not those targeted are racial minorities. See, e.g., Craig Green, "Ending the Korematsu Era: An Early View from the War on Terror Cases," *Northwestern University Law Review* 105 (2011): 985–87, arguing that while conventional wisdom has viewed Korematsu narrowly as "a singular error in Supreme Court history concerning the racist internment of United States citizens[,] . . . the decision extends beyond its racist facts and embodies a general theory of presidential war powers." Other commentators, while drawing parallels between the targeting of Japanese Americans and the targeting of Muslims and Arab Americans, have noted a changed climate in which individuals have reminded the country not to repeat what it did during World War II. David A. Harris, "On the Contemporary Meaning of Korematsu: 'Liberty Lies in the Hearts of Men and Women,'" *Missouri Law Review* 76 (2011): 1–42.

31 Amy Goldstein, "A Deliberate Strategy of Disruption," *Washington Post*, Nov. 4, 2001, A1. "Some . . . were apprehended because they were in the same places or engaged in the same activities as the hijackers: learning to fly airplanes, traveling or—as in [Mohammed] Mubeen's case—getting a driver's license [at the same time and place as one of the suspected terrorist leaders]. Others appear to have been detained more randomly, because they come from a set of Middle Eastern countries and had immigration violations." Ibid.

32 William Glaberson, "A Nation Challenged: The Government's Case; Support for Bush's Antiterror Plan," *New York Times*, Dec. 5, 2001, B6; see also William Glaberson, "War on Terrorism Stirs Memory of Internment," *New York Times*, Sept. 24, 2001, A18.

33 Associated Press, "Republican Defends WWII Internments," *CBS News*, Feb. 7, 2003, http://www.cbsnews.com/news/republican-defends-wwii-internments/. See also Yamamato et al., *Race, Rights, and Reparation*, 397, 399–400. In July 2002, a commissioner of the U.S. Civil Rights Commission, Peter Kirsanow, was criticized for suggesting that another terrorist attack could lead to a groundswell of support for ethnicity-based internments like the one that happened during World War II. He clarified later that he himself did not support such an internment. Niraj Warikoo, "Arabs in U.S. Could Be Held, U.S. Official Warns," *Detroit Free Press*, July 20, 2002, 1A; Chisun Lee, "Rounding Up the 'Enemy': Sixty Years after It Jailed Japanese Americans, Would U.S. Consider Another Ethnic Internment?" *Village Voice*, July 30, 2002, www.villagevoice.com/issues/0231/lee.php.

34 See, e.g., Daniel Pipes, "The Japanese Internment's Effects Today," *New York Sun*, Dec. 28, 2004, also available as Daniel Pipes, "Japanese Internment: Why It Was a Good Idea—And the Lessons It Offers Today," *History News Network*, Jan. 10, 2005, http://hnn.us/articles/9289.html, arguing that characterizing the Japanese American internment as the result of racism "pre-empt[s] efforts to build an effective defense against today's Islamic enemy."

35 Professor Natsu Taylor Saito speaks of the "racing" of Arab Americans: "Just as Asian Americans have been 'raced' as foreign, and from there as presumptively disloyal, Arab Americans . . . have been 'raced' as 'terrorists': foreign, disloyal, and imminently threatening." Saito, "Symbolism Under Siege," 12. See also Thomas W. Joo, "Presumed Disloyal: Executive Power, Judicial Deference, and the Construction of Race before and after September 11," *Columbia Human Rights Law Review* 34 (2002): 1–47; Leti Volpp, "The Citizen and the Terrorist," *UCLA Law Review* 49 (2002): 1575–99; Susan Akram and Kevin R. Johnson, "Race, Civil Rights, and Immigration Law after September 11, 2001: The Targeting of Arabs and Muslims," *NYU Annual Survey of American Law* 58 (2002): 295–355; and Margaret Chon and Donna E. Arzt, "Walking While Muslim," *Law & Contemporary Problems* 68 (2005): 222–23, 238.

36 Eric Fournier, interview by author, Aug. 25, 2010. For information regarding the documentary *Of Civil Wrongs and Rights: The Fred Korematsu Story*, see "Of Civil Wrongs and Rights: The Fred Korematsu Story," POV, accessed Dec. 29, 2014, http://www.pbs.org/pov/pov2001/ofcivilwrongsandrights/storyline.html. The project to produce a documentary of Fred's life was originally begun by Shirley Nakao and Fred's son, Ken. Ken Korematsu, interview by author, Jan. 7, 2011. Karen relates that Ken sacrificed his career to make the film happen. It was the gift he gave his father. The film went on to win two Emmy Awards. Karen Korematsu, interview by author, May 24, 2009.

37 Kathryn Korematsu, interview by author, May 23, 2008, 30; "Fred Korematsu," Robert H. Jackson Center, accessed Dec. 29, 2014, http://www.roberthjackson.

org/the-man/speeches-articles/articles/remembering-korematsu/fred-korematsu/.

38   Fred Korematsu, "Do We Really Need to Relearn the Lessons of Japanese American Internment?" *San Francisco Chronicle*, Sept. 16, 2004, http://www.sfgate.com/opinion/openforum/article/Do-we-really-need-to-relearn-the-lessons-of-2724896.php#ixzz1G4XdDKkU. See also Yamamoto et al., *Race, Rights, and Reparation*, 160–65; Michelle Malkin, *In Defense of Internment: The Case for "Racial Profiling" in World War II and the War on Terror* (Washington, DC: Regnery Publishing, 2004).

39   Brief of Amicus Curiae Fred Korematsu in Support of Petitioners, Rasul v. Bush, 542 U.S. 466 (2004) (Nos. 03-334, 03-343), 2004 WL 103832, 4 (Jan. 14, 2004). See Yamamoto et al., *Race, Rights, and Reparation*, 403–7.

40   *Rasul*, 542 U.S. 466, 480–82.

41   Brief Amicus Curiae of Fred Korematsu, the Bar Association of San Francisco, the Asian Law Caucus, the Asian American Bar Association of the Greater Bay Area, Asian Pacific Islander Legal Outreach, and the Japanese American Citizens League in Support of Respondents, Rumsfeld v. Padilla, 542 U.S. 426 (2004) (No. 03-1027), 2004 WL 791897 (Apr. 10, 2004).

42   Kathryn Korematsu, interview by author, May 24, 2008; Riemer and Biggs to Fred Korematsu, Sept. 7, 1983, *Korematsu* Coram Nobis Litigation Collection, UCLA, Collection 545, Box 10, Folder 5.

43   Kathryn Korematsu, interview by Bannai and Kashima, May 14, 1996; remarks, Fred Korematsu, ACLU Bill of Rights Day, recorded for *Unfinished Business*. On June 15, 2001, in Miami, Florida, the National ACLU awarded Fred and Gordon Hirabayashi its Roger N. Baldwin Medal of Liberty award, which honors "individuals who have made lifetime contributions to the advancement of civil liberties." "ACLU Awards Prestigious Medal of Liberty to Japanese Americans Who Challenged Internment During WWII," ACLU, June 13, 2001, http://www.aclu.org/racial-justice/aclu-awards-prestigious-medal-liberty-japanese-americans-who-challenged-internment-du.

44   "Justice Fighter to Receive ADL Award," *J Weekly*, June 26, 1998, http://www.jweekly.com/article/full/8589/justice-fighter-to-receive-adl-award/.

45   "Celebs Gather in Beverly Hills to Fete Jesse Jackson's 58th Birthday and Salute Rainbow/PUSH Honoree," *JET* 97, no. 22 (Nov. 1, 1999): 12.

46   Fred received honorary doctor of law degrees from the City University of New York Law School, the University of the Pacific McGeorge School of Law, the University of San Francisco School of Law, and the California State University, East Bay. On its conferral of an honorary degree to Fred in 1988, the City University of New York Law School at Queens College wrote, "The [university] confers the degree of Doctor of Law, *honoris causa*, upon you, Fred Toyosaburo Korematsu, for your service as a leading figure in the struggle to preserve individual freedoms and Constitutional guarantees in this country." Commencement program, the City University of New York Law School at Queens College, May 27, 1988.

47 Karen Korematsu, interview by author, May 25, 2009.

48 William J. Clinton, "Remarks on Presenting the Presidential Medal of Freedom (Jan. 15, 1998)," in *Public Papers of the Presidents of the United States: William J. Clinton*, Book I, Jan. 1 to June 30, 1998 (Washington, DC: U.S. Government Printing Office, 1999), 56–58; Karen Korematsu, interview by author, May 25, 2009.

49 Ibid.

50 "Clinton Presents Medal of Freedom to Korematsu," *Hokubei Mainichi*, Jan. 17, 1998; Karen Korematsu, interview by author, May 25, 2009.

51 Ibid.

52 "*San Francisco Examiner*: Medal for Korematsu was Long Overdue," *Hokubei Mainichi*, Jan. 21, 1998. Gordon Hirabayashi was awarded the Presidential Medal of Freedom posthumously in May 2012. "An Honor from the President," *New York Times*, May 30, 2012, http://query.nytimes.com/gst/fullpage.html?res=9 E03E3D8133EF933A05756C0A9649D8B63&module=Search&mabReward=relb ias%3Ar%2C%7B%222%22%3A%22RI%3A18%22%7D. Efforts are being taken to similarly honor Min Yasui. Frances Kai-Hwa Wang, "The Life and Legacy of Minoru Yasui," accessed Apr. 15, 2015, http://www.nbcnews.com/news/asian-america/will-minoru-yasui-get-presidential-medal-freedom-n325826.

53 Bill Hosokawa, "Why Is the President Honoring Fred Korematsu?" *Pacific Citizen*, Jan. 23–Feb. 5, 1998. Reader Fred Y. Hirasuna agreed, "[Fred's] was not a straight-forward attack on evacuation. He wanted to stay with his non-Japanese girlfriend." "Medal of Freedom Undeserved, Agrees with Hosokawa," *Pacific Citizen*, Feb. 6–19, 1998.

54 John Tateishi, interview by author, May 26, 2009.

55 "Korematsu Receives Presidential Medal of Freedom," *Pacific Citizen*, Jan. 23–Feb. 5, 1998.

56 Joanne Kataoka, interview by author, Jan. 8, 2011; Ken Korematsu, interview by author, Jan. 7, 2011.

57 Kathryn Korematsu, interview by author, May 24 and 25, 2008; Karen Korematsu, interview by author, May 24, 2009; Leigh-Ann Miyasato, interview by author, Dec. 14, 2010. Fred met many distinguished people during his travels, too many to recount. For example, while Fred was visiting Boston, Justice Steven Breyer asked to meet him. Eric Fournier, interview by author, Aug. 25, 2010. He greatly enjoyed getting to know Senator Paul Simon, who invited Fred to speak at the Paul Simon Public Policy Institute at South Illinois University. And he shared a special respect for Rose Bird, former chief justice of the California Supreme Court.

58 Holly English, "Meeting a Famous Case: Fred Korematsu," *New Jersey Law Journal* 114 (1988): 645.

59 Karen Korematsu, interview by author, May 24, 2009; Kathryn Korematsu, interview by author, May 25, 2008.

60 JANM Conference, *Judgments Judged and Wrongs Remembered: Examining the Japanese American Civil Liberties Cases of World War II on Their 60th Anniversary*, Los Angeles, Nov. 5–6, 2004.

61 Kathryn Korematsu, interview by author, May 25, 2008; Karen Korematsu, interview by author, May 23 and 25, 2008; Ed Chen, e-mail to author, July 29, 2014; editorial, "Ordinary Man, Extraordinary Courage," *Seattle Times*, Apr. 6, 2005, B6; Claudia Luther, "Fred Korematsu, 86, Fought World War II Internment, Dies," *Los Angeles Times*, Mar. 31, 2005; Richard Goldstein, "Fred Korematsu, 86, Dies," *New York Times*, Apr. 1, 2005, 13.

EPILOGUE

1 Neal Katyal, "Confession of Error: The Solicitor General's Mistakes during the Japanese-American Internment Cases," accessed Apr. 11, 2015, http://blogs. justice.gov/main/archives/1346. See also Yamamoto et al., *Race, Rights, and Reparation*, 304–5; David G. Savage, "U.S. Official Cites Misconduct in Japanese American Internment Cases," *Los Angeles Times*, May 24, 2011.

2 Pub. L. No. 112-81, 125 Stat. 1298 (2011). Portions of this discussion of the NDAA, as well as the discussion of *Hedges v. Obama* that follows, are drawn Lorraine K. Bannai's contribution "Indefinite Detention 2012: The National Defense Authorization Act and the Continuing Import of the Japanese Americans Internment Cases," in Yamamoto et al., *Race, Rights, and Reparation*, 417–19.

3 Senator Dianne Feinstein, statement, and Lorraine K. Bannai, testimony, *The Due Process Guarantee Act: Banning Indefinite Detention of Americans, Hearings before the Senate Judiciary Committee on S. 2003*, 112th Cong., 2nd Sess. (Washington, DC: U.S. Government Printing Office, 2012), accessed Apr. 11, 2015, http://fas.org/irp/congress/2012_hr/dueprocess.pdf.

4 Brief of Amici Curiae Karen and Ken Korematsu, Holly, Iris, and Laurel Dee Yasui, Jay Hirabayashi, Sharon Mitsu Yuen, and Marion Setsu Oldenburg in Support of Plaintiffs-Appellees and Affirmance, Hedges v. Obama, 724 F.3d 170 (2d Cir. 2013) (Nos. 12-3176, 12-3644), *cert. denied*, 134 S. Ct. 1936 (2014), 2012 WL 6622648 (Dec. 17, 2012).

5 "Portrait of Fred Korematsu Unveiled," facetoface, Feb. 2, 2012, http://face-2face.si.edu/my_weblog/2012/02/portrait-of-fred-korematsu-unveiled-february-2-2012.html. Other schools named for Fred include the Fred T. Korematsu Elementary School at Mace Ranch, California, which opened in 2005. San Leandro High School's Fred T. Korematsu Campus was dedicated in 2010. And on July 9, 2014, Portola Middle School in El Cerrito, California, was renamed Fred T. Korematsu Middle School. Kathryn Korematsu interview by author, May 25, 2008; Karen Korematsu, interview by author, May 25, 2009; Rick Radin, "Middle School Rename OK's: Korematsu," *Contra Costa Times*, July 11, 2014, B1. To learn more about the work of the Fred T. Korematsu Institute, see "About Us," Korematsu Institute, accessed Dec. 29, 2014, http://korematsuinstitute.org/.

6 Kevin Fagan, "History in the Making: State's Fred Korematsu Day First to Honor an Asian American," *San Francisco Chronicle*, Jan. 29, 2011. In Hawai'i, January 30, 2013, Fred's birthday, was designated Civil Liberties and the Constitution Day, a day to remember the efforts of Fred, Gordon, Min, and Mitsuye Endo. News Re-

lease, "Governor Signs Bill Establishing 'Civil Liberties and the Constitution Day,'" *Hawai'i Free Press*, June 7, 2013, http://www.hawaiifreepress.com/ArticlesMain/tabid/56/ID/9852/Governor-Signs-Bill-Establishing-Civil-Liberties-and-the-Constitution-Day.aspx. Utah, Illinois, Georgia, Pennsylvania, and Virginia have also recognized Fred's birthday as Fred Korematsu Day. Rachel Lowry, "Utah Gov. Gary Herbert Signs Declaration Establishing Fred Korematsu Day," *Deseret News*, Jan. 18, 2013, http://www.deseretnews.com/article/865571053/Utah-governor-signs-declaration-establishing-Fred-Korematsu-Day.html?pg=all; "Honoring a Japanese-American Who Fought Against Internment Camps," NPR, Jan. 30, 2014, http://www.npr.org/blogs/codeswitch/2014/01/30/268917800/honoring-a-japanese-american-who-fought-against-internment-camps; "Fred Korematsu Day in Georgia," *Rafu Shimpo*, Jan. 17, 2014, http://www.rafu.com/2014/01/fred-korematsu-day-in-georgia/; resolution designating January 30, 2014, as the Fred Korematsu Day of Civil Liberties in Pennsylvania, available at http://www.legis.state.pa.us//cfdocs/Legis/CSM/showMemoPublic.cfm?chamber=H&SPick=20130&cosponId=13975; "Commonwealth of Virginia Establishes January 30 as Fred Korematsu Day of Civil Liberties and the Constitution," Feb. 25, 2015, http://www.alexandrianews.org/the-commonwealth-of-virginia-establishes-january-30-as-fred-korematsu-day-of-civil-liberties-and-the-constitution/; U.S. Commission on Civil Rights to Barack Obama, Mar. 28, 2014, http://www.usccr.gov/press/2014/Chavez_Korematsu.pdf (also requesting that a national holiday be created to honor Cesar Chavez).

7   For an excellent discussion of the legacy of the wartime incarceration and Japanese American redress as it relates to social justice initiatives both nationally and globally, see Yamamoto et al., *Race, Rights, and Reparation*, 329–419; Eric K. Yamamoto, "The Evolving Legacy of Japanese American Internment Redress: Next Steps We Can (and Should) Take," *Seattle Journal for Social Justice* 11 (2012): 85–87.

8   For more about the work of the Korematsu Center at Seattle University School of Law, see Robert S. Chang, "The Fred T. Korematsu Center for Law and Equality and Its Vision for Social Change," *Stanford Journal of Civil Rights and Civil Liberties* 7 (2011): 197–212; "Fred T. Korematsu Center for Law and Equality," Seattle University School of Law, accessed Dec. 29, 2014, http://www.law.seattleu.edu/centers-and-institutes/korematsu-center.

9   For more about the Korematsu professorship at the University of Hawai'i School of Law, and Eric K. Yamamoto, the holder of that professorship, see "Korematsu Professorship," University of Hawai'i, accessed Dec. 29, 2014, https://www.law.hawaii.edu/korematsu-professorship, and "Eric K. Yamamoto," University of Hawai'i, accessed Dec. 29, 2014, https://www.law.hawaii.edu/personnel/yamamoto/eric.

10   Audrey McAvoy, "Scalia: 'Kidding Yourself' If You Think Internment Camps Won't Return," *Washington Times*, Feb. 3, 2014.

GLOSSARY

JAPANESE TERMS

Issei. Immigrants of Japanese ancestry, first generation in the United States.

Nikkei. Generally refers to "Japanese emigrants and their descendants living outside (and sometimes inside) Japan."[1] I use the term "Nikkei" interchangeably with the term "Japanese American."

Nisei. Second-generation persons of Japanese ancestry, born in the United States.

Sansei. Third-generation persons of Japanese ancestry.

Yonsei. Fourth-generation persons of Japanese ancestry.

LATIN LEGAL TERMS

Amicus curiae brief. "Amicus curiae" means "friend of the court." An amicus curiae brief is submitted by an individual or group that is not directly involved in the litigation as a party, but "that is allowed by the court to advise it on a matter of law or policy directly affecting the litigation."[2]

Petition for writ of error coram nobis. A legal proceeding brought to challenge the validity of a conviction after the sentence has been served "under circumstances compelling such action to achieve justice."[3]

Petition for writ of habeas corpus. A legal proceeding brought "to obtain immediate release from an unlawful confinement," for example, "when the confinement has occurred through a means that violated the person's constitutional rights."[4]

---

1   *Densho Encyclopedia*, s.v. "Nikkei," last updated March 19, 2013, http://encyclopedia.densho.org/Nikkei/.

2   *American Heritage Dictionary of the English Language*, s.v. "amicus cur-

iae," accessed April 16, 2015, https://www.ahdictionary.com/word/search.html?q=amicus+curiae.

3   Hirabayashi v. United States, 828 F.2d 591, 604 (9th Cir. 1987), citing United States v. Morgan, 346 U.S. 502, 511 (1954).

4   *American Heritage Dictionary of the English Language,* s.v. "habeas corpus," accessed December 19, 2014, https://www.ahdictionary.com/word/search.html?q=habeas+corpus&submit.x=0&submit.y=0).

A NOTE ON TERMINOLOGY

IN RECENT YEARS, JAPANESE AMERICANS HAVE ASSERTED THE right to describe their own wartime experience, rejecting euphemistic terms originated by the government that mask the reality of their incarceration.[1] Many of my choices grow from those discussions. Although during World War II many spoke of the "evacuation" of Japanese Americans, because that term usually evokes the movement of individuals for their own safety, I use the terms "removal" or "expulsion." Similarly, while in the terminology of the wartime government Japanese Americans were sent to "assembly centers" until more permanent camps could be built, I do not use the term because it fails to describe the coercive and harsh environment of these camps.

Similarly, while the more permanent camps were termed "relocation centers," I do not use that term because, again, it does not represent the camps as they were—sites for the confinement of over 110,000 individuals behind barbed wire with armed guards. While the use of the term "concentration camps" has caused some controversy, I use the term because the camps were, using the term's dictionary definition, "a type of prison where large numbers of people . . . are kept during a war and are usually forced to live in very bad conditions."[2] In addition, as discussed in this book, the government actors at the time of the incarceration referred to the camps as, and intended them to be, concentration camps.

The word "internment" has been rejected by many because it has a specifically defined legal meaning, referring to the lawful incarceration of citizens of a foreign country with which the United States is at war.[3] It is said that the term is not properly applied to the incarceration of the Nisei, who were U.S. citizens. Although I do believe that "internment" as used in reference to the Japanese American incarceration has acquired a broader meaning, I have generally avoided using "internment," preferring instead "imprisonment," "incarceration," or "confinement."

Finally, I have used the term "Japanese Americans" to refer collectively to both Issei and Nisei, even though the Issei were not American citizens. I do this because the Issei made this country their own but were prohibited from becoming citizens by discriminatory laws.

1   See, e.g., Karen L. Ishizuka, *Lost and Found: Reclaiming the Japanese American Incarceration* (Urbana, IL: University of Chicago Press, 2006), 8–13, 154–72; "Terminology and Glossary," Densho: The Japanese American Legacy Project, accessed December 31, 2014, http://www.densho.org/default.asp?path=/assets/sharedpages/glossary.asp?section=home; James Hirabayashi, "'Concentration Camp' or 'Relocation Center?' What's in a Name?" *Japanese American National Museum Quarterly* (Autumn 1994): 5.

2   *Merriam-Webster*, s. v. "Concentration Camp," last updated March 19, 2013, http://www.merriam-webster.com/dictionary/concentration%20camp.

3   See Roger Daniels, "Words Do Matter: A Note on Inappropriate Terminology and the Incarceration of the Japanese Americans," Discover Nikkei, February 1, 2008, http://www.discovernikkei.org/en/journal/2008/2/1/words-do-matter/.

SELECTED BIBLIOGRAPHY

There are numerous resources regarding the broader history of Japanese Americans, their incarceration, others who resisted, and the movement for redress. There are also numerous websites addressing these issues; the Densho website, www.densho. org, is one excellent site that also has a helpful resource list. The following list includes just some of the many sources addressing the history of Japanese Americans and their incarceration, with specific focus on Fred Korematsu's life and case.

Adams, Jane Meredith. "To Clear His Name." *Biography* 2, no. 9 (Sept. 1998): 66.

Aoki, Keith. "No Right to Own?: The Early Twentieth-Century 'Alien Land Laws' as a Prelude to Internment." *Boston College Law Review* 40 (1998): 37.

Bannai, Lorraine K. "Taking the Stand: The Lessons of Three Men Who Took the Japanese American Internment to Court." *Seattle Journal for Social Justice* 4, no. 1 (Fall 2005): 1–38.

Bannai, Lorraine K., and Dale Minami. "Internment during World War II and Litigations, in Asian Americans and the Supreme Court: A Documentary History." In *Asian Americans and the Supreme Court: A Documentary History,* edited by H. Kim, 755–88. Westport, CT: Greenwood Press, 1992.

Briones, Matthew. *Jim and Jap Crow: A Cultural History of 1940's Interracial America.* Princeton, NJ: Princeton University Press, 2012.

Chan, Sucheng. *Asian Americans: An Interpretive History.* Boston: Twayne Publishers, 1991.

Chemerinsky, Erwin. "Korematsu v. United States: A Tragedy Hopefully Never to Be Repeated." *Pepperdine Law Review* 39 (Dec. 2011): 163–72.

Chuman, Frank, *The Bamboo People: The Law and Japanese-Americans.* Del Mar, CA: Publisher's Inc., 1976.

Commission on Wartime Relocation and Internment of Civilians (CWRIC). *Personal Justice Denied.* Washington, DC: U.S. Government Printing Office, 1982.

Conn, Stetson, Rose C. Engelman, and Byron Fairchild. *United States Army in World War II: The Western Hemisphere: Guarding the United States and Its Outposts.* Washington, DC: Office of the Chief of Military History, Department of the Army, 1964.

Daniels, Roger. *Concentration Camps USA: The Japanese Americans and World War II.* New York: Holt, Rinehart, and Winston, 1972.

———. *The Decision to Relocate the Japanese Americans.* J. B. Lippincott Co., 1975.

———. *The Japanese American Cases: The Rule of Law in Time of War.* Lawrence: University Press of Kansas, 2013.

———. *The Politics of Prejudice.* 2nd ed. Berkeley: University of California Press, 1962.

———. *Prisoners Without Trial.* New York: Hill and Wang, 1993.

Dembitz, Nanette. "Racial Discrimination and the Military Judgment: The Supreme Court's Korematsu and Endo Decisions." *Columbia Law Review* 45 (1945): 175–239.

DeWitt, John L. *Final Report: Japanese Evacuation from the West Coast 1942.* Washington, DC: United States Government Printing Office, 1943.

Elinson, Elaine, and Stan Yogi. *Wherever There's a Fight.* Berkeley: Heydey Books, 2009.

Fighting for Justice: The Coram Nobis Cases. Documentary. Directed by Dianne Fukami and gayle k. yamada. El Macera, CA: Media Bridges, 1999. VHS, 105 mins.

Fujita-Rony, Thomas Y. "Korematsu's Civil Rights Challenges: Plaintiffs' Personal Understandings of Constitutionally Guaranteed Freedoms, the Defense of Civil Liberties, and Historical Context." *Temple Political and Civil Rights Law Review* 13 (2003): 51–70.

Gee, Emma, "Issei: The First Women." In *Asian Women's Journal,* 8–9. Berkeley: University of California Press, 1975.

Harris, David A. "On the Contemporary Meaning of Korematsu: 'Liberty Lies in the Hearts of Men and Women.'" *Missouri Law Review* 76 (2011): 1–42.

Hashimoto, Dean Masaru. "The Legacy of Korematsu v. United States: A Dangerous Narrative Retold." *Asian Pacific American Law Journal* 4 (1996): 72–128.

Hirabayashi, Gordon K., with James A. Hirabayashi and Lane Ryo Hirabayashi. *A Principled Stand: The Story of Hirabayashi v. United States.* Seattle: University of Washington Press, 2013.

Hirase, JoAnne. "The Internment of Japanese Americans: The Constitutional Threat Fifty Years Later." *Journal of Contemporary Law* 19 (1993): 143–83.

Hosokawa, Bill. *JACL in Quest of Justice.* New York: William Morrow, 1982.

Iijima, Chris. "Reparations and the 'Model Minority' Ideology of Acquiescence: The Necessity to Refuse the Return to Original Humiliation." *Boston College Law Review* 40 (1998): 385.

Irons, Peter. *Justice at War: The Story of the Japanese American Internment Cases.* New York: Oxford University Press, 1983.

———. *Justice Delayed: The Record of the Japanese American Internment Cases.* Middletown, CT: Wesleyan University Press, 1989.

Iyeki, Marc Hideo. "The Japanese American Coram Nobis Cases: Exposing the Myth of Disloyalty." *N.Y.U. Review of Law & Social Change* 13 (1984–85): 199–221.

Kang, Jerry. "Denying Prejudice: Internment, Redress, and Denial." *UCLA Law Review* 51 (Apr. 2004): 933–1013.

Kawaguchi, Gary. *Living with Flowers: The California Flower Market History.* San Francisco: California Flower Market, 1993.

Kikuchi, Charles. *The Kikuchi Diary: Chronicle from an American Concentration Camp*, ed. John Modell. Urbana: University of Illinois Press, 1973.

Kutulas, Judy. "In Quest of Autonomy: The Northern California Affiliate of the American Civil Liberties Union and World War II," *Pacific Historical Review.* vol. 67. Berkeley: University of California Press, 1998.

Maki, Mitchell, Harry H. Kitano, and S. Megan Berthold. *Achieving the Impossible Dream: How Japanese Americans Obtained Redress.* Urbana: University of Illinois Press, 1999.

Matsuda, Mari J. "Foreword: McCarthyism, the Internment, and the Contradictions of Power." *Boston College Law Review* 40 (1998): 9.

Minami, Dale. "*Coram Nobis* and Redress." In *Japanese Americans: From Relocation to Redress*, 200–201. Edited by Roger Daniels et al. Seattle: University of Washington Press, 1986.

Muller, Eric L. *American Inquisition: The Hunt for Japanese American Disloyalty in World War II.* Chapel Hill: University of North Carolina Press, 2007.

———. *Free to Die for Their Country: The Story of the Japanese American Draft Resisters in World War II.* Chicago: University of Chicago Press, 2003.

Murray, Alice Yang. *Historical Memories of the Japanese American Internment and the Struggle for Redress.* Stanford, CA: Stanford University Press, 2008.

Nakano, Mei T. *Japanese American Women: Three Generations, 1890–1990.* Berkeley: Mina Press Publishing, 1990.

Of Civil Wrongs and Rights: The Fred Korematsu Story. Documentary. Directed by Eric Paul Fournier. New York: Docurama, 2006. DVD, 70 mins.

Okada, John. *No-No Boy.* Tokyo: Charles E. Tuttle Co, 1957.

Okubo, Miné. *Citizen 13660.* New York: Columbia University Press, 1946; repr., Seattle: University of Washington Press, 1983.

Pascoe, Peggy. *What Comes Naturally: Miscegenation Law and the Making of Race in* America. New York: Oxford University Press, 2009.

Patel, Marilyn Hall, Karen Korematsu, and Dale Minami. "Justice Restored: The Legacy of Korematsu II and the Future of Civil Liberties." *Asian American Law Journal* 16 (2009): 228.

Petersen, William. "Success Story, Japanese American Style." *New York Times Magazine*, Jan. 9, 1966, 21.

Robinson, Greg. *A Tragedy of Democracy: Japanese Confinement in North America.* New York: Columbia University Press, 2009.

———. *By Order of the President: FDR and the Internment of Japanese Americans.* Cambridge, MA: Harvard University Press, 2001.

Rostow, Eugene. "The Japanese American Cases—A Disaster." *Yale Law Journal* 54 (June 1945): 489–533.

Saito, Natsu Taylor. "Symbolism Under Siege: Japanese American Redress and the 'Racing' of Arab Americans as 'Terrorists.'" *Asian Law Journal* 8 (2001): 12.

Sarasohn, Eileen Sunada. *The Issei: Portrait of a Pioneer, An Oral History.* Palo Alto, CA: Pacific Books, 1983.

Serrano, Susan Kiyomi, and Dale Minami. "Korematsu v. United States: A 'Constant Caution' in a Time of Crisis." *Asian Law Journal* 10 (Jan. 2003): 37–50.

Shibata, Yoshimi. *Across Two Worlds: Memoirs of a Nisei Flower Grower.* San Jose, CA: Mt. Eden Floral Company, 2006.

Takahata, Sandra. "The Case of Korematsu v. United States: Could It Be Justified Today?" *University of Hawai'i Law Review* 6 (1984): 109–75.

Takaki, Ronald. *Strangers from a Different Shore: A History of Asian Americans.* Boston: Little, Brown and Company, 1989.

Tanaka, Chester. *Go For Broke: A Pictorial History of the Japanese American 100th Infantry Battalion and 442nd Regimental Combat Team.* Richmond, CA: Go For Broke, 1982, 49.

Tateishi, John. *And Justice for All: An Oral History of the Japanese-American Detention Camps.* Seattle: University of Washington Press, 1984.

tenBroek, Jacobus, Edward N. Barnhart, and Floyd W. Matson, *Prejudice, War, and the Constitution.* Berkeley: University of California Press, 1954.

Tritter, Daniel F. "In the Defense of Fred Korematsu: Vox Clamantis in Deserto Curiarum." *Thomas Jefferson Law Review* 27 (2005): 255–316.

Unfinished Business: The Japanese American Internment Cases. Documentary. Directed by Steven Okazaki. Berkeley, CA: Farallon Films, 1985. DVD, 58 mins.

Walker, Samuel. *In Defense of American Liberties: A History of the ACLU,* 2nd ed. Carbondale: Southern Illinois University Press, 1990.

Weglyn, Michi. *Years of Infamy.* New York: Morrow Quill Paperbacks, 1976.

Wei, William. *The Asian American Movement.* Philadelphia: Temple University Press, 1993.

Woodward, Mary. *In Defense of Our Neighbors: The Walt and Milly Woodward Story.* Bainbridge Island, WA: Fenwick Publishing, 2008.

Yackle, Larry W. "Japanese American Internment: An Interview with Fred Korematsu." *Boston University Public Interest Law Journal* 3 (1993): 95–104.

Yamamoto, Eric. "Korematsu Revisited—Correcting the Injustice of Extraordinary Government Excess and Lax Judicial Review: Time for a Better Accommodation of National Security Concerns and Civil Liberties." *Santa Clara Law Review* 26 (1986): 1–62.

Yamamoto, Eric, Dale Minami, and May Lee Heye. "One Man Seeks Justice from a Nation: *Korematsu v. United States.*" In *Untold Civil Rights Stories,* edited by Stewart Kwoh and Russell C. Leong (2009).

Yamamoto, Eric, Margaret Chon, Carol L. Izumi, Jerry Kang, and Frank H. Wu. *Race, Rights, and Reparation: Law and the Japanese American Internment.* 2nd ed. New York: Wolters Kluwer Law & Business, 2013.

Yoo, David K. *Growing Up Nisei.* Urbana: University of Illinois Press, 2000.

INDEX

Note: page numbers in *italics* refer to figures;
those followed by "n" indicate endnotes.

THE SCOTT AND LAURIE OKI SERIES IN ASIAN AMERICAN STUDIES